FOR THE SURVIVAL OF LIBERTY
GREAT PRESIDENTIAL DECISIONS

Elton B. Klibanoff

First published by Dog Ear Publishing
4010 W. 86th Street, Ste H
Indianapolis, IN 46268
www.dogearpublishing.net

ISBN: 978-1-4575-1367-1

This book is printed on acid-free paper.

Printed in the United States of America

For my family—past, present, and future.

By the rude bridge that arched the flood,
Their flag to April's breeze unfurled,
Here once the embattled farmers stood,
And fired the shot heard round the world.

Lines from *Concord Hymn* by Ralph Waldo Emerson, as engraved on the pedestal of the Concord Minute Man Statue, Minute Man National Historic Park, Concord, Massachusetts. Sculpted by Daniel Chester French and pictured on the cover.

TABLE OF CONTENTS

PREFACE

In putting this volume together, I referred to many of the most notable books by historians relative to the subject matter of each chapter, including those presenting the most recent scholarship. I have also consulted most of the letters and public papers of the Presidents themselves in order to access their ideas directly and not second-hand. Finally, I have synthesized this material in ways that I think make for coherent stories and logical generalizations, although I have tried to recognize alternative conclusions where appropriate. My purpose was to distill the expertise of decades of research and writing that would not easily be accessible to the general reader and to describe the impact of six momentous Presidential decisions on American liberty. I could not have produced this book without the resources available at the Library of Congress, The Boston Athenaeum, the Harvard Law School Library, and the Minuteman Library System. I am also appreciative of the efforts of my family, friends and colleagues who have unselfishly given of their time to attempt to improve my product.

I am especially grateful for the wisdom, patience, support, and editorial skill of my wife, Susan, without whom this project might never have come to fruition. To my children—John, Jennifer, and Daniel Klibanoff—I want you to know how proud I am of you for being the extraordinary people you are. My pride also extends to my grandchildren, Paige and Tess Klibanoff, in whose hands the future of the country partially, and, capably, rests.

I hope that, by shining a new light on past events, this book can help readers rededicate themselves to the true nature of American liberty and appreciate the importance of character and vision in our national leaders.

E.B.K.

LIST OF ILLUSTRATIONS

1

INTRODUCTION.

Presidential Foundations of American Liberty

On January 20, 1961, the youngest elected President of the United States declared that America would do anything it could "to assure the survival and success of liberty."

Not every American endorsed the unlimited nature of Kennedy's commitment, but few disagreed with his general message. Assuring the survival and success of liberty is, in a very real sense, America's 'state religion.' It has inspired and motivated generations since before the Revolution of 1776 and it will undoubtedly continue to do so into the foreseeable future.

This book examines the six Presidents who have most profoundly shaped American liberty and defined its mission at home and abroad. They have provided basic policy foundations that are to a great degree responsible for the vitality and survival of American liberty. These critical accomplishments are the following:

a <u>national economic structure</u> established by George Washington;

<u>continental geographic expansion</u> set in motion by Thomas Jefferson;

<u>freedom and equal opportunity for all Americans</u> made national policy by Abraham Lincoln;

<u>a national commitment to encourage and protect the liberty of those in foreign countries</u> as first articulated by James Monroe;

<u>the linking of America's mission with international cooperation</u> as more fully developed by Woodrow Wilson; and

<u>federal governmental responsibility for providing economic and social security</u> as enshrined by Franklin Roosevelt.

The substance of these policy decisions has been vitally important to American history; equally influential has been the example of strong federal leadership set by Presidents with a clear and deeply held vision for the country's future.

The United States Constitution and its Bill of Rights erected American liberty's general framework: government with the consent of the governed; freedom of thought and religion; respect for the rights of the minority; and governmental limits such as 'separation of powers' and 'checks and balances.' The three branches of government established by the Constitution have had to fill in the blanks, resolve the ambiguities, and respond to unforeseen events and new circumstances—in short, to give shape and substance to that liberty and to more clearly define American values. These six Presidents took up the challenge left open by the Constitution and provided the basic principles that have given American liberty its meaning.

To appreciate the enormous impact of these particular achievements, one has only to consider the possible consequences if these decisions had not been made at the time and in the manner that they were.

Had Washington not established a national economic framework, the country would have developed a fragmented, state-based economic system incapable of providing the vigorous economic growth it has enjoyed from its birth. It would thus not have become, as it did, one of the world's great powers, primarily responsible for the survival of liberty around the world during the 19th and 20th centuries.

Had Thomas Jefferson not seized the opportunity to double the size of the country and set the example for further expansion west to the Pacific, south to Texas and Florida, and north to Alaska, the United States would have had to constantly deal with strong European powers on its borders. The American character would never have reflected an individualist, "frontier" spirit, courageously seeking economic opportunity; the country would have suffered from a paucity of natural resources; and it never would have realized the moral and economic benefits of large-scale immigration.

Had James Monroe not established via the Monroe Doctrine a mission of encouraging and protecting liberty in other countries, much of Central and South America might have remained in European hands, thus confronting the United States with the burden of balance of power politics in its own backyard. Moreover, the United

States would not have been as prepared to enable so many countries to withstand the great threats to liberty that materialized in the 20th century.

Had Abraham Lincoln not devised a strategy for halting the expansion of slavery, emancipating those slaves within his authority, and setting in motion the complete abolition of the institution, the United States may have permanently split apart or, at a minimum, might have been burdened by long-term civil strife and political paralysis. It would not have become a beacon of hope for those desiring liberty, thus making it impossible to exercise what became its role in the 20th and 21st century role as the most powerful defender of liberty in the world.

Had Woodrow Wilson not linked the idea of liberty with a framework for international cooperation to help prevent war, the country may have succumbed to an isolationist, self-defeating foreign policy during the entire 20th century, with world prospects for liberty and peace, as well as economic growth, greatly reduced. Moreover, multi-lateral alliances of free nations might not have been established, the United Nations might not have been born, and millions of people in Europe, Africa, and Asia might not have had the opportunity to escape colonial rule and live in freedom.

And, finally, had Franklin Roosevelt not established economic and social security as a federal government responsibility and an inherent part of American liberty, human suffering in the 1930's would have reached even more catastrophic levels. Moreover, the country may have been subject to class conflict and political revolution or, at a minimum, strikes and civil unrest, for the foreseeable future, thus putting in doubt the outcome of the Second World War and the great challenges to liberty of the 20th century.

These six decisions have earned their place in America's political tradition because successor Presidents and later Congresses have built on their foundation and followed their example.

Washington's national economy led to Teddy Roosevelt's trust-busting, Wilson's Federal Trade Commission and creation of the Federal Reserve System, and Franklin Roosevelt's establishment of broad regulation of the financial and investment systems.

Jefferson's model for the Louisiana Purchase led to Monroe's acquisition of Florida and Oregon, Andrew Johnson's purchase of Alaska, and McKinley's acquisition of Guam and Hawaii.

Monroe's Doctrine protected the independence of our southern neighbors, and inspired the independence of the Philippines, the Marshall Plan for Europe, and the protection of Greek and Turkish freedom after World War II.

Lincoln's Emancipation Proclamation eventually led to the desegregation of public schools and to the landmark civil rights legislation of the 1960's outlawing racial segregation and discrimination.

Wilson's League of Nations principles inspired the establishment of the United Nations, the Marshall Plan to rescue European liberty after World War II, Kennedy's nuclear test ban treaty, Reagan's Strategic Arms Limitation Treaty, and George H.W. Bush's leadership of an international coalition to protect the independence of Kuwait.

Franklin Roosevelt's New Deal inspired the G.I. Bill, the passage of Medicaid and Medicare in the 1960's, national health insurance in 2010, and a myriad of federal aid to education and job training programs.

Equally important, these decisions have become part of the framework of American liberty because, over time, they have become an integral and accepted part of American culture. Americans no longer question the mission President Monroe established for them of encouraging and protecting the liberty of those in other countries, although debates may continue over the appropriate means to that end. And Lincoln's call for equal opportunity for all regardless of the circumstances of their birth is deeply felt as the essence of American liberty, not only within the nation, but around the world.

In the early 21st century, American liberty is threatened, both by foreign terrorists, by domestic decisions believed necessary to fight terrorism, and even by domestic political extremism. The national political environment has been polarized to such an extent that some of America's most important political principles, such as the separation of powers, the right to privacy, freedom of thought, the separation of church and state, and a commitment to international cooperation are now at the center of debate. Controversy continues about how America should assert itself in the world and whether the Wars in Iraq and Afghanistan are an effective way to achieve the nation's objectives.

Americans face great international challenges in responding to terrorism, the proliferation of weapons of mass destruction, global warming and environmental degradation, and regimes denigrating human rights. What lessons do these six framework decisions carry for those issues? In brief, they teach the wisdom of international or multi-lateral rather than unilateral solutions, and they equate the encouragement of liberty and economic opportunity throughout the world with American national security.

In the domestic sphere, Americans confront: a failing health care system; increasing economic inequality between the middle class and poor, on the one hand, and the very rich, on the other; an education system that does not serve all students well; a Social Security system that is under-funded and provides inadequate security; a political system in which money and manipulation have the effect of denying fair representation to all; and continued societal discrimination based on gender, race, religion, or sexual preference that hinders equal opportunity for everyone. Our study of the six framework decisions points to solutions to these problems based on national programs that create a protective floor of economic, health, and social security and that effectively enforce equal opportunity.

What these decisions tell us about the Presidents who made them is as important as their impact on American liberty. In each case, the action was an outgrowth of both strong intellect and varied life experience. Each man brought with him to the office a vision for the country that was formed and tempered by his past. George Washington became convinced of the need for strong federal leadership after having great difficulty obtaining adequate military resources during the Revolutionary War from the fragmented and weak Continental Congress. Jefferson's profound political thinking and observation of European revolution established his commitment to the government's responsibility to enable and protect individual freedom. James Monroe learned first-hand about the efforts of colonial powers to discourage independence and freedom as a result of his diplomatic experience in Europe. Abraham Lincoln, with his 'common man' background, spent his entire political life seeking a realistic political strategy to end the scourge of slavery. Wilson's religious faith and study of world history resulted in his dedication to international peace and human welfare. And Roosevelt's prior government experience and long battle against polio left him with insights and character traits that enabled him to rescue his country's economy as well as its spirit.

Each of these Presidents was also able to take a flexible approach to the nation's problems, even to deviate from previously held political views when differing circumstances or new challenges presented themselves. They were able to recognize and seize the moment of opportunity when it came to them, revealing an inner confidence and a facility of mind not often present in political leaders. And each of them took actions as President whose primary objective was strengthening American liberty, not solely American power.

If there is one lesson the study of history teaches, it is the fragile nature of a country's good fortune. To preserve a nation's strength, as well as its freedom, its leaders must have both vision and courage and its citizens must be both well-informed and politically vigilant.

History is truly relevant to the choices made today. Not because history repeats itself, for situations change and times are different. But understanding the character of past Presidents is critical to an understanding of how the United States became the great and powerful nation it is. When Americans vote for the Presidential candidate they prefer, too often their choice is based on negative campaigning or advertising slogans. Sometimes, the focus is on what the candidate says about his or her political program and how voters believe that program will affect their own self-interest. Voters try to predict what a leader will do based on what he says about himself or what others say about him. However, when we study American history, we come to realize that the Presidential decisions that have shaped America the most have been ones that would have been difficult to anticipate or predict in advance. They have resulted from circumstances and challenges that presented themselves after the candidate was elected. And they were ones that often required the President to look beyond his normal political program, or beyond the interests of his region or of his class, to the long-term welfare of the country.

All of the foundational decisions were made by Presidents who were able to fit their initiative into a coherent and forward-looking political vision, and who were conscious of the likely impact on the nation and the world. To a significant extent, each man brought that vision into focus as a result of life experience that prepared him to confront national challenges and to address them both creatively and courageously. As Presidents, they exhibited an inner strength and confidence that reflected the nature of their personality.

Such decisions take vision and intellectual courage—qualities that can be discerned only by a careful study of a man's character and background. History does tell us that the ability to identify such qualities may be critical to America's future.

CHAPTER 1.

George Washington and the Foundation of a National Economy

George Washington, the first President, built an economic foundation that could support the country's unity and growth. He overcame the failures and inherent weaknesses of the government that existed prior to the adoption of the Constitution in 1787. Creatively assisted by Alexander Hamilton, he established a blueprint for a strong, growing national economy that enabled the United States to develop its system of liberty and play a significant role on the world stage. In doing so, he established a precedent for a strong federal government and showed that a President with vision could overcome major challenges to American liberty.

1. After the Revolution

When America defeated Great Britain in 1783 after a seven year Revolutionary War, it became a beacon of hope to people everywhere who desired liberty. At the time, citizens of foreign countries were governed either by tyrannical regimes or by hereditary monarchs and aristocrats anointed solely by the accident of birth. The United States embarked on a noble experiment to determine whether a government dedicated to human liberty could survive and prosper. Never before had a people sought to build a country based totally on the consent of the governed and on equal opportunity for leadership. And nowhere had the Enlightenment values of freedom of thought and religious freedom yet coexisted with security and order. From the perspective of a 21st century citizen of the world's only superpower, one may think the experiment was destined to be successful, but it was truly not inevitable. There were many opportunities for failure along the way; a foreign threat, internal dissension, political instability, fragmentation of the union—any one could have caused tragic collapse. American liberty has survived because of the Constitution on which it was grounded, the balanced structure of the government that it prescribed, the heroic sacrifices of its people, and the fortuitous leadership of a few great Americans.

No single person is more responsible for the success of the brave experiment in liberty than George Washington. He was a riveting symbol of the character and endurance of the new nation—through a torturous war against the most powerful empire on earth, during a period of loose confederation among thirteen disparate colonies, and throughout a precedent-setting first Presidency. His leadership and policies gave the ideals of the Revolution lasting substance. He set an example for his nation's future that established the importance of strong federal government policies carried out by a President whose confidence and vision equipped him to provide critical leadership. It was inevitable that the country's first President would powerfully influence the conduct and decision-making of future Presidents. Fortunately for the country and for the future of liberty, Washington was a man of dependable character and unequaled integrity, whose life experience gave him firm ideas about how America could not only survive, but flourish.

2. Washington's Background

A Virginian from his birth on February 22, 1732 to his death on December 14, 1799, George Washington was born into an upper middle class landowning family. Eleven years old when his father died in 1743, the majority of the family's 10,000 acres, including Mount Vernon near Alexandria, was inherited by his older half-brother, Lawrence, in accordance with the custom of the time. Fourteen years older than George, Lawrence was a cultured, European-educated man who had acquired significant military experience and became an ideal role model. George admired and emulated him, visiting him often to join in hunting, farming, and horseback riding, and to listen to stories about the honor of a soldier's life.

By his early teens, George had become physically mature and was eager to embark on adult responsibilities, learning from Lawrence many social graces, including how to dress respectably and dance proficiently. He learned the value of showing poise and decorum in social situations, copying in longhand at age 15 a popular self-improvement guide originated by 16th century Jesuits, specifying 110 "Rules of Civility & Decent Behavior in Company and Conversation."[1]

Lack of financial resources for higher education did not discourage George's determination to better himself and his status in life. He both observed others and taught himself, acquiring the applied sciences of surveying, mathematics, geography, and accounting that would prove useful in the ensuing years. By 16, he earned money on occasion by assisting the country surveyor in plotting land, with the neatness of his handwriting and the accuracy of his surveys becoming legendary. Nevertheless, George's interests lay in another direction; years of listening to his brother's tales of military exploits, as well as Lawrence's advice to join the navy or merchant marine, appealed more to his adventurous spirit. Yet, his practical and responsible nature led him to acquiesce to the wishes of his mother, and George continued to develop a surveying career. Significant profits could be made in buying the uncharted territory west of the nearby Blue Ridge Mountains, and the ambitious young man used his surveying talent to help increase the meager property he had been bequeathed and, consequently, to improve his social status. By the time of his death, he owned over 56,000 acres.

The sense of responsibility he later exhibited to the new nation was a natural extension of the "family values" he always displayed. When Lawrence began to exhibit signs of the serious lung disease that would later claim his life, George volunteered to accompany him to the more favorable Caribbean climate on Barbados and to help with his care. While there, George contracted smallpox, a common scourge of young men of the time, but his overall strength enabled him to survive it. The trip helped him to understand the great economic potential of the markets of the West Indies, and the advantages of trade as a key element in the economic growth of the country. As time passed, Lawrence's health failed to improve and he died in 1752, leaving the family estate at Mount Vernon to his wife and daughter and, upon their death, to George. Following the deaths of both women, he took ownership of Mount Vernon in 1761, living there for the remainder of his life.

At age 27 Washington married Martha Dandridge Custis, a prominent widow who brought him significant wealth and dramatically increased his family responsibilities. Although the couple never conceived children together, Martha brought two children to their marriage, John (called Jackie), age three, and Martha (called Patsy), age two. Patsy suffered from epilepsy and died at the premature age of 17 in 1773. John grew up with a lack of motivation, finally becoming an aide to his father during the Battle of Yorktown in 1781, but he became ill in the rough, unfamiliar military environment and died within days. The grief George and Martha felt was partially assuaged by their decision to raise their only grandchildren, John's two children, George Washington Parke Custis (called 'Little Washington') and Eleanor Parke Custis (called 'Nelly').

The Washingtons extended their compassionate largesse at Mt. Vernon to nephews, nieces, cousins and other extended family. George assumed responsibility as caretaker to a variety of people within his household, whether they were slaves, temporary workers, or family. Neighbors and colleagues valued his advice on personal or agrarian problems and called upon him to write their will, act as guardian to their children, and extend needed financial loans. His word was his bond and he expected the same in return. Although a slave owner, he respected the worth of each individual and, at his death, freed all his slaves and bequeathed funds sufficient for their education and welfare.

Washington actively cultivated his property, occasionally borrowing from British lenders to ensure a livelihood from his tobacco crop. Some of his fellow property owners felt mistreated by British creditors as a result of the high interest rates they had to pay and the strict, unforgiving enforcement of loan obligations. Washington was farsighted enough to convert part of his property from the depletive effects of tobacco farming to the more profitable and more restorative wheat crop, reducing his dependency on loans and thereby avoiding the plight of other landowners. Notwithstanding his good fortune, he always felt sympathy for the grievances Virginia planters had against the British.

The personal integrity Washington exhibited and the trust he was given by others combined to make each succeeding step in his military and political career appear to build inexorably to leadership of the new nation. He joined the Virginia militia in the early

1750's, fighting alongside the British in the French and Indian War, defending Virginia's claims to territory in the Ohio region. Like many others of his generation, his concern was for the defense of his own colony rather than any overriding interest in the British Empire. Relishing the military life, Washington wrote to his brother, "I heard Bulletts [sic] whistle and believe me there was something charming in the sound."[2] As he had done with his education, determination and ambition enabled him to learn the military arts through tutoring, observation, and combat experience. Showing great leadership ability and rising quickly in responsibility, he received a British commission as lieutenant colonel at the age of 22 and became colonel in charge of the Virginia Regiment at the age of 24. The highlight of his pre-Revolution military career occurred when he successfully led his Virginia Regiment in the retaking of Fort Duquesne from the French in 1758. Travel to conferences with British commanders in Boston and Philadelphia during these years allowed him to gain familiarity with the situation in other colonies and to become one of the country's few founders with personal knowledge of colonies other than their own—a prime reason why others looked to him for leadership during the later Revolutionary period.

Washington's political career began in late 1758 with his election to the Fairfax County legislature, eventually becoming its representative to the Virginia state legislative body, the House of Burgesses, and remaining a member throughout the revolutionary period of the 1760's and 1770's. Composed of elite landowners with similar interests, this body operated on the basis of mutual respect and consensus building; their power and prestige increased steadily during the 1760's. At various points during that decade, as the British enacted taxes and commercial restrictions on the colonies, the House of Burgesses viewed these acts as infringements of their own rights and privileges. Washington firmly and consistently opposed these British measures.

Already widely recognized in Virginia as a leader, he was elected as a representative to the First Continental Congress, held in Philadelphia in 1774, to determine a coordinated response to British rule—the first attempt of the thirteen original colonies to act as one "nation". He was later elected to the Second Continental Congress in May, 1775, convened to consider an appropriate response to the first battles of the Revolution in Lexington and Concord, Massachusetts. Washington attended the opening session of that Congress in his military uniform as commander of the Virginia militia, intentionally foreshadowing the likely result of the deliberations. It was clear that the citizens of Boston needed military help against the British from more than their nearby militias. The Congress decided to summon that support from throughout the colonies and asked George Washington to become "General and Commander in Chief of the American Forces." John Adams of Massachusetts nominated him to that post and, to some extent, Washington's Virginia background was influential in obtaining the support of colonies outside New England for the resistance effort. He accepted the commission but declined salary to perform it, believing that a man of means should be willing to serve his country without compensation, preserving government resources for other critical purposes.

Washington's military role in the Revolution was one that demanded strong character as much as strategic ability. He was required to act simultaneously as leader of men, administrator and organizer of complicated logistics, balancer of political interests, and diplomat par excellence. Time and time again, in order to preserve manpower for future battles, he was able to parry more numerous military forces and undertake tactical retreats, most notably in New York, Trenton, and Valley Forge.

The consequences of having a weak national government became quickly obvious to General Washington. Leading an army dependent on the Continental Congress for both men and money, he realized early in the war that he would have to carry on without all the necessary resources. The Congress had neither the power nor the political will to provide what he needed, relying as it had to on the vagaries of political decisions in each colony to raise tax revenue for the cause; such decisions were unpredictable, often made in response to the results of the latest battle or the newest rumor about the coming of peace. In addition, because Congress provided only for voluntary one-year enlistment periods, and had no authority to conscript recruits, Washington was deprived of experienced troops over an extended time, severely handicapping his military planning. He protested these circumstances in a letter to the President of the Congress in 1780:

> ...the system appears to have been pernicious beyond description...Had we formed a permanent Army in the beginning, which by the continuance of the same men in

Service, had been capable of discipline we never should have had to retreat with a handful of Men across the Delaware in Seventy Six; trembling for the fate of America, which nothing but the infatuation of the enemy could have saved…We should not have remained all the succeeding Winter at their mercy…liable at every moment to be dissipated…We should not have been at Valley Forge with less than half the force of the enemy…destitute of every thing, in a situation neither to resist nor retire…[3]

Despite the lack of support, Washington, in a compelling demonstration of patriotism, never wavered from his loyalty to the Congress and was never tempted to take power into his own hands in a military coup, although several of his inferior officers urged him to do so.

To compensate for its inability to exercise effective wartime authority, the Congress asked France, Britain's enemy, for military assistance; General Rochambeau's army and Admiral LeGasse's navy provided aid that proved crucial to Washington's ultimate victory. The colonies were able to obtain critical financial resources for the war by negotiating loans from France and the Netherlands, with John Adams' skillful diplomacy instrumental in that effort. As it turned out, the inability of the Continental Congress to meet the loan payments during the war led to one of President Washington's greatest challenges as President almost a decade later.

Victory in the long and exhausting Revolutionary War was recognized in the Treaty of Paris in 1783. Washington immediately thereafter surrendered his military command to the civilian government, setting a powerful and enduring precedent for the supremacy of civil over military authority. He was ever a "republican", in the sense that he was committed to representative government—elected by those who would be governed. But the lessons of his experience as the military commander under the weak Continental Congress remained with him for the remainder of his public career.

3. Government After the Revolution

Thirteen spirited, but fragmented, states had successfully fought the powerful British, but the weak confederacy they constituted was not yet capable of taking its place among the major nations of the world; they had barely begun to evolve into a nation.[4] The Articles of Confederation the states had adopted in 1781 had created only one institution of national government, the Continental Congress, but its powers were limited and very much at the mercy of the individual states.[5] Because Congress had no ability to levy taxes, it was forced to depend not only on the willingness of each state to provide funds voluntarily, but on the readiness of foreign countries to extend critical loans.

The Articles created no executive branch and, therefore, no President to lead it. Congressional Committees performed all administrative functions, constituting an inefficient executive, at best. With neither a national Justice Department nor a judicial branch to enforce the laws Congress passed, obedience to national law depended on whether state legislatures passed statutes that mirrored those enacted by the Congress.

The Continental Congress was crippled in its attempts to establish the basis for a true national economy. Each state could, and often did, levy its own tariffs on imports from foreign countries. State tariffs were discriminatory and haphazard, never constituting a consistent plan to protect domestic commerce, and never permitting a united negotiating front to the world. Congress did not even have an effective mechanism to encourage commerce between individuals or among the states. It could make treaties with foreign countries, but could not override state laws that were inconsistent with any treaty provision. The country was saddled with heavy war debts that had to be addressed before its economy expanded, yet there was no power to raise taxes to pay them or to establish a national currency.

It was by no means certain the government could withstand these centrifugal pressures. To strengthen it by modifying the Articles, unanimous consent of the states was required. The most prominent supporters of our independence and founders of the country, men such as George Washington, John Adams, Thomas Jefferson and James Madison, idealistically thought that state political leaders, coming together out of patriotism and good will, would agree to the amendments necessary for an effective national government. But the cooperative spirit of the Revolution quickly gave way and the hopes of the founders were sorely disappointed; unanimous consent could never be obtained.

Victory in the Revolutionary War should have resulted in great enthusiasm among the citizenry for building a nation; it did not. Instead, with British oppression gone, people concentrated on meeting local priorities and satisfying material needs. With their newly won freedom, many state legislatures unwisely used their power to enact whatever laws favored the short-term economic interests of the majority of their own constituents. The ability to build a country was dealt a near fatal blow by these laws, enacted in the years between the Treaty of Paris in 1783 and Washington's Inauguration in 1789. States favored debtors over creditors, especially penalizing those creditors who had been loyal to Great Britain during the Revolution. They printed money that was not supported by gold or silver or by any confidence-building economic institution, with the result that it quickly depreciated.

Since each state printed its own currency, with varying values, interstate commerce was very cumbersome, and was made even more difficult by legislation protecting each state's selfish economic interests. "Tender laws" required creditors and businessmen to accept their state's currency at face value, even though its true worth was usually much lower. "Staying laws" automatically extended the term of debts and contractual obligations and "special acts" overrode specific judicial decisions favoring particular creditors. "Ex post facto" laws were commonly passed to nullify contracts and legal obligations after they were agreed to. As one historian has put it: "These attacks on property rights were, in the eyes of many, symptomatic of the excesses that were inherent in democracy."[6] Such shortsighted actions convinced many that the country could not afford to trust its political future to those who were lacking in the character necessary to shape it.[7]

All this had the effect of undermining confidence in government, increasing inflation and unemployment, inhibiting trade with other nations, particularly Great Britain, and causing a widespread economic depression. Many of the founders became convinced that the structure of the national government had to be drastically changed—not merely because the powers of the Continental Congress were inadequate for building a nation, but because state legislatures were abusing their power and perverting the liberty for which the founders fought.[8] George Washington verbalized this concern:

> Virtue, I fear, has…taken its departure from our Land, and
> the want of disposition to do justice is the source of the
> national embarrassments[9]

In response to growing concern for the future of national unity,
the Continental Congress decided in February, 1787 to call a convention of representatives from each state "for the sole and express purpose of revising the Articles of Confederation and reporting to
Congress and the several legislatures such alterations and provisions
therein."

4. Washington and the Making of the Constitution

George Washington was elected as a delegate from Virginia to
the Constitutional Convention of 1787, giving him an opportunity
to restructure the government he had long believed was too weak.
He was distressed that states failed to comply with Congressional
directions, and that Congress was unable to prevent individual states
from printing paper money—thus devaluing their currency—and
from wreaking havoc with the relationship between creditor and
debtor. He was particularly disappointed at the inability of the states
to coordinate any common approach to building canals and improving
river transportation, which would have allowed for increased internal
trade and western development. He envisioned a government that
could take the lead in encouraging the growth of commerce, both
within the country and internationally; he foresaw a government that
had the power to raise taxes and armies when necessary; and, most of
all, he wanted a government that could be respected by other countries. He wrote in 1785 of his concern that the failure of the states to
support the national government would "…Sap the Constitution of
these States (already too weak), destroy our National character, and
render us as contemptible in the eyes of Europe as we have it in our
power to be respectable."[10]

The 55 delegates to the Constitutional Convention included
prominent and able men from each state. Taking a national rather
than parochial view of the government's shortcomings, these men
"revised" the Articles by proposing their complete replacement with
the document that has been the guiding charter of the country ever

since, the Constitution of the United States. That this document, created in the 18th century for thirteen states with 3 million people, is still vital in the 21st century for 50 states with 300 million people, is a tribute to the wisdom of those framers and to the citizens in each state who later voted to adopt it.

His fellow delegates unanimously elected Washington to be President of the Convention on the basis of his great reputation; ironically, in that capacity, the Convention's rules prevented him from taking part in any of the debate. However, during the four months the Convention was in session, Washington listened to and learned from some of the most brilliant oratory and argument about the structure of government that have ever been developed. The speeches of Alexander Hamilton, James Wilson and James Madison resonated most clearly for him because they advocated the strong national government he favored.[11]

Each delegate was conscious of the likelihood that Washington would be the first holder of executive authority in the new government, which escalated the gravity and drama of the occasion. Some were apprehensive about the scope of that power, since the Revolution was fought primarily against oppressive executive authority. By this time, though, there was consensus that each state had too much discretion under the Articles of Confederation while the national government had too little effective power. The delegates fashioned Article II of the Constitution, which described the powers of the President, with reference:

> ...to what they already knew of Washington. What they decided, in short, was whether the strength they wanted, as well as the restraint, were to be found in Washington, and whether the weakness they feared, or the despotism they abhorred, were likely to appear under Washington's hand.[12]

The resulting Article II granted extensive powers to the President, and it is unlikely that a Constitution with such strong executive authority would have been written if Washington had not been seen as the obvious first choice. After all, the Revolution was fought to end the arbitrary power exercised by King George III of England and the former colonials were loath to replace one arbitrary executive with another. However, George Washington was already a great man in the eyes of his countrymen, having been the symbol of determination and courage throughout the Revolution. His integrity reassured almost everyone that there would be no danger of abuse of power with him in the office. Historians believe that one major reason the people approved the new Constitution, as they later voted in state constitutional conventions, was the reassurance they felt at the prospect of Washington as the first President.[13] In the famous quotation of Henry Lee, he was "...*first in war, first in peace, and first in the hearts of his countrymen.*" As Pierce Butler, a delegate from South Carolina, put it, the President's powers would not have been so great:

> ...had not many of the members cast their eyes towards General Washington as President; and shaped their Ideas of the Powers to be given to a President, by their opinions of his Virtue.[14]

The delegates spent more time on drafting Article II than any other part of the document. Although the Article established a strong executive, its general language left room for each future President to develop his particular relationship to Congress, to state governments, to foreign countries and to the people of the United States.

The new instrument, by its own decree, became the supreme law of the land, binding judges and legislators in every state—even if local law was inconsistent with it. Article VI stated:

> This Constitution, and the Laws of the United States which shall be made in Pursuance thereof; and all Treaties made, or which shall be made, under the Authority of the united States, shall be the supreme Law of the Land; and the Judges in every State shall be bound thereby, any Thing in the Constitution or Laws of any State to the Contrary notwithstanding.

This provision, called the Supremacy Clause, cured the major weakness of the Articles of Confederation. In addition, states were specifically prohibited from enacting ex post facto laws, from impairing the obligations of contracts, from issuing money, and from accepting anything but gold and silver coin in payment of debts. These measures prevented the abuses of legislative power by transient state majorities that had been most disturbing to the Constitution's framers. Although James Madison proposed a provision granting Congress the power to nullify any act of a state legislature, the proposal did not receive sufficient support in the Convention to be enacted. Ironically, only a decade later, Madison (and his political ally, Thomas Jefferson) reversed his position and claimed that an individual state had the power to nullify any act of Congress![15]

Intent on ensuring that national legislative power would not be abused, the delegates established the principle of "separation of powers," placing responsibility for making law, executing law, and interpreting law in separate parts of government.[16] Since 1700, a similar principle was at the center of the British constitutional system, but it was largely an unwritten one. The drafters of the American Constitution were convinced that King George III had abandoned it in the years before the Revolution by acquiring too much influence over Parliament, and causing the American colonies to suffer as a result. They were determined that the American version of the principle would be structured so that it could not be ignored by any political leader or leaders seeking arbitrary power.

The heart of the system of separation of powers was the establishment of three independent and co-equal branches of government: the legislative, the executive and the judicial. Each governmental element had its separate yet essential functions and was able to exercise "checks and balances" against the others, thus preventing any from acquiring too much power. The legislature was divided into two houses, the House of Representatives, elected directly by the people every two years, and the Senate, elected indirectly by each state legislature (until the 17th Amendment, adopted in 1913, provided for direct popular election), with each state equally represented. The executive was led by a President who was indirectly elected by electors in each state. The judiciary was appointed by the President, with the consent of the Senate, but was protected from political pressure from the other branches by virtue of lifetime appointments. Congress was given the power to remove executive and judicial officers for serious misconduct by means of impeachment. As a final "check", two of the branches, the executive and the legislative, although detached from the people, were "representative" of them and, thus, ultimately controlled by them. These operational elements of the separation of powers have provided the basic framework of the American Republic to this day. They constitute a marvelously effective barrier to tyranny and deserve to be understood clearly by all the citizens who benefit from them.

Specific powers were delegated to the three branches that were lacking under the Articles; primarily, the powers to tax, to regulate interstate and foreign commerce, to raise and support standing armies and to supervise state militias. The new document also authorized more general enabling powers, permitting each branch to respond to future conditions that were unknown or unforeseen when the Constitution was created. For example, Congress was given authority to pass all laws "necessary and proper" for carrying out the defined powers, yet, it was not clear how far those "implied" powers could extend in specific applications. Similarly, the Constitution "vested" executive power in the President and designated him as "Commander in Chief", but it was not clear about the extent of his authority over foreign policy, or his ability to put soldiers in harm's way without Congressional approval.[17] Opinions differ on that issue even today. Some relatively recent Presidential decisions, such as John Kennedy's ill-fated Bay of Pigs invasion, Richard Nixon's bombing of Cambodia, George W. Bush's imprisonment of alleged terrorists at Guantanamo Bay without charge or trial, and his NSA eavesdropping program without court approval, remain controversial exercises in Presidential authority.

The Constitution did not spell out precise boundaries for federal-state relations and was silent on whether the states could exercise a power that was not specifically assigned to the federal government. In 1791 the Tenth Amendment was adopted in an attempt to answer that question, stating "The powers not delegated to the United States by the Constitution, nor prohibited by it to the States, are reserved to the States respectively, or to the people." The meaning of this Amendment in particular cases has not been obvious and has been the subject of many Supreme Court cases throughout American history.

Such ambiguities sowed the seeds of political debate and conflict and have provided opportunities for decisions that have had positive impact on the survival of liberty. George Washington was the first to grapple with the lack of clarity when, as President, he was faced with structuring the country's economic framework. He responded to the Revolutionary War debt and to the need for a national bank by taking an expansive view of implied powers and exercising a broad role for the federal government in relation to the states. Washington's decisions set the pattern for disputes regarding federal/state relations that have continued to the present day. They also had a profound impact on the growth of the young republic and helped to elevate its standing in the world.

The government established by the Constitution was, in a very real sense, an experiment, whose outcome was not predictable with certainty. Would it be possible for a government representative of and responsive to the people—a republic—to reconcile order and liberty, power and justice, security and freedom in an effective manner? Could it survive in a dangerous world of empires, wars, and greed? Washington knew that a young republic would need to be seen as capable, both militarily and economically, in order to preserve its independence.

5. The First President

At the age of 56, George Washington was unanimously elected the first President of the United States on February 4, 1789. The results could not be made official until the ballots cast by the designated electors were counted by both houses of Congress, as remains true today. Travel was slow and tedious, and several weeks elapsed before a quorum of Congress was present in New York City (the original national capital) to do the counting. Washington, at his home in Mount Vernon, did not learn of his election until April 14 and, when he was told, he wrote in his diary of his genuine apprehension about whether he would succeed as the first President:

> About ten o'clock I bade adieu to Mount Vernon, to private life, and to domestic felicity; and, with a mind oppressed with more anxious and painful sensations than I have words to express, set out for New York…with the best dispositions to render service to my country in obedience to its call, but with less hope of answering its expectations.[18]

His fellow countrymen had no such apprehension; the ceremonial journey from Mount Vernon to New York City, a distance of about 300 miles, lasted almost two weeks and provided an opportunity for average citizens to express their admiration and adulation. Washington was greeted by large crowds in each city and town along his route, often accompanied by bands, fireworks, public officials, and military officers. At the site of the battle of Trenton, New Jersey, where he had repulsed the British attack seven years previously during the Revolutionary War, Washington passed under a great arch, supported by pillars and festooned with evergreen and flowers. Young girls offered bouquets to him and sang ceremonial songs. When he finally reached Elizabeth, New Jersey, across the water from his destination, he was ushered onto a barge with a crimson canopy that brought him to New York. Each boat in the harbor displayed flags and their seamen shouted support as fireworks boomed in the background. Thousands of New Yorkers left work to witness Washington's arrival, the equivalent of a modern day ticker tape parade down Fifth Avenue.

Although the celebration at the beginning of Washington's Presidency showed widespread confidence in the man, Americans did not necessarily have faith that the new federal government would be a lasting one. Some feared that it would abuse its power and oppress its citizens as the British had done, perhaps with excessive taxation or aristocratic rule. This group included "anti-federalists", like Patrick Henry, who had campaigned against the ratification of the Constitution, but also included, from time to time, some of the nation's greatest patriots—Thomas Jefferson and James Madison among them. In the First Inaugural Address on April 30, 1789 Washington himself succinctly summarized the challenge awaiting both him and the nation:

> …the preservation of the sacred fire of liberty, and the destiny of the Republican model of Government, are justly considered as deeply, perhaps as finally staked, on the experiment entrusted to the hands of the American people.[19]

The country's unity and liberty would truly be put to the test during Washington's Presidency. His first term would require him to provide specific definition to the general powers the Constitution granted the national government. The most prominent founders of the country—Washington, John Adams, Alexander Hamilton, Thomas Jefferson, and James Madison—hoped and trusted that the nation could do so without encouraging factions and political parties. They believed that people of high morality, with "republican" virtues and a national outlook, would form political consensus on all major issues. In the event, they underestimated the depth of the political disagreements that would ensue and separate these former allies and friends from one another. And they failed to foresee the clash of economic and regional interests that were inherent in the administration's first legislative proposals. It was not clear in 1789, but the tension between national unity and states' rights would soon lead to the creation of the first United States political parties, and to recurring political battle for the remainder of the country's history.

6. The National Debt

The talents, skills, and personal dignity developed during a lifetime of leadership responsibility were crucial to President Washington's ability to maintain the unity of the country and the trust of its citizens. Conscious of the critical role the first administration would play, he gathered around him some of the great men of the revolutionary generation, men whose ideas and courage had already laid the foundation for freedom and liberty. Thomas Jefferson, John Adams, and John Jay were among the very few Americans with any diplomatic experience abroad. Adams became the first Vice President, Jefferson was appointed Secretary of State, and Jay, key negotiator of the Treaty of Paris ending the Revolution, became the first Chief Justice of the Supreme Court. By far the most influential member of the administration was the brilliant and ambitious Secretary of the Treasury, Alexander Hamilton of New York, who, at 32 years of age, was the youngest member of the Cabinet. Washington's administrative style required each of his department heads to obtain approval from him on any significant administrative or policy proposal, the same approach he used as Commander of the revolutionary army. However, Hamilton enjoyed more freedom than other Cabinet members as a result of the depth of his financial knowledge and his great creativity in solving problems.[20]

As General Washington's chief military aide during the Revolutionary War, Hamilton had managed with ingenuity the scarce human and material resources that were made available for combat. When the British threatened to attack the Southern states, Hamilton boldly recommended that slaves be made soldiers and given their freedom.[21] Convinced that the army's lack of resources was a result of the inability of the Continental Congress effectively to manage the economy of the new nation, he took the initiative to become an expert in economics, reading Adam Smith, among other English economists. Hamilton produced a variety of recommendations detailing how the Continental Congress could manage its debt and provide adequate resources, although few were adopted. Washington was impressed by Hamilton's analytic abilities and the young man's capacity to help build the country, entrusting him with the most sensitive diplomatic and political missions. He went on to be a key contributor to the Constitutional Convention and the principal author (the others being James Madison and John Jay) of *The Federalist Papers*, a persuasive collection of analyses and arguments in support of the ratification of the Constitution. He had risen from quite humble origins in the Virgin Islands to graduate from what is now Columbia University, have a successful military career under General Washington, and become a respected lawyer in New York. He was President Washington's most important advisor and a prominent example of the generous opportunities for advancement available to the citizens of the new republic.

Washington immediately faced policy choices that would determine where power to shape the economy would lie in the new nation—with the national government or with the states, with the commercial and manufacturing interests or with the landholders and the farmers. Hamilton's role was to recommend a framework for a sound financial and monetary system. Shortly after Congress established the Department of the Treasury in September, 1789, it passed a resolution instructing the first Secretary to prepare a plan to manage the outstanding debt of the new country.

The problem of public finance was not only one of great importance but of great complexity. It was, in actuality, a four-sided paradox:

1) unless the new country could borrow funds, its economy would not be able to grow and its very existence would be threatened by economically stronger, rival nations;

2) no one would want to lend the country money (usually by buying its bonds) unless they were sure it would be able to pay the interest and principal the debt required;

3) no prospective lender or investor, whether foreign or domestic, could be sure the country would pay future debts while those acquired during the Revolution remained unpaid; and

4)   the country could not pay the Revolutionary debts unless it
could establish good credit and borrow necessary funds.

Some politicians advocated potentially disastrous, "quick" solutions, such as ignoring or repudiating the debt, or immediately raising enough taxes to pay all of it. Repudiation of the debt would have caused the collapse of the country's trade and commercial welfare, effectively discouraging anyone from extending credit to it. Yet, immediate payment of the debt from tax revenues would have required such high tax burdens that most citizens would have wondered whether the Revolution had merely replaced one oppressive government with another. Some states had tried these "quick" solutions during the 1780's, with predictable results. Rhode Island's legislature, controlled by radical agrarian interests, tried to repudiate the state's debt by issuing paper money that quickly lost its value, hurting almost everyone.   Massachusetts took the opposite approach, raising enough taxes to pay off all its bonds, but many farmers in the state did not have the funds to pay their taxes and feared foreclosure, stimulating a civil uprising called Shay's Rebellion after its leader, Daniel Shays. The rebels attempted to prevent the courts from functioning and issuing orders against farmers and their property; the rebellion had to be put down by local militias that remained loyal to the state government. At the time, Washington was so alarmed by the these events that he strongly supported the call for the 1787 Constitutional Convention in order to give the national government more effective power to guide the economy and ensure public tranquility. As President he resolved not to allow the new federal government to put the entire country in a comparably humiliating position by adopting one of the "quick" but impractical and self-defeating solutions.

Hamilton meticulously researched and identified the size of the debt, together with the domestic and foreign creditors that would have to be satisfied.[22] After reviewing the problem and his proposed solutions with President Washington, the two were convinced that they needed to develop faith in the credit of the United States and place the new country on a firm economic footing. The Constitution itself authorized such a policy, stating in Article VI:

All Debts contracted…before the Adoption of this Constitution, shall be as valid against the United States under this Constitution, as under the Confederation.

Both men understood that the reputation of the country in the eyes of the world required that the national government take the lead in honoring its debts. With Washington, this belief was intrinsic to his personal sense of honesty and fairness and consistent with the lessons of his experience as commander of the revolutionary forces. He had stated in a letter to the Marquis de Lafayette in 1789:

> ...my endeavors [as President] shall be unremittingly exerted (even at the hazard of former fame or present popularity) to extricate my country from the embarrassments in which it is entangled, through want of credit...[23]

With Hamilton, the conviction was based on years of studying history and observing in-depth the economies of European countries, particularly those of England and France. He concluded that a market economy and free trade were essential to growth, since they established incentive for man's natural desires and interests to be acted upon. He also believed that the government should actively administer the economic system to ensure the availability of an adequate supply of money, and to direct it to the hands of those who would use it most productively for the country's benefit. This included the merchants, industrialists, investors and financiers—in short, the people who were in the best position to put capital to work.[24]

In January, 1790, Hamilton presented to Congress the *Report on Public Credit*, the first explanation of his and Washington's grand design for the economic framework of the United States. The Report set out the principle that the entire debt needed to be honored, with no part of it ignored, in order to establish the Government's creditworthiness. Rather than outright or quick payment, the document proposed "funding" of the debt, whereby the Government would pledge a sufficient amount of the country's annual income to pay the interest and principal gradually. Hamilton called properly funded debt "a national blessing"; when citizens had confidence in the government's commitment to pay, they would treat the "bonds" or "notes" (then called 'certificates') issued to do so as money.[25] If they had faith that value would always be there, they did not need to hold the paper until the due dates in order to redeem them, using them instead to pay each other for goods and services. Thus, funding could greatly increase the amount of liquid capital available for economic growth because the annual taxes levied by the government for this purpose would need to be only a fraction of the total indebtedness. The bonds issued to cover the entire debt would provide resources many times the amount of those taxes and would significantly stimulate the economy. The funding scheme would thus solve the four-sided paradox.[26]

The Report proposed the establishment of a stable tax base to support debt service. The Constitution had specified the power to impose import duties as an exclusively federal power and they were an important part of the plan. As a result, continued commerce with Great Britain, our most significant trading partner, became essential to the country's economic well-being. The Report also recommended the use of an excise tax on alcoholic beverages to raise the money necessary to fund the debt. These two taxes were intended to cure one of the weaknesses Washington perceived under the Articles of Confederation—the inability of the national government to command a stable source of tax revenue.

There was some opposition in Congress because the Report proposed that only the current holders of certificates would benefit. Many of the poorest and most deserving members of society would be disadvantaged by it, particularly those original holders of government certificates who had since sold them to investors and speculators rather than wait for the government to redeem them. James Madison, then a Congressman from Virginia, advocated paying both the current and original holders, arguing that since many soldiers, their widows, and orphans were induced to sell their certificates at greatly devalued prices, the government should allow these original holders to share in the payments. He recommended issuing new certificates to then current holders at the highest market value their certificates had attained; original holders would be paid the difference between that value and the original face value. He called his plan "discrimination" among potential creditors.

Most Congressmen disagreed with Madison. His scheme would have been much more costly than Hamilton's; it would have been extremely difficult to track down original holders and find adequate records, and the opportunity for fraud would have been rampant. Hamilton persuaded a majority of Congress that discrimination was, in effect, a breach of contract with the current holders and would render the government's bonds difficult to negotiate freely. Therefore, the ability of the country to develop a liquid money supply would be compromised and its ability to borrow in the future would be undermined.   Even though Madison's plan was soundly defeated, it earned for him the reputation of being in support of the "common man" and against the "moneyed interests."

More serious opposition was directed at the administration's proposal for the immediate "assumption" of the state debts, whereby the national government would assume responsibility for all the financial obligations incurred by the states to prosecute the Revolution. Although it would add another $25 million to the total needing funding, the Report claimed that assumption would result in two major benefits to the country.   Because there would be a unified group of creditors, the government would acquire a powerful interest group to support its economic program.[27]   It would also forestall a battle between the states and the federal government over tax revenue, leaving the best sources for the federal government.

The problem then became how to identify the debts and apportion them fairly.   Those states that had been careless in their bookkeeping—mostly in the South—feared they would be shortchanged if the audit standards were too strict; those that were efficient—mostly in New England—feared the audit standards would be too lenient, thereby permitting false claims by others.[28] The Report suggested that the debts would be assumed as they existed in 1790, penalizing those states, like Virginia, which had already paid off a good part of its debt. As a political son of Virginia and susceptible to its political pressure, James Madison strongly objected to this part of the plan, proposing instead that the government should assume the debts of each state as they had stood in 1783. Although this would have benefited those states that had paid off debt, it would have nearly doubled the burden on the federal government.   President Washington, another political son of Virginia and still a major landowner, was able to see beyond the narrow interests of his home state and viewed the assumption plan as fair to all the states that sacrificed for the Revolution.[29]

Hamilton was surprised by Madison's political stance, since, when they co-authored *The Federalist Papers*, the Virginian favored a strong federal government and did not emphasize states' rights. However, political pressure from his home state, as well as Madison's growing antagonism to the nature of the Washington administration's entire economic system, made his opposition not so surprising, after all. Madison was concerned about policies that favored creditors over debtors and about economic measures that mirrored those British institutions that the Revolution resisted. As one writer has put it:

> Historians may reasonably conclude that...Hamilton's ideas were better calculated than [Madison's] to foster national prosperity and to promote the nation's long-term interests. But...for Madison, prosperity and rapid economic growth were not the only—not, indeed, the most important—points to be considered.[30]

Although the President took no active part in the assumption debate, most Congressmen understood that Washington would not have permitted the plan to be proposed had he been against it. Secretary of State Jefferson bolstered this view with his own concern that, unless funding and assumption were passed, thus establishing the credit standing of the United States, the country might not have the economic strength required to stay neutral in the face of war in Europe.

Madison's opposition delayed Congressional action for months; it appeared that assumption would not pass the House of Representatives. The stalemate was resolved by one of the most fascinating political compromises the country has ever witnessed—a unique event involving Jefferson, Hamilton and Madison that has been called the "Dinner Deal" or the "Compromise of 1790". The compromise involved both the issue of assumption and the relocation of the nation's capital, at that time in New York City. Washington, Jefferson, Madison, and most mid-Atlantic and southern politicians wanted it moved to the banks of the Potomac River in Virginia or Maryland. They felt that, to maintain the unity of the nation, the center of political gravity of the country needed to be further south than it had been. Opposition came not only from New Yorkers and New Englanders, who did not wish the capital moved at all, but, also, from Pennsylvanians who believed the capital should be permanently moved to Philadelphia, birthplace of the Declaration of Independence and the Constitution.

It is not clear who initiated the dinner meeting in late June, 1790 that produced the compromise. The only written recollection of it was penned by Jefferson in 1818, some 27 years after the event, and was undoubtedly influenced by his subsequent disagreements with the Washington Administration's policies and with Hamilton that crystallized much later than 1790. In *The Anas*, Jefferson claimed that Hamilton, distraught by the unwillingness of Congress to pass the assumption bill, accidentally came upon Jefferson while walking to the President's house and begged for his help to convert the votes of some Virginia Congressmen.[31] Jefferson alleged that while he merely offered to host a dinner with Madison to discuss the issue, Hamilton used the occasion to "dupe" the other two into arranging for Virginia support for assumption, in exchange for Hamilton's effort to attract northern votes to move the capital to the Potomac.[32] Despite these claims, it is more likely that all parties were, at some point, equally interested in a bargain and entered into it fully aware of its significance.[33] In the event, Congress voted to move the capital; Hamilton adjusted his assumption formula and accounting method slightly to give Virginia a better deal; and the assumption bill was passed on July 29 with key support from Virginia Congressmen.

The trade-off was more than a routine political compromise; all the principals viewed the agreement as essential to national unity and strength. President Washington put it clearly:

> The two great questions of funding the debt and fixing the seat of government...were always considered by me as questions of the most delicate and interesting nature...They were more in danger of having convulsed the government itself than any other points.[34]

Had the bill to move the capital not been passed, some states might have seceded from the Union long before the Civil War of 1861. Had funding and assumption not been adopted, and the nation's credit had not been established, the country would have faced an equally serious threat to its survival—a financially weakened nation might not have been able to withstand an attempt by either Great Britain or France to extend the European war by invasion or blockade of the United States. Perhaps America would have become a colony once again.

7. The National Bank

The President greeted the First Congress upon its return in December, 1790 for its second session by observing that the strengthening of the nation's credit as a result of funding and assumption had brought economic prosperity at home and respectability abroad.[35] At the same time, there was growing disenchantment in Virginia and the southern states about the passage of that legislation. James Monroe, a Virginian who was later to become the fifth President, wrote to Jefferson complaining that the legislation was a blow to the power of the states because it undermined their ability to levy taxes and greatly strengthened the authority of the federal government.[36] Monroe's concerns about national power were to lessen in later years as experience broadened his vision. Despite such political dissent, Hamilton obtained Washington's approval to submit for Congressional action the *Report on a National Bank*, which constituted the second phase of the administration's economic program.

The proposed national bank was to be a critical facilitator in achieving the strong economic growth intended to follow the passage of funding and assumption; it would create the currency the country so desperately needed by issuing its own notes, redeemable in gold or silver on demand. Under the Articles of Confederation, there had been a constant shortage of money—gold and silver were scarce, no national paper currency existed and the notes issued by state banks varied greatly in value and did not enjoy national circulation. The bank, conceived as a partnership between the government and the bank's private directors, would have an authorized capitalization of $10 million, at the time an enormous sum—greater than the combined capitalization of all banks then existing in the country.[37] The bank would also perform many of the financial functions required by the government— collecting taxes, acting as fiscal agent in foreign transactions, loaning the government money, and serving as the national depositary bank. Finally, ample and secure capitalization would allow the bank to be a financier for entrepreneurs, thereby fueling business expansion and economic growth.

The Report was acknowledged to be a well-reasoned and persuasive document which offered great benefits to the new government yet contained no clear preferences for one interest group over another, unlike the funding and assumption legislation. Most Congressmen recognized the wisdom of its proposals and their importance to the country. There was some opposition based on the fear that the entire economic framework the administration was building—one part of which was the bank— favored the commercial and moneyed interests of the North, rather than the property owners and agrarian interests of the South. Hamilton vigorously disputed that concern, convinced that all classes and all regions would benefit from the system once it was established. Some Congressmen worried that the establishment of the bank in Philadelphia, as the legislation provided, would make less likely the eventual relocation of the nation's capital to the shores of the Potomac. James Madison was the focus for this Virginia-based opposition, and he attempted unsuccessfully to amend the legislation to limit the bank's life to the ten years of Philadelphia's temporary designation as the capital.

Madison next argued that the bank bill was, by its very nature, in violation of the Constitution. The ensuing constitutional arguments over the limits of the power of the federal government formed the basis for the true historical significance of this political event. In the House of Representatives, Madison claimed that, unless the specific power to charter a bank was found in the Constitution, Congress had no power to enact the legislation necessary to do so. This approach to the meaning of the Constitution has become known as "strict constructionism" and has influenced political debate in the United States to the present day. Madison examined the powers granted in Article I and did not believe the authority to charter a bank was included in the powers to tax, to pay debts, to borrow money, to regulate commerce or to provide for the common defense and welfare. Nor did he believe that the power "To make all Laws which shall be necessary and proper for carrying into Execution the foregoing Powers" gave Congress any authority beyond what had already been specified.[38] In any event, he denied that the bank was "necessary" to carry out any of the specified powers, rendering the clause irrelevant in that context. His colleagues were not persuaded and voted 39-20 in favor of the bill. Nineteen of the twenty votes against came from the South, twelve of those from Virginia and Maryland.

The political battle to kill the bank did not end with the bill's passage. Madison next turned his attention to President Washington, hoping to convince him to veto the bank on constitutional grounds.

Washington favored the bank but was sufficiently concerned about these new legal arguments that he requested formal opinions on the matter from two other Virginians, Attorney General Edmund Randolph and Secretary of State Thomas Jefferson. Their opinions essentially agreed with Madison's arguments and went even further by citing, as a basic principle, the language of the soon to be enacted Tenth Amendment to the Constitution: "…all powers not delegated to the United States, by the Constitution, nor prohibited by it to the States, are reserved to the States or to the people."[39] Jefferson's opinion set forth the classic strict constructionist interpretation of the Necessary and Proper Clause:

> "…the Constitution allows only the means which are "*necessary*," not those which are merely "convenient" for effecting the enumerated powers…the Constitution restrained [the enumerated powers] to the *necessary* means, that is to say to those means without which the grant of power would be nugatory."[40]

The opinions intensified Washington's dilemma; to him, the Constitution was sacred and he was unwilling to add his name to legislation that the great document did not authorize. Nor did he want to endanger the movement of the national capital to the banks of the Potomac, something he deeply desired. With fresh doubts, he asked Alexander Hamilton to respond to the constitutional arguments and to do so expeditiously, since the Constitution gave the President only ten days to sign or veto a bill. Simultaneously, the President asked Madison to draft a veto message for him in the event he decided not to sign.

More was at stake than merely the fate of the bank bill. If the Constitution were to be strictly limited to the enumerated powers, it would become almost impossible for the new country to grow strong and take its place among the great nations of the world. To achieve Washington's goal of overcoming the weaknesses inherent in the Articles of Confederation, the new Constitution must permit "implied powers," giving the government flexibility to deal with crises and new situations that were not envisioned when the Constitution was written. Hamilton's challenge was clear and he spent most of his waking hours working on his response.

The opinion Hamilton delivered only two days before the deadline is the classic statement of "broad construction" and implied powers. While acknowledging that sovereignty in the United States was divided between the national and the state governments, he argued that this did not mean that each level of government could not exercise complete authority to carry out its appropriate functions. To the contrary, "each has sovereign power as to *certain things*, and not as to *other things*." Hamilton claimed that, in interpreting the Necessary and Proper Clause, Jefferson added a word that was not there—either "absolutely" or "indispensably" before necessary. With either word added, Hamilton correctly concluded that few actions of any government would be constitutional. Rather, the word "necessary" must take the normal meaning of *"needful, requisite, incidental, useful,* or *conducive to."*

Hamilton demonstrated that the bank was 'necessary' to all of the following enumerated powers: to collect taxes, to borrow money, to regulate foreign and domestic commerce, to provide for the common defense, and to regulate the property of the United States. In one of the most famous statements of Constitutional interpretation, he wrote:

> If the end be clearly comprehended within any of the specified powers, & if the measure have an obvious relation to that end, and is not forbidden by any particular provision of the constitution—it may safely be deemed to come within the compass of the national authority.[41]

Hamilton's formulation influenced our greatest Supreme Court Chief Justice, John Marshall, when he adhered to it almost verbatim in upholding the constitutionality of the successor national bank in the 1819 case of *McCulloch v. Maryland.* After receiving Hamilton's opinion, President Washington decided that the constitutional questions had been adequately answered; he signed the bill on June 25, 1791.

8. The Effects of Washington's Economic Policies

Washington was more than satisfied with the impact of the establishment of the national bank, believing that his administration had rescued the credit standing of the country.[42] In his message to Congress in October, 1791, he reported that:

The rapid subscriptions to the Bank of the United States, which completed the sum allowed to be subscribed, in a single day, is among the striking and pleasing evidences which present themselves…The subscription in the domestic debt of the United States, has embraced by far the greatest proportion of that debt;[43]

The combination of funding of the debt and establishment of the bank yielded the predicted benefits for the new republic. An ample and stable money supply was provided, a reliable system of credit was made available both domestically and internationally, a national tax system was established, a reliable source of loans to the government strengthened its stability, and economic growth was significantly stimulated. Hamilton wrote to Washington that:

…the most incorrigible theorist among its [the bank's] opponents would in one months experience as head of the Department of the Treasury be compelled to acknowledge that it is an absolutely indispensable engine in the management of the Finances and would quickly become a convert to its perfect constitutionality.[44]

Washington and Hamilton's economic system was intended to unify the country and, over the very long run, it had that effect. But, ironically, in the 1790's and early 1800's, it had somewhat of the opposite, though, perhaps, inevitable result. Both Jefferson and Madison had grave concerns about the economic direction of the Washington administration and did not favor federally-led commercial growth, centered in New England and the Northeast. Rather, they envisioned a country whose economy was more dependent on agrarian interests, less willing to tolerate debt and more sensitive to the interests of Virginia and the South. They feared that a strong federal government, particularly with Hamilton at its center, would be overly focused on national growth and insufficiently concerned with individual liberties. Ultimately, their fight against the bank, coming after the battles over funding, discrimination, and assumption, was the start of bitter political conflict among Washington's most trusted colleagues and friends that continued throughout the 1790's. In response to a letter from the

President seeking to mediate the disputes, Hamilton wrote of the growing differences between his supporters and those of Jefferson:

> One side appears to believe that there is a serious plot to overturn the State governments, and substitute a monarchy to the present republican system. The other side firmly believes that there is a serious plot to overturn the General Government and elevate the separate powers of the States upon its ruins. Both sides may be equally wrong & their mutual jealousies may be materially causes of the appearances which mutually disturb them, and sharpen them against each other."[45]

The disagreements were to become even more contentious, ultimately leading to the creation of the Jeffersonian Republican Party, formalizing the political opposition to the Federalists and establishing the American two-party system.

The debate over constitutional interpretation between Madison and Jefferson, on the one hand, and Hamilton and Washington, on the other, has reverberated throughout the nation's history. "Strict constructionism" has been used frequently as an argument against a particular political action with which an individual might disagree. Such historic decisions as the nation's expansion westward, the abolition of slavery, the movement to control the monopoly power of big business with anti-trust laws to benefit consumers, the New Deal's social and economic program to counteract the depression of the 1930's, the racial integration of schools and public accommodations in the 1960's, and national health insurance enacted in 2009 have been attacked as violations of strict construction. The doctrine is often voiced by the party out of power against the policies of the party in power. Despite the belief that strict constructionism serves a "conservative" point of view, in reality it serves whatever group favors federal inaction, whether conservative, liberal or something in between. Ironically, individual political leaders have taken opposing sides of the argument at various times in their careers as it suited their political goals. When Washington and Hamilton favored a strong Presidency, with discretionary authority that could further their economic program, Jefferson believed that such power could be abused and ran counter to the prerogative of the legislature, the people's representatives. Yet, when the

Presidency was in Jefferson's hands, he eagerly used executive discretion in the service of his basic political objectives—specifically, westward expansion enabled by the Louisiana Purchase.

The national bank facilitated economic growth during the late 18th and early 19th centuries. Yet, it provoked ongoing, spirited political conflict between those that believed it was essential for economic expansion and those that thought it favored the commercial and wealthy classes as opposed to farmers and poorer citizens. President Andrew Jackson's Democrats vehemently opposed the national bank as contrary to the interests of the common man and Jackson vetoed the bill to re-charter it in 1832. Thousands of banks and tens of thousands of varieties of paper money plagued the nation's economy as a result of his decision. During the Civil War, some standardization in bank notes was finally mandated and, in 1879, a metallic exchange rate was established for the dollar. However, it was not until 1913, with the creation of the Federal Reserve System, that a central bank on the model of that established by Washington was again at the center of the country's economy. It is a tribute to the vision of both Washington and Hamilton that such an institution proved critical to the development of the United States into the world's leading economy—an economy that was primarily responsible in the 20th century for the victory of liberty over several forms of tyranny, in two World Wars and one Cold War.

9. Washington's Legacy

Nothing was more important to George Washington than that the United States command respect, both at home and abroad.[46] As President, he nurtured the establishment of a system that replaced thirteen weakly confederated states with a strong national government, forever to remain at the center of the economic life of the country. Washington's foresight resulted in a foundation for economic strength that enabled the United States to retain its political liberty and to play a major on the world stage, from his era to the present.

Lacking the economic education and historical knowledge that allowed Hamilton to design the new country's economic framework, Washington understood and supported its value from the outset. Historians have, at times, given Washington too little credit for these achievements because he was not the author of the legislative measures or the primary advocate for them with the Congress.[47] But others have recognized what was more important to the country—the wisdom of his leadership in the service of a strong national economy.[48] Washington recognized the advantages of the economic plan and had the foresight to comprehend from the outset what the United States could become as a result of it. He also had the courage to rise above the parochialism of his Virginia and agrarian origins, and subordinate local interests—including his own—for the good of the country.

Washington is often, though unfairly, viewed in the shadow of Madison, Hamilton and others in assigning responsibility for the substance and adoption of the United States Constitution. In a very real sense, Washington made possible the success of the government created by the Constitution by establishing the tradition in the United States of the supremacy of the popularly elected government over the military. As a leading critic of the weak Articles of Confederation and the excesses of legislature-dominated state governments during the 1780's, he was a crucially important voice for adoption of the Constitution. He realized that the future of liberty could better be served by a strong nation than by a weak federation.

As much as anyone, Washington determined the practical meaning of the Constitution's general principles. He was the first to be called upon to give life to the powers of the President set forth in Article II and, in doing so, established that the President must be subordinate to the rule of law, that he had a similar right and responsibility to interpret the Constitution as did the legislature and judiciary, that the President bore special responsibility over foreign policy as defender of the people, and that the President should act as spokesman for the people in both domestic and foreign affairs.[49] Yet, Washington's most profound influence on the Presidency lies in the high standard of character he set for his successors. Always reluctant to take power and to retain it, he was universally trusted to exercise it wisely.

Washington symbolized and exemplified, in his person and in his character, the strength and the optimism of the new republic. His calm, yet confident demeanor, his honesty and responsibility, his fairness and tenacity, his regal bearing and forward-looking attitude, all combined to render indispensable leadership. In his second term, he would steer the young country on a course of neutrality in the environment of European War, permitting it to husband its growing resources until better able to hold its own in the world. He warned in his Farewell Address against letting faction and party politics influence foreign policy and compromise what was in the best interests of the country. Always aware that lack of unity could weaken America's position in the world, he set the precedent for the country's tradition of a bipartisan approach to foreign policy where, in the well-known phrase of a great diplomatic historian, Samuel Flagg Bemis, "politics stops at the water's edge."

It is deceptively simple, from the perspective of the 21st century, to see loyalty to a strong national government as inevitable. But, in the late 18th century, many questioned whether all Americans shared a commitment to the Constitution and to "republican" government. Only a decade had passed since a group of fragmented yet proud colonies declared their independence; a national consciousness was only in its infancy. In this context, Washington set a visionary, powerful and courageous example of strong federal leadership for his countrymen to follow. His actions set a precedent for how future challenges to American liberty and unity, even if outside the economic sphere, should be met. These challenges included the geographic expansion of the country, immigration policy, the great conflict over slavery, and the extension of the opportunity for liberty to other parts of the world. Without Washington's example, the country's growth would have been delayed and uncertain, its strength less likely to be realized, and the future of its liberty less surely guaranteed.

<u>CHAPTER 2.</u>

Thomas Jefferson and the Expansion of the Nation

President Thomas Jefferson doubled the size of the country as a result of the Louisiana Purchase, setting the course for continental expansion. He created what he called an "Empire of Liberty," to carry into the future the ideals of freedom for which the Declaration of Independence had inspired his countrymen to fight. To accomplish this objective, Jefferson deviated from some of his previous political positions and clouded the future for African Americans and Native Americans. In so doing, he left an impressive, yet inconsistent, legacy.

1. Jefferson the Man and His Early Career

Thomas Jefferson's service as Secretary of State in President Washington's Cabinet lasted only three years, whereupon he "retired" to Monticello, his Virginia estate and sanctuary, without any plan to serve his country again. Had his public career ended at that point, with his primary accomplishment being the drafting of the Declaration of Independence, Jefferson's unique place in the country's history would have been secure. Yet this remarkable man is also remembered now as a great champion of intellectual and religious freedom; as the author of precedent-setting legislation furthering political rights, freedom of speech and public education; as the creator of the two-party system; and as one of the country's most notable Presidents.

Jefferson stands in sharp contrast to George Washington, in both leadership style and personality. The two were but ten years apart in age, Washington born in 1732 and Jefferson in 1743, and both were members of the gentrified Virginia society of landowners who were also slaveholders. Each was left fatherless in early adolescence, and each man's wealth was vastly increased through both inheritance and marriage. They were each wed once, coincidentally to widows named Martha, and each acted as father to an extended family of relatives' children. Yet, there the similarity ended.

Washington's informal education, military experience, and life-long marriage were cornerstones of a steady, confident personality that made him the natural choice to become the nation's first President and the "father of our country"; Jefferson's life experience, independence of thought, and formal education produced a less traditional leader. The solidity and trustworthiness of Washington enabled him to maintain the unity of the country; Jefferson's innovative ideas in opposition led to the division of the country into two political parties. Washington's noble bearing, in and of itself, engendered confidence in the future of America; Jefferson inspired the country with noble ideas of liberty in both the Declaration of Independence and his First Inaugural Address. President Washington, the former military commander, delegated significant responsibility to trusted subordinates; President Jefferson, the political theorist, diplomat, and philosopher, reserved to himself key political decisions and maintained an aversion to military action. Washington was able to transfer to the new government some of his own strength by creating a solid economic framework; Jefferson's greatest contribution as President, the Louisiana Purchase, was an audacious and unexpected doubling of the size of the nation, opening the way for a dynamic expansion of liberty. It can be truly said that if George Washington was a leader through character and example, Thomas Jefferson was a leader through ideas and inspiration. And if Washington's contribution to liberty was the design of an economy strong enough to support it, Jefferson's was the geographic expansion that facilitated the development of individual freedom.

While Washington was exactly what he appeared to be, Jefferson was a more complicated man, a free thinker who was ahead of his time in many ways. He was a "Renaissance Man" and a gentleman farmer, both amateur philosopher and humanist, and a student of the great classical thinkers and the major writers of the English and French Enlightenment. Jefferson designed practical machines, developing a horse-powered threshing device, a mold-board plow for farming, and a multi-level, revolving book stand for consulting more than one volume at a time. He was an omnivorous reader, adept at mathematics and knowledgeable in meteorology, and carried on lifelong studies of

plants, agriculture, migrating birds, extinct animals, and spring flowers. He loved music, playing the violin, cello, and keyboard. Having
studied ancient Roman as well as contemporary English architecture,
he meticulously designed all the buildings that constituted Monticello,
the extensive estate that still stands as a tribute to his ingenuity atop a
hill outside Charlottesville, Virginia, and created the classically beau-
tiful campus of the University of Virginia, which he founded a few
miles away.

Jefferson was the third child, and first son, of Peter Jefferson, a
self-taught surveyor and mapmaker, whose landowning status and
wealth was enhanced by his marriage to Jane Randolph, a member of
one of Virginia's most prominent families. Peter was an active explorer
of the undeveloped land beyond the Alleghenies and east of the Mississippi River, and the son inherited his father's love of nature, hunting,
and the outdoors. When Thomas was only fourteen, Peter Jefferson
died, denying the boy a father's guidance and companionship during
adolescence. Thereafter, he grew up in a female led family and there
are indications he resented his mother's authority. Dumas Malone,
Jefferson's most prominent biographer, states, "…the only remark he
is known to have made about her influence was negative, and he probably did not value her counsel very highly."[50] He was, however, close
to his two older sisters—Jane, who died when Jefferson was 19, and
Martha, who, years later, as a widow with six children, became part of
his Monticello household.

Jefferson's early education was under the tutelage of local clergy,
and was based on a classical curriculum that featured Greek and Latin.
Showing great intellectual potential, he entered the College of
William and Mary in Williamsburg, Virginia at the age of 17. He was
inspired there by older mentors who were influential in forming his
political and moral philosophy—Professors William Small, George
Wythe, his law instructor, and Governor Francis Fauquier. These
men not only strengthened the rational and scientific cast of his mind,
but they filled a void in Jefferson's life left by the death of his father.
After completing his legal studies at William and Mary, he returned
home to Charlottesville in 1767 to practice law.

Jefferson's personal life has been the subject of both curiosity and
debate over the years. While at Williamsburg, his shyness and indecision resulted in the loss of his first love, Rebecca Burwell, when she
became engaged to another suitor. Nine years later, at the age of 28 on

New Year's Day, 1772, he married Martha Wayles Skelton, a wealthy widow with a great love of music, whose four-year-old son had died the year before. The couple shared a life of both happiness and sadness, giving birth to five daughters and one son, only two of whom lived past age three—his daughter Martha, known as Patsy, and his daughter Maria, called Polly. In late 1774, when his father-in-law died, he inherited extensive land holdings and more than 100 slaves, becoming the largest slaveholder in Albemarle County. In their tenth year of marriage, Jefferson suffered the greatest tragedy of his life when Martha passed away on September 6, 1782 at the age of 33. Her dying wish was that he never marry again so that her daughters would not be brought up as stepchildren as she had been.[51] He was to abide by that wish. He mourned her loss deeply, and for several weeks thereafter his major activity consisted of riding on horseback for hours, with daughter Patsy at his side. In November he wrote that he had only recently emerged "...from the stupor of mind which had rendered me as dead to the world as she was whose loss occasioned it."[52] Following Martha's death, Jefferson, ever reticent about his personal life, burned the voluminous correspondence between the two, forever guaranteeing the privacy of their thoughts.

Jefferson's relationships with women were part of his effort to live a cultured life, one where reason was capable of restraining passion. While in France as the country's Ambassador during the 1780's, he had an intimate, two-year friendship with Maria Cosway, an educated English woman who, with her artist husband, lived much of the time in Paris. She and Jefferson often shared visits to museums and accompanied one another to concerts. Although historians are divided on the romantic nature of this relationship, there is no doubt that it was warm, personal, and close, as his letters indicate.[53] There was speculation during Jefferson's lifetime and since, that, following Maria's return to London in 1787, he began a long-term romance with Sally Hemings, the teenage slave who accompanied Jefferson's younger daughter Polly to Paris in July, 1787. While it has been alleged that he fathered some of Sally's children, there is no consensus among historians on whether there was a sexual tie between them, notwithstanding a DNA link to Jefferson's family.[54] Whether either relationship went beyond the platonic is unknown, and is likely to remain so, which, it is safe to assume, is exactly how Jefferson would want it.

He had an enduring friendship with Abigail Adams, the wife of the second President, John Adams. The many letters between them are frank and heartfelt, providing a revealing look at the personalities of two eloquent and noteworthy Americans.[55] Their families became close when they were both in Paris and continued so as Abigail and John moved to London, where they cared for Jefferson's younger daughter Polly when she first traveled to join her father in Europe. Though sorely tested when the two men were political foes during their respective Presidencies, the relationship (as well as the correspondence) between Jefferson and both Abigail and John endured throughout their lifetimes. Coincidentally, and fittingly for heroes of the Revolution, the death of the two former Presidents occurred on the fiftieth anniversary of the country's independence, July 4, 1826.

If Jefferson's personal life can be seen as an attempt to pursue friendship, civility, and order, his public life featured a commitment to abolish oppressive government in the service of individual liberty. His political career began even before the birth of the nation, when he was elected to the colonial Virginia House of Burgesses in 1769. He strongly opposed British rule in the ensuing years, writing his first major work, entitled *A Summary View of the Rights of British America*, in 1774. In it, he established the philosophical underpinning of the American Revolution by stating that people had a "natural right" to freedom and liberty. This concept was a revolutionary one in the late 18th century because it provided people with a powerful justification for separation from a repressive, established government. Jefferson advocated repudiation of the authority of the British Parliament over the American colonies and recommended that the British Empire become a loose confederation of independent countries, much like the British Commonwealth of the present day. Though he never fired a musket in combat, his ideas were as incendiary as the shots fired in Lexington and Concord a mere year later. His battle for liberty would always be fought with words and not weapons.

The power of Jefferson's political ideas would be enshrined forever as the result of his appointment to a five-man committee of the Continental Congress to draft the Declaration of Independence.[56] In June, 1776, Jefferson became the committee's choice as principal draftsman, primarily because of the admiration he earned from his authorship of the *Summary View*. He borrowed extensively from that work in drafting The Declaration, including the famous notion that "all men are created equal" and are "entitled" to independence by "the Laws of Nature and of Nature's God." Abraham Lincoln later said of this natural rights concept:

> All honor to Jefferson—to the man, who in the concrete pressure of a struggle for national independence...had the coolness...and sagacity to introduce into a merely revolutionary document an abstract truth, applicable to all men and all times, and so to embalm it there, that to-day, and in all coming days, it shall be a rebuke and a stumbling-block to the very harbingers of re-appearing tyranny and oppression.[57]

When presented to the Continental Congress for approval, the only major modification to the draft Declaration was the deletion of Jefferson's provision on slavery. He had placed responsibility on King George III for continuing the transport of slaves to the colonies and asserted that the new country would discontinue it. Jefferson regretted the change and attributed it as much to northern protection of their slave traders as to southern dependence on slave labor.[58] Written in only two weeks, the majority of the draft was adopted and the country's independence from Great Britain was thus declared. Although Jefferson was only 32 years old at the time, he created the nation's most cherished national document and utilized little more than his pen and writing table to produce it.

Returning to the Virginia legislature during the years 1776 to 1779, Jefferson submitted two bills that were both radical and controversial for their time, one for religious freedom and one supporting public education.[59] Although only the latter was enacted, and that some nine years later, both proposals reveal a great deal about Jefferson and his political thought. His controlling philosophic principle was that each man should be free to determine his own moral framework, aided solely by his capacity to reason for himself. He objected to the special privileges and status granted to clergy of the established Anglican Church of Virginia. Dissenting sects such as Presbyterians, Baptists and Methodists were becoming numerous and vocal politically and Jefferson believed that the more religious opinions, the better, including non-Christian ones, in order to prevent the established church from becoming oppressive.[60] From the perspective of 21st century America, this may not seem remarkable, but, in 18th century Virginia, it was both contentious and courageous. He went so far as to oppose a proposal for a general tax in support of religion, even though it included a proviso that a citizen could direct the revenue to his own sect; and he wanted to eliminate "religious crimes" such as heresy, denial of the Trinity, or rejection of divine authority, despite the fact they were no longer prosecuted.

Jefferson's view of the proper relationship between politics and religion was based on his conviction that mankind had a natural right to complete intellectual freedom. The bill he submitted set forth the principles of freedom of religion and separation of church and state that were later embodied in the First Amendment to the United States Constitution. Finally enacted in 1786, Jefferson regarded it as one of the three great achievements of his life.[61]

Decades before he founded the University of Virginia, Jefferson's belief in the importance of education was embodied in his proposed 1777 bill on public education. The legislation represented a radical attempt at reform in 18th century Virginia, proposing two levels of schools, primary and grammar, throughout the Commonwealth. At the primary level, three years of free public education would be offered to all non-slave children, male and female, whose family could not afford to pay; at the grammar school level, poor children of exceptional ability would be supported at public expense. The goal was to ensure that liberty (which he defined most basically as government with the consent of the governed, together with the right of freedom of thought) would survive by means of an informed citizenry.

The education system Jefferson proposed was intended to ensure the survival of his vision of American liberty by producing a regular supply of capable leaders who were knowledgeable of and committed to free, representative government. In preparing for the future of his country, Jefferson called upon his own understanding of the past: the key element in his recommended curriculum was the study of history, so that examples of tyranny could be understood and prevented. (Regretfully, the study of history remains frequently undervalued in the schools of 21st century America.) Although the bill was not enacted, it foreshadowed the commitment to universal public education that has become a key building block for all modern developed nations.

In the midst of the Revolutionary War, Jefferson, then 36, was elected Governor of Virginia, a role in which his performance was to be criticized as inadequate to the threat posed by the British. His hesitation in mobilizing military resources in anticipation of the British invasion made it easier for British troops to capture the capital, Richmond, in 1781; he quickly evacuated the city in the face of the attack and barely escaped his own capture when he retreated to Monticello. Criticism of him as an indecisive military planner plagued Jefferson throughout the remainder of his political career, particularly in the context of the Louisiana crisis in his first Presidential term and during the maritime conflict with Great Britain in his second.

In 1783, several months after his wife's death, Jefferson renewed his public service as a delegate to the Continental Congress. Showing great interest in the country's expansion, he drafted and submitted a legislative proposal for governing the land west of the Appalachians and east of the Mississippi. Congress later adopted those parts of his plan organizing northwestern land into territories and prescribing methods for surveying and selling public land. The remainder of the proposal, setting boundaries for new states and prohibiting slavery in those states, served as a model for the Northwest Ordinance adopted in 1787. That act resulted in the eventual addition to the union without slavery of the states of Indiana, Illinois, Michigan, Ohio, and Wisconsin.

Although worldly in so many ways, Jefferson had never left America until after he accepted an appointment by the Congress in 1784 as Minister Plenipotentiary to France, joining Benjamin Franklin, then Ambassador to France, and John Adams to obtain critical economic cooperation and support from European countries. In 1785, Jefferson succeeded Franklin as Ambassador to France, shortly after Adams was appointed Ambassador to Great Britain.

Early in Jefferson's tenure in France he published the only full length book he ever wrote, *Notes on the State of Virginia*. Intended as a response to questions from French acquaintances about the nature of life in Virginia, it ultimately constituted the most extensive explanation by Jefferson of: 1) his political ideas regarding public education, freedom of religion and thought, and the relationship of farmers to government; 2) his interconnected approach to the economy, free trade, peace and war; and 3) his thoughts and attitudes towards Native Americans, slavery, and black people generally.

In the *Notes*, Jefferson reiterated his advocacy of broad public education as a means to ensure that government would be free from corruption and tyranny. Focusing on the right of freedom of thought, he wrote, "It is error alone which needs the support of government. Truth can stand by itself."[62] For him, stable government depended on those who labor on the land and he expressed contempt for "the mobs of great cities", equating the success of republican government with the growth of an agrarian population, uncorrupted by commerce, manufacture, and financial transactions:

> Those who labour in the earth are the chosen people of God, if ever he had a chosen people, whose breasts he has made his peculiar deposit for substantial and genuine virtue...Corruption of morals...is the mark set on those, who not looking up to heaven, to their own soil and industry, as does the husbandman, for their subsistence, depend for it on the casualties and caprice of customers. Dependance begets subservience and venality, suffocates the germ of virtue, and prepares fit tools for the designs of ambition.[63]

Although he understood the great value of free trade, Jefferson wanted the country to avoid the old-fashioned power diplomacy of Europe, which too often led to economic conflict and war. War between nations could only be destructive of liberty, wasting resources that would be better dedicated to internal development. He envisioned a self-sufficient, agrarian-based United States that was capable of maintaining its distance and independence from Europe. As America took its place on the world stage during the 19th and 20th centuries, these ideas became increasingly anachronistic, but the isolationist impulse they expressed has been echoed, from time to time, in political debates over foreign policy, including those conducted prior to United States participation in both World Wars I and II.

Jefferson could not find a way to incorporate America's non-European peoples into the republican government he cherished. Although he recognized the bravery, sensitivity and family loyalty of the Indians of North America, he called them a "barbarous people" needing to be shown the way to civilization. He hoped to prohibit the further import of African slaves and movingly recognized the destructive nature of the master-slave relationship on both parties, especially lamenting the depraved example slave masters set for their own children. He feared for his country in the event some way was not found to emancipate all slaves. On the other hand, he wrote that "blacks" were intellectually inferior to "whites," an idea that was, to him, empirically based and consistent with the thought of the day. Taking a scientific rather than an emotional approach to the problem of race, he suggested that the only eventual solution would be to emancipate the slaves, remove all "blacks" from American society, and settle them elsewhere.

These attitudes are difficult to reconcile with Jefferson's otherwise enlightened world-view and his fervent commitment to individual freedom. It is improbable that he espoused them as a means to acquire political power, for power was never his conscious objective. Yet, as one historian has put it, "He was not tormented enough by racial injustice to risk his political career on this issue."[64] He was an integral part of the society of rural Virginia and showed no inclination to divorce himself from it; moreover, his landholdings and livelihood would have suffered by loss of his slaves, and he was often plagued by personal debt. It is likely he was sincere in his belief that the growth and strengthening of liberty—his primary passion—would be more easily achieved without the need to integrate three different races. From a modern perspective, this concept of liberty is anachronistic and immoral, yet, Jefferson deserves to be judged as part of his age and environment rather than the present one.

During Jefferson's more than five-year stay in France, his political philosophy became more intolerant of outmoded political systems. He was deeply interested in the nascent French Revolution and acted, unofficially, as an informal advisor to members of the Revolutionary Parliament, the Estates General. To assist in developing a rationale for ending the French monarchy's restrictions on individual freedom, he developed the idea that Constitutions and laws should be revised every generation, since no government would always remain truly representative of the will of the majority. He also came to believe that revolutions were necessary to ensure that governments were representative of the people, writing in 1787, "The tree of liberty must be refreshed from time to time with the blood of patriots & tyrants. It is its natural manure."[65] He applied his doctrines to the upheavals in France, convinced that the French and American revolutionary causes were the same, conveniently ignoring the excesses of mob rule in Paris and, later, downplaying the effects of the political executions known as the "reign of terror."

2. The Emergence of a National Political Leader, 1790-1800

Jefferson returned to the United States in late 1789 with his children, servants, and the extensive collection of books he had acquired in Europe, intending to stay only as long as necessary to establish new roots at home for his daughters. However, in 1790, when he was offered the post of Secretary of State in George Washington's first Cabinet, he bowed to the President's wish and accepted the appointment. Despite his respect for Washington, he became uncomfortable with what he perceived to be the aristocratic tone and style of the administration, too much like the "corrupt" English and too little like the newly "democratic" French. More important, his three-year Cabinet service was punctuated by continuing disagreements with Treasury Secretary Alexander Hamilton over economic policy and their ongoing rivalry for the ear of the President.

Eventually, Jefferson decided that Washington and Hamilton favored an excessively strong federal government, at the expense of states' rights and individual liberty, and that they encouraged commercial interests at the expense of farmers. Believing that the Constitution should be interpreted strictly, with all but specifically delegated powers reserved to the states, he felt the administration was exercising unauthorized "implied" powers. President Washington was not at all pleased with the lack of consensus in his Cabinet and attempted unsuccessfully to bring the two combatants closer together.[66] Washington most often resolved these disagreements by favoring Hamilton's arguments, causing Jefferson to prematurely depart the administration in 1793, after its first term.

He retired to Monticello, his mountaintop home in Virginia, to live "in the bosom of my family, my farm, and my books,"[67] and to begin the design and re-design of his home and landholdings that were to occupy his creative interests in architecture and agriculture for nearly two decades. Monticello was to serve, again and again, as his strategic retreat from the political conflicts he inspired in theory, yet shied away from in practice.

Jefferson's stay proved to be anything but a quiet retirement. The political infighting he stimulated had the effect of planting the seeds of growth for a political party reflective of his own political philosophy. With the energetic partnership of James Madison, then Speaker of the House of Representatives and his long-time political alter ego, he began to build the new Republican Party.[68] It was to provide the opposition to those supporting Washington and Hamilton, who formed the Federalist Party.

Jefferson's political opposition went beyond domestic economic issues to include the administration's approach to foreign policy, primarily because he never reconciled himself to the reality of the need for economic cooperation with Great Britain.[69] The French Revolution was causing political divisions in the United States, with the Jeffersonian Republicans favoring what they saw as its democratic strivings, and the Federalists opposing what they viewed as its excessive disorder. Northern merchants, ship owners, and financiers, dependent on trade with Great Britain, lined up as Federalists. Southern and western farmers and landowners, sympathetic with the fight for individual rights of the French Revolutionaries, joined the new Republican Party. President Washington was able to keep the government and the country formally unified during his terms in office; however, the election of 1796 featured the first contest for the Presidency driven by rival political parties.

No formal party nomination process existed then as it does today, and there was no opportunity for people to vote directly for the President. The Constitution provided that only Presidential electors, chosen in each state, would select the President. Although private discussions among local and national political leaders recommended candidates for President and Vice President, electors could vote for any individual candidate, even one not recommended by the parties, with the first place finisher elected President and the second place finisher Vice President. The Federalist Party chose John Adams of Massachusetts for President and Thomas Pinckney, war hero, former Governor of South Carolina, and recently negotiator of an important treaty with Spain, for Vice President. The Republicans chose Jefferson for President and made no formal recommendation for Vice President, although Aaron Burr, Senator from New York, was most often mentioned. Jefferson proved to be a reluctant candidate in 1796, taking no active part in the election process and remaining secluded at Monticello. Adams was elected President by three electoral votes and Jefferson became Vice-President with the second highest total, even though the two were nominated by different parties. Jefferson professed not to be dismayed at the outcome, writing to the

President-elect, "I have no ambition to govern men. It is a painful and thankless office."[70] Jefferson no doubt respected Adams, but, more important, he regarded him as the only hope to forestall Hamilton from eventually coming to power. As he wrote to James Madison:

> I can have no feelings which would revolt at a secondary position to Mr. Adams. I am his junior in life, was his junior in Congress, his junior in the diplomatic line, his junior lately in the civil government...If mr. Adams can be induced to administer the government on it's true princi-ples, & to relinquish his bias to an English constitution, it is to be considered whether it would be on the whole for the public good to come to a good understanding with him as to his future elections. He is perhaps the only sure barrier against Hamilton's getting in.[71]

During Adams' Presidency, Jefferson became an opposition critic, as events related to Revolutionary France conspired to separate their paths. Unwilling to cede control of the high seas to England, France interfered with American ships seeking to trade with the West Indies and Europe. Many Americans believed that France aimed at worldwide empire and anti-French sentiment grew rapidly. It was exacerbated by the so-called "X, Y, Z affair" during which the French Foreign Minister, Talleyrand, appeared to require both a bribe for his personal use, and a subsidized loan to France, in order to embark upon negotiations with the emissaries sent by the United States to end the maritime hostility.[72] The diplomats forcefully rejected the insulting French request, which had stimulated substantial war fever in America and inspired a popular toast: "Millions for defense, but not one cent for tribute!" In truth, the country was divided on the issue and ill-pre-pared to fight. Jefferson and the Republicans, favoring France as they did, fervently demanded that Adams withstand the popular clamor for war.

Political vitriol reached significant heights (or depths) in news-papers, magazines and on the floor of Congress. It led to the passage by Congress of the Alien and Sedition Acts, which sought to limit the rights of foreigners and to prosecute anti-patriotic opinion, defined broadly to include speech or writing against the President or Con-gress. Jefferson decried the potential political impact of these laws as well as their denial of the basics of individual liberty—free speech and due process in criminal proceedings. Vigorous opposition to them became a cornerstone of his Republican Party. His draft of the Kentucky Resolutions declared that the laws were an expansion of the powers delegated to the national government in the Constitution and, therefore, invalid infringements on state power.[73]

To President Adams' great credit, he was able to withstand the war fever and steer the country on a peaceful path, allowing it to continue to grow stronger economically, politically and militarily. For Jefferson, the country's flirtation with English alliance and French war convinced him that the Republican Party needed to increase its opposition to a powerful federal government, capable of making war, and to the inevitable accompaniment of a large national debt, high taxes, standing armies and navies, and an excessive diplomatic establishment. These ideas became the platform of the party he led into the Presidential election of 1800.

3. Jefferson's Election and Inauguration, 1800-1801

The Republican Party in 1800 nominated Thomas Jefferson and Aaron Burr as candidates for President and Vice President, respectively, and the Federalists named President John Adams and Charles Cotesworth Pinckney of South Carolina, one of the diplomats involved in the X, Y, Z affair. The Republicans energetically espoused Jefferson's political philosophy during the campaign, asserting that the economic system conceived by Hamilton, implemented by Washington, and continued by Adams, ran counter to the interests of the farmers and landowners who were essential to the survival of the revolutionary principles of 1776. These were the men who exhibited the self-discipline, independence, and moral virtue that were essential to Jefferson's ideal of liberty, yet they bore the heaviest tax burden in support of a growing government and military; they also benefited least from what he called "corruption" caused by financial transactions to support the debt and the National Bank.

At the core of the evolving Republican political program was Jefferson's view of human nature, influenced as it was by his study of Enlightenment philosophers such as Locke, Bacon, and Newton—in his opinion the three greatest men who ever lived.[74] He believed that man had unlimited potential to do good, especially if his environment encouraged free thought, he possessed the requisite virtue, and his outside influences were wholesome. The smaller the government, the fewer the corruptive influences, and the healthier that environment would be— an idealistic and somewhat wishful view of human behavior.

Jefferson and the Republicans won the presidential election of 1800, carrying almost the entire west and south, the strongholds of farmers and landowners. His election has been called the "Revolution of 1800" and is notable in our history because it represents the first American transition of power from one political party to another. Although Jefferson carried the clear majority of states, the election proved to be a marathon affair, finally decided in the House of Representatives. Jefferson and Burr actually received the same number of electoral votes. President Adams finished third, and Pinckney fourth. With no separate designation on the electors' ballots for President and Vice President, ties were possible even between candidates of the same party. In that event the House of Representatives, with each state having one vote, had to choose the President from among all the candidates in the election.

Federalist Congressmen sought to make political deals to elect either Adams or Pinckney, despite the fact that neither man came close to receiving a majority of the electoral votes.[75] They then attempted to elect Burr in preference to Jefferson. All their efforts failed, and after 36 ballots, Jefferson was finally elected on February 17, 1801, ironically as a partial result of support from his political rival Alexander Hamilton and the silent acquiescence of John Adams. Although disagreeing with most of Jefferson's policies, Hamilton saw him as much more honest and straightforward than Burr and by far the lesser of two evils. Hamilton and Burr, two New York politicians with very different political agendas, had carried on a bitter political rivalry for years, one that was to end in a duel on July 11, 1804 which resulted in Hamilton's death the following day. Despite Hamilton's support in the 1800 election, Jefferson showed no reciprocal appreciation for the former Treasury Secretary, bitterly disagreeing with his political ideas and failing to give him credit either for his patriotism or for the consistent adherence to principle demonstrated throughout his career. As years went by, Jefferson mellowed and developed a grudging admiration of Hamilton, displaying a bust of the man that still stands, appropriately, opposite his own in the foyer at Monticello.

Jefferson's inauguration on March 4, 1801 stands in sharp contrast to that of Washington twelve years earlier. He intentionally eliminated most of the pomp and circumstance, and acted as one of the "people"; even his dress was humble and common. But his Inaugural Address was far from ordinary. To this day, it is regarded as one of the most eloquent political speeches ever given. In it, Jefferson was able to equate the principles of civil liberty in the Republican platform with the destiny of America. His words deserve a detailed reading, and are as meaningful and relevant today as they were more than 200 years ago.

In response to the rancor of the election, Jefferson called for unity:

> Let us, then, fellow-citizens, unite with one heart and one mind. Let us restore to social intercourse that harmony and affection without which liberty and even life itself are but dreary things. And let us reflect that, having banished from our land that religious intolerance under which mankind so long bled and suffered, we have yet gained little if we countenance a political intolerance as despotic, as wicked, and capable of as bitter and bloody persecutions.

On political conflict he said:

> ...every difference of opinion is not a difference of principle. We have called by different names brethren of the same principle. We are all Republicans, we are all Federalists. If there be any among us who would wish to dissolve this Union or to change its republican form, let them stand undisturbed as monuments of the safety with which error of opinion may be tolerated where reason is left free to combat it.

He foreshadowed both his foreign policy and his expansionist ambitions by stating:

> Kindly separated by nature and a wide ocean from the exterminating havoc of one quarter of the globe; too high-minded to endure the degradations of others; possessing a

chosen country, with room enough for our descendants to the thousandth and thousandth generation...with all these blessings, what more is necessary to make us a happy and prosperous people?

He answered his own question by summarizing his philosophy of government:

Equal and exact justice to all men, of whatever state or per-suasion, religious or political; peace, commerce, and honest friendship with all nations, entangling alliances with none; the support of the State governments in all their rights, as the most competent administrations for our domestic con-cerns and the surest bulwarks against antirepublican ten-dencies...absolute acquiescence in the decisions of the majority, the vital principle of republics, from which is no appeal but to force, the vital principle and immediate parent of despotism.[76]

Ironically, the greatness of the speech was appreciated only after people had read his words, for Jefferson's delivery was flat and barely audible to his audience. When one reads this Address along with the Declaration of Independence, one readily understands Jefferson's rep-utation as the greatest articulator of the values and mission of Amer-ica. He had the capacity and the unique ability to express human and national ideals in a way that allowed Americans to see themselves as part of a noble effort. He served as a visionary for America's political responsibility to protect and expand liberty, in its own country and throughout the world, and, in doing so, he gave voice to the better angels of America's nature.

4. The Louisiana Purchase and the Empire of Liberty

President Jefferson's ambitious political agenda included revers-ing as many of the policies of the Federalists as possible, particularly by reducing the size of government and by lowering or eliminating both the national debt and taxes. He replaced Federalist officeholders with Republicans—the first Presidential exercise of political patronage, which came to be known as the "spoils system." But more dramatic change was to follow.

History sometimes allows the opportunity to view events that render great visions a reality, something we can clearly do with Jefferson's first term. The President who wanted smaller government chose, at the same time, to ensure the growth of liberty by expanding the country westward. He hoped to spread the benefits of representative government, elected by literate citizens with freedom of thought and speech, by extending American control to all the land east of the Mississippi River. The yeoman farmers who settled this land would have the requisite Republican virtues and morality to make liberty work. They would be committed to individual freedom and would establish what Jefferson called an "Empire of Liberty". Equally important to the strength of the expanding country was the need for freedom to utilize the Mississippi. Despite Spain's ownership of the southern banks of the river, Jefferson claimed a "natural" right to navigate its entire length, from its source in Minnesota to its basin in the Gulf of Mexico, an assertion that was unprecedented in international law and diplomacy to that time. Critical to that right was the ability to exercise control over the strategic port of New Orleans.

To realize his vision, Jefferson had to confront the colonial ambitions of European powers, specifically Spain, France, and Great Britain. After France's 1763 defeat in the Seven Years' War, the land she had controlled east of the Mississippi was divided between Great Britain and Spain. Under the Treaty of Paris, which settled the American Revolution in 1783, the United States obtained most of this land from Great Britain. However, remaining under Spanish control was New Orleans, the Floridas, and the vast areas west of the Mississippi, extending to the Rockies and beyond, misleadingly called the Louisiana Territory.

By treaty with Spain in 1795, the United States had gained free navigation of the Mississippi and permission to deposit goods in New Orleans pending their export, to the great benefit of American farmers and tradesmen.[77] The treaty also formalized the boundary between the United States and the Floridas, with West Florida constituting the land from approximately the current southern boundary of Mississippi, Alabama, and Georgia to the Gulf of Mexico, and East Florida constituting approximately the current state of Florida.[78]

When Jefferson took office, Great Britain and France, then led by First Consul of the French Revolutionary government, and eventual Emperor, Napoleon Bonaparte, were battling over colonial territory. The two countries reached a temporary end to their imperial wars in the Peace of Amiens in 1802, providing Jefferson with an opportunity to enact his domestic program, which included drastic reductions in Army and Navy strength, without fearing involvement in European war. Ironically, peace also provided Napoleon with an opportunity to plan for the revival of the French empire in North America, which had been lost in the Seven Years' War. The Frenchman who desired power through the forcible expropriation of the land of others, and the American who desired peaceful development of an Empire of Liberty, were about to embark on a struggle for America's future. The French General had a diplomatic and military plan he intended to implement; the American politician relied on caution and faith in his vision to withstand the General's initiatives. While fortune was on Jefferson's side, the decisions he made along the way contributed to the ultimate outcome so decidedly in America's favor.

Jefferson learned in 1801 that Spain had agreed, in a treaty kept secret to avoid any strong reaction from Great Britain, to cede the Louisiana Territory (supposedly including the Floridas) to France at an undisclosed future time. To have New Orleans and Louisiana under the aegis of the relatively weak Spain was not a significant threat to the American economy or to American expansion. However, control by a strong and ambitious Napoleonic France[79] could threaten free navigation of the Mississippi and present a dangerous challenge to the security and growth of the United States.

Napoleon's first step in this undertaking was to recapture the island of Santo Domingo (today divided between the countries of Haiti and the Dominican Republic), which had revolted against French rule in the mid 1790's. Led by a former slave, Touissant L'Ouverture, the native Domingans had been successful for the remainder of the decade in preventing the French from regaining control of the island. The Federalists at that time, under President Adams, had been openly sympathetic to Touissant's efforts to establish an independent government of emancipated slaves. President Jefferson was unwilling to continue Adams' support of the independence of Santo Domingo because he desired French acquiescence in American expansion. He also believed that an independent Santo Domingo, run by former

slaves, would pose a threatening example to his slave-owning supporters in the South.[80] Thus, when Napoleon decided to send his brother-
in-law, General LeClerc, at the head of an army contingent to regain
it, Jefferson told the French Ambassador, Pichon, that the United
States would not stand in the way of the expedition.

Napoleon's next objective, assuming LeClerc's success in Santo
Domingo, would be to invade and control New Orleans and, hence,
the Mississippi River and the Louisiana Territory, thereby providing
the economic support necessary for a French North American empire.
Jefferson was aware of this and wanted to pacify, to delay, and, to some
extent, appease Napoleon, a strategy aimed at reducing the French
threat to American expansion.

Jefferson had faith in the superior virtue of America's objective
and that it would, in the end, prevail. His faith was bolstered by the
growing number of American settlers with commercial and agricultural interests in the territory.[81] Moreover, he wanted to avoid a costly
war and was personally averse to planning for military action. Therefore, he gambled that, by playing for time, all would not fall into place
for Napoleon and that the First Counsul's ambitious plan would fail.
Despite the somewhat idealistic optimism on which it was based, the
strategy had some practical prospects for success. Several contingen-
cies all had to turn out in Napoleon's favor for him to realize his North
American objectives. First, France had to subdue the rebels in Santo
Domingo before being able to take possession of New Orleans. Second, Great Britain had to stand idly by and witness the revival of
French power in North America. And third, France had to implement
its side of the secret treaty under which it promised to install the Duke
of Parma (Spanish King Charles IV's brother-in-law) on an Italian
throne in Tuscany.

Jefferson's diplomacy was designed to avoid both war with France
and an alliance with England, since, in either case, his domestic political goals would be compromised. He had confidence his unique tactics would succeed. Even if France was successful in controlling the
Mississippi Valley initially, he believed that the large numbers of anticipated American settlers to the territory eventually would present
France with an impossibly hostile population. As Jefferson put it, he
was prepared "to palliate and endure" until either France had to give
way to American claims, or war between France and Great Britain
would have made New Orleans easy for the United States to occupy.

Jefferson's strategy can be contrasted with that championed at the time by the leading Federalists' spokesman, Alexander Hamilton, who recommended: "First, to negotiate and endeavor to purchase, and if this fails go to war. Secondly, to seize at once on the Floridas and New Orleans and, then negotiate."[82] His advice stemmed from a conviction that the United States needed to take control of its own destiny and not shrink from using force along with diplomacy. Jefferson was reluctant to bring matters to a climax; for him, war (and the planning for it) was always a great threat to liberty and to the republican form of government. These two distinct approaches to foreign affairs—one trusting in peaceful diplomacy, a limited military, and the good will of others—and the other being always prepared to use force if necessary, became opposing paths for the country's foreign policy.

Jefferson took charge of all the diplomatic moves regarding Louisiana. Unlike Washington, he was not satisfied with delegating to his subordinates and reserving only the major decisions for himself. He was at the center of the day-to-day maneuvering, although he utilized his long-time political ally and Secretary of State, James Madison, as an active partner.

At the end of 1801, Jefferson designated Robert Livingston, who had been a member of the committee to draft the Declaration of Independence and foreign affairs coordinator under the Continental Congress, to undertake a mission to try to convince France not to go through with the cession of Louisiana. Livingston was instructed that, if the cession had already happened by the time he arrived in France, which could take many weeks, he was to attempt to convince the French to grant New Orleans and the Floridas to the United States. These particular holdings, together with the unfettered right to navigate the Mississippi, were Jefferson's true priorities since possession of them would facilitate the commerce of new American settlers and prevent the areas from falling under the control of a strong European power. However, Livingston became so frustrated by the difficulties of negotiating with the French that he wrote to Secretary of State Madison: "There never was a Government in which less could be done by negotiation than here. There is no people, no Legislature, no counselors. One man is everything."[83]

Jefferson then decided to engage in a very subtle piece of diplomacy. He wrote what has become a famous letter to Livingston in April 1802, which he decided to have delivered by Pierre DuPont de

Nemours,[84] a former French statesman living in the United States and well known to the French government. In it, he warned of the dangers of the French possession of New Orleans, and threatened an alliance with England and possible war against France:

> There is on the globe one single spot, the possessor of which is our natural and habitual enemy. It is New Orleans, through which the produce of three-eighths of our territory must pass to market, and from its fertility it will ere long yield more than half of our whole produce and contain more than half our inhabitants...France placing herself in that door assumes to us the attitude of defiance. Spain might have retained it quietly for years...The day that France takes possession of N. Orleans...seals the union of two nations who...can maintain exclusive possession of the ocean. From that moment we must marry ourselves to the British fleet and nation...If anything...[could reconcile us to French possession of Louisiana]...it would be the ceding to us the island of New Orleans and the Floridas.[85]

Jefferson utilized DuPont as an emissary with the calculated intent that the substance of the letter to Livingston would reach the French government and affect their behavior without his having to threaten them directly. It may be that Jefferson was bluffing, given Great Britain's unwillingness to upset the Peace of Amiens; nevertheless, he had gradually but, surely, raised the stakes. And he did so in an audacious and surprising way, given his previous aversion to any alliance with Great Britain.

By the spring of 1802, Jefferson received from Livingston a copy of the treaty ceding the Louisiana Territory to France, even though the French had not yet disclosed the treaty's existence. Both sides were acting cautiously. The United States' offer to purchase the land east of the Mississippi (New Orleans and the Floridas), rather than to persuade France to cede it, apparently originated with Madison, when he requested that Livingston determine the potential price. DuPont, acting on his own initiative, had advised the President to offer gold for the real estate and probably also discussed the matter with both Talleyrand and Napoleon.[86]

No further progress was made until an event in October, 1802 forced the issue. The Spanish Intendant, the local administrator of New Orleans, revoked the right of the United States to deposit its exports and closed the port to foreign commerce. This threatened the international trade of the United States, economically injuring the east coast shippers as well as western farmers, whose produce traveled down the Mississippi and waited for export from New Orleans. The public assumed that France was behind the step taken by its ally and anti-French war fever again gripped the United States. The Federalists strongly encouraged military action, hoping to weaken Jefferson's political hold on the west, and even Republicans expressed outrage.

Jefferson maintained grace under pressure and, consistent with his long-standing reticence regarding military action, redoubled his effort to pursue a diplomatic solution. His administration attributed the New Orleans revocation to the unauthorized act of a local Spanish official, and, therefore, did not consider it a justifiable cause for war. The President did, however, nominate his long-time Republican ally and retiring Governor of Virginia, James Monroe, as Minister Extraordinary to join Livingston in negotiating a settlement. Monroe was trusted in the western territories as an advocate of free navigation of the Mississippi, and had previously been a minister to both France and Spain.

Jefferson not only hoped to neutralize political pressure at home, but to gain a close confidante on the ground in France. Although he authorized Monroe to bring about the purchase of New Orleans and the Floridas, with no mention of territory west of the Mississippi, he encouraged the use of whatever mix of diplomacy and threats of belligerency Monroe thought appropriate. As Jefferson put it, the mission would determine whether such a purchase would "insure to ourselves a course of perpetual peace and friendship with all nations…[or cause us to] get entangled in European politics, and…be much less happy and prosperous."[87] Congress later appropriated $2 million to cover any expenses of the mission, including the purchase price. No one at the time imagined that Monroe would be negotiating to double the size of the country.

While stalling for time, Jefferson simultaneously sought to secure the borders of the western lands against potential French possession by relocating the Indians who were native to those areas,[88] and replacing them with politically dependable white settlers. He departed from what had been his quasi-romantic admiration for the Indians and their culture, rationalizing the action as one that would ultimately benefit the Indians, who would be taught to be agriculturally self-sufficient on new, more productive land. He also took some very minor steps to bolster military preparedness in the forts along the Mississippi.

In anticipation of success with Napoleon, the President secretly asked Congress, in January, 1803 for funds to support what, one year later, became the Lewis and Clark Expedition. In order not to alarm European powers, he described the effort publicly as literary and scientific, but his primary purpose was more strategic. Anticipating the ultimate expansion of the United States after gaining New Orleans and the Floridas, Jefferson hoped to find a navigable water route across the continent to the Pacific Ocean as well as opportunities for commercial development, including the diversion of the fur trade with the Indians from Canada to the United States. He also wanted to prepare the geographic basis for future military outposts west of the Mississippi.[89] The impending good fortune of the Louisiana Purchase was to make this famous mission much more timely and important than he originally supposed it would be. The United States was on the verge of controlling all the territory the Expedition was to explore and would be able to begin immediately to make the President's Empire of Liberty a reality.

The turning point for both Jefferson and Napoleon came when General LeClerc's mission to Santo Domingo turned out to be a costly failure. The combination of malaria among the French troops, which claimed many lives, including LeClerc's, and stiff resistance by the Domingans, meant that the French quest for empire could not be easily achieved in North America. Napoleon reportedly said, after learning of his brother-in-law's death, "Damn sugar, damn coffee, damn colonies."[90] He had decided, instead, to turn his attention again to the English, opting to contest for some of their possessions in Europe and the Middle East. The sale of all of Louisiana to the United States would bring the capital necessary for his new imperial plan. In Napoleon's mind, such a sale would also prevent the territory from falling into British hands and render the United States a potential ally in his pursuit of empire at the expense of the British. He commented on April 10, 1803:

They ask of me only one town in Louisiana, but I already consider the colony as entirely lost, and it appears to me

that in the hands of this growing power it will be more useful to the policy and even to the commerce of France, than
if I should attempt to keep it.[91]

One day later, he is reported to have asserted, "I renounce
Louisiana. It is not only New Orleans that I cede; it is the whole
colony, without reserve."[92]

The two-year chess match between Jefferson and Napoleon over
land for two very different versions of empire was about to be resolved
in favor of the President. Talleyrand immediately asked Livingston if
the United States wanted to buy all of the Louisiana Territory.
Stunned by this unanticipated invitation, Livingston initially refused it
and merely repeated his desire to discuss solely the purchase of land
east of the Mississippi. Talleyrand replied that the remaining territory
west of the Mississippi would be of little value to France and asked
what the United States would pay for it all. Livingston made a low
offer of $3 million, and Talleyrand told him to consider a more gener-
ous response, whereupon Livingston said that he needed to confer
with newly 1903appointed minister, Monroe, who would be arriving
in a few days. These two immediately realized that the French offer
could be epoch-making and decided to deviate from their limited
instructions. Unlike 21st century diplomats, equipped with instanta-
neous global communication, they did not have the luxury of quickly
conferring with Jefferson or Madison. The agreed upon price was $15
million, one-quarter of which was offset by the assumption by the
United States government of debts owed to Americans by the French
government for interference with American shipping during the late
1790's. France and Spain gained the privilege of paying duties no
higher than those of American ships in the ports of the ceded territory.
The United States promised that the inhabitants of Louisiana would
be incorporated as citizens as soon as this could be done consistent
with the Constitution. In return, the United States received all the
territory given by Spain to France. Although the precise boundaries
were unknown and the territory uncharted, it was clear that the land
area of the United States had been at least doubled. Ultimately, the
territory became all or part of 14 states.[93]

5. Implementation and Jefferson's Political Principles

On July 3, 1803 Jefferson learned that his representatives in Paris had signed a treaty gaining all of Louisiana. Along with his great satisfaction came the realization that some complicated diplomatic, political, and constitutional issues needed to be resolved before the purchase could be implemented. At first, no one was certain of the actual size of the territory, particularly whether West Florida was included, because the Treaty's language was somewhat ambiguous in referring to the previous secret agreement between Spain and France. Jefferson also wanted East Florida also (most of the present state of Florida), but no case for it could be made by any interpretation of the words of his treaty with France.

The American emissaries were convinced that the language gave the United States a valid claim to West Florida. While in Monticello in mid-July, researched the question of the boundaries of Louisiana and concluded that he agreed with Monroe and Livingston. However, Henry Adams, John's great grandson, in his classic history of the Jefferson Administration, characterized the emissaries' interpretation this way:

> ...he [Livingston] was forced at last to maintain that Spain had retroceded West Florida to France without knowing it, that France had sold it to the United States without suspecting it, that the United States had bought it without paying for it, and that neither France nor Spain, although the original contracting parties, were competent to decide the meaning of their own contract.[94]

Not surprisingly, neither France nor Spain agreed with the United States' version of their treaty and West Florida remained in Spanish hands for seven more years.[95]

As an advocate of strict construction, Jefferson was greatly troubled by the question of the constitutionality of his own Purchase, doubting that the government had legal authority to acquire territory. Initially, he was unwilling to implement it without passage by Congress of a constitutional amendment ratifying his and the Congress' action. He wrote in August 1803:

Our confederation is certainly confined to the limits established by the revolution. The general government has no
powers but such as the constitution has given it; and it has
not given it a power of holding foreign territory, & still less
of incorporating it into the Union.[96]

Jefferson was even more definitive when he wrote a few days
later:

The Constitution has made no provision for our holding
foreign territory, still less for incorporating foreign nations
into our Union. The executive in seizing the fugitive occur-
rence which so much advances the good of their country,
have done an act beyond the Constitution.[97]

Jefferson's close political ally, Treasury Secretary Albert Gallatin,
took the position that the United States had an inherent right to
acquire territory—a power that should be implied from the constitutionally delegated authority to negotiate treaties with foreign countries. He argued that Congress had the power to admit such territory
as a state, annex it to an existing state, or govern it directly. Gallatin's
formulation became the constitutional doctrine on which expansion of
the United States was based for much of the 19th century and was iden-
tical to the broad construction of the Constitution taken by Alexander
Hamilton when the national bank was created in 1791. However, the
approach was diametrically opposed to the position taken at the time
by Jefferson himself when he argued, unsuccessfully, that President
Washington should not sign the bank bill.

Constitutional principles did not, for long, prevent implementation of the Purchase. When Livingston warned that Congress' delay
in ratification of the treaty threatened the agreement itself, Jefferson
acceded to the advice of many of his own political allies and allowed
congressional action without the amendment. He has been criticized
for inconsistency by this action, but, in his defense, he had to face the
real impatience of France as well as tremendous political pressure at
home to consummate the popular treaty. Moreover, he knew that to
press his constitutional doubts would be to endanger an incomparable
opportunity for the realization of his Empire of Liberty. Jefferson
foresaw the impact the acquisition had and would have on the nation

and took the action he believed correct and in the national interest. At the same time, he put his constitutional views on record, hoping they would be taken into account in any future similar situation. After he was out of office, when asked whether public officials had, at times, to act beyond the law, he made the following revealing reply:

> A strict observance of the written laws is doubtless *one* of the high duties of a good citizen, but it is not *the highest*. The laws of necessity, of self-preservation, of saving our country when in danger, are of higher obligation. To lose our country by a scrupulous adherence to written law, would be to lose the law itself, with life, liberty, property and all those who are enjoying them with us; thus absurdly sacrificing the end to the means.[98]

Jefferson did not hesitate to sacrifice other long-valued principles to the goal of rapid implementation of the Purchase. When choosing a method for governing the inhabitants of the territory corresponding to the current state of Louisiana, he opted, at first, to impose on them an authoritarian system. He believed these former subjects of Spanish aristocratic rule, half of whom were slaves and the rest predominantly of French Creole descent, were too unfamiliar with democratic government and not yet ready for liberty. In essence, he governed them by martial law. Two years later, pressure from these new Americans for the blessings of liberty, together with support for their plight from his own Republican colleagues in Congress, finally convinced him to agree to establish representative government.

As he had done prior to the Purchase, Jefferson once again put aside his policy with respect to the American Indian in order to solve what he regarded as a political problem presented by the Louisiana Purchase. He had been acquiring Indian land through negotiation of treaties, leaving the Indians in control of their own commerce, and, at the same time, establishing programs to teach them agricultural skills and gradually to integrate them into American society. He wrote in early 1803:

> ...the ultimate point of rest & happiness for them is to let our settlements and theirs meet and blend together, to intermix and become one people. Incorporating themselves

with us as citizens of the U.S., this is what the natural progress of things will of course bring on, and it will be better to promote it than to retard it.[99]

Even though this approach was showing great promise, particularly north of the Ohio River, Jefferson chose to abandon it in order to facilitate the early settling of the newly acquired territory east of the Mississippi. This time, he displaced Choctaws, Chicasaws, Cherokees and Shawnees, and resettled them, forcibly when necessary, in the newly acquired uncharted territory west of the Mississippi.[100]

Notwithstanding the great potential the new territory offered a growing country, it was not immediately clear that all of it could be easily assimilated. Some Federalists expressed concern that the country would be fragmented, perhaps permanently divided into more than one republic. Jefferson's response to these doubts was quick and clear:

> Whether we remain in one Confederacy, or form into Atlantic and Mississippi confederacies, I believe not very important to the happiness of either part. Those of the western Confederacy will be as much our children and descendants as those of the Eastern, and I feel myself as much identified with that country, in future time, as with this.[101]

For him, the important issue was not the unity of the country; it was the survival of his vision of liberty, in whatever national form was required. He had long considered the Mississippi River essential to the economy and the political strength of the country, and it was now in American hands. That was more critical to Jefferson than political subdivisions. The West itself was sacred. Only with its continuous development by those committed to individual liberty would the goals of the American Revolution, and his Revolution of 1800, be secure. For that great political purpose, other principles could be sacrificed.

6. The Louisiana Purchase and Jefferson's Legacy

The most notable consequence of the Louisiana Purchase was the most obvious one—it doubled the size of the country, made likely the growth of the United States to the Pacific Ocean, and laid the foundation for the acquisition of Florida and Texas.[102] Without the Purchase, such growth was not foreordained. The United States was not destined to become one country, rich in natural resources, from the Atlantic to the Pacific. European powers had owned many parts of the continent before the Purchase and, had it not come about, they may well have sought new colonies west of the Mississippi. Whether America would have had the economic and military resources to forestall this development is uncertain. Nor is it clear whether any President would have had the political will to do so, especially one who was not driven by Jefferson's revolutionary commitment to liberty.

The Purchase was a logical result of Jefferson's evolving political thinking over three decades. It grew out of his devotion to a unique American mission as the engine of liberty, together with his distaste for the power politics practiced by "aristocratic" and "undemocratic" European governments. Foreign control over the Mississippi basin would threaten the livelihood of American farmers and was likely to draw the United States into foreign wars. Removing that presence would eliminate the likelihood of war, and with it the threat to republican values represented by a government that wages war. Only American control of all the unexplored and unsettled lands west of the Appalachians could make real his vision of an expanding, continuously self-renewing Empire of Liberty. As a corollary benefit, westerners would acquire new political clout in United States politics, and, in fact, they did, keeping Jefferson's Republican Party and its policies dominant for two decades. The Purchase also extended the promise of Jefferson's revolution beyond the country's shores, by sowing the seeds of the Monroe Doctrine of 1823 which made American power protective of the democratic potential of the entire hemisphere.[103] It was critical to the spread of American political ideals and the growth of American power.

Jefferson had faced the crisis that led to the Purchase with the fear that he would have to choose between a British alliance and a French war; he wanted neither. His faith that the passage of time would resolve his dilemma had been grounded more in his philosophy and temperament than in shrewd diplomatic strategy. Indeed, his tactics carried the risk of French success in building a North American empire. As a recent study of Jefferson has concluded:

At best, Louisiana taught that a strategy of playing for time sometimes works, despite the dangers it may incur. Contending forces may balance themselves out. A dangerous adversary may get over committed elsewhere. But this modest lesson was not the lesson Jefferson appeared to have learned from his one success in foreign policy. Instead, he learned that passivity and a reliance on the power of others was the course of wisdom. Not surprisingly, Louisiana was not followed by similar diplomatic triumphs.[104]

It is true that Jefferson's success was primarily a result of choices made by Napoleon, and it has created a misleading example for future Presidents. Hoping for the best, believing in the inevitability of progress, and entering the diplomatic fray without a realistic capability or willingness to use force can be a very dangerous approach in a brutal world. In fact, Jefferson himself found this out in his second term, when he tried to pressure Great Britain and France to reverse their belligerent maritime policies against the United States by a passive embargo prohibiting all exports from American ports. His aversion to balance of power politics, as well as to war, resulted, in the short run, in economic deprivation to the United States and, in the long run, in the war he desperately wanted to avoid.[105]

Yet, during the Louisiana crisis, Jefferson's grace under pressure and willingness to consider alternatives to war, resulted in a great advance for liberty, matched in the 19th century only by Monroe's Doctrine and Abraham Lincoln's emancipation of the slaves. The Louisiana Purchase added natural resources that have been critical to the survival of the political system of the United States and to making the country a world power. Although Jefferson owed much to the ambitions of Napoleon, as well as to good fortune, credit for having a timely vision and for taking advantage of the opportunity belongs to him alone. His action set an example for future Presidents that patience and diplomacy can, at times, achieve geo-political objectives facilitating liberty as well as power politics or military campaigns.

No achievement of this scale comes without consequences, and the Purchase brought controversy to Jefferson that has never abated. The methods by which he implemented it has raised questions about his consistency, character, and motivation that have been debated for 200 years. His willingness to put aside the philosophy of strict construction of the Constitution has weakened the vitality of that doctrine, because, if a man as eminent as Jefferson could utilize it only when his political interests benefited, one should not expect any different behavior from lesser political figures. The same, of course, might be said for the philosophy of implied powers. In a sense, Jefferson helped to dilute both doctrines, showing that they are subservient to the particular political goal at issue. One can defend Jefferson's actions only by accepting, as he did, the overriding need for an expanding, agrarian-based empire in order to have liberty survive.

His willingness to impose an authoritarian government on part of the territory raises questions about just how deep Jefferson's commitment to democracy really was. It is hard to square with his devotion to republican government, unless we remind ourselves that he sincerely believed that some people are better equipped to practice liberty than others. He favored those with education and "republican virtue." This is certainly not a modern American notion, but we hold him, as a man and as a President to an impossibly high standard if we fail to judge him in the context of his own time. Even today, Americans continue to strive for an educated, informed electorate, with an appreciation for democratic government.

Most troubling have been the consequences of Jefferson's treatment of American Indians and his approach to slavery. He changed the country's policy from one of education and integration of the Indian, to one of removal to make way for expansion by the favored settlers. It remained so throughout the 19th century and resulted in severe cruelty and forcible removals, such as the suppression of the Creeks during the War of 1812, the Battle of Tippecanoe, the Seminole Wars, and the infamous Cherokee "Trail of Tears". Yet, despite the racial and cultural bias inherent in the policy, it set the precedent for American expansion and offered a path to fame for those officials who carried it out, including future Presidents Andrew Jackson and William Henry Harrison.

One seldom recognized consequence of the Louisiana Purchase was that the issue of slavery could no longer be ignored. Would it be permitted in the new territory? Congress addressed the issue previously when it enacted the Northwest Ordinance of 1787, prohibiting the extension of slavery to the Northwest Territory—legislation that was modeled after Jefferson's 1784 draft. However, the Louisiana Territory proved much more controversial, partially because slavery existed there when the United States acquired it. President Jefferson did not follow his 1784 example despite the fact that there were opportunities to do so. He was urged in 1804 to support Representative Hillhouse's amendment prohibiting slavery in the entire territory, but declined to do so, and he could have proposed a compromise that permitted slavery only in the limited area where it already existed.[106] Jefferson did support the abolition of the slave trade in 1808, but, without a clear prohibition against its proliferation in the new territory, the future would produce decades of political struggle that threatened the unity of the country and, in 1861, resulted in a cataclysmic Civil War.

Acknowledging the importance of the Purchase to the country's history, we must also recognize that Jefferson was unable or unwilling to find ways to solve humanely the problem of the integration of the Indian and the African-American that the Purchase made ripe for solution. Yet he cannot be blamed for the country's continuing, tragic failure peacefully to resolve those issues. We can, however, lament the fact that he did not utilize his enormous popularity and political power to seize the opportunity for courageous solutions that the Purchase offered. As a consequence, the full potential of that great event—and of President Jefferson—was never realized. Perhaps this only proves that Jefferson was, indeed, human, but, given the courage of his revolutionary ideas, Americans have often wanted his image in their memory to be much more extraordinary than that.

The mixed Louisiana legacy does not diminish Jefferson's profound impact on the country. Nothing can detract from the power of his thoughts and words—his ability to express ideals that still motivate Americans. He had that rare talent in American history, comparable only to Abraham Lincoln, to lift political ideas to the level of universal truths. Although he was a better judge of political ends than of means, he personified that faith in liberty that has become quintessentially American. Yet his faith was never limited to Americans; his ideas about liberty and individual freedom are applicable to all of mankind. Although he focused too much on restraining the abuse of political power and too little on how to benefit from the use of it, he defined for the ages the true meaning of government oppression. And his commitment to freedom for the individual—for his mind and his creativity—has never been exceeded. No one who reads of Jefferson's life can fail to be awed by the breadth of his knowledge and interests, and the intellectual courage he often exhibited. As President John F. Kennedy said of him at a White House dinner honoring western hemisphere Nobel Prize winners:

> ...[this is] the most extraordinary collection of talent, of human knowledge, that has ever been gathered together at the White House, with the possible exception of when Thomas Jefferson dined alone.[107]

CHAPTER 3.

James Monroe and the Establishment of America's Place in the World

President James Monroe defined a special role for the United States in international affairs, one that has inspired and motivated his successors ever since. He significantly expanded the nation's borders and created a guiding mission in foreign policy by skillfully building on unity at home and division in the world. A man of great character, he left a powerful, patriotic, and enduring legacy.

1. President Monroe's Opportunity

Thomas Jefferson's partner in creating the Republican Party, and his Secretary of State, James Madison, succeeded him as President in 1809. Despite the limited government philosophy of his party, Madison, like Jefferson, undertook policies that strengthened the federal government and energetically exercised the powers of the President. By his side as his Secretary of State, as he led the country through the War of 1812, its "second" War of Independence from Great Britain, was James Monroe, a fellow Virginian.

In 1816, Monroe himself was elected President and was faced with issues as momentous as those that faced President Washington at the nation's birth. His decisions were some of the most far-reaching in the history of the country. Yet, his image in the pantheon of America's heroes is pale compared with that of Washington, and it fails to match those of Jefferson and Madison, his close political allies. That image deserves to be much brighter.

President Monroe was able to realize the full potential of the Louisiana Purchase, which had eluded Jefferson, by acquiring all of Florida and by extending the border of the Louisiana Territory all the way to the Pacific Ocean. The natural resources of the United States thereafter would be unmatched by any other country—vast fertile plains, mineral rich soil, abundant forests, plentiful navigable waterways, and harbors ideally situated for commerce with the world. Monroe accomplished all this by a shrewd mixture of force and diplomacy, fully the equal of any statecraft practiced by older, established European countries.

Building on the stalemate resulting from the War of 1812 against Great Britain,[108] Monroe firmly established the United States as a world power, one that could not be ignored by Europe. He took advantage of the European balance of power after the end of the Napoleonic Wars, and declared, in the Monroe Doctrine, that the western hemisphere was off-limits to European colonization. Challenging stronger European nations who had colonial ambitions in the new world, he set a precedent for the country's relationships with the powers of Europe and helped ensure that the hemisphere would be safe for the expansion of liberty.

Monroe established a unique place for the new nation on the international stage by focusing on America's commitment to liberty as the primary motivation of its foreign policy. He succeeded because he brought to the job a vision of the country's mission, forged from his own diplomatic experience, and he was able to reconcile the political differences that had severely tested the country's unity in the two decades preceding his election.

Monroe was the last President from the generation of men who fought the Revolution. Like Washington, he could claim a heroic military contribution, suffering life-threatening wounds in the Battle of Trenton. He also shared with Washington a soldier's bearing—strong, tall, and distinguished. Neither had a brilliant mind, but each was seen by contemporaries as a firm, wise, and natural leader. Both carried from their Revolutionary experience a conviction that the United States needed a national government capable of maintaining a strong defense against other nations. And each man valued national unity above party, factional, or sectional divisions. Washington and Monroe were doers and leaders, called to service at critical moments in their country's history.

Unlike his three predecessors, John Adams, Thomas Jefferson, and James Madison, Monroe was not a notable political thinker or writer. He contributed no inspirational ideas to the country's revolutionary ferment. Yet, with the exception of the Louisiana Purchase, no

Presidential decision by Adams, Jefferson or Madison affected the growth and development of the United States, and of liberty, as profoundly and as positively as either of President Monroe's major contributions, the Transcontinental Treaty and the Monroe Doctrine.

2. Monroe's Early Life and Career

James Monroe was born on April 28, 1758 into a Virginia family with modest land holdings. His father owned 500 acres[109] (as compared to 10000 acres for George Washington's father), and, from a young age, James was attracted to agriculture as a career. Despite subsequent training as a lawyer and his many governmental positions, he always considered himself a farmer by profession. Like Jefferson, he loved the outdoors, learning at an early age to fish, hunt, climb and swim, and acquiring an intimate knowledge of nature. He was the eldest Monroe child, the others being brothers Andrew and Joseph and sister Elizabeth. At the age of eleven, James entered what was then considered the finest preparatory school in Virginia. He walked many miles each morning with his schoolmate, John Marshall, future Chief Justice of the United States, who was to write several opinions during Monroe's Presidency that strengthened and upheld the powers of the national government.[110] His father died in 1774, leaving the 16 year old James all his property as the eldest son. In accordance with convention, James also took on the responsibility for the welfare of his younger siblings. While his relationship with them was always close, his brothers proved to be unsuccessful in earning a living throughout their lives, and were a constant worry and financial burden. It is interesting to note that Monroe's loss of a father in early adolescence matches the experience of both Washington and Jefferson, as does the ensuing responsibility for the care of extended family. There is little doubt that the character of each was shaped by the emotional loss as well as the resulting family duties.

Monroe was fortunate to have an uncle, Judge Joseph Jones, who acted as a substitute father in many ways, offering guidance and advice about education and career. Judge Jones was a prominent and wealthy member of Virginia's ruling elite, serving in the House of Burgesses and in the Continental Congress. He proved to be an important political influence on Monroe, setting an example of a dedicated revolutionary, and was highly instrumental in Monroe's successful political career. Due primarily to his advice, Monroe entered the College of William and Mary in the capital, Williamsburg, in June, 1774. Monroe soon became caught up in the revolutionary struggle between the House of Burgesses and England's colonial Governor Dunmore over the rights of the colonists, joining a small group of men on June 24, 1775 to steal hundreds of rifles and swords from the Governor's palace and transfer them to the local militia. Finally, after almost two years at William and Mary, Monroe left prematurely to enlist in the Virginia militia and spent the following two years actively fighting for the Revolutionary cause.

Monroe achieved early recognition from his military colleagues and superiors, primarily because of his admirable interpersonal qualities. Sincere and completely without malice, he was a patient listener, able to put others at ease and make them feel comfortable. He tended to consider problems carefully and exercised good judgment consistently. As a result, he was quickly made an officer and earned the respect of all those in his command. These traits served him well in his later political career, allowing him to be an effective consensus builder and respected leader. Jefferson's later assessment of Monroe's character was shared by almost all who came to know him: "…turn his soul wrong side outwards, and there is not a speck on it."[111]

The Third Virginia Infantry, of which Monroe's brigade was a part, traveled to New York to join General Washington's Army. Monroe's outnumbered unit participated in several skirmishes with the British, holding its own but taking many casualties. He was part of the force that followed Washington across the Hudson to New Jersey, in preparation for the Battle of Trenton. Prior to the battle, Washington ordered that Thomas Paine's *Crisis* be read to every company, and the words, which resonate today as movingly as at that time, had a lasting impact on Monroe:

> These are the times that try men's souls. The summer soldier and sunshine patriot will, in this crisis, shrink from the service of his country; but he that stands it NOW deserves the love and thanks of man and woman. Tyranny, like hell, is not easily conquered; yet we have this consolation with us, that the harder the conflict, the more glorious the triumph. What we obtain too cheap, we esteem to lightly…[112]

Lieutenant Monroe accompanied Washington across the Delaware, and was one of the first officers to encounter the Hessians at Trenton. He led his men into battle and was badly wounded in the shoulder by a musket ball, which cut an artery. If it had not been for the quick action of a local surgeon, he would undoubtedly have bled to death in the field. As it was, he carried the ball in his body the remainder of his life.

Monroe returned to Virginia to recover from his wounds, and later attempted to raise recruits for the Continental Army, experiencing firsthand the difficulties of doing so without either conscription or adequate pay for the soldiers. The consequences of the meager powers of the continental government made him a strong advocate in later years for the authority of Congress to raise an army through the draft. Because no other military command was available, he spent most of the next two years as an aide to one of Washington's brigade commanders, Lord Stirling. Monroe was a witness to the deprivations of the army at Valley Forge and, like Washington, he consistently supported measures to ensure an adequate military. He acquired valuable knowledge and experience in military operations, which served him in good stead as Secretary of War under President Madison during the War of 1812. At the young age of twenty, he had already participated, as combatant or staff, in battles at Harlem Heights, White Plains, Trenton, Brandywine, Germantown, and Monmouth.

Monroe's view of the world was broadened by contact during the Revolution with men from other regions of the country, as well as from Europe. Included among his friends were Alexander Hamilton, Aaron Burr, the Marquis de Lafayette, and a French intellectual named Pierre DuPonceau. From him, Monroe became acquainted with the political philosophers of the European Enlightenment and their criticism of the oppression of the old regimes. He began to see the American Revolution as one part of mankind's struggle for freedom from authoritarian government.[113] As President, he translated this early thinking into a unique mission for America—to help spread the blessings of liberty beyond its shores.

When Monroe returned to Virginia in early 1779, he met Thomas Jefferson, then Governor of Virginia, and, like many other bright, young Virginians, became a political follower of Jefferson as well as the beneficiary of his advice on life and career. At Jefferson's urging, Monroe decided to study law at William and Mary in accordance with an extensive reading curriculum prepared by Jefferson that extended to history, philosophy and literature. Jefferson's influence resulted in a life-long love of books, particularly in the area of politics and political theory. After a brief time at Williamsburg, Monroe continued his studies by following Governor Jefferson to Richmond, the new capital, where he undertook some intelligence gathering for the Governor related to the British capture of Charleston and the impending attack on Richmond. When the Revolutionary War ended successfully, Monroe turned his sights toward a political future.

In early 1782, Monroe was elected to Virginia's legislature, succeeding his uncle, Judge Jones, who became a delegate to the Continental Congress. In a short time, he was also named to the Governor's Council where he was a vigorous supporter of the development of land west of the Alleghenies; indeed, he invested in real estate in what later became the state of Kentucky. Monroe's legislative contributions were recognized quickly by his peers, who elected him to the Continental Congress in June, 1783, where he served with distinction for three years. With the Revolution behind them, the majority of the delegates were distrustful of federal power; Monroe was not. Mindful of his Army experience, he believed that a more effective national government was necessary for the welfare of the country. He respected legislators who represented the interests of people from sections and backgrounds other than his own, such as those from commercial areas; his was a non-dogmatic and realistic approach to politics.

During this period, Monroe shared lodgings with fellow delegate Thomas Jefferson, continuing to learn from his mentor, including improving his already significant proficiency in the use of the French language. When Jefferson was appointed an emissary to France, Monroe purchased much of Jefferson's library from him. Jefferson also brought Monroe into close political association with James Madison, a fellow delegate and close confidante. This relationship further identified Monroe with delegates who favored a strong national government and, over the next four decades, Madison was inextricably, but not always harmoniously, linked to Monroe's political career.

Conscientious and hard-working as a delegate to the Continental Congress, Monroe was instrumental in measures to incorporate the Northwest Territory and strongly supported granting to Congress the power to regulate commerce. Alone among the members, he had taken an extended journey to familiarize himself with the territory west of the Appalachians. His most noteworthy effort was his attempt to ensure that the United States maintained an unfettered right to navigation of the Mississippi. When it appeared that the American negotiator,

John Jay, was willing to sacrifice that right in order to obtain other concessions from Spain, Monroe fought effectively to ensure that no such treaty could obtain the requisite two-thirds approval. Monroe was, from then on, looked upon as a major national spokesman for the expansion of the country, and for the interests of the people of the west. His effective political performance gave notice that he would be a prominent figure in national politics for a long time to come.

3. Senator, Diplomat, Cabinet Member

Following his marriage in 1786 to Elizabeth Kortright, from a prominent New York family, Monroe embarked upon a career in law and politics in Virginia. The couple had two daughters—Eliza, who later acted as Presidential hostess when her mother was incapacitated, and Maria, who was to be the first daughter of a President to be married in the White House. The Virginia/New York nature of Monroe's family came to symbolize the national unity his political career was later to foster. He was elected to the Virginia legislature in 1787 and the following year was elected as a delegate to the Virginia convention, called to decide whether to ratify the new United States Constitution. Nominally, Monroe was an anti-federalist, objecting to several Constitutional provisions: the establishment of a Senate with each state having an equal number of senators (he favored a Senate proportional to population as more protective of the interests of westerners); the Congressional power of direct taxation (he preferred federal tariffs, local taxes and federal requisitions); and an indirectly elected President (he preferred direct popular election). He also favored the addition of a Bill of Rights to the original document. Such positions placed him on opposite sides of the debate from his friend, James Madison. The Constitution was approved as written, in Virginia and in the entire country, and the two men soon found themselves political rivals once again in the election to the first House of Representatives. In 1788, Monroe was asked to run as an anti-federalist against Madison in an attempt to obtain passage of the modifying amendments; however, Madison handily won the election.

Upon Jefferson's return from diplomatic service in France, Monroe, Jefferson, and Madison began their famous political collaboration, which continued throughout the 1790's and gave birth to the Jeffersonian Republican movement. In the spring of 1790, Monroe was persuaded to run for the United States Senate as a moderate anti-federalist, easily winning election. He proved to be a hard-working and diligent Senator, who opposed the practice of conducting Senate business in private and consistently labored to open its sessions to the public. During this period, his concern about the economic policies of Alexander Hamilton increased, his admiration of the French Revolution grew, and his political alliance with Jefferson matured. The two began to see the American and French Revolutions as similar, with any threat to the latter capable of weakening the government created by the former.

Monroe played a role in the Senate similar to that played by James Madison in the House—leader of the nascent Jeffersonian Republican movement. Together with Jefferson they devised strategy for the development of the Republican Party and, thus, the establishment of the two-party system in America. They organized political factions in each state and, most important, pioneered the use of print media to affect public opinion. Monroe's newspaper articles focused primarily on his belief that the French Revolution deserved American support and that Federalist pressure to undertake a war against France must be resisted.

In the late spring, 1794, President Washington surprised Monroe by offering him the post of Ambassador to France, an appointment that had already been turned down by Madison.[114] Monroe had been critical of the President's authorization of a diplomatic mission to Great Britain by John Jay, a key Hamilton supporter, and was generally skeptical of the administration's neutral stance on the French Revolution. However, Washington believed that it was important to name a "Republican" to this post in order to counter any accusation that he was anti-French and pro-British. By doing so, the President hoped to forestall the development of political parties and wanted to present a politically and geographically balanced administration.[115]

Monroe's tenure in France nearly sidetracked his political career, as his partisanship toward the French Revolution overcame his diplomatic objectivity and led to embarrassments for the Washington administration. Upon his arrival, he presented his credentials for recognition directly to the ruling legislative body, the Convention, instead of to the customary foreign affairs officials, and did so with a very public speech emphasizing solidarity with the recent French political changes. He was overly conciliatory to French views of Great Britain, and presented to the French a description of the purposes of the Jay mission which was partly Monroe's wishful thinking, and partly an underplay of its true purposes. The new Secretary of State, Timothy Pickering, a partisan

Federalist, was convinced that Monroe did not effectively explain the Jay Treaty to the French and, thereby, unnecessarily provoked French opposition. He convinced Washington that Monroe did not support the administration's neutrality policy and in July, 1796, the ambassador was recalled.

It is certainly true that Monroe was no traditional diplomat. Throughout his tenure in France, he was a visible public figure, taking positions on French political issues and openly supporting radicals such as Thomas Paine. He championed the cause of many imprisoned supporters of the Revolution and achieved the release of the wife of Jefferson's friend, the Marquis de Lafayette, who had been a prominent supporter of the American Revolution. Monroe urged his government to be bolder and more aggressive with the European powers, particularly Great Britain; he came to believe that the United States should not shrink from advancing its interests with the use of force as an adjunct to diplomacy. This conviction was the foundation for his actions as President two decades later when he took advantage of Andrew Jackson's military exploits to obtain Florida during the negotiation of the Transcontinental Treaty.

Monroe was unable to support his extended family obligations solely through income from agriculture after his return, so he resumed the practice of law and his role in Virginia politics. In 1799, he became the Republican candidate for Governor and was easily elected, becoming an outstanding Governor and gathering administrative experience that would be valuable during his later Presidency. He expansively interpreted his powers and was an activist executive, supporting a strengthened state militia to more effectively contribute to the national defense. Following Jefferson's earlier example, he proposed a broad statewide system of public education as critical to the survival of liberty. He stated that:

> In a government founded on the sovereignty of the people the education of youth is an object of the first importance. In such a government knowledge should be diffused throughout the whole society, and for that purpose the means of acquiring it made not only practicable but easy to every citizen. To preserve the sovereignty in the hands of the people it is not necessary, however desirable, that every person should be qualified to fill every office in the State. It is sufficient that the mass of the people possess a correct knowledge of the principles of the government...[116]

Although a slave owner himself, Monroe believed slavery to be evil, but, as Governor, he witnessed the great public panic that accompanied slave insurrection and knew that a purely domestic solution was highly unlikely. He, therefore, supported the colonization of freed slaves in Africa as the only acceptable solution. Ever a strong partisan of the union, he would later work to avoid the permanent political division of the country based on slavery. He acknowledged slavery's potential cloud over the American form of government, he often lauded the country's unique devotion to equality:

> Called to act in an enlightened age, having never recognized
> hereditary orders, all the citizens born with equal rights and
> expectations…equally sanctioned by nature, by early habits,
> and political institutions. With such advantages we have it
> in our power, and it is our duty, to transmit this blessing to
> our latest posterity. Should that be the case America will
> remain an instructive, an illustrious example to nations.[117]

With the election of Thomas Jefferson as President in 1800, Monroe's diplomatic career was renewed, with not altogether happy results. He served as Special Envoy to France in 1803 during the negotiations leading to the Louisiana Purchase (see Chapter 2), Ambassador to Great Britain, and Special Envoy to Spain in an attempt to obtain all of Florida. After Louisiana, he negotiated a treaty with Great Britain, later disavowed by Jefferson as inadequate because it didn't solve the problem of the impressment of American sailors. In addition, Monroe was unable to make progress to obtain Florida in negotiations with Spain. These apparent failures caused a rift between Monroe and James Madison, Jefferson's Secretary of State.

From Monroe's point of view, the rift was the result of the weakness of the Jefferson administration's foreign policy. He believed that Jefferson should have been more willing to take risks and consider the use of force to affect the negotiations, especially regarding Florida. Only then could the United States garner the respect of the European powers that was necessary for success in foreign affairs. He advocated a hard-headed approach to diplomacy, writing at the time:

> The respect one power has for another is in the exact pro-
> portion of the means which they respectively have of injur-
> ing each other with the least detriment to themselves.

[Each negotiation is an] affair of calculation, dependent upon the physical forces which each has at its command, the relative exposure of their possessions and the probability of the interference in the case of war of other powers.[118]

Although Monroe's differences with Jefferson and Madison were eventually reconciled, he felt humiliated by his European experience, certain that France, Spain, and Great Britain had failed to treat the United States, or its minister, with respect. One historian has stated that "During a century of American diplomatic history, a minister of the United States has seldom if ever within six months suffered, at two great courts [France and Spain], such contemptuous treatment as had fallen to Monroe's lot."[119] After returning to England, Monroe described the English Foreign Minister as "far from being conciliatory," "not in the spirit of amity," without a "friendly sentiment toward the United States," and complained that "Everything he said was uttered in an unfriendly tone, and much more was apparently meant than was said."[120] His experience convinced him that, henceforth, the United States must face the world with strength and unity, unafraid to further both its ideals and its interests. That conviction directly resulted in The Monroe Doctrine—the major achievement of his Presidency.

After Monroe's return to the United States, he decided to challenge Madison for the Republican nomination for President in 1808, much to the chagrin of Jefferson, who wrote to Monroe:

I see with infinite grief a contest arising between yourself and another, who have been very dear to each other, and equally to me...I have ever viewed Mr. Madison and yourself as two principal pillars of my happiness. Were either to be withdrawn, I should consider it among the greatest calamities which could assail my future piece of mind.[121]

Despite Jefferson's concerns, the election contest went forward, with Madison the clear victor and Monroe retiring, once again, to his Virginia farm in Albemarle County. He reestablished his friendship with Jefferson after the former President retired to Monticello, but it wasn't until 1810, when Monroe was invited to the White House, when the quarrel with Madison was finally smoothed over. Ever the politician, Monroe was elected to the Virginia House of Delegates in April, 1810 and was chosen Governor for the second time in January,

1811, with the support of Madisonian Republicans. He served little more than three months later before another call to national service, this time as Madison's Secretary of State.

Monroe entered Madison's administration at a time when the President was struggling with serious maritime and trade issues with Great Britain. These grew out of British restrictions on American commerce intended to pressure the United States to abandon its "neutral" position in Great Britain's conflict with Napoleonic France. Political leaders from the western states further complicated the matter by pushing for expansion into British territory in Canada. Madison's attempts at resolution had foundered and Monroe was able to bring a strong voice to the administration, determined to defend America's honor and its maritime rights as a non-belligerent. The new Secretary of State was widely respected in Congress and was effective in marshaling support for the administration's efforts when negotiations failed, leading to the War of 1812.

Following two years of indecisive military engagements on the Great Lakes, Canada, and what now comprises the American Midwest, the fall of Napoleon in 1814 permitted the British to significantly increase their military effort. They utilized thousands of newly available troops to launch a three-pronged campaign against the United States. One group was sent to Canada to invade from the north, another was to attack Atlantic Coast cities, and a third was sent to New Orleans to capture territory obtained by the United States in the Louisiana Purchase. The attacks in the north and south were aimed at conquering territory, the one against the coastal cities was intended only to intimidate.

Concerned that defenses around Washington were inadequate, and convinced that a British invasion was imminent, Monroe advocated for the establishment of a central intelligence capacity together with improved coastal defenses. Unfortunately, an ineffective Secretary of War Armstrong declined to implement either measure. With the British approaching Washington, Monroe took the extraordinary step for a Cabinet officer of offering personally to obtain the necessary military intelligence to evaluate the threat to the capital. He proceeded to lead a small group of cavalry and accurately estimated the size and location of the advancing British troops, correctly judging their number at 5000 and their position as approaching Bladensburg, Maryland. Monroe and many administration members, including President Madison, gathered near that town to observe the impending battle. Despite outnumbering the British, the young American amateurs were quickly routed, with Madison and his government officials fleeing south towards Washington. Monroe warned the President of the imminent threat to the capital, which he feared could not be defended. Madison followed Monroe's advice and ordered the civil servants to continue their flight to Fredericksburg, Virginia, taking with them as many important documents as they could quickly gather.

They fled none too soon, because British General Ross led his troops to Washington where, in a 24-hour period, they burned and destroyed every government building except the patent office.[122] So precipitous was the departure that the President and his wife, Dolley, left dinner on the table when they fled. British General Ross and Admiral Cockburn reportedly ate the abandoned meal, personally set fire to the White House,[123] then, just as quickly, retreated from Washington. However, the havoc they wrought had a profound effect on the citizens. One prominent socialite, upon her return to Washington, described the scene:

> The poor capitol! Nothing but its blacken'd walls remained!…We afterwards look'd at the other public buildings, but none was so thoroughly destroy'd as the House of Representatives and the President's House. Those beautiful pillars in that Representatives Hall were crack'd and broken, the roof, that noble dome, painted and carved with such beauty and skill, lay in ashes in the cellars beneath the smouldering ruins.[124]

As a result of the debacle, Secretary of War Armstrong was fired, replaced by none other than James Monroe who, for the duration of the war, also held the post of Acting Secretary of State. He worked tirelessly to shore up the ability of the Americans to save the capital from permanent capture and focused effort on defeating the British forces in Baltimore, their next destination. To that end, he concentrated on recruiting troops, improving logistics and creating an adequate intelligence network. So total was his commitment that he slept on a cot in his office, maintaining his post throughout the day and night. As the words of the Star Spangled Banner indicate, "our flag was still there" at the end of the battle of Fort McHenry in Baltimore; the Americans held the city and forced the British to retreat from the capital area, this time permanently.

Monroe was determined that the United States should never again suffer the humiliation of an invasion of its hallowed capital. He supported the idea of a conscript army, deviating from previous Republican philosophy that the Constitution could not be interpreted to grant the federal government such power. Monroe focused on the good of the country and used the same implied powers argument to justify conscription that Alexander Hamilton had used to justify the first national bank. Monroe also favored re-chartering the national bank (the first charter had expired in 1811), believing it critical to the ability of the government to raise funds and to tie commercial interests to the Republican Party, again taking a page from Hamilton. He did so despite the opposition of former President Jefferson, recognizing, as Jefferson did not, the changing nature of the country's needs and the desirability of broadening the political platform of the Republican Party. However, neither conscription nor the re-chartering of the bank were adopted at the time he supported them.

In December, 1814, The Treaty of Ghent ended The War of 1812 by returning the combatants to their relationship before the war started. Many historians have viewed the war as, at best, a draw, with the United States fortunate that Great Britain chose not to pursue it with all available resources. However, Monroe saw it as a critical test of American independence that the young country passed with flying colors. By standing up to the most powerful nation in the world, the United States strengthened the foundation of its national character, acquitted itself with honor, and earned the respect of its rivals. Great Britain concluded that disagreements with the United States would henceforth be settled only through diplomacy. As President some four years later, Monroe built on the positive results of the war and carried them further in the service of liberty.

4. The Expansion of the Country, First Term

Monroe won the Presidential Election of 1816 by easily defeating the Federalist candidate, Rufus King, with 183 electoral votes to 34. The country remembered his courageous military record in the Revolution, rewarded his four decades of honorable public service, recognized his integrity, and trusted his sound judgment. If Monroe did not elicit passionate admiration, his distinguished appearance, sincerity, and kind disposition brought great respect. After 20 years of internal division and conflict with Europe, people yearned for what even Federalists looked forward to as "The Era of Good Feelings" under the new President.[125] He was widely viewed as having the character and personality to unify the nation and take advantage of the coming of peace.

The Napoleonic Wars in Europe had ended in 1815, freeing the United States from constant concern about the impact on its economy of the actions of European belligerents. No longer did the country have to worry about interception of its ships or restrictions on its trade. It could concentrate on the economic growth so necessary for a still young nation, its unfinished territorial expansion, and the strengthening of its national identity. In the words of Henry Adams:

> With the disappearance of every immediate peril, foreign or domestic, society could devote all its energies, intellectual and physical, to its favorite objects...The continent lay before them, like an uncovered ore-bed. They could see, and they could even calculate with reasonable accuracy, the wealth it could be made to yield.[126]

To assist him in addressing the new opportunities, Monroe chose two of the most outstanding Americans in history, John Quincy Adams of Massachusetts as Secretary of State and John C. Calhoun of South Carolina as Secretary of War. Adams, son of the second President, was destined from his youth for prominence in the service of his country. At the age of 14, he accompanied his father to Europe as the elder served in several diplomatic posts, and was exposed at an early age to the sources of western culture as well as the rough and tumble of high level diplomacy. He was an independent minded, moderate Federalist, a prominent lawyer, and the holder of a professorship at Harvard University, who often supported the foreign policy of Republican administrations. He had served as this country's ambassador to Holland, Great Britain, Portugal, Prussia and Russia, and as the head of the commission that negotiated the Treaty of Ghent. As Ambassador to Great Britain, he reported to Secretary of State Monroe and, most important, shared Monroe's belief in the need for a realistic, tough approach to international affairs.

Arguably one of the brightest public servants we have ever had, Adams admired Monroe's deliberate approach to decision-making, the firm nature of his decisions once taken, and the President's ability to listen to differing opinions. Adams called Monroe's capacity to evaluate the advice of others "a disposition which in so high a place is an infallible test of a great mind."[127] Although there is no doubt that Monroe ultimately controlled foreign policy decisions, the advice he chose was usually that of Adams. The two represented one of the closest and most successful collaborations of President and advisor in our history, comparable to Washington and Hamilton, Wilson and House and John and Robert Kennedy.

John C. Calhoun shared Adams' brilliance, intellectual interests, and support for a nationalist program, despite the fact that he came from South Carolina, a region with strong sectional interests. Like Adams, he viewed political judgments as moral ones, enabling him to rise above sectional and factional concerns to see the greater good of the country. Later in his political career, his political focus changed and in the 1840's he became the leading spokesman for states' rights on the issue of slavery, laying the philosophical foundation for the South's political position prior to the Civil War. But in the first Monroe administration he was an extremely effective Secretary of War who teamed with Adams to give the President strong support for an aggressive foreign policy, designed to advance the national interest.

The President hoped Speaker of the House Henry Clay of Kentucky would join his Cabinet as well, but Clay would have accepted appointment only as Secretary of State, the most prestigious post, had it been offered. However, in his role as Speaker, he was a critical figure in the politics of the Monroe Presidency, not only because of his political rivalry with senior members of the Cabinet, but because Clay was an even more vigorous nationalist than Adams, and usually pushed the administration to go further and faster in enlarging the country and challenging the European powers than it otherwise would have.

Looming in the political background, but very much a key player in the first Monroe Administration, was General Andrew Jackson, military hero of the Battle of New Orleans during the War of 1812. Jackson was a rough-hewn American from Tennessee, who did not hesitate to utilize his military role in the service of opening the country to settlers with the same rugged, rustic background as his. Viewed from a modern perspective, his methods were, at times, unacceptably extreme, particularly when directed against Indian tribes, yet he was enormously popular with the average American citizen of the time.

Monroe was a strong executive, despite the traditional Republican doctrine favoring limited executive power. His triumphant tours of the northeast in 1817 and the south and west in 1819 provided a model for future Presidents who wanted to encourage national political unity. Foreshadowing Abraham Lincoln's rededication to Union at Gettysburg more than two score years later, Monroe visited the site of the Revolutionary Battle of Bunker Hill on July 4, 1817, declaring:

> The blood spilt here roused the whole American people and united them, in common cause in defense of their rights. That union will never be broken.[128]

Monroe used his great interpersonal skills to cajole and persuade individual Congressmen to support his positions. He also set precedent by urging his Cabinet members to deal directly and intensively with Congress, but only after consensus on administration policy was achieved through intra-Cabinet deliberations.

With political unity came renewed efforts to obtain Florida from Spain and to establish a firm boundary for the Louisiana Purchase. The Napoleonic Wars had weakened Spain so that it was no longer in a position to maintain all her possessions in both North and South America. In fact, independence movements were active in much of South America, taking the experience of the United States as inspiration for their freedom and liberty. Henry Clay led those advocating giving these movements immediate American support, but for Monroe, the problem was not that simple. If the United States recognized the independence of the Latin republics prematurely, would Spain refuse to cede Florida and agree on expansive borders for Louisiana? The authoritarian regimes in Europe were not likely to sit idly by and watch revolutionary movements succeed in undermining the Spanish Empire. If Spain was too weak to resist, perhaps France, or even Russia would attempt to make the colonies theirs. For Monroe, the problem was how to gain Florida and expand the country without causing war with Spain and, possibly, her European allies.

The Treaty of Ghent had left unresolved the question of the Canadian-American border, from the Great Lakes to the West Coast. Contemporaneous with the effort to determine the final extent of Louisiana, Monroe directed Adams to settle geographical issues with Great Britain in the northwest, so that the borders of the United States would reach to the Pacific Ocean. Adams guided negotiations that produced the Convention of 1818, which designated the 49th parallel as the Canadian border, thus placing the entire Mississippi River within the United States, and forever ending any challenge to the primacy of America on that waterway. The two countries could not agree on the border west of the Rockies to the Pacific, in what was then called Oregon Country and what now constitutes the states of Oregon and Washington. The treaty, therefore, provided that the disputed land would be open to settlement (including contested exploitation by fishermen and fur traders) by either country for ten years, with this provision renewable with both parties' consent.

Even before the Convention of 1818 with Great Britain became final, Monroe and Adams were focusing their attention on Florida and the uncertain boundary of the Louisiana Purchase. The War of 1812 had made the United States keenly aware of the importance of the Floridas to its national security, for, if either part of it came into the hands of a strong European power, the continent would face grave danger. As one noted historian has written:

> In the hands of any foreign power they were a pistol pointed at the heart of the future Continental Republic. East Florida was the butt of the pistol, Pensacola the trigger-guard, and the "panhandle" of West Florida was the horizontal barrel with its muzzle pressed against the nation's life-artery, the Mississippi River, just above New Orleans. Spain had been too feeble to load the pistol and pull the trigger, but not her ally England, nor her enemy Napoleon if he could lay his hands on the weapon.[129]

Spain also desired a resolution of the Florida issue, unsure that it could hold the territory for long against aggressive settlers, hostile Seminole Indians, and runaway former slaves, some of whom had been organized by Great Britain during the war to make trouble for both Spain and the United States. The Spanish were not likely to be able to control these activities and resist a determined United States government. Moreover, Spain's greater concern was the loss of its colonies in South America to independence movements; it did not want the United States to offer support to the rebels, an objective for which Speaker Henry Clay had been pressuring the Monroe administration. Aware that an accommodation on Florida might forestall any such anti-Spanish action by the United States, their Minister to the United States, Don Luis de Onis, initiated negotiations with Secretary Adams in December, 1817 to determine the fate of the Spanish Empire in North America.

In a memorandum of instructions to Adams in February, 1818, President Monroe recorded the first written proposal to extend the boundary of United States all the way to the Pacific Ocean.[130] The Spanish, for their part, did not want to cede Florida without an agreement that the western border of the United States would extend no further than the Mississippi River, much further east than the ambitious target set by Monroe. At this point in the negotiations, the situation "on the ground" intervened to move things much more quickly to a conclusion. The military aggressiveness of General Andrew Jackson intimidated the Spanish and gave Monroe an important opportunity.

For a considerable time, the Seminole Indians in Spanish Florida had been posing problems for the citizens of Georgia, bitter over the Seminoles' protection of runaway slaves. Frequent border incursions from both sides were taken as evidence of Spain's inability to control its own territory. When the Seminoles refused to attend a conference organized in November, 1817 to try to resolve the problems, Georgians burned the Seminole town of Fowltown, just north of the Florida border. In retaliation, the Seminoles attacked an American ship, slaying 45 people, including women and children. Secretary of War Calhoun sent orders to General Edmund Gaines, the American commander in Georgia, to pursue the Seminoles across the Spanish border until they reached a Spanish post, *but to stop at that point*, notify the War Department, and wait for further instructions. General Andrew Jackson, Gaines' superior, received a copy of these orders and saw an opportunity to go beyond them to seize all of Florida, but thought it best to ensure that President Monroe was of the same mind. He sent a letter on January 6, 1818 to the President urging the seizure and, although Monroe did not respond, Jackson went ahead without a written Presidential directive.[131]

With 3,000 troops from Fort Scott in Georgia and, ironically, 2,000 Creek Indian allies, General Jackson marched into Florida, routed the Indian resistance and pursued the fleeing Seminoles to the Spanish town of St. Marks, where, on April 6, he overwhelmed the Spanish defenders and lowered their flag, replacing it with the American. The General then turned east, showing no mercy either for the Indians or the residents in his path. Along the way, Jackson captured two English citizens he believed were aiding the Seminoles, Alexander Arbuthnot and Lieutenant Robert Ambrister, and, after a hastily convened court martial, the two were executed on April 29, an act which was to haunt Jackson's reputation for the remainder of his life. Jackson showed no remorse, writing on May 5:

I hope the execution of these two unprincipled villains will prove an awful example to the world, and convince the Government of Great Britain, as well as her subjects, that certain, though slow retribution awaits those unchristian wretches who, by false promises, delude and excite an Indian tribe to all the horrid deeds of savage war.[132]

Emboldened by the executions, Jackson proceeded to overtake Pensacola, the center of Spanish rule in Florida, and sent orders to Gaines to capture St. Augustine, the only remaining major Spanish outpost. He unilaterally proclaimed Spanish rule ended and established a provisional government for Florida with Col. William King as governor. He wrote to Calhoun:

So long as Spain has not the power…to preserve the Indians within her territory at peace with the U States no security can be given to our Southern frontier…The moment the American Army retires from Florida, The War hatchet will be again raised, and the same scenes of indiscriminate murder with which our frontier settlers have been visited, will be repeated…[133]

Jackson's exploits presented Monroe with a dangerous crisis and, because they were undertaken without a declaration of war, resulted in a Congressional investigation of the entire episode, which later exonerated the popular General. The public supported Jackson's actions, but the Cabinet was divided on how to deal with them. Secretary of War Calhoun, who immediately reversed Jackson's order to Gaines to capture St. Augustine, was outraged that his original orders to stop at St. Mark's had been ignored, and wanted Jackson reprimanded or subject to court martial. Secretary of the Treasury Crawford saw Jackson as a potential political rival and agreed with Calhoun. For Speaker Clay, eager to criticize both Jackson and the administration, the war was both a violation of the Constitution and an unconscionable exercise of military power.

Where some saw only malfeasance, others saw opportunity. Adams supported Jackson's actions as self-defense, mindful of the opportunity to further American interests in the negotiation with Spain. President Monroe concurred, but did not want to give an outright endorsement to Jackson. Thus, he directed that a note be sent to the

Spanish stating that the Florida seizures were the product of Jackson alone, outside of orders, yet understandable in the circumstances of Spanish failure in Florida. He offered to return the seized territory only when the Spanish could adequately control the Seminoles.

President Monroe's decision was a product of the variety of advice he received from his Cabinet, the lessons of his diplomatic experience in Europe, his geographic vision for America, and the strength of character that allowed him to make difficult choices. He was thus able to turn away from sanctioning a violation of international law, cleverly gain the diplomatic advantage Jackson's action had brought, sidestep a confrontation with Congress, and avoid repudiating an admired national hero.

Throughout the summer and fall of 1818, Adams and Onis continued their negotiations, while Jackson's actions and the administration's reluctance to denounce them had a significant intimidating effect on Spain. The Spanish wanted to avoid a similar military thrust by General Jackson in territory they controlled in Texas and Mexico and the British, whose two citizens had fallen victim to Jackson, had to take into account the newly aggressive Americans in planning their future in the new world. Adams drafted a diplomatic note for Ambassador Erving to deliver in Madrid which defended Jackson and attacked the British for meddling in Florida. As one noted diplomatic historian concluded:

> Adams drove home the real lesson of the Florida invasion: Spain must either exercise responsible authority in the derelict province or cede it to the United States...Adams's great gun cleared the air everywhere...It settled the Florida question.[134]

The Spanish became much more open to an American borderline to the Pacific Ocean. The more critical issue for them was to hold Texas, and President Monroe decided that he was willing to give up any Texas claim in exchange for Florida and the line to the Pacific.[135] This compromise, coming as it did in the face of domestic political pressure from Clay to obtain Texas, demonstrated the political courage and good judgment of Monroe, who did not want to go so far as to provoke a war with Spain and her European ally, France. Adams and Onis were left with the details of where the eastern border of Texas should be drawn and at what parallel the line to the Pacific should be placed. The latter was settled at the 42nd parallel (the current southern border of Oregon and Idaho) and the former at the Sabine, Red, and Arkansas Rivers (the modern border between Texas and Louisiana, the southern border of the current state of Oklahoma, and through the middle of the present state of Colorado). On February 22. 1819, the two men signed the Transcontinental Treaty; Adams wrote in his diary of the momentous event:

> It was near one in the morning when I closed the day with ejaculations of fervent gratitude to the Giver of all good. It was perhaps, the most important day of my life."[136]

Two days later, the Senate unanimously ratified the document and sent it to President Monroe for signature.

The Spanish Government proved less enthusiastic and did not quickly approve the treaty. The Council of State believed that too much territory was ceded without assurance that the United States would refrain from recognizing the independence of Spain's rebellious Latin American colonies. Spanish emissaries were directed to attempt to obtain better terms. A livid Adams urged President Monroe to have the military occupy all of Florida. Henry Clay, on the other hand, was pleased, urging Monroe to abandon the treaty, recognize Latin independence, and forcibly seize both Florida and Texas. Even former President Jefferson suggested that ratification be rescinded until Texas was included in the Treaty, prompting Adams to write that Jefferson's advice reminded him "that an old sea-captain never likes that his mate should make a better voyage than himself."[137] Monroe did not follow Jefferson's advice, concerned that a move on Texas would further complicate sectional conflict over slavery and expansion, recently quieted with the Missouri Compromise. He wrote to the former President:

> ...the further acquisition, of territory, to the West & South, involves difficulties, of an internal nature, which menace the Union itself. We ought therefore to be cautious in making the attempt.[138]

In the end, Monroe steered a middle course, knowing that an aggressive Latin policy at the time would end all hope of Spanish approval of the treaty, and an immediate military campaign would bring unpredictable domestic and foreign reaction. He asked Congress to grant him authority to take possession of Florida at his discretion, then requested that any action on the matter be delayed to give diplomacy an opportunity to bring the desired result.

Monroe's policy of moderation was rewarded with success when a democratic revolution in Spain forced King Ferdinand VII to re-establish parliamentary government, one that reflected Spanish domestic opinion favoring peacefully resolving the dispute with the United States. Moreover, the non-democratic European powers were not inclined to support the new Spanish parliamentary government in any American conflict. The King bowed to the new forces and signed the treaty on October 14, 1820.

For President Monroe, the final conclusion of the Treaty capped decades of effort to realize the potential of the Louisiana Purchase he helped negotiate. Although Adams and Jackson played their part in facilitating the great achievement, Monroe deserves the greatest credit—for the consistency of his vision, for recognizing how circum-stances could be used to implement that vision, and for his masterly guidance of the ship of state through dangerous domestic and foreign waters. Even Adams, who had claimed that it was his idea to propose a line to the Pacific in the negotiations,[139] gave most of the credit to Monroe:

> ...can there be a doubt in considering it as the most magnif-icent supplement to our national Independence presented by our history...which more than doubled the territories...the leading mind of that great movement in the annals of the world, and thus far in the march of human improvement upon earth, was the mind of James Monroe?[140]

5. The Monroe Doctrine, Second Term

James Monroe was elected President for his second term in 1820 with only one electoral vote cast against him,[141] an achievement exceeded in American history only by George Washington. To some extent, this was due to the weakness of the Federalist Party, but it was also testament to the fact that there was no organized opposition to Monroe's policies. The expansion of the country was enormously pop-ular and, in the resolution of the great domestic issue of the day—the status of slavery in the proposed new state of Missouri—the President had supported a compromise that preserved political balance in the country and avoided any immediate threat to the union. In so doing, he offended no section or faction. Those who had an appetite for political contest were looking forward to the election of 1824, when an expected battle among Adams, Clay, Crawford, Calhoun, and Jackson held the promise of what a Virginia newspaper labeled the "war of the giants."[142]

With his election by a unified country, Monroe saw great opportunity to strengthen the nation and its commitment to liberty. Having overcome foreign threats to America's geographic expansion in his first term, he created an American role in reducing foreign threats to liberty's expansion in his second term. The growing independence movements in the Spanish colonies of Latin America presented him with his opportunity. In the negotiations leading up to the Transcontinental Treaty, he had maintained a scrupulously neutral stance in order not to remove a major incentive for Spain to come to agreement on territory. He did this in the face of strong domestic pressure from Henry Clay, who reflected a considerable body of public opinion in favor of recognizing the new Latin republics. With the Treaty ratified, Monroe, too, was ready to do so.

Adams, however, was skeptical of the ability of the new Latin nations to maintain democratic societies and was not enamored of America's "duty" to support liberty in other places. He was disdainful of what he considered the self-defeating impulse of some of his countrymen during the French Revolution—namely, to get involved in a foreign war to defend another country's "liberty". He believed that neutrality in European affairs was America's best course and favored a policy of anti-imperialism and non-intervention. For him, a more aggressive foreign policy would not only lead to war, but "change the very foundations of our own government from *liberty to power*."[143] This sentiment is still echoed in American foreign policy debates, most recently regarding United States military efforts in Afghanistan and Iraq.

Monroe was the first President to grapple in real terms with the classic ongoing dilemma for America's foreign policy: Is the country's security best served by aggressively helping to establish, protect, and safeguard liberty around the world, or, would it be better to set an example for all those seeking liberty by improving equality, justice, and freedom at home? Henry Clay was pushing the administration towards the former approach; Washington's Farewell Address and Jeffersonian Republican principles pointed to the latter. Each of Monroe's successors has had to resolve this dilemma in the context of specific foreign policy situations.

When resolved in favor of an aggressive approach, some of the greatest mistakes and greatest successes have occurred—the Cuban

Bay of Pigs invasion and the Vietnam War are frequently cited as examples of mistakes, and the ouster of Panamanian dictator Manuel Noriega and the rescue of Kuwait in First Gulf War have been offered as examples of successes. It is more difficult to determine when the "liberty by example" approach succeeded or failed, since cause and effect are more difficult to identify as a result of inaction. One could say that the unwillingness of the United States to intervene in the Hungarian Revolution of 1956, and, possibly the entire Cold War, constituted examples of failure because America stood by while Eastern European countries desiring freedom remained oppressed. On the other hand, American military intervention to liberate Eastern Europe from communism could have caused World War III, and, eventually, these countries became free without it, so, possibly, the "liberty by example" Cold War policy could be claimed as a success.[144] With his famous Doctrine, Monroe managed the classic dilemma by seeking a middle course—one that could be called "prudent aggressiveness."

By 1822, President Monroe believed that it was time to support Latin American independence and thought he could do so without jeopardizing American neutrality. The countries of Chile, the United Provinces of the Plata (Argentina), Peru, Colombia and Mexico had already declared their independence and, in response to Monroe's request, Congress formally recognized them on May 4. The action offered encouragement to the fledgling countries and, at the same time, Spain and its allies accepted the recognition as inevitable. Monroe directed Adams to instruct the newly appointed ambassadors on the principles of United States policy toward Latin America, the cornerstone of which would be support for civil, political, commercial and religious liberty. The President was now ready to fit Latin recognition into a broader role for United States' foreign policy.

In the aftermath of the Napoleonic Wars, the autocratic states of Europe agreed to act in concert to suppress movements for independence and democracy. France, Russia, Prussia and Austria formed the "Holy Alliance," which approved the 1823 French military action in Spain that overthrew the new Spanish parliamentary government and restored the absolute monarchy of Ferdinand VII. The new Minister of Foreign Affairs in Great Britain, George Canning, concerned at the growth of French power as well as the attack on a democratic government, sought ways to redress the balance of power to his country's advantage. His approach was to mend fences with the United States and, in combination, serve as a counterweight to French and Spanish interests in the western hemisphere. The two nations shared the objective of helping to maintain the newly declared independence of the Latin American republics, Great Britain to protect its enormous commercial potential there and the United States to help strengthen sister democratic governments. Both were concerned that the French restoration of Ferdinand VII might provoke an attempt to crush the new governments and reinstate Spanish rule.

In a conversation with the American Ambassador to Great Britain, Richard Rush, Canning suggested that the two countries issue a *joint declaration* to neutralize any potential Holy Alliance effort in Latin America.[145] Rush responded that the United States would be favorably inclined if Great Britain would immediately recognize the independence of the Latin republics. While waiting for an answer, he sent the proposal to the President for consideration.

Monroe initially found the idea of a joint declaration an appealing one, acknowledging, as it did, the elevated status of the United States in international affairs and enlisting the naval power of Great Britain to guarantee Latin independence. Yet, he recognized that joining with Great Britain departed from the policy of non-involvement in European politics initiated by George Washington, and followed in previous Republican administrations. He was mindful of tradition, but not necessarily bound by it in new circumstances, but he forwarded the proposal to former Presidents Jefferson and Madison for their advice. Both favored accepting Canning's offer, despite the entanglement with Great Britain. Jefferson wrote that the United States should:

> ...have a system of her own, separate and apart from that of Europe...One nation, most of all, could disturb us in this pursuit; she now offers to lead, aid, and accompany us in it. By acceding to her proposition, we detach her from the band of despots, bring her mighty weight into the scale of free government and emancipate a continent at one stroke which might otherwise linger long in doubt and difficulty.[146]

As Monroe was preparing to submit Canning's proposal to the Cabinet for decision, Adams received a somewhat threatening note from the Russian Ambassador, Baron Tuyl, implying that if the United States went beyond recognition of the Latin republics by offering overt support, Czar Alexander, on behalf of the Holy Alliance, would assist France and Spain in defending their interests in the new world. The Cabinet debated how to respond to both Tuyl and Canning, with Secretary of War Calhoun in favor of accepting Canning's proposal in order to offset what he viewed as a significant military threat from the Holy Alliance.

Monroe was also worried about that threat. According to Adams, the President was:

> ...alarmed, far beyond anything that I could have conceived possible, with the fear that the Holy Allies are about to restore immediately all South America to Spain...the news that Cadiz has surrendered to the French has so affected the president that he appeared entirely to despair of the cause of South America.[147]

Nonetheless, Monroe did not want to place the United States in a subservient position to Great Britain and, although he recognized the wisdom of his Republican predecessors, he chose not to mention the letters from Jefferson and Madison at the Cabinet meeting.[148] Adams focused the meeting on the Russian note:

> It affords a very suitable and convenient opportunity for us to take our stand against the Holy Alliance and at the same time to decline the overture of Great Britain. It would be more candid, as well as more dignified, to avow our principles explicitly to Russia and France, than to come in as a cock-boat in the wake of the British man-of-war.[149]

The Cabinet authorized a direct response to Russia, which Adams drafted and Monroe toned down. It defended the recognition given to the new Latin Republics as consistent with America's founding principles, but indicated that the United Sates would observe formal neutrality between Spain and her former colonies only so long as Russia and the Holy Alliance remained neutral as well. The response was delivered on November 8. Nine days later, when Monroe asked Adams to obtain a clarification of Russian policy from Tuyl, the Russian Minister indicated that the Czar would view favorably the re-establishment of Spanish control over Latin republics, crushing their independence. In a Cabinet meeting on November 21, 1823, Adams and Monroe were concerned at the time not only with the fate of the Latin republics, but, also, with the recent attempt by Russia to stake a claim in the Pacific Northwest.[150] They agreed that the United States needed to go further than the statements in the note delivered to Russia and to declare:

> ...our expectation and hope that the European powers will equally abstain from the attempt to spread their principles in the American hemisphere, or to subjugate by force any part of these continents to their will.[151]

While Adams would have limited the expression of American policy to traditional diplomatic notes, President Monroe had a broader vision. He had previously indicated to Jefferson that he wanted the United States to "take a bolder attitude...in favor of liberty",[152] and now saw the opportunity and occasion to do so in a very public way. He wanted to prepare a comprehensive statement of American policies and announce it with the seriousness and solemnity of a formal State of the Union Message to Congress. After hearing from Ambassador Rush that Canning was no longer pushing for a joint declaration, Monroe made the final decision to issue a unilateral statement of policy.

Adams produced ideas for the President's message that focused on Latin independence and American ideals. Monroe broadened the document to include support for the Greek democratic revolt against the Turks, criticism of French aid to Ferdinand VII, and a call for the restoration of the Spanish parliamentary system. He warned of grave danger to the United States, and to liberty everywhere, from the Holy Alliance. During Cabinet and private discussions, Adams convinced Monroe that such strong statements that might threaten the peace and the two reached agreed that the message should focus on the American hemisphere and the American system of government. Monroe accordingly modified the text to avoid provoking the Holy Alliance with a defiant tone, and to set forth an American position clearly distinguishable from that of Great Britain. As tradition dictated, the message was read to Congress by an official reader, but the President braved the snow and mud on a cold December 2, 1823 to travel to Capitol Hill personally to answer questions on the solemn occasion. Since 1850, we have known the message as the Monroe Doctrine, although at the time it was referred to the "American System."

The substance of the Monroe Doctrine appeared in two separate portions of Monroe's State of the Union Message and constituted three major principles: 1) Non-colonization of North and South America, 2) Abstention by the United States from European wars, and

3) Non-interference with the independence of the countries of North and South America (sometimes referred to as the "Hands Off" principle). With respect to the first, the President made reference to upcoming discussions among Russia, Great Britain and the United States about the Pacific Northwest, and enunciated the following guideline:

> ...the occasion has been judged proper, for asserting as a principle in which the rights and interests of the United States are involved, that the American continents, by the free and independent condition which they have assumed and maintain, are henceforth not to be considered as subjects for future colonization by any European Powers...

Later in the message, the President turned to the relationship of the United States to Europe in pronouncing the second principle:

> In the wars of the European powers in matters relating to themselves we have never taken any part, nor does it comport with our policy so to do. It is only when our rights are invaded or seriously menaced that we resent injuries or make preparation for our defense. With the movements in this hemisphere we are of necessity more immediately connected...The political system of the allied powers is essentially different in this respect from that of America.

Finally, in the most enduring principle of American foreign policy, the President sought to place a blanket of protection over newly won liberty:

> ...we should consider any attempt on their [European powers] part to extend their system to any portion of this hemisphere as dangerous to our peace and safety. With the existing colonies or dependencies of any European power we have not interfered and shall not interfere. But with the Governments who have declared their independence and maintained it, and whose independence we have, on great consideration and on just principles, acknowledged, we could not view any interposition for the purpose of oppressing them, or controlling in any other manner their destiny, by any European power in any other light than as the manifestation of an unfriendly disposition toward the United States.[153]

Monroe was issuing a moral call in his message—for the extension of the ideals of the Declaration of Independence to the remainder of the hemisphere. Although it is not clear whether he was prepared, at the time, to go to war to prevent interference with the independence of the Latin countries, his words were greeted as a signal that the United States would have a major impact on the fate of the peoples of the world. Public opinion in the United States was overwhelmingly positive, resonating to the President's plea for national awareness of the role of the country's role as advocate for and, if necessary, protector of, the liberty of others.

Partisans of democracy in Europe were equally enthusiastic. The Marquis de Lafayette thought it "the best little bit of paper that God had ever permitted any man to give to the World."[154] The reactionary powers of Europe were not so enthusiastic. Prince Metternich of Austria deemed the declaration "indecent," declaring that the United States had "...astonished Europe by a new act of revolt, more unprovoked, fully as audacious, and no less dangerous than the former."[155]

Latin America's response was cordial, but muted, as the new governments viewed support from Britain's navy more relevant to their security than the American President's noble words. Monroe worried that the Holy Alliance might send troops to Latin America, and would have been willing to form an alliance with Great Britain, if necessary, to resist. But no such tandem materialized, nor was it necessary. The Holy Alliance focused its attention on Europe and the countries of Latin America remained independent.

The remaining year of Monroe's second term was anti-climactic, with attention focused on political jockeying for advantage carried on by the contestants in the 1824 Presidential election—Adams, Calhoun, Clay, Crawford and Jackson. At the conclusion of his Presidency, Monroe moved to his new Oak Hill estate in Louden County, Virginia, which had been designed by Thomas Jefferson and constructed during Monroe's second term by James Hoban, builder of the White House. His retirement was a happy one and included continued public service, most notably as Regent of the University of Virginia in 1826 and as a delegate to the Virginia Constitutional Convention in 1829. Like Jefferson, his long years in the service of his country left him in difficult financial straits and, shortly before his death, Congress appropriated $30,000 as partial reimbursement of his expenses as a public servant. In a coincidental footnote of history, Monroe, like both Jefferson and Adams, died on Independence Day—in his case in 1831, at the age of 73.

6. Monroe's Legacy

James Monroe's two great accomplishments as President were among the most courageous and enduring of any in American history. The Transcontinental Treaty firmly enlarged the country's geographic ambitions and achieved the potential inherent in the Louisiana Purchase. From then on, it was virtually inevitable that the boundaries of the United States would stretch across the breadth of the North American Continent, from Atlantic to Pacific, from Canada to Mexico, and, with them, the great American experiment in liberty. The natural resources acquired, and the human opportunities created, have fueled the engine of democracy ever since.

The Monroe Doctrine declared to the world that the United States was a unique nation, whose foreign objectives were rooted in the survival of liberty, and whose determination to accomplish them would have a permanent place in the country's tradition. No other country can say that its relations with other nations are grounded primarily on the survival and protection of liberty. The Doctrine did not constitute law, either domestic or international. It was merely a unilateral declaration of foreign policy by the President of the United States. Yet, it has had a profound effect on the nation and on all of Monroe's successors as President, more than most statutes passed by Congress and as much as any provision of the Constitution. While there is frequent political debate over how America's unique foreign policy objective should be implemented, Monroe's great declaration is the major reason the objective exists.

The subsequent history of the Doctrine, its use and misuse, its effectiveness and impotence, has been a fascinating, if inconsistent one. It has been invoked by Presidents for a multiplicity of purposes— by James K. Polk to assert rights in Oregon and Texas and to protect the Yucatan against British claims; indirectly by Andrew Johnson to prevent France from taking Mexico; by Grover Cleveland in a dispute between Great Britain and Venezuela; by Franklin Roosevelt to protect Latin America from the Axis Powers during World War II; and by John Kennedy to force the Soviet Union to remove its offensive missiles from Cuba. It has also represented different things at different times to different people—the American Secretary of State (and later Presidential candidate) Lewis Cass called it the American doctrine of self-preservation; the Spanish philosopher Jose Ortega y Gasset thought it transferred the center of the universe from Europe to

America; the German Chancellor Bismarck considered it an imperti-
nence; and Abraham Lincoln believed it applied only to the circumstances of Monroe's day. Latin Americans themselves have embraced
it when they thought it protected them and criticized it as United
States imperialism when they felt oppressed by it, particularly after
President Theodore Roosevelt issued his famous Corollary that justified the exercise of international police power by the United States.

There is no question, however, that the Doctrine remains an
important foundation of America's approach to the world. It was
intended by Monroe as a clarion call for liberty and a declaration of the
constructive purposes of American foreign policy. It also served as a
second Declaration of Independence, as much to inspire the American
people as to warn the Europeans.

Monroe's entire career can be seen as building to the message he
delivered.[156] It expressed his deeply held belief that there was a fundamental difference between the authoritarian governments of the old
Europe, and the commitment to liberty that had been born and nurtured in America. From the time of his early diplomatic assignments,
Monroe wanted to set America apart in the world, and garner for it the
respect of the European powers and the admiration of all people desiring liberty. With the indispensable assistance of John Quincy Adams,
he took advantage of the opportunities presented to him during his
second term to do just that.

Although Monroe's legacy is based in large measure on the two
great acts of his Presidency, his character set him apart in equally
important ways. He established an example for future Presidents in
what Calhoun called his "intellectual patience":

> ...above all men, that I ever knew, when called on to decide
> an important point, hold the subject immoveably [sic] fixed
> under his attention, till he had mastered it, in all of its rela-
> tions. It was mainly to this admirable quality that he owed
> his highly accurate judgment. I have known many much
> more rapid reaching the conclusion, but very few, with a
> certainty so unerring.[157]

To many, he embodied Washingtonian traits that were ideal for a
public servant—sincerity, honesty, dependability, and dedication to
country. His very presence reminded citizens of the nobility of their
Revolution and of their first Commander. He had a capacity for wise

judgment that seldom erred, a commitment to integrity that always looked to the public good, and a firmness upon which his friends and enemies, alike, could unfailingly depend. Moreover, he had the courage to step outside the norm and implement a compelling vision for the country.

Monroe is sometimes criticized for failing to solve the nation's great burden, the existence of slavery, but he deserves credit even in this area for supporting the Missouri Compromise, despite opposition from his fellow southerners. He was dedicated to the Union, as he eloquently made clear when he became President:

> The American people have encountered together great dangers and sustained severe trials with success. They constitute one great family with a common interest.[158]

Had the country remained committed to the Compromise, preserving all states north of the 36th parallel as free states, instead of departing from it in the 1850's, the Union may well have stayed together and the tragic Civil War may well have been avoided. Undoubtedly, Monroe would have fondly hoped for such an outcome. It is noteworthy, too, that Monroe supported efforts which were widespread in the 1820's to colonize freed slaves in Africa, at the time considered a progressive and humane way to ameliorate the slavery issue. His backing for this effort was recognized by the beneficiaries of his support when the capital of the new African country of Liberia was named for him, as "Monrovia."

Like Jefferson, he was convinced that only an educated and informed electorate could understand what it would take to help liberty survive. Ever a supporter of public education and civic responsibility, he set a tone in his First Inaugural Address for future public policy:

> It is only when the people become ignorant and corrupt...that they are incapable of exercising the sovereignty...Let us by all wise and constitutional measures promote intelligence among the people as the best means of preserving our liberties.[159]

Monroe was the last of the revolutionary heroes to lead the nation. The lessons of that experience—the value of unity and non-partisanship—always served to guide his actions as a political leader. Yet, he didn't hesitate to deviate from previously held political positions if he thought the interests of the country required him to do so, most notably, the Jeffersonian fear of a strong chief executive. He learned as a diplomat in Europe the realities of international affairs and the great differences between authoritarian and republican government. He became a committed nationalist, confident that American liberty could survive only if the world saw the country as a determined defender of its interests.

Monroe was the first President to realize the importance to the nation's security of an effective intelligence capability and he set an influential precedent for a formidable national defense by supporting both conscription and effective coastal fortifications. He knew that the welfare of the nation would be forever threatened if the great powers in the world sought to maintain a presence on our doorstep. Monroe expressed the essence of his legacy better than anyone:

We must support our rights or lose our character, and with it, perhaps, our liberties. A people who fail to do it can scarcely be said to hold a place among independent nations. National honor is national property of the highest value. The sentiment in the mind of every citizen is national strength. It ought therefore to be cherished.[160]

James Monroe combined a sincere and conciliatory political personality with a vision of a strong America that grew out of his broad experience, and the combination served the country well, indeed. When he died on Independence Day, 1826, then President John Quincy Adams said in his eulogy:

Thus strengthening and consolidating the federative edifice of his country's Union, till he was entitled to say, like Augustus Caesar of his imperial city, that he had found her built of brick and left her constructed of marble.[161]

President George Washington, Father of the Country

Alexander Hamilton, Secretary of the Treasury

President Thomas Jefferson

President James Monroe

John Quincy Adams, Secretary of State

President Abraham Lincoln

114   Elton B. Klibanoff

First Reading of the Emancipation Proclamation Before Lincoln's Cabinet

President Woodrow Wilson

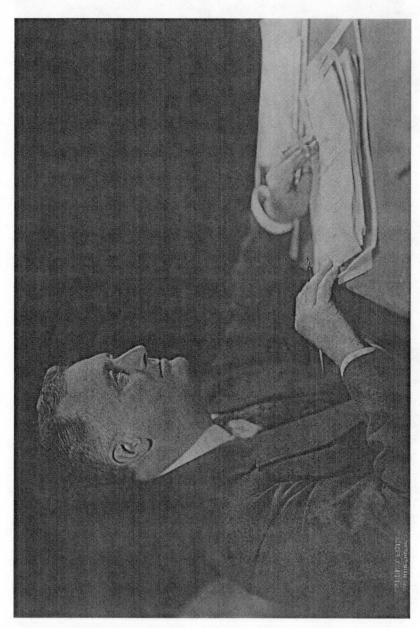

President Franklin D. Roosevelt

Frances Perkins, Secretary of Labor

Harry Hopkins, Works Progress Administrator

CHAPTER 4.

Abraham Lincoln and the Revitalization of American Liberty

Slavery existed in America at the time of the Revolution and was not abolished by the framers of the Constitution. As the South became increasingly dependent on slavery, and the system became an entrenched part of Southern culture, the continuous geographic expansion of the nation resulted in bitter debate over slavery's future. Abraham Lincoln and the Republican Party created the political environment in which the inconsistency between slavery and American liberty had to be resolved and, as President, Lincoln provided the vision and inspiration necessary to lead the nation through the tragic path of resolution.

1. Slavery and Race as an Obstacle to Liberty and America's Mission

The four decades following the Presidency of James Monroe were a time of great change for the United States. The economy grew rapidly, continual political battles were fought over the relative powers of the federal and state governments, the expansion of the country proceeded dramatically, and major national political parties were created and died. Throughout this period, the critical threat to American liberty proved to be the existence and expansion of the institution of slavery.

From a modern perspective, slavery clearly appears as the single most controversial, emotional, and regrettable part of the American experience. Its effects, and those of the Civil War it caused, are reflected today in America's ongoing struggle to overcome a society divided by race and by geography. As modern politicians debate issues such as affirmative action and racially fair redistricting, some in the

South[162] still fly the Confederate flag, 140 years after the War. It remains a symbol of separation, and, to many Americans, is a reminder of the cruelty, bigotry, and hatred that bedevil the country's history.

The growth of slavery during the 19th century was a greater threat to the nation's liberty than any since the Revolutionary War. It spawned decades of political conflict that undermined the "spirit of 1776" and it painted a picture to the world of a hypocritical and heartless society, whose promise of equal opportunity would never be fully realized. Incongruous with a Revolution based on the liberty of the common man, slavery was nevertheless tolerated and accepted even by the founders of the nation. Thomas Jefferson blamed the English for imposing it on the colonists against their will and claimed that it was alien to the nature of the new world. In truth, slavery gradually became critical to southern agricultural production and, therefore, to America's early economic growth. The rise of liberty coincided with the rise of slavery to such an extent that one influential historian has concluded that Americans "bought their independence with slave labor."[163]

Southerners defended slavery as a national institution, protected by the Constitution. Northerners disagreed and, in the first half of the 19th century, the sectional division was dramatically reflected in ongoing political battles over the status of each new territory added to the United States. It is ironic that the expansionist nationalism that helped the American experiment in liberty survive and prosper also sowed the seeds of its own potential destruction in the conflict over slavery.

Some of the country's greatest political figures—Thomas Jefferson, James Monroe, John Quincy Adams, John Calhoun, Daniel Webster, Henry Clay, Stephen Douglas and Abraham Lincoln—argued and compromised in vain attempts to prevent slavery from undermining either liberty or union. Few of them believed they would be successful, even in a country that prided itself on optimism, energy, practicality, and an "anything is possible" attitude. Most were convinced that nothing could be done to end slavery and bring sectional harmony. Jefferson's prophetic words in 1820, after the Missouri Compromise, poignantly expressed this feeling:

> This momentous question, like a fire bell in the night, awakened, and filled me with terror. I considered it at once

as the knell of the Union. It is hushed, indeed, for the moment. But this is a reprieve only...we have the wolf by the ears and we can neither hold him, nor safely let him go. Justice is in one scale, and self-preservation in the other.[164]

This seemingly unresolvable dilemma existed in the minds of many Americans of the time, primarily because they could not bring themselves to look upon the slave as a fellow human being, entitled to full membership in American society. To be sure, there were those who believed that slavery was immoral, worked for its abolition, and even envisioned an integrated society. However, the eradication of slavery proved much more difficult in the United States than anywhere else in the world.[165] This was as a result of four factors: 1) a Constitution that was less than clear about slavery's status, 2) the balance of power between the federal government and the states, 3) the economic importance of slavery to the American economy, and, perhaps, most critically, 4) the political power of the slaveholding states in both Congress and the Presidency throughout the first six decades of the 19th century. These elements contributed to a great, ongoing debate over the meaning and future of liberty, and, ultimately, the nature of America.

It would fall to Abraham Lincoln and his Republican Party finally to find a way to break the country's subservience to the slaveholding interest. In doing so, Lincoln revitalized American liberty by emancipating the slaves and extending to them the right to full and equal citizenship in American society. He established the principle that for liberty to maintain its relevance for future generations, it must be combined with equal opportunity for each citizen to develop his full potential. The "consent of the governed" must include all those governed and civil rights must be shared by all the nation's citizens. By freeing the country from the political shackles of slavery, Lincoln recaptured for America the ability to exercise leadership in the struggle for freedom around the world. He fully embraced this mission, concluding in his Gettysburg Address that the Civil War, as the culmination of the struggle over slavery, would determine "whether this nation or any nation so conceived and so dedicated can long endure." To comprehend the enormity of Lincoln's accomplishment, it is vital to understand how American slavery developed and became the most serious threat to the country's values and mission.

2. Slavery and the Early Republic

As the Spanish, then the English, Portuguese, and French built colonies in North and South America, they found it impossible to benefit from the newly discovered natural resources without the importation of slave labor to work the soil. The Spanish introduced the first African slaves into the New World in Santo Domingo in 1502 and the British brought Africans to their North American settlement of Jamestown, Virginia, in 1609. The Europeans developed what has been called a "vast commercial system that brought a profound transformation of African culture."[166] The Africans they uprooted were distributed throughout the Americas, the greatest concentrations being in the Caribbean and Brazil,[167] and the black slave gradually became an integral part of the history of the New World.

As the world's greatest naval power, Great Britain dominated the slave trade from the 16th to the middle of the 19th century, transporting human cargo to colonies throughout the Americas, from Argentina in the south to Canada in the north. Africans arrived as captives, after a long and grueling passage of untold suffering.[168] It has been estimated that more than ten million involuntarily crossed the Atlantic from 1500 to 1900, with 85% going to Brazil and the Caribbean and approximately 600,000, or 6% to the United States.[169] Their families grew rapidly. By the time of the Declaration of Independence, 80% of blacks in British America were native born—90% in those living in the North and 50% of those in the South.[170]

During the 1760's and 70's, American colonists began to raise questions about the morality of slavery, and to take action against it. They were influenced by the political thought of the European Enlightenment, which taught about natural rights, the inherent goodness and dignity of man, and the governmental objective of producing the greatest good for the greatest number. Slavery also violated the economic principles of free enterprise and free labor that were popularized by the economist Adam Smith in England and, later, incorporated in the economic policies of George Washington and Alexander Hamilton in the United States. Moreover, many Protestant sects in the colonies questioned the morality of the institution.

A geographic divide was clearly etched by the time of the Revolution, with the social and economic system of the South built upon the foundation of slavery. Southerners utilized slaves to support their agriculture because doing so was economically more beneficial to them than utilizing their own labor or paid workers. In the early 1780's, the one million American slaves constituted one sixth of the population; two of every five Southerners were slaves.[171] However, the slave owning class was relatively small, with modest-sized landholdings; most of the white population was non-slaveholding. By the late 18th century, the advent of steam power in Britain, as well as the widespread use of water power in the northern United States, dramatically increased the demand for southern cotton. Great Britain imported three quarters of the cotton produced in 1790; New England's textile industry purchased most of the remainder.

Northern states were unsuited by climate and topography to the production of staple agricultural products, but they were intimately involved in providing the slaveholding states with goods and supplies, prominent among which were the slaves themselves. The slave trade was supported from many northern cities, including Newport and Providence, Rhode Island, and Boston and Salem, Massachusetts. The most prominent families in these cities acquired financial fortunes by owning ships that carried weapons, rum, and other goods to Africa in trade for slaves.

When the American Revolution began, slaves and free blacks were accepted as soldiers and fought at the Battle of Bunker Hill, though the Continental Congress soon thereafter barred black recruits and all slaves until later in the Revolution when the need was great. It authorized payments to the owners of slave soldiers of up to $1,000 per man and the slaves were granted freedom when their service was over.[172] The Revolutionary era brought the abolition of slavery in several northern states—Massachusetts, New Hampshire, Rhode Island, Connecticut and, gradually, in Pennsylvania, New York and New Jersey. By 1810, three-quarters of the blacks in the North were free, and by 1840, almost all were.[173] Some northern states abolished the trade in slaves as well, but enforcement was spotty, and New England benefited commercially by providing ships for the purpose. Although the upper border states of Virginia, Maryland and Delaware encouraged private manumission (voluntary emancipation by slave owners), and saw an increase in freed blacks, the slave population in the South continued to grow and the region emerged from the Revolution with slavery a strengthened institution.

As Southern slavery was increasing, the new country was developing its constitutional framework, but the founders of the United States were not able to set clear policy or precedent to guide their countrymen on the issue. Their differing geographic origins produced basic disagreement about slavery and their primary focus was on resistance to British actions that impinged on the freedom of the colonies. Consequently, the great documents that built the foundation for the nation's political system failed to deal with it in any definitive way.

Jefferson's first draft of the Declaration of Independence blamed King George III for the slave trade, for enslaving Africans, and for inciting American blacks to rise in arms against their masters. He wrote:

> He has waged cruel war against human nature itself, violating its most sacred rights of life and liberty in the persons of a distant people who never offended him, captivating & carrying them into slavery in another hemisphere, or to incur miserable   death   in   their   transportation thither...Determined to keep open a market where MEN should be bought & sold, he has prostituted his negative for suppressing every legislative attempt to prohibit or to restrain this execrable commerce.[174]

The full Second Continental Congress deleted this language from Jefferson's draft, although their motivation for doing so is unclear. Jefferson blamed slaveholding interests in South Carolina and Georgia and Northerners sensitive about their role in the slave trade. Some delegates just believed Jefferson had stretched the truth too much in absolving colonists of any responsibility for slavery. For whatever reason, the specific anti-slavery references did not survive.

The most famous passage of the Declaration, "...that all men are created equal" and are "entitled to life, liberty, and the pursuit of happiness" seemed to carry implications for slavery. However, the question of whether that clause was intended to include blacks became the subject of political disagreement and debate for the succeeding 85 years.

The delegates to the 1787 Constitutional Convention were openly divided over slavery with each group eager to ensure that the new document supported their side of the issue. Gouverneur Morris of Pennsylvania criticized the South's "nefarious institution" which had turned some southern states into "barren wastes" of misery and poverty, and which induced a slave trader to go to Africa, where, "in defiance of the most sacred laws of humanity, [he] tears away his fellow creatures from their dearest connections & dam[n]s them to the most cruel bondage."[175] Nonetheless, Southerners were not at all defensive on the topic. Charles Cotesworth Pinckney of South Carolina announced that he would vote against the Constitution if it lacked some security against the future emancipation of southern slaves.[176]

Three provisions of the new document dealt with aspects of slavery. The "Three Fifths Clause" was applied to apportion both direct taxes and representation in the House of Representatives.[177] It was agreed that three-fifths of the total of "other persons" would be added to the total of "free persons" to determine a state's population for these two purposes. The South read this language as legitimizing slavery as it existed, with slaves the property of slaveholders. The North viewed it as only limited recognition of slavery and took solace in the fact that the clause never used the terms "slave" or "slavery."[178] The ratio was intended as an estimate of the wealth producing capacity of a person, consistent with the 18th century notion that representation should be related to a person's wealth or economic value. Thus, although the ratio reflected the generally accepted belief that slave labor was not as economically efficient as free labor, it did not necessarily imply that a slave equaled three-fifths of a human being, nor did it expressly recognize the property-holding aspect of slavery.[179]

A second provision addressed the existence of the slave trade, with some delegates favoring a total ban on the practice, while others advocating no restriction whatsoever. In the end, a compromise was reached which prohibited Congress from outlawing the slave trade for a twenty-year period, ending in 1808.[180] Southerners saw in this a sanction of slavery as a property right. Northerners viewed the provision as a confirmation of Congress' power to regulate the slave trade under the Commerce Clause, and treated it as repudiation, although delayed, of the controversial institution. As soon as the time limit expired, Congress did, indeed, take the action authorized by the Clause and outlawed importation under the Slave Trade Act of 1807.

The provision that was to create the most divisiveness in the country was one whose adoption was little debated in the Convention and came to be known as the "Fugitive Slave Clause." Without mentioning slavery as such, the provision essentially made it unlawful for any state into which a fleeing slave had escaped to render him a free man. This clause was widely understood to be an acknowledgement of the existence of chattel slavery, and it formed the basis for the enactment of a federal fugitive slave law and, eventually, an extensive administrative system for returning slaves to their masters. It provoked the radical abolitionist William Lloyd Garrison decades later to label the Constitution "a covenant with death, and an agreement with hell."[181]

Although Southerners claimed that the Constitution endorsed their right to hold slaves as property, the relevant provisions really did not articulate any clear principle. One could just as easily have read the Slave Trade Clause, together with the previously adopted Northwest Ordinance[182], as indicating a determination by the framers to make slavery a dying institution in a dynamic new nation. Nowhere does the Constitution either authorize slavery or forbid its abolition; delegates were looking for compromises in order to produce a Constitution that would be ratifiable by the people of each state. Achieving a new federal union required recognizing reality—that slavery existed in many states and that there was no consensus on its abolition. The most that could be done against slavery was to create a strong federal government to deal with the problem at a later date. In the insightful image of the historian Don E. Fehrenbacher, "It is as though the framers were half-consciously trying to frame two constitutions, one for their own time and the other for the ages, with slavery viewed bifocally—that is, plainly visible at their feet, but disappearing when they lifted their eyes."[183]

As Northern states gradually emancipated their slaves, the South continued to pass oppressive laws aimed at tighter and tighter control over them. Although these "slave codes" varied from state to state, all were based on the notion that slaves were personal property or "chattel." Statutes commonly required lifetime service, prohibited leaving the plantation without permission, severely restricted a slave's legal rights, and established elaborate regulations of the master/slave relationship in order to ensure social control. As chattel, slaves could not enter into contracts, making even their marriages non-binding, and they suffered serious discrimination in the criminal law, being subjected to punishments much more severe than those given whites for the same offense. The Louisiana code provided that "The master may sell him, dispose of his person, his industry, and his labor: he can do nothing, possess nothing, nor acquire anything but what must belong to his master."[184] And in Kentucky, a court stated that "A slave by our code, is not treated as a person, but...a thing."[185]

The basic purpose of the codes was to prevent any potential slave uprising or resistance to the social system. Thus, manumission was commonly prohibited or severely restricted, free blacks were prevented from immigrating to a slave state, and those who were already there were subjected to severe limits on their activity. The codes targeted sympathetic whites as well, forbidding them from engaging in activities that were seen as subversive, such as distributing abolitionist literature, teaching slaves to read and write, gambling with them, or supplying them with liquor, drugs, or guns. Restrictions were most severe in the deep South, less so as one moved west. Even in the North, where blacks had received their freedom, they were not welcomed into white society, but were subjected to ostracism, deprivation, and rampant discrimination in rights and services, particularly outside the New England states.

Southern political power in Congress continuously pressed the question of how the federal government should act with regard to slavery. Although pro-slavery policies were not required by the new Constitution, many were not forbidden, either. Thus, Congress enacted the Fugitive Slave Law of 1793, authorizing a slave owner to cross state lines in pursuit of a fleeing slave, seize the escapee, go before a federal magistrate to prove ownership, and obtain a certificate entitling the master to return home with the slave. Essentially the law permitted a federal override of normal state legal processes and sanctioned what otherwise would have been the crime of kidnapping. To a very real extent, the federal government acted as a protector of slavery until the coming of the Civil War.[186]

Congress did, however, take the first opportunity permitted by the Constitution to outlaw the slave trade, passing the Slave Trade Act of 1807. However, antislavery advocates were disappointed by the ineffective enforcement of the law in the decades following its passage. W.E.B. Du Bois, a black historian and educator, estimated that more than 250,000 slaves were brought into the country illegally between 1807 and 1862.[187] During this period, "violation of the slave-trade laws was common enough to raise doubts about the government's sincerity and enhance the impression of the United States as a slaveholding nation at heart."[188] This perception grew in the minds of progressive people throughout the world, to the point that it began clearly to erode America's entitlement to its unique role as champion of human liberty.

3. The Nature of Slavery in 19th Century America

Slavery in America grew rapidly over the first half of the nineteenth century. In the census of 1790, there were 697,897 slaves; by 1860, the number had risen to 3,953,760 (out of a total population of approximately 12,000,000).[189] Fifteen states had slaves as of 1845, although the pattern of ownership varied widely: in South Carolina and Mississippi, almost half the families owned slaves; in Georgia, two-fifths; in Florida, Alabama, and Louisiana, one-third; in Virginia, North Carolina, Kentucky, Tennessee and Texas, one-fourth; in Arkansas, one-fifth; in Maryland and Missouri, one-eighth; and in Delaware, one-thirtieth.[190]

Southerners built their institution with little regard to the long-term economic, social and political choices they were making. In the early years, the system made agriculture profitable, and Southerners were motivated primarily by economics. Ironically, they became so dependent on slavery, and on the single cotton crop, that they neglected investment and innovation in areas that would have led to productivity enhancements and long-lasting economic growth. They used their capital to acquire slaves rather than to stimulate invention and mechanization. It is no wonder that the South badly trailed the North in technological advances and human efficiency, whether measured by improvements in transportation and infrastructure, or literacy, as measured by participation in public education.

Part of the reason for Southern short sightedness was the paralyzing power of tradition. Slavery created a hierarchical social structure built around cultivation of the soil with slave labor. Even though the economic and social benefits of the plantation system extended only to a small portion of the population, it offered the great mass of people the less measurable benefits of feeling "superior" to blacks and aspiring to rise to the master class. The system ensured that blacks could not compete with whites, either economically or socially.

White Southerners were eager to defend their system, claiming for it and their slaves great advantages over the Northern economic and social system. They observed that slaves received care and protection, including free food, housing, clothing and medical care, contrasting their condition favorably with that of poor laborers in the North. They boasted of a stable social order in the South—free of class conflict, radical politics, or materialistic individualism. And they took satisfaction from the fact that slaves had developed their own subculture and they rationalized that the master-slave relationship, while held in place by fear and force, had within it a good deal of closeness and affection.

The perspective of the slave and his family was, of course, very different. The material "care and protection" they received was far from that available to whites. And their lives were totally dependent on the whim of each slave holder and slave master. To ensure that slaves would be obedient and productive, slave owners resorted to instilling fear in the slave and controlling every aspect of his life. The tyranny can be compared to that of a modern totalitarian state. Frederic Douglass, an escaped slave who became a writer and world famous antislavery lecturer, described the fear in the mind of a slave who decided to try to escape:

> At every gate through which we had to pass, we saw a watchman—at every ferry, a guard—on every bridge, a sentinel—and in every wood, a patrol...Upon either side we saw grim death, assuming the most horrible shapes.[191]

The slave had no right to exercise his own will or judgment. The owner determined the length of a work day—usually from the first morning light until well after dark, with little time for rest or refreshment. The slave was forbidden to leave the plantation without permission from his master and was forced always to show subservience to whites—in their communication and their physical movements. Even the slave's religious instruction was aimed at perpetuating the pernicious system, teaching that the Bible required them to obey their masters and that eternal salvation would be the reward for obedient service. The slave was discouraged from ever having any contact with free blacks or with whites, primarily to avoid the possibility that he entertain any idea of freedom or enlargement of rights. For violation of any of these rules and constraints, there existed frequent and cruel punishment, including the use of stocks, chains and irons, imprisonment in private jails, even branding and bodily mutilation. Slaves were also subjected to mob justice, including burning or hanging, if they were suspected of a particularly heinous crime. But the master's most ubiquitous tool was the whip, the legendary and very real symbol of the master's authority. It was used on almost every plantation and almost every adult slave was subjected to it at one time or another.

The slave was not merely a legal non-person; he was treated as a piece of human property. He could not marry without permission of the slave owner and his marriage had no legal sanction; it existed at the pleasure of the master and was often ended by the sale of one of the partners. He couldn't acquire title to property or make an enforceable contract. If a slave owner died with debts, his estate was entitled to sell one or more of his slaves, even if it resulted in breaking up a slave family. Often, children were torn from their parents to be sold to new owners far from home because young slaves, with a lifetime of economic potential, were worth much more than older ones. Slaves were offered as prizes in raffles or made the object of gambling bets. They would be given as gifts to a slave owner's children or grandchildren, sometimes even before the slave child had been born.

Like any victims of tyranny, slaves wished for freedom and tried in a variety of ways to resist authority or even to escape, but the system which was established to control them was all too successful. Resistance was seldom organized and usually took the form only of individual acts of conscience. Nonetheless, Southerners were often irrationally fearful of slave uprisings and were concerned for their own physical safety. For that reason, they felt easily threatened by outsiders preaching liberation. This reinforced their defensiveness and made it even more difficult to learn from others how to modernize their economy. As one writer has put it, "Slavery to them represented not just an economic interest but also a way of life; abolition threatened not just the loss of money but also the loss of a world."[192] Future freedom for the slave, and for the country, could not be won solely by the action of the victims. It would have to be determined on the national political stage.

4. The Politics of National Expansion and Slavery

At the turn of the 19th century, Southerners believed themselves to be in control of their political destiny and did not foresee the day that their political power would be seriously challenged. As the century progressed, the political battles became more divisive, the rhetoric more extreme, and the South's psychological defenses more fragile.

Congress organized the Southwest Territory without the antislavery clause of the Northwest Ordinance, and Kentucky and Tennessee became slave states in 1792 and 1796, respectively. The Mississippi Territory was organized in 1798 in a similar fashion and Mississippi (in 1817) and Alabama (in 1819) were later admitted as slave states. The major focus of disagreement, however, was to result from Thomas Jefferson's great Louisiana Purchase. Although several amendments were offered in Congress to restrict or prohibit slavery in the Louisiana Territory, Jefferson did not support them and they were defeated. The slave status of states created out of the new areas was left to be determined at a later date. In 1812, the Orleans Territory portion was admitted as the slave state of Louisiana and the remainder of the Purchase was renamed the Missouri Territory.

The War of 1812 diverted political attention in the country away from slavery but, once it was concluded, antislavery concerns increased, fueled by the unclear status of territory beyond the Mississippi River all the way to the Pacific Coast. When the issue of statehood for Missouri and Arkansas came before Congress in 1819, Representative James Tallmadge of New York added an amendment to the Missouri bill prohibiting slavery in that state, which passed the House, sending shock waves among Southern politicians and making them realize that Northern antislavery sentiment was formidable. The Senate, influenced by pressure from the proslavery citizens of Missouri, overturned Tallmadge's amendment. But Senator Thomas of Illinois inserted a provision in a Maine statehood bill declaring that slavery would be "forever prohibited" in the remainder of the Missouri (formerly Louisiana) Territory north of latitude 36 degrees/30 minutes (the "36/30 line"). The Thomas Amendment was intended to make the removal of the slavery prohibition in the state of Missouri more acceptable to the North. The entire package—the admission of Missouri as a slave state, Maine as a free state, and the Thomas Amendment—constituted the Missouri Compromise.[193] It was passed by Congress and presented to President Monroe for signature.

Monroe asked former Presidents Jefferson and Madison for their opinion on the Compromise and both advised against signing it. Jefferson claimed that diffusing slavery to the west would benefit both the slaves and the country, perhaps making it less divisive, and Madison questioned whether Congress had the power to prohibit slavery in the territories. Monroe and his Cabinet decided that Congress did have such power and he signed the bill, although the same issue would later be bitterly debated in the 1850's, leading to the Supreme Court's Dred Scott decision and to the final political crisis prior to the Civil War.

In the early 1830's, Americans began to organize to demand the emancipation of all slaves, a political stance that became known as abolitionism. One of the original pioneers of the movement was William Lloyd Garrison of Boston, who published the most widely known abolitionist periodical, *The Liberator*, in 1831, and who served as President of the American Anti-Slavery Society for 22 years. He represented the radical wing of the abolitionist movement, which favored immediate, wholesale emancipation. The "gradualists" focused, by contrast, primarily on the threat slavery posed to the unity of the nation and less on the injustice suffered by the slaves, and were willing to support a phased ending to the institution together with compensation for slave owners. In addition, they were prominent in the effort to colonize freed slaves outside the United States as a solution both to slavery and to white antipathy to the integration of blacks. Many gradual abolitionists belonged to The American Colonization Society, which was organized in 1816 by Henry Clay and George Washington's son, Bushrod. The Society founded the country of Liberia in Africa as the object of their colonization efforts and attracted many leading Americans to their cause, including Abraham Lincoln in the 1850's.

The radical abolitionists not only aimed at immediate, unconditional emancipation, but were unconstrained in their tactics. They used inflammatory rhetoric and were totally dedicated to the cause, at times urging personal assault on those who supported slavery and encouraging slave revolts, thus intensifying the antagonism and fears of Southerners. Radicals believed in an egalitarian society, assuming that once slaves were free, they would become full participants in American life. They had the confidence of idealists that blacks could overcome their disadvantages and whites their prejudice. Leadership of this faction was centered in evangelical Protestants and Unitarians, chiefly from New England, who believed in the "Protestant ethic"—faith that hard work and individual freedom would benefit the entire society and uplift everyone. Radical abolitionism was also related to the rise in the feminist movement, dating back to 1840 when Lucretia Mott and Elizabeth Cady Stanton, duly chosen American delegates, were denied participation in the World Anti-Slavery Conference in London. William Lloyd Garrison protested their exclusion by declining to speak as scheduled, taking a seat beside his "sisters in the cause." These two female abolitionists went on to organize the first national women's rights convention at Seneca Falls, New York in 1848.

As the abolitionist movement grew in strength, Southerners increasingly justified slavery as not only essential to their economic well-being, but necessary to social stability, particularly after the slave uprising in 1831 led by Nat Turner. Inspired by a religious motivation to punish the wickedness of slave holders, Turner had led a group of approximately 80 slaves in a two day insurrection in Southampton County, Virginia, during which 59 whites were murdered. After most of his band were captured or killed by local citizens, Turner hid in the woods for two days, but was finally captured, tried and hanged. The rebellion had few precedents—one in Richmond in 1800 led by a slave named Gabriel Prosser and another in Charleston in 1822 headed by a former slave named Denmark Vesey. Prosser planned to have thousands of blacks attack Richmond and Vesey hoped to capture Charleston. Each of these earlier uprisings was discovered with information from slave informants and ended before any injury or death, except that most of the conspirators were themselves hanged. The Turner action made the South acutely more sensitive to political and psychological pressure from abolitionists, and more fearful of the potential effect of freedom for millions of slaves.

Southern political leaders transformed their defensiveness into a belief in slavery as a positive good rather than an unfortunate legacy. They convinced themselves that, since slavery was integral to their way of life, it must be beneficial to all, justifying their pride in the stability and distinctiveness of the South. Senator John C. Calhoun of South Carolina, who had served in President Monroe's Cabinet and had been a spokesman for nationalist expansion, led the political conversion to sectional pride. In 1838, he summarized the Southern attitude on the floor of Congress:

> Many in the South once believed that [slavery] was a moral and political evil; that folly and delusion are gone; we see it now in its true light, and regard it as the most safe and stable basis for free institutions in the world.[194]

The ante-bellum historian Kenneth M. Stampp has expressed a different perspective on Southern attitudes: "In the hardened pattern of southern law and custom the twin functions of the slaves were now clearly defined: they were to labor diligently and breed prolifically for the comfort of their white masters."[195]

Southerners reacted to criticism of their institutions with increasing oppression and limitations on freedom, almost to the extent of establishing a closed society. Viewing abolitionist propaganda as incendiary, they established restrictions on mail, tightened control over free blacks and generally harassed northern travelers.[196]   The effort to silence dissenting views about slavery was carried to the floor of Congress where Southern political power successfully enacted a "gag rule" in 1836 that automatically tabled any antislavery bill that was introduced. Its supporters argued that Congress should not consider any legislation that "violated the Constitution." For eight years thereafter, former President John Quincy Adams, then a Congressman from Massachusetts, fought a courageous battle against the rule, ultimately succeeding when the House repealed it in 1844.[197]

The prolonged fight over the gag rule foreshadowed the difficulty in later years of coming to agreement on the meaning of the Constitution and of accommodating the values of both North and South. Senator Calhoun had laid the basis for slavery's advocates to argue, on the one hand, that slavery was a local concern, beyond the authority of Congress to prohibit, yet, on the other, was so vulnerable that the Constitution required the federal government to protect it in the territories. But, despite the appeal to the Constitution, slavery's defenders really had in mind "a southern version of higher law...Slavery was untouchable and, indeed, unmentionable except in respectful, protective tones."[198]

During the 1840's, the battleground in Congress focused on the country's continued expansion westward. This growth came to be known as "Manifest Destiny," a term coined by John L. O'Sullivan, editor of the New York Morning News, to give moral and political justification to that movement.

> "[America has] by the right of our manifest destiny to overspread and to possess the whole of the continent which Providence has given us for the development of the great experiment of liberty and federative self government entrusted to us."[199]

The idea that America's expansion was justified by its special mission to spread liberty had fired the imagination of Washington, Jefferson, Jackson, and later, Lincoln. It also inspired ordinary men from all sections of the country seeking opportunity.

> Pitting their muscle against the elements, these men were independent, aggressively individualistic, and fiercely hostile to external controls. Prizing the opportunity to become unequal in personal achievement and hating the inequality

of pretension to status, they cherished an unsleeping distrust of public authority and glorified the virtues of simplic-
ity, frugality, liberty, and self-reliance. Despite the nuances
of regional difference, Americans conformed to this basic
pattern from one end of the Union to the other.[200]

Unity over expansion of the country began to crumble when the
question of the slaveholding status of a potential new territory came
before Congress. The issue was joined in the 1840's over the questions
of the annexation of Texas and the status of the Oregon Territory.
Slaveholders from the South had settled Texas, then a part of Mexico,
and in 1836, had waged a struggle for its independence. They captured
the Mexican President Santa Anna and forced him to agree to independence for Texas in exchange for his own release, whereupon Texans
formed the Lone Star Republic. Santa Anna's concession was repudiated by the Mexican Congress, and Texans began to lobby strongly for
annexation to the United States. In order to avoid war with Mexico,
the American government refrained from annexation until after the
expansionist James K. Polk was elected President in 1844. Even before
Polk could take the oath of office, then President John Tyler quickly
obtained approval of an annexation bill in February, 1845. During the
Congressional debate, the echoes of Manifest Destiny were loud and
clear. Congressman Wentworth of Illinois asserted:

> ...the God of Heaven, when he crowned the American arms
> with success [in the Revolutionary War did not] design that
> the original States should be the only abode of liberty on
> earth. On the contrary, he only designed them as the great
> center from which civilization, religion, and liberty should
> radiate and radiate until the whole continent shall bask in
> their blessing.[201]

Notwithstanding Wentworth's claims, many Northerners were
concerned over the inconsistency between adding territory where slavery was established and America's mission to nurture and spread liberty. Their concern was heightened when President Polk negotiated
the Oregon Treaty with Great Britain in which he accepted a division
at the 49th parallel, rather than push for a boundary further north,
made famous by the popular cry of "54/40 or fight!" Northerners
believed that the slave interest cared only for the annexation of the

slave state of Texas and sacrificed half of the free territory of Oregon. Sectionalism now became the prevailing political motivator.

Although the North and South were divided by economic and cultural interests, the true differentiator was slavery. Politicians became conscious of the possibility that choices might have to be made between slavery and union. And they began to see the opposing side in terms that would make accommodation more and more difficult. Historian David Potter summarized the crisis in the following way:

> As they became isolated, instead of reacting to each other as they were in actuality, each reacted to a distorted mental image of the other—the North to an image of a southern world of lascivious and sadistic slavedrivers; the South to the image of a northern world of cunning Yankee traders and of rabid abolitionists plotting slave insurrections...ordinary, resolvable disputes were converted into questions of principle, involving rigid, unnegotiable dogma. Abstractions, such as the question of the legal status of slavery in areas in which there were no slaves and to which no one intended to take any, became points of honor and focuses of contention which rocked the government to its foundation.[202]

The most contentious political battles over slavery occurred in the aftermath of the Mexican War, when vast new territory needed to be absorbed. President Polk started the war in May, 1846, in an attempt to satisfy claims by Texas for land beyond the existing border, extending to the Rio Grande River. It was not a popular war, with many northerners, including Whig Congressman Abraham Lincoln, questioning its wisdom. When Polk asked Congress for funds to finance the potential acquisition of the Mexican territory of California and New Mexico, a Pennsylvania Congressman named David Wilmot proposed, in August, 1846, that slavery never be permitted in any territory acquired from Mexico. His motivation was to redress the political balance that had been lost by the North when, in Wilmot's view, Polk negotiated away half of Oregon; more broadly, his amendment was intended to justify the Mexican War in the eyes of the northern electorate.

Thereafter known as the Wilmot Proviso, this proposed legislation did more than anything else previously to define the great political division between North and South. Southerners were shocked and angered by it. They pointed to the Missouri Compromise 36/30 line, which had barred slavery only north of that line, and observed that most of the territory likely to be won from Mexico lay south of it. They greatly feared being surrounded by free territory on both their northern and western borders, thus signaling the eventual end of their beloved institution.

Once again, the spokesman for Southern honor and its legal position was Senator John C. Calhoun of South Carolina. In the debate before Congress, he argued that the territories were the "common property" of the states and that Congress, as merely the "joint agent" of the states, could not prevent citizens from emigrating to the territories with their slaves as property. Therefore, he said, slavery was legal in all the territories. He also was candid enough to oppose the Proviso because it would give the North political preponderance in the country, ending the careful balance that had been maintained since the Missouri Compromise. He warned that:

"The day that the balance between the two sections of the country—the slaveholding States and the non-slaveholding States—is destroyed, is a day that will not be far removed from political revolution, anarchy, civil war, and widespread disaster."[203]

Calhoun and many Southerners were afraid that the resulting political power of the North would be used to end slavery even where it existed. The Wilmot Proviso was defeated in the House by the vote of 102-97, and the question of the status of any Mexican Territory was left to be determined by future Congressional action.

The war proved to be a decidedly one-sided affair, as the Americans not only took the land claimed by Texas, but also ousted the Mexicans from California and New Mexico. The United States obtained more than one million square miles of territory, including the current states of California, Nevada, Utah, most of Arizona and New Mexico, and parts of Oklahoma, Colorado and Wyoming. What appeared to be the logical fulfillment of the nationalism inherent in the idea of Manifest Destiny would become the stimulus for national disunion in the fight over slavery in the new territory.

North and South each sought to make the new territory over in its own image. For many Northern Congressmen, it was one thing to acquiesce to slavery where it had existed, particularly since the Constitution did not clearly forbid it. But, it was quite another to be asked to permit slavery where it was not yet established, particularly when Congress clearly had the power to prescribe the government of new territories. For Calhoun's Southern supporters, Congress had no power to exclude slavery from a territory prior to admission of any part of that territory as a state. For other political leaders, party pressures pushed them to look for compromises to avoid choosing either extreme and jeopardizing the Union. At times each faction justified its position with appeal to constitutional or legal principles, but, from a modern perspective, these appear as rationalizations to avoid dealing directly with the morality of slavery.

General Zachary Taylor, hero of the Mexican War, was elected President as a Whig in 1848, and asked Congress, in December, 1849, to admit California as a free state, thereby precipitating the most serious national crisis over slavery since the Missouri Compromise. Some Northern Congressmen sought to resurrect the Wilmot Proviso to expand the orbit of freedom. Some Southerners were so concerned about the potential Congressional actions that they convened a convention at Nashville in 1850 to consider secession.

The debates in Congress concerning California featured great personal drama along with major consequences for both liberty and national unity. John Calhoun, old and frail—just twenty seven days from his death—delivered what has been called his "dark valedictory," warning of a divided nation:

> "It is a great mistake to suppose that disunion can be effected by a single blow. The cords which bind these states together in one common Union are far too numerous and powerful for that. Disunion must be the work of time...Already the agitation of the slavery question has snapped some of the most important, and has greatly weakened all the others..."[204]

Daniel Webster of Massachusetts, disappointing antislavery advocates, gave his famous Seventh of March Speech, pleading for compromise: "I wish to speak today not as a Massachusetts man, nor as a Northern man, but as an American...I speak today for the preservation of the Union."[205] Henry Clay, Whig Senator from Tennessee, broke with President Taylor, leader of his party, to propose a series of compromise resolutions involving the admission of California as a free state but organizing the Utah and New Mexico Territories without restriction on slavery, an idea that, four years later, evolved into the doctrine of "popular sovereignty" under which local settlers would themselves decide about the legality of slavery.

Clay's proposals, the basis for what was to become the Compromise of 1850, initially met with great resistance and leadership of the effort was taken over by Senator Stephen Douglas of Illinois. The drama of the occasion was further increased with the sudden death of President Taylor on July 9, thus removing an opponent of compromise and resulting in the installation as President of Millard Fillmore, a supporter of the objectives of Clay and Douglas. Had Taylor lived, there most likely would have been no compromise—either secession and a Civil War might have happened in 1850, or, the South would have acquiesced in a provision such as the Wilmot Proviso. Fillmore was not only more conservative on slavery, but clearly recognized Clay as the true leader of his party. Douglas engineered separate votes on each of Clay's measures, uniting supporters of compromise with the supporters of each individual proposal, and preventing a united opposition; that, along with the changed political environment, allowed the entire package to pass in a series of close votes.

The Compromise of 1850 was adopted because a majority in Congress believed that the only alternatives to it were secession and war. Southerners had argued vigorously that Congress had no power under the Constitution to prohibit slavery in the territories, yet they had no difficulty in concluding that it had ample power, and even the duty, to protect it. In fact, what Southerners most desired was an end to the pressure they felt from slavery's opponents and a revival of their honor and self-respect as a region. They got only a brief reprieve in Congress on the former, though it can be argued that they obtained ten years of the latter. During that period, however, the North grew in strength while the South stagnated, a harbinger of the outcome of the Civil War when it came.

The most tangible victory for the South in the Compromise was a revised Fugitive Slave Law, which greatly expanded the power of the federal government to override state law in determining whether fugitive slaves should be returned. The act established a federal administrative and judicial system for the sole purpose of enforcing the new law. During the years 1850 to 1860, federal tribunals released only 11 of the 191 slaves whose cases were adjudicated.[206] In a very real sense, Southerners maintained their attachment to the Union only so long as they believed the government would enforce this law and not enact any new "aggressions" on them. On the other hand, no other factor contributed as much to the growth of anti-slavery sentiment in the North than that very enforcement.

Slavery's prospects depended on non-political efforts, as well. In June, 1851, Harriet Beecher Stowe began to publish, in serial form, her novel entitled *Uncle Tom's Cabin or Life Among the Lowly*, describing the cruel effects on individuals and families of both slavery and the fugitive slave law. The work was later distributed as a book and presented as a stage play across the country. Her heart-rending tale had as much influence on Northern public opinion as the propaganda of abolitionists. After Lincoln was elected President he was reported to have greeted Mrs. Stowe with the words, "So you're the little woman who wrote the book that started this great war."[207]

Despite strong sectional differences, many political figures, including Presidents Fillmore and Pierce and the chief legislative strategist, Senator Stephen A. Douglas, hoped that the Compromise of 1850 would bring a permanent settlement to the slavery question. Ironically, Douglas himself made this unlikely when, in 1854, he introduced even more divisive legislation to deal with slavery in the context of national expansion. He was in a difficult position because he had a strong ambition to become President and needed Southern Democratic support to do so, yet, he didn't want the federal government to take direct action to extend slavery. He developed a revised definition of non-intervention, calling it "popular sovereignty", which he defined as leaving "the people free to form and regulate their domestic institutions in their own way, subject only to the Constitution of the United States." He coupled this idea with a concession to the South—declaring "null and void" the prohibition of slavery north of the 36/30 line enacted in the Missouri Compromise. These two provisions were passed by Congress on May 30, 1854 and came to be known as the Kansas-Nebraska Act. As a believer in Manifest Destiny, Douglas hoped his legislation would pave the way for successful national expansion. What he did not fully appreciate was the dramatic impact the combination of popular sovereignty with repeal of the 36/30 line would have on both the advocates of slavery and their opponents.

The Kansas-Nebraska Act produced two devastating effects on the country. First, it gave rise to a bloody struggle in the Kansas Territory between pro- and anti-slavery forces to establish themselves in the area in greater numbers than their adversaries. That conflict lasted several years and earned the sobriquet "Bleeding Kansas." It also bitterly divided the Congress, tragically symbolized by the beating with a cane of Senator Charles Sumner of Massachusetts by Preston S. Brooks, a South Carolina Congressman, after Sumner had given an angry speech decrying Kansas violence and criticizing Senator Andrew Pickens Butler of South Carolina. Sumner's recovery took over three years; that of the Union took more than a decade.

The second major effect of the Act was the creation of a serious rift in the Democratic Party over the potential impact of popular sovereignty on the institution of slavery. The party maintained fragile unity by papering over its division over when the local decision about slavery could be made. Southerners asserted that it could only be at time of petition for statehood, after slave holders had populated the territory. Northerners claimed it had to be during the territorial stage, soon after the area was annexed and before slavery could take root. The Democratic Party had been the broadest national organization to support the Federal Union. The gradual loss of its unity during the 1850's was one of the reasons why political solutions could not be found to avoid the Civil War.

The Missouri Compromise exclusion of slavery north of the 36/30 line had established anti-slavery as national policy, but its repeal put the nation in the uncomfortable position of no longer disapproving of the oppressive system. As Northerners began to see popular sovereignty as having a pro-slavery orientation, political support for it began to erode. The question of the meaning and future of American liberty was now open, as was the door for new ideas and new leaders.

The 1850's saw the weakening of both the Democrats and the Whigs— the two national parties that had preserved the unity of the nation since the 1830's. The Democrats were divided sectionally by the Kansas-Nebraska Act and by popular sovereignty; the Whigs were practically destroyed by the reduction in controversy over issues that had brought them together in the 1830's—antipathy to Andrew Jackson, internal improvements, tariffs and the national bank. Several organizations sought to fill the void, among them the Know Nothing Party, a group that capitalized on prejudice against immigrants, in general, and Catholics, in particular. In 1855, Abraham Lincoln, then a lawyer in Illinois, said of this new party:

> How can anyone who abhors the oppression of negroes, be in favor of degrading classes of white people?...As a nation, we began by declaring that "all men are created equal." We now practically read it "all men are created equal, except negroes."

When the Know-Nothings get control, it will read "all men
are created equal, except negroes, and foreigners, and
catholics." When it comes to this I should prefer emigrating
to some country where they make no pretense of loving liberty—to Russia, for instance, where despotism can be taken
pure, and without the base alloy of hypocrisy."[208]

Lincoln focused his efforts on helping to build the new Republican Party.[209] Founded in 1854, the party consisted of reformist, anti-
slavery Protestants, economic growth capitalists, as well as northern
Whigs and Know-Nothings. Republicans aimed at opposing the
South's growing political power and supporting equal economic
opportunity for all, advocating what they called "free soil" principles.
They decried equally the oppression of slaves as well as the lack of economic advancement of poor southern whites. To them, nothing less
than the country's future was at stake—the primary question being
whether the expanding west would be organized more like the North
than the South. One of the pioneer Republicans, William Seward of
New York, believed that "Southern society, with its aristocracy based
on slaveholding, seemed the direct antithesis of the egalitarian ideals of
the North."[210] In an 1858 speech, Seward anticipated Lincoln and created a political stir when he declared: "It is an irrepressible conflict
between opposing and enduring forces, and it means that the United
States must and will, sooner or later, become either entirely a slaveholding nation, or entirely a free-labor nation."[211]
    Lincoln was strongly drawn to the new Republican philosophy—
its emphasis on economic opportunity and its implications for America's role in the world. Republicans, as the historian Eric Foner has
concluded, "saw their anti-slavery program as one part of a world-wide
movement from absolutism to democracy, aristocracy to equality,
backwardness to modernity…They accepted the characteristic American vision of the United States as an example to the world of the social
and political benefits of democracy, yet believed that so long as slavery
existed, the national purpose of promoting liberty in other lands could
not be fulfilled."[212] Lincoln shared the definition of the American
mission as articulated by Seward:

[America's] destiny is to renovate the condition of
mankind…[its system of government] is founded on the

natural equality of all men—not alone American men, nor alone all white men, but all MEN of every country, clime, and complexion...[America's responsibility is to prove at home that] the experiment in self-government could succeed...[and abroad to aid in] the universal restoration of power to the governed.[213]

It was to become Lincoln's role to develop a strategy for eliminating slavery, the greatest obstacle to that mission.

5. The Rise of Abraham Lincoln

Conventional wisdom has it that, because of his humble background, lack of formal education, and dearth of financial resources, Abraham Lincoln was an unlikely American hero. On the contrary, he was uniquely equipped to revitalize American liberty. He brought to political life, and to the Presidency, a combination of ability and character that have seldom been equaled, at a time when the country desperately needed those qualities. His self-reliant early life rendered him a rugged realist, uninfluenced by emotionalism or by prejudice. He continually exhibited great interpersonal skills and perceptiveness about human nature and consistently received the admiration and affection of others. Despite being self-taught since childhood, or, possibly because of it, he possessed a thoughtful, logical mind that was adept at strategic planning to achieve his goals. An extremely ambitious man, he was able, nevertheless, to avoid the Caesarian abuse of ambition that sometimes renders political men tragic failures. He did so out of dedication to a vision for America that he nurtured and fine-tuned for decades before being called to act upon it. Lincoln was committed to America's unique political mission as the great example of liberty for the world.

He was born on February 12, 1809, in the slave owning state of Kentucky, the son of Thomas Lincoln, a simple, self-employed farmer, and Nancy Hanks Lincoln. Abraham was the second child, three years younger than his sister Sarah, with whom he had a close relationship until she left the family home to marry at age 17; she died in childbirth two years later.

Young Abraham's parents adhered to a strict, Baptist moral creed, including a belief in the immorality of slavery. He shared his parents'

views, believing all his life in the unfairness and unwholesome nature
of slave society.   Thomas Lincoln suffered economic hardship, partly
due to the competition from plantations worked by slaves and partly as
a result of his difficulty in acquiring legal title to profitable land.
When young Lincoln was seven years old, his father moved the family
from Kentucky to Indiana, where slavery did not exist and where
Thomas could avoid feeling looked down upon by slave owners. Eight
year old Abraham suffered his own hardship when his mother died in
1817. However, within a year his father married Sarah Bush Johnson,
who brought both love and organization to the Lincoln home and was
a major influence on the young boy. Long after Lincoln's death, she
called him "the best boy I ever saw or ever expect to see."[214]

His stepmother encouraged him to become an educated man and,
although he had less than one year of formal schooling, he was remembered as reading "everything that he could lay his hands on...never for-
getting what he read."[215]   He had a particular fondness for literature,
history, and math and showed an early capacity for telling stories, writing
poetry, and public speaking. Although his family attended church, Lincoln apparently was not very interested in religion. Sarah Bush Johnson
Lincoln later said that "[Young] Abe had no particular religion—didn't
think of these questions at that time, if he ever did."[216] His lack of interest in religion caused political discomfort and defensiveness when he ran
for public office in later life, yet, during the darkest days of the Civil War,
he seemed to be affected by a certain fatalism based on submission to a
power beyond himself, or to "God's will."

Lincoln's relationship with his father was not a close one, and
became more distant as the two grew older. From an early age, Abraham knew that he wanted to rise above his father's lack of education
and inability to read, write, or speak publicly. At 21, he left his family
home determined not to be a poor farmer like his father. Lincoln's
estrangement from his father and his father's social environment lasted
a lifetime, and when Thomas died in 1850, the son did not attend the
funeral. Curiously, he also maintained distance from his more empathetic and literate stepmother, since Sarah never was to meet Lincoln's
wife or any of his children.

In his early twenties, Lincoln took a variety of jobs in search of self-
awareness, including riverboat hand, carpenter, retail clerk, blacksmith,
and surveyor, but soon developed a strong political ambition and
became a politician and self-taught lawyer before he was 30, settling in
New Salem, Illinois. His own life gave him an appreciation of the day-

to-day struggles of the common man, as well as a realistic understanding of the opportunities offered by the American economy to a person willing to learn and work hard.

Much of the information about the formation of Lincoln's character and personality as a young adult comes from recollections of family and friends recorded well after Lincoln became famous and might well be colored by the perceived need to make Lincoln's development comport with his historical reputation.[217] Nevertheless, some generalizations can reliably be made from the weight of the evidence.

Lincoln carried his family's moral antipathy to slavery into his adulthood, but his own life experience deepened his belief. When he was a riverboat hand, he traveled at least twice down the Mississippi to New Orleans, where he witnessed for the first time the actual marketing of human beings and he never forgot the cruelty inherent in the process. One of the legends about Lincoln is that, after seeing the way prospective slave buyers inspected one young mulatto girl, he angrily said, "If I ever get a chance to hit that thing [slavery] I'll hit it hard."[218] We can reasonably conclude that he carried such images with him and they helped to motivate him to achieve important political goals.

Biographers of Lincoln have always stressed his qualities of fortitude and forbearance; friends were eager to tell of instances in which Lincoln dealt with interpersonal conflicts by relying on his good humor and self-assurance rather than his outstanding physical strength and his exceptional height at six feet four inches. He participated in sports, particularly wrestling, but was always reluctant to use his strength to settle disputes by fighting and often acted as a peacemaker for others.

Although Lincoln's clothes and appearance at this age reflected his poor, rural origins, his intelligence always shone through. From childhood, he designed for himself a determined program of reading and learning. He would frequently carry a book with him wherever he went and was often seen pausing in the middle of the street or sitting under a tree to continue a particularly interesting passage. Some thought him lazy because he appeared to prefer reading to physical labor. Poetry fascinated him and he immersed himself, at different times, in Shakespeare, Robert Burns and Lord Byron. He studied grammar in order to distinguish himself from farmers and country folk. In New Salem, Lincoln actively participated in a debating club and developed his talent for public speaking. From his childhood, he was known as a witty story teller, one who in later years was fond of telling tales that were off color. Although prone to moodiness and depression at times during his lifetime, he never lost his love of humor, his talent for performing, and his affinity for good company.

Lincoln showed a capacity for leadership early in his life, frequently being the most popular among his group of friends. When he volunteered to fight the Black Hawk Indians in Illinois, who were trying to retake land that had been theirs, his fellow soldiers chose him to lead them. Lincoln later called the selection "a success which gave me more pleasure than any I have had since."[219]

Elected to the state legislature in 1834, at the age of 25, Lincoln began a life in politics and the law, distinguishing himself in both roles. While in the legislature, he concentrated on issues of banking and economic development. He was one of the few legislators to call slavery immoral, although, at the same time, he cautioned against the excesses of abolitionism. After being admitted to the bar in 1837, he moved from New Salem to Springfield, the new state capitol, where he practiced law for the next 24 years, becoming one of the most accomplished attorneys in Illinois.

In 1838 Lincoln gave a notable speech that indicated that the effects of slavery were central even to his early political thinking. He spoke to the Young Men's Lyceum shortly after a violent mob destroyed the printing presses of a local anti-slavery editor, Elijah P. Lovejoy, before shooting him to death. Lincoln decried "the vicious portion of the population [who] throw printing presses into rivers and shoot editors." He went on to mention an incident in St. Louis in which a newly freed slave was chained to a tree and burned to death "all within a single hour from the time he had been a free man, attending to his own business, and at peace with the world." Lincoln warned of political violence and advised a remedy:

> Let reverence for the laws, be breathed by every American
> mother, to the lisping babe, that prattles on her lap—let it
> be taught in schools, in seminaries, and in colleges…in short
> let it become the political religion of the nation.[220]

He also took the opportunity to discuss the nature of political leadership by observing that a politician with "ambition and talents" who "thirsts and burns for distinction" could use power either for beneficial or harmful ends. To control such individuals, he urged that the public needed to avoid the dangers inherent in the politics of passion, and to be guided by good judgment: "Reason, cold, calculating unimpassioned reason, must furnish all the materials for our future support and defence."[221] Lincoln was undoubtedly lecturing himself, as well, since he, too, was embarked on a political life and would seek to satisfy his own sizable ambition. He recognized how a talented politician could manipulate people and become a demagogue for base or selfish ends. He would avoid that by constructing a principled vision of the meaning of American liberty and taking appropriate action to guide the country to it.

Before entering national political life, Lincoln settled his personal life. Often ill at ease with women, he finally fell in love with Ann Rutledge of New Salem, whom he met in late 1834, and they agreed to become engaged. However, her untimely death in August, 1835 sent Lincoln into a period of grief and depression. A few years later, he met Mary Todd, a cultured woman from a wealthy family, who, unlike Lincoln, had many social graces, yet shared with him a passion for politics, literature and good conversation. After a somewhat troubled courtship, during which Lincoln felt some guilt about his simultaneous involvement with a woman named Matilda Edwards, Mary and he were married in November 4, 1842.

The Lincolns went on to have an enduring and supportive relationship, at times troubled by both his moods and heavy responsibilities, and her temper and frequently fragile emotional condition. Their marriage produced four sons: Robert, born in 1843 and the only one of the Lincoln children to live to adulthood; Eddie, born in 1846 but dead in 1850; Willie, born in 1850 and tragically dead in the White House in 1862; and Thomas, or Tad, who was born in 1853 and died in 1871. Lincoln was a devoted father, giving Willie and Tad as much time as possible even while he was a War President. Willie's death, after two weeks of agonizing illness from typhoid fever contracted from polluted White House water, left both parents stunned with grief. On February 20, 1862, Lincoln said to his secretary, "Well, Nicolay, my boy is gone— he is actually gone!" The President then broke down in tears and rushed to comfort his son, Tad, who was suffering from the same illness.[222] The great sadness resulting from the untimely death of Eddie, Willie, and Tad, as well as the assassination of a husband, led to the progressive deterioration of Mary's mental health in her later years.

Lincoln cast his early political lot with the Whig Party, whose philosophy of national growth and development, expansion of the country, and increasing opportunity resonated with him, a self-made man. Lincoln believed deeply all his life in the overall benefits of national economic expansion. In another sense, his identification as a Whig, contrary to the Jacksonian loyalty of most of his family and neighbors, represented his own "Declaration of Independence." In Illinois, the Democrats were by far the stronger party and Lincoln's political career prior to the Presidency undoubtedly was more limited than it might have been as a result of his party affiliation.

Elected to Congress in 1846, Lincoln chose to serve only one term, distinguished primarily by his opposition to the Mexican War and his vote in favor of the Wilmot Proviso. Although, at the time, he did not work to abolish slavery where it existed, he believed that its natural death should not be delayed by finding new areas for it to thrive.

His political model was Henry Clay, who opposed slavery and supported colonization in Liberia of free blacks in order to encourage increased manumission and emancipation. From the 1840's Lincoln, too, supported the idea of colonization, convinced that it was the only politically acceptable solution to the slavery problem. Despite the fact that many prominent Americans shared that view and supported the American Colonization Society, it never had a realistic chance for implementation in any widespread fashion. American blacks, who, by the middle of the 19th century had almost all been born in the United States, did not wish to emigrate to Africa or anywhere else; Southern slave owners were not inclined to end their way of life by emancipating their slaves, even in return for compensation; and Northerners could not possibly have contributed the vast amounts of money it would have required to emancipate, transport and settle millions of blacks overseas. But Lincoln took a broader inspiration from Clay, saying in his eulogy of the man in 1852, that "Mr. Clay's predominant sentiment, from first to last, was a deep devotion to the cause of human liberty—a strong sympathy with the oppressed everywhere, and an ardent wish for their elevation."[223]

Lincoln's political philosophy was a product of a careful thought process, informed by a deep knowledge of the country's history and always coupled with a keen appreciation for the requirements of practical politics. As a consequence, his positions were subject to adjustment based on new political circumstances. And his views on the assimilability of the slave population were influenced by the generally accepted prejudices of the white electorate. He not only supported colonization, but avoided endorsing political and social equality for blacks, and, until the Emancipation Proclamation, never advocated mandated abolition where slavery was already part of a functioning social system. But he also never wavered in his belief that slavery was morally wrong and, ultimately, inconsistent with American political values.

The passage of the Kansas-Nebraska Act in 1854 was a turning point for Lincoln, as well as for the nation. He viewed it as setting the United States in the wrong direction on slavery. He had recognized that the Constitution did not outlaw slavery and that, as a lawyer and follower of the rule of law, he was willing to tolerate slavery where it existed, at least until the law of the land were amended. But he was unwilling to accept the possibility that slavery could be introduced into land that Congress, under the Missouri Compromise, had previously put off limits to the institution. Doing so would mean the expansion of slavery rather than its contraction—a prospect that would not only be a tragedy for blacks, but would prevent white settlers from enjoying the full benefits of American economic opportunity.

To Lincoln, American liberty and slavery were incompatible and, equally important, any growth in slaveholding would completely undermine America's special mission of showing the world the way to freedom. His Speech on the Kansas-Nebraska Act, given on October 16, 1854 in direct response to Senator Douglas's previous oration, is one of Lincoln's most profound and learned addresses. In it, he traced the history of the country's response to slavery and then made clear the essence of his maturing political philosophy:

> The declared indifference, but as I must think, covert real zeal for the spread of slavery, I can not but hate. I hate it because of the monstrous injustice of slavery itself. **I hate it because it deprives our republican example of its just influence in the world**—enables the enemies of free institutions, with plausibility, to taunt us as hypocrites—causes the real friends of freedom to doubt our sincerity, and especially because it forces so many really good men amongst ourselves into an open war with the very fundamental principles of civil liberty—criticising the Declaration of Independence, and insisting that there is no right principle of action but self-interest.[224] [emphasis added]

Lincoln was concerned that the meaning of the Revolution, in particular, and of America, in general, might fade throughout the world. To prevent this, he applied the principles of the Declaration of Independence to the definition of American liberty—by adding an inclusive political equality to that definition—thus making it even more relevant to people everywhere. He explained his idea this way:

> No man is good enough to govern another man, without that other's consent, I say this is the leading principle—the sheet anchor of American republicanism…The master not only governs the slave without his consent; but he governs him by a set of rules altogether different from those which he prescribes for himself. Allow ALL the governed an equal voice in the government, and that, and that only is self-government.[225]

The only way to do something about the expansion of slavery would be to place the issue squarely at the center of American political debate.

Lincoln's dedication to practical politics would make his ideas truly influential. Aware that he could not affect change within the dying Whig Party, he became a prime mover in the formation of the Republican Party in Illinois, supporting a platform that advocated "free soil" doctrine, with its inherent criticism of slavery because it made labor inefficient and condemned slaveholding society to slow economic development. He decided at about this time that he was willing to take leave of his extremely successful law practice whenever necessary to work toward political objectives. At the 1856 Republican convention that nominated John C. Fremont as President, Lincoln was known well enough to come close to obtaining the nomination for Vice President. His candidacy gave him visibility that would help him win the Presidency four years later. But Lincoln's notoriety wasn't quite enough for success in his try for the United States Senate from Illinois later in 1856, where he lost a vote in the legislature to Lyman Trumbull. Notwithstanding this defeat, Lincoln remained quite active in politics and became one of the national spokesmen for the new Republican Party.

The crises of the years of 1857 and 1858, stimulated by the Dred Scott case and the fight over Kansas' Lecompton Constitution, shook the foundation of the Union and brought Lincoln to the forefront of

American political life. On June 26, 1857, the Supreme Court, for only the second time in its history, declared an act of Congress unconstitutional when it handed down its most infamous decision regarding slavery in the case of Dred Scott v. Sandford. The Southern Chief Justice, Roger B. Taney, hoped that the decision would put an end to the conflict between North and South over the power of Congress to prohibit slavery in the territories. Ironically, this issue was really moot since there were no restrictions on slavery in territories at the time of this decision.[226] In further irony, the decision hardly put an end to conflict, but only exacerbated the gulf between the sections, making the Civil War even more likely.

Dred Scott was a slave who was taken by his owner, an army surgeon on temporary duty, from the slave state of Missouri to the free state of Illinois, then to Wisconsin, a territory made free by virtue of the Northwest Ordinance under a slavery prohibition similar to that used by Congress in establishing the Missouri Compromise 36/30 line. Upon the death of the slave owner, Dred Scott sued the owner's heirs for his freedom, first in Missouri, whose courts refused it, then in federal court after Sandford, the owner's heir, moved to New York. Scott lost in the lower court then appealed to the Supreme Court. In a draconian opinion, which went much further than the scope of Dred Scott's suit required the court to go, Taney handed down three major rulings, each of which utilized illogical, prejudiced, and politically motivated reasoning. First, he decided that "Negroes" were not citizens of the United States and, therefore, Scott did not have the privilege to sue. The Chief Justice claimed that the neither the Declaration of Independence nor the Constitution was intended to benefit blacks because:

> They were at that time considered as a subordinate and inferior class of beings, who had been subjugated by the dominant race, and whether emancipated or not, yet remained subject to their authority, and had no rights or privileges but such as those who held the power and the government might choose to grant them...They had for more than a century before had been regarded as beings of an inferior order, and altogether unfit to associate with the white race, either in social or political relations; and so far inferior, that they had no rights which the white man was bound to respect; and that the Negro might justly and lawfully be reduced to slavery for his benefit.[227]

Although the case would have been decided if the opinion had stopped there, thus effectively denying Dred Scott his freedom, Taney went on to rule that the 36/30 line of the Missouri Compromise was unconstitutional because Congress had no power to prohibit slavery in the territories. He claimed that the due process clause of the 5th Amendment protected the right to property from interference by Congress or by any territorial government. Therefore, no slave could achieve freedom by being in a "free" territory. This undermined the Northern interpretation of popular sovereignty that permitted a territorial government to decide on slavery prior to statehood, driving deeper the wedge within the Democratic Party. Finally, the Chief Justice stated that slaves similarly could not become free by being in a free state temporarily. Their status would depend solely on the laws of the state in which they finally resided—in Scott's case, the slave state of Missouri. Taney's opinion did not go unchallenged on the Court. In a learned and powerful dissent, Justice Benjamin Curtis of Massachusetts pointed out errors in the Chief Justice's interpretation of history and persuasively refuted his reasoning on almost every point, giving the opinion's opponents effective political ammunition.

The Dred Scott case provoked extreme antagonism in the North, tearing down the foundations of previous compromise, and raising fears that slavery would be the wave of the future, rather than an expiring institution of the past. The Court basically read the Constitution as a proslavery document, with the Fifth Amendment protecting rights in slave property and the Tenth Amendment giving states power denied to the federal government. David M. Potter, noted historian of the ante-bellum period, concluded that the Court had completely reversed the Constitutional principles of the United States:

> It made freedom local—an attribute of those states which abolished slavery, but not of the United States; it made slavery national, in the sense that slavery would be legal in any part of the United States where a state government had not abolished it.[228]

Indeed, then President Buchanan interpreted the opinion to mean that even if Kansas ultimately came into the Union as a free state, slaves already there would remain slaves, regardless of the decision of a majority of the state's citizens.[229]

The Court's ruling resulted in strengthening the Republican Party, whose members refused to accept the judgment as final. They warned that the Court intended to make slavery legal everywhere, consistent with John C. Calhoun's doctrine that only states could impact the rights of slave owners. For Abraham Lincoln, the offensive decision presented a dilemma because of his devotion to the rule of law. He never advocated disobedience of the ruling, but he was acutely alarmed by Chief Justice Taney's assertion that neither the Declaration of Independence nor the Constitution included blacks.

In a speech on June 26, 1857, Lincoln responded to the Court. First, he felt constrained to reassure his audience by saying, "I think the authors of that notable instrument [Declaration of Independence] intended to include *all* men, but they did not intend to declare all men equal *in all respects*." He then laid out what he thought the drafters did intend: "They defined…in what respects they did consider all men created equal—equal in 'certain inalienable rights, among which are life, liberty, and the pursuit of happiness.'" Finally, Lincoln proceeded to revitalize the definition of American liberty by giving life to the element of equality, for his generation and for all people:

> They meant simply to declare the right, so that enforcement of it might follow as fast as circumstances should permit. They meant to set up a standard maxim for free society, which should be familiar to all, and revered by all; constantly looked to, constantly labored for, and even though never perfectly attained, constantly approximated, and thereby constantly spreading and deepening its influence, and augmenting the happiness and value of life to all people of all colors everywhere.[230]

Without broadening liberty to include a politically acceptable formula for equality, Lincoln realized that America's values and mission would be hollow and hypocritical, unsuited to the world of the future. As President, he would have the opportunity to apply his new philosophy.

Following quickly on the Dred Scott decision came the second major crisis of these years, the battle over the Lecompton Constitution in Kansas. As a result of establishment of popular sovereignty in the Kansas-Nebraska Act, pro- and anti-slavery settlers in Kansas battled fiercely to achieve a majority. To implement popular sovereignty, a Constitutional convention was called at Lecompton but the vote for delegates to it was boycotted by antislavery forces, who feared that the pro-slavery legislature would perpetrate some sort of fraudulent process. The unsurprising result from the convention was a proslavery state constitution that was clearly contrary to the wishes of the majority of Kansans, as shown in subsequent votes.

In early 1858, President Buchanan submitted a bill to Congress for admission of Kansas as a slave state, essentially endorsing the Lecompton Constitution, despite its unrepresentative nature. This prompted Senator Stephen A. Douglas to break ranks with his party's President and oppose the bill as a perversion of his favored popular sovereignty principle. Douglas' action brought out into the open the long-simmering feud within the Democratic Party over whether slavery actually could be prohibited under popular sovereignty. In the end, a compromise bill sent the Lecompton Constitution back to Kansas voters, where it was rejected, thus delaying statehood and retaining territorial status, but essentially ending local bloodshed. Buchanan emerged from this debacle earning the opprobrium of future historians as an ineffective leader who bore some responsibility for the coming of the Civil War.[231] Douglas, on the other hand, resuscitated his reputation in the North as a moderate whose policies did not necessarily work in favor of slavery, but earned the undying enmity of Southern Democrats that was to dim his political future and help elect Abraham Lincoln President.

The fight over Lecompton, though as bitter as any previous political battle regarding slavery, was really fought over very little of substance. There were, after all, no slaves in Kansas and its future was destined to be as a free state. Yet the South latched on to the "fraudulent" Constitution as "another chapter in its perpetual quest for reassurance."[232] Northerners saw it as a chance to at least preserve some hope for a "free soil" future in the event popular sovereignty could be made to work. To Lincoln and the Republicans, however, the prospect of Northern acquiescence to popular sovereignty, particularly after the Dred Scott case, represented a potential step backward, one that was dangerous to the future of liberty and, not coincidentally in their mind, to the growth and viability of the Republican Party.

As the Lecompton debate was being carried on in Congress, the Republicans nominated Abraham Lincoln to run for the Senate from Illinois against Stephen A. Douglas. In accepting the nomination, Lincoln gave one of his most notable, but least understood, speeches, the "House Divided." In it he stated, "A house divided against itself cannot stand. I believe this government cannot endure, permanently half *slave* and half *free*." He was not predicting or advocating a Civil War; rather, he was expressing his not unrealistic belief that the Kansas-Nebraska Act had set the nation on a course of slavery's expansion rather than its ultimate extinction. The Dred Scott decision had reinforced his belief that the Supreme Court would go even further in its next slavery case and, perhaps, forbid the prohibition of slavery everywhere.[233]

> We shall lie down pleasantly dreaming that the people of Missouri are on the verge of making their State free; and we shall awake to the reality, instead that the Supreme Court has made Illinois a slave state.[234]

Lincoln even professed to see a conspiracy among "Stephen, Franklin, Roger, and James" [Douglas, former President Pierce, Chief Justice Taney, and President Buchanan] to advance the cause of slavery.[235]

For Lincoln, the direction of slavery policy needed to be reversed, so that the ultimate extinction of the institution could, once more, be considered likely. At the same time, he was setting out a practical political program that distinguished the Republican Party from Douglas and the Northern Democrats, thus making the young party the logical leader of that movement. Although the notion that a country divided over slavery could not continue in that mode was not new, Lincoln was the first to foresee a solution that assumed continued unity—either in freedom or slavery.[236] He wanted to forestall potential Republican supporters from being won over by the anti-Lecompton, popular sovereignty coalition in Congress. One rhetorical tactic he used was to remind his listeners of Douglas' controversial statement during the Lecompton debates—"I care not whether slavery was voted down or voted up"—to indicate the morally bankrupt nature of popular sovereignty.[237] Lincoln intended to render insignificant the disagreement between Northern and Southern Democrats over popular sovereignty, and to draw a clear difference in principle on slavery between Douglas and the Republicans. He hoped to mold public opinion in such a way to achieve a Republican majority in the nation, thus putting the country [once again, in his mind] on the side of freedom, leading to the peaceful and eventual end of slavery. In hindsight, we can see that Lincoln overestimated the South's willingness to accept a national Republican majority and underestimated the South's movement toward secession.

In his Senatorial campaign, Lincoln's primary objective was to convince the electorate that Douglas' indifferent attitude would result in further gains for the institution of slavery, either through the lack of legal prohibition in the territories or more extreme judicial decisions. The danger was that slavery would become legal in all states and its extinction would be postponed or even made impossible. Douglas wanted to persuade the voters that the House Divided Speech was an encouragement to civil war and that Lincoln supported radical abolitionist policies. Douglas was not above pandering to the widely held prejudice against blacks, while Lincoln was sensitive to the need to avoid provoking that prejudice. Although Senatorial elections were, at the time, conducted within the state legislature, the amount of interest generated by the contest was great, receiving national attention, and the candidates agreed to hold a series of debates that would be open to the public.

The Lincoln-Douglas Debates have acquired a legendary status because of their consequences in American history. Without them, the Republicans probably would not have nominated Lincoln in 1860, Douglas might have been elected President, the Civil War would, at the very least, have been delayed, and slavery would have continued unabated. Even at the time, people understood that these exchanges held importance beyond the borders of Illinois. One newspaper exclaimed, "The prairies are on fire…It is astonishing how deep an interest in politics this people take."[238] The two debaters held the floor for several hours, and the attendees, who numbered from ten to twenty thousand for each of the seven debates, had to stand for the entire time. Special trains were arranged to carry the multitudes from cities all over Illinois to the sites. They were not disappointed in what they heard.

Lincoln emphasized the immorality of slavery and argued that blacks had been included in the Declaration of Independence. He referred repeatedly to the idea that the founders wanted to declare the right to equality, but leave the timing of its implementation up to appropriate political circumstances. He denied that the Constitution gave slavery a privileged position, concluding that the framers intended to put it on a course to extinction, as evidenced by the exclusion of slavery from the Northwest Territory and the limited reprieve for the African slave trade. He cast the issue in draconian terms: "[The real issue] is the eternal struggle between these two principles—

right and wrong—throughout the world...The one is the common right of humanity and the other the divine right of kings...It is the same spirit that says, 'You work and toil and earn bread, and I'll eat it.'"[239] Here, again, Lincoln is linking the idea of equal opportunity with America's mission to be an example of liberty for the world. His primary criticism of Douglas' popular sovereignty was its inconsistency with that mission. Mimicking Douglas' reference to his "gur-reat purrinciple," Lincoln said that it meant simply that "if one man would enslave another, no third man should object."[240] He tried to persuade his audience that such moral indifference could lead to an unlimited expansion of slavery, even to existing free states.

Douglas did not issue a moral verdict on slavery, but concentrated on his desire to preserve the Union, even if it were half slave and half free. He saw popular sovereignty as the path to removing the issue of slavery from national politics, letting it be resolved on the local level, thereby cooling passions and making disunion less likely. He gave higher priority to self-government and majority rule than he did to the morality of slavery or the rights of minorities. He was also motivated by a belief in Manifest Destiny and his version of the American mission—to spread liberty to the Pacific Ocean and even to Cuba and Central America, areas that might, under popular sovereignty, choose to benefit from the existence of slavery. The fact that Douglas considered blacks inferior to whites made acquiescing in the potential expansion of slavery much easier for him. While Lincoln accepted that the races were different and that actual equality did not exist, he fervently pleaded with his audience to accept that, for the right to enjoy the fruits of his labor, the black person "is my equal and the equal of Judge Douglas, and the equal of every other man."[241]

During the second debate at Freeport, Lincoln put Douglas on the defensive by posing his famous question about the Dred Scott decision, asking whether, under the court's ruling, the people of a territory could exclude slavery prior to the formation of a state Constitution. Douglas knew that he couldn't completely agree with the court's view that it would be unconstitutional to so exclude slavery, since that would be inconsistent with his own popular sovereignty doctrine. Instead, he responded with a torturous rationale, stating that it didn't matter what the Supreme Court ruled in theory, because the people of a territory could refuse in actuality to apply their police power to protect slavery. The answer, which became known as the "Freeport Doctrine," avoided an extreme pro-slavery position and satisfied some of his listeners in Illinois, but it permanently alienated Douglas from southern Democrats who demanded full agreement with the Dred Scott decision. Lincoln also asked Douglas whether he would follow a hypothetical future Supreme Court decision which decided that no state could exclude slavery from its limits. Douglas' reply again pointed to the ability of citizens to refrain from using the police power to protect slavery, but the answer did not calm the great fear in the North that the Dred Scott decision could lead to the unlimited extension of slavery. That fear would underlay a great deal of the North's hostility to the South prior to the Civil War.

It is difficult to determine who won the Lincoln-Douglas debates, although they increased the prominence of both men. In the Senatorial election, conducted in the Illinois legislature, Douglas was the victor, but, when the popular vote is analyzed for the various legislative districts, Lincoln's supporters garnered more votes.[242] Lincoln emerged a national figure, prominent in the Republican Party and a contender for the nomination for President in 1860. He actively campaigned for that office by organizing supporters in most Northern states, writing an autobiography, and traveling to make speeches outside of Illinois. Similarly, Douglas had taken positions in the debates that unified his support among Northern Democrats, leading to his own nomination for President in 1860. However, his alienation of Southern Democrats fractured the party, created a valuable political opportunity for the Republicans in 1860 and made Southern secession from the Union more likely.

The schism in the Democratic Party widened during the Congressional session of 1859 as the South pushed for a federal slave code for the territories. Even though the slave population in the territories was small, and unlikely to grow, Southerners viewed the issue as a symbolic test of its way of life. Douglas' opposition further infuriated Southern Democrats, already convinced that the Freeport Doctrine undermined the Dred Scott decision. President Buchanan sided with the Southern Democrats, claiming that popular sovereignty was really a Republican idea. Although some have viewed the emotional debate over slavery in the territories as proof that the Civil War itself resulted from a disproportionate response to a practically non-existent problem, this ignores the fact that the debate mirrored sectional differences that were very real and irresolvable with available political remedies. As Civil War historian Eric Foner has written:

Only by a comprehension of this total conflict between North and South, between Republican and southern ideologies, can the meaning of the territorial issue be fully grasped. Its importance went even beyond the belief shared widely in both sections that slavery required expansion to survive, and that confinement to the states where it already existed would kill it. For in each ideology was the conviction that its own social system must expand, not only to insure its own survival but to prevent the expansion of all the evils the other represented.[243]

In a memorable address at the Cooper Institute in New York (more familiarly Cooper Union) on February 27, 1860, Lincoln dealt directly with the apparent irreconcilable nature of the conflict. He reiterated his conviction that the founders of the country had intended to put slavery on a course to extinction, then cautioned his followers to oppose the Dred Scott decision lawfully, with the hope that the Supreme Court would reverse it. He advised Republicans to work toward a peaceful resolution with the South by considering their demands "even though the southern people will not so much as listen to us."

Lincoln then asked a most challenging question—how the South could ever be satisfied. His answer: "We must not only let them alone, but we must, somehow, convince them that we do let them alone. This, we know by experience, is no easy task." He concluded with his assessment of how the conflict stood: "What will convince them [that we wish to leave them alone]? This, and this only: cease to call slavery *wrong*, and join them in calling it *right*." He spelled out what this would mean in practical terms:

And this must be done thoroughly—done in acts as well as in words. Silence will not be tolerated…We must arrest and return their fugitive slaves with greedy pleasure. We must pull down our Free State constitutions. The whole atmosphere must be disinfected from all taint of opposition to slavery, before they will cease to believe that all their troubles proceed from us.[244]

Lincoln built skillfully on his reputation from the debates with Senator Douglas in developing a strategy for receiving the Republican nomination for President in 1860. Sensitive to the requirements of practical politics, he took a position on slavery that was viewed as not too conservative for the Republican Party but not too radical to obtain an electoral majority. Although William Seward from New York was the initial favorite, Lincoln's character, moderation, and organization prevailed. This was partly the result of some fortuitous geographic circumstances in that Lincoln's Midwestern background and support for internal improvements put him in good position to win the four northern states that helped elect Buchanan President in 1856—Indiana, New Jersey, Pennsylvania and Illinois.

The Democrats were fragmented, with Southerners separating and nominating John C. Breckinridge of Kentucky on a platform that promised federal protection of slavery. Northern Democrats nominated Douglas under a platform that was almost as pro-slavery. In addition, a fourth party, called the Constitutional Union, nominated John Bell of Tennessee, who supported a program that simply promised loyalty to the Constitution and the Union, and enforcement of existing law.

Lincoln won the election, with 180 electoral votes to 72 for Breckinridge, 39 for Bell and 12 for Douglas. In the popular vote, Lincoln tallied 1,866,452, Douglas 1,376,957, Breckinridge 849,781, and Bell 588,879. Contrary to common opinion, Lincoln's victory was not a result of the fact that his opposition was divided, but, rather, because of "advantageous distribution of his votes among populous states where the large minority votes of his opponents, even if combined, would have failed to "carry" the states..."[245]

Lincoln's election was devastating to the South. Despite his promise not to interfere with slavery where it existed, Southerners interpreted his election as a complete change in the nature of the national government as it had existed since the origin of the Constitution—from one supportive of slavery to one committed to a new revolutionary attitude regarding it. Because Lincoln never campaigned in the South nor sought the support of Southerners, they were left to believe the worst of him. They thought that his administration and his party would begin by controlling the House of Representatives, then add many new free states, proceed to control the Senate, appoint an antislavery majority on the Supreme Court, undercut the Fugitive Slave Law, distribute abolitionist literature, encourage slave rebellions, and, in the end, destroy the Southern way of life.

Lincoln took a conciliatory stance in the period between his election and his inauguration, promising that he would not threaten slavery where it existed and urging the South to remain within the Union.

However, he also was clear about his view of American liberty. On his way to Washington, he said during a speech in Cincinnati, "I hold that while man exists it is his duty to improve not only his own condition, but to assist in ameliorating mankind." In Philadelphia ten days later, he said that the United States and its Declaration of Independence provide "hope to the world for all future time," promising that, in due time, weights "should be lifted from the shoulders of all men, and that *all* should have an equal chance."[246]

Prior to Lincoln's taking office, one last attempt was made in Congress to settle the territorial issue in the hope of averting a Southern secession. Known as the Crittendon Compromise after its sponsor, Senator John J. Crittendon of Kentucky, it contained a series of Constitutional Amendments favoring slavery, including protection of it south of the 36/30 line, all the way to the Pacific Ocean, and anywhere else it was permitted, and forever forbidding changes to the Fugitive Slave and Three-Fifths Clauses. Largely as a result of President-elect Lincoln's admonition to Republican legislators to permit "no compromise on the question of *extending* slavery,"[247] the measure died in committee.

With the defeat of the Crittendon Compromise, the South saw no further reason for remaining within the Union. Its leaders were convinced that its traditions and way of life were inconsistent with the prevailing political philosophy of the federal government. The movement toward secession was started by South Carolina in December, 1860, and was joined by the remainder of the seven states of the Deep South—Mississippi, Florida, Alabama, Georgia and Louisiana in January, 1861 and Texas in February. Representatives from these states met in Montgomery, Alabama on February 4 and, four days later, established a provisional government for the Confederate States of America, naming Jefferson Davis of Mississippi as President.[248] Davis was inaugurated on February 18, two weeks before Abraham Lincoln.

6. President Lincoln and the Emancipation Proclamation

On March 4, 1861, the Republican President whose election resulted in a divided nation relied on common history to urge conciliation. In his Inaugural Address, Lincoln refused to recognize the secession, maintaining that the Union was unbroken. He again tried to reassure the South by promising not to interfere with slavery in the states where it existed and holding out the hope of peace:

> We are not enemies, but friends. We must not be ene-
> mies...The mystic chords of memory, stretching from
> every...patriot grave to every living heart and hearthstone,
> all over this broad land, will yet swell the chorus of the
> union, when again touched, as surely they will be, by the
> better angels of our nature.[249]

Notwithstanding Lincoln's moderation, the gulf between the sections was too wide to be bridged and, at dawn on April 12, 1861, Confederate General Beauregard opened fire on Union troops at Fort Sumter, South Carolina, beginning the Civil War. Soon after the commencement of hostilities, four additional states seceded to join the Confederacy—Virginia, Arkansas, Tennessee and North Carolina.

Lincoln's strategy at the outset of the Civil War consisted of three objectives: 1) to hold the Union together, 2) to prevent the loss of any more states, particularly the slave-owning border states of Delaware, Maryland, Kentucky and Missouri, and 3) to defeat the Confederate Army. To accomplish these, he had to balance many conflicting political interests and keep their advocates together behind the Union cause. He needed both radical Republicans, like Senator Charles Sumner of Massachusetts, and conservative "War Democrats" like Senator Stephen A. Douglas. He needed both vehement abolitionists, like William Lloyd Garrison, and Union supporters with prejudice against blacks, such as Congressman Samuel S. Cox of Ohio. And he had to manage the conservative but able commander of Union forces, General George A. McClellan, whose overly cautious objective was to gradually plan to capture the Confederate capitol, Richmond, rather than aggressively attack the Confederate Army, as Lincoln thought critical.

Despite his desire to weaken the institution of slavery, Lincoln was unwilling to do anything that would jeopardize support for the Union. The existence of slavery in the border Union states created conflicting concerns. On the one hand, it was an embarrassment that affected foreign policy. European countries would find it difficult to view the American Civil War as a contest between freedom and slavery so long as states within the Union sanctioned the institution. Ever since the 1830's, when Great Britain had abolished slavery in its empire, liberal opinion in Europe favored ending the slave trade and viewed America as reactionary on this issue. On the other, the continued loyalty of the Union slave states—Delaware, Kentucky, Maryland, and Missouri— gave the North critical psychological and material advantages over the South. If Lincoln had, at the outset, described the war as one against slavery, he would have risked losing these states as well as alienating many Northern Democrats, whose commitment was to the preservation of the Union and not to abolition.

Unwilling to ignore the profound issue that caused the war, the President developed an initial policy that was aimed at gradually ending slavery while avoiding a crisis in the loyal border states. First, he decided that states should be the instrument for emancipation, partially because he had real doubts about the constitutionality of any action by the federal government and partially because he thought that only the states could take such action in a politically acceptable way. Second, he believed that slave owners should be compensated for the taking of their "property". Again, practical political considerations were primary for him. Third, he was convinced that the federal government would have to provide much of the financing for any emancipation since the costs would be beyond the capacity or willingness of any state. Fourth, he wanted the timetable for emancipation to be extensive, setting the year 1900 as the required end date. Finally, he wanted freed blacks to be colonized on a voluntary basis outside the country because he harbored doubts whether blacks and whites could live together peacefully in an integrated society.

The course of events during 1861 and early1862 would gradually change Lincoln's thinking. Always conscious that slavery was morally reprehensible, he had hoped that the rebellion could be readily defeated and the Union restored under a gradual, state-based emancipation program. Events proved that neither goal would likely be achieved in the foreseeable future. He would need to call on all his political and tactical skills to adjust to changing circumstances.

The military impact on slavery presented the first set of challenges. Soon after the opening skirmish at Fort Sumter, Senator Sumner advised Lincoln that the emancipation of the slaves of a military opponent would be within the war powers of the Commander in Chief. The notion of using emancipation as a war measure probably owed its authorship to John Quincy Adams who, as a Congressman from Massachusetts in 1842, claimed that an antislavery militia commander from a free state who had to intervene to help put down a slave insurrection, nonetheless had the right to emancipate some or all of those slaves.[250] Lincoln's first Secretary of War, Simon Cameron of Pennsylvania, had sent him a report in December, 1861 that recommended slaves be freed and enlisted in the Union army. Unwilling at the time to utilize blacks as soldiers, Lincoln directed that the report be modified to say only that slaves could be a military resource of some type and should not be returned to their owners.

In the field, Lincoln's generals had to make immediate decisions as escaping slaves sought asylum. In May, 1861, General Benjamin Butler, Commander at Fortress Monroe in Virginia, refused to return three men to their owner, calling them 'contraband of war,' claiming they were employed in the erection of enemy batteries, and declaring that the Fugitive Slave Law did not apply in a foreign country (meaning in Virginia). Butler found work for the slaves within the Union lines. Lincoln did nothing to reverse Butler's actions.

Major General John C. Fremont, head of Union forces in Missouri, presented the President with a more serious dilemma. He declared martial law throughout Missouri on August 31, 1861 and declared all the slaves in that state free. Lincoln was livid because he knew that many of those who had volunteered to fight for the Union would refuse to do so to support emancipation. This was particularly true for recent volunteers from Kentucky, a pivotal border state. Lincoln immediately overturned Fremont's order, saying "I think there is great danger that...liberating slaves of traitorous owners, will alarm our Southern Union friends, and turn them against us—perhaps ruin our rather fair prospect for Kentucky."[251] He continued:

> I think to lose Kentucky is nearly the same as to lose the whole game. Kentucky gone, we can not hold Missouri, nor, as I think, Maryland. These all against us, and the job on our hands is too large for us. We would as well consent to separation at once, including the surrender of this capitol.[252]

Finally, Major General David Hunter, Union Commander of the Department of the South began, in March, 1862, to issue certificates of emancipation to all slaves who were part of the Confederacy. In April, he freed slaves held at Fort Pulaski and Cockspur Island, and on May 9 he issued a similar proclamation for his entire command area (parts of South Carolina, Georgia and Florida). Lincoln did not let the order stand, saying that emancipation should be undertaken only if it was a military necessity, and made it clear that he, alone, as Commander in Chief, would make that judgment. Although no slaves were emancipated under Lincoln's directive, it was a precursor to the justification he used later in the year when he issued his own Emancipation Proclamation.

Congressional actions during 1861 and 1862 built momentum toward a modification in Lincoln's policy. The First Confiscation Act, passed on August 6, 1861, provided that "when slaves were engaged in hostile military service, the owners claims to the labor of such slaves were forfeited."[253] While the law was less than clear in defining "forfeiture," Congress clearly intended to move toward a policy of at least limited, uncompensated emancipation. They were concerned that, as assets of war, slaves should not remain in the hands of the enemy. In March, 1862, Congress prohibited the use of military forces to return slaves who had escaped into the hands of the Union Army. On April 16, 1862 Congress abolished slavery in the District of Columbia, but agreed, at Lincoln's request, to provide one million dollars for compensation to slave owners in the District, permitting up to $300 per slave. By contrast, in June Congress abolished slavery in all territories without providing for either compensation for the owners or colonization of the freed slaves. Despite the fact that the bill did not contain these two elements of Lincoln's policy, the President signed it because neither the border states nor the District of Columbia would be affected. In July, the Militia Act was passed that provided that any enemy-owned slave who came to Union lines and rendered military service would be free, together with his mother, wife and children.[254]

The Second Confiscation Act passed on July 17, 1862. This theoretically far ranging statute emancipated the slaves of all those who supported the rebellion by confiscating their property. They were made "forever free of their servitude and not again held as slaves." Lincoln secured additional funds under the act to finance his plans for voluntary colonization of freed slaves. The act's promise was greater than its delivery since, prior to the slave's liberty, there needed to be a legal determination of whether the owner was in rebellion. Nevertheless, its passage added to the political momentum propelling Lincoln to change his policy.

The most significant single influence on Lincoln was likely the heroic action of black slaves themselves in the course of the war. Given opportunities to resist authority, they did so with many individual acts of "self-liberation," including running away, slowing work down, breaking disciplinary rules, and making it difficult for mistresses to manage plantations while their husbands were away fighting. These acts of disobedience helped persuade both the President and the country to change the nature of the war and face emancipation squarely. W.E.B. DuBois, in his 1935 book *Black Reconstruction in America*, claimed that slaves engaged in a large general strike that helped the North win the war. Although historians have not found clear evidence of such mass action, there is no doubt that slave resistance was a critical contributor to their own emancipation.[255]

When Union troops approached the plantations, slaves became bolder and more defiant, sensing the coming of liberation. They ran away in groups to Union lines, crowding into makeshift refugee camps, forcing northern generals to decide how to make use of them. Modern historians have generally agreed that blacks helped to end their own slavery by taking "…advantage of weakened authority resulting from the war to engage in acts that undermined the ability of masters to govern and that persuaded federal officials the time had come to bury the peculiar institution…By refusing to act like slaves, blacks throughout the South struck a mortal blow to slavery."[256] As the war progressed, more and more Northerners, and particularly radical Republicans, began to see an opportunity to completely change the social system of the South. It was as if people said, "if we're going to suffer all this horror, let it be for a noble cause."

Lincoln's thought process changed as these anti-slavery influences grew. By the summer of 1862, hopes for an early military victory had faded. General McClellan's campaign in Virginia was a failure and Lincoln felt a desperate need for more troops to break the military stalemate. Yet, recruiting them would be a formidable task because patriotic fervor had waned as the war dragged on and casualties increased. Emancipation would have the potential to revive enthusiasm for the war, thus increasing the willingness of northerners to volunteer for service. Equally important, manpower needs could be readily met if blacks, including newly freed slaves, were allowed to become soldiers.

A new war strategy centered on emancipation would have two additional benefits, one domestic and one international. First, the loss of slave labor would seriously undermine the Confederate economy, hampering the South's ability to carry on the war. As it was, the North was much richer in resources to fight a protracted war and the new policy would increase its advantage. Second, the strategy would fore-

stall Great Britain, and, possibly, other European countries, from recognizing the Confederacy. Although it maintained a position of neutrality, Great Britain was supportive of the southern cotton economy
and British politicians were sympathetic to a war for self-government.
However, public opinion there would probably prevent any British
government from supporting a war to preserve slavery.

Lincoln had tried in early 1862 to induce the Union slave states
to accept his slavery policy. He proposed legislation that offered
federal financing to states for a gradual, compensated abolition program. In a letter to a California Senator, he observed that "Less than
one half-day's cost of this war [$719,000] would pay for all the slaves in
Delaware...[and] less than eighty seven days cost of this war
[$174,000,000]...would pay for all in Delaware, Maryland, District of
Columbia, Kentucky, and Missouri."[257] Congress passed the measure
but it met with little interest in the key states. On July 12, Lincoln
called border state representatives to the White House personally to
appeal for support for his program of gradual, compensated emancipation coupled with colonization for those receiving freedom. Two
days later, the attendees rejected his request by a vote of 20 to 8.

By the summer, the President believed the time had come to
move against slavery in a more aggressive way than he had previously.
The rejection of voluntary emancipation by the Union border states
had left only more radical options. Moreover, the war was more difficult and long lasting than Lincoln had initially hoped, and there was
desperate need for additional soldiers. A more ambitious slavery policy might attract increased numbers of white enlistees and make available thousands of newly freed black men. The Northern public also
seemed ready to entertain a broadening in the war's objectives. They
were affected by the example of hundreds of thousands of slaves
already supporting the Union cause, as well as the growing foreign
sentiment for abolition.

In June, Lincoln had begun to compose the outlines of a document that would place the government clearly on the side of freedom.
Legend has it that he worked alone, most of the time at the telegraph
office of the War Department, where he had more peace and quiet
than he would receive at the White House. As an added convenience,
he could receive the latest, direct reports from the battlefields.[258] He
took several weeks to draft the Proclamation himself and, by early July,
was ready to share his ideas with his closest advisors. According to
Secretary of the Navy Gideon Welles, Lincoln first discussed the idea

on July 13, 1862, during a carriage ride to the funeral of the infant son of Secretary of War Stanton, telling Welles and Secretary of State Seward that he intended to emancipate the slaves in the event the war did not end in the very near future. He saw it as a military necessity, since the war was not going well at the time. As Welles described it,

> ...the reverses before Richmond and the formidable power and dimensions of the insurrection...impelled the Administration to adopt extraordinary measures to preserve the national existence. The slaves, if not armed and disciplined, were in the service of those who were.[259]

The President had become convinced that it was "absolutely essential for the salvation of the Union, that we must free the slaves or be ourselves subdued." Both Welles and Seward recognized the idea as a new direction for Lincoln and both offered him their support in shaping it.

On July 22, the President convened the Cabinet and read a draft proclamation, written in his own hand on two pages of lined note paper. He did not ask for approval, but, rather, for input as to the schedule and the wording. Postmaster Blair advised that it would engender a terrible political backlash. Seward felt that, given recent military reverses, the timing was wrong and that the measure would be viewed as an act of desperation. Lincoln later recalled that Seward thought "it would be considered our last *shriek*, on the retreat."[260] The President was persuaded and decided to delay the promulgation until the military prospects were more favorable—perhaps after a victory on the battlefield. "As ever, the art of political timing dictated Lincoln's course."[261]

Awaiting an opportune moment for its announcement, Lincoln acted in the next weeks as if no great change in policy was pending. He told visitors from Indiana that he still believed that enlisting black men in the army would risk losing the state of Kentucky to the Confederacy. He remained concerned that the primary objection to emancipation would be the widespread belief that blacks and whites could not live together. After inviting a representative group of free black men to visit the White House in August, Lincoln took the opportunity to try to obtain their support for a new program of colonization in Central America. He told them: "You and we are different races...It is better for us both, therefore, to be separated."[262] The men gave the President a polite hearing but showed no great enthusiasm for his idea.

Lincoln decided to respond to an influential editorial by Horace Greeley in the New York Tribune dated August 20, 1862, entitled "The Prayer of Twenty Millions," that was critical of the President's timid antislavery policy. The President wrote:

> My paramount object in this struggle is to save the Union, and is not either to save or destroy slavery. If I could save the Union without freeing any slave I would do it, and if I could save it by freeing all the slaves I would do it; and if I could save it by freeing some and leaving others alone I would also do that. What I do about slavery, and the colored race, I do because I believe it helps to save the union; and what I forbear, I forbear because I do not believe it would help to save the Union.[263]

Since he had already decided to issue a strong antislavery proclamation, the response to Horace Greeley seems strange. But one must remember that Lincoln was a master of political timing and preparing the political path. He did not want to appear, either in the North or the South, to be waging the war only to abolish slavery, for many in both sections would be alienated by such a stance. However, the issue of preserving the Union and ending slavery, were inextricably linked together in his mind. He did not want a Union in which the meaning of American liberty was distorted by the prospect of a future that included oppression of fellow human beings.

On September 13, Lincoln met at the White House with a delegation of Christian ministers from Chicago and made statements that were as equivocal as those in his letter to Greeley. In response to their assertion that God wished immediate emancipation of the slaves, Lincoln said it would be of help to him if God revealed himself "directly...on a point so connected with my duty." He went on to explain his hesitancy on emancipation:

> What good would a proclamation of emancipation from me do...I do not want to issue a document that the whole world will see must necessarily be inoperative, like the Pope's bull against the comet! Would my word free the slaves, when I cannot even enforce the Constitution in the rebel states?...But I am not so sure we could do much with the blacks. If we were to arm them, I fear that in a few weeks the arms would be in

the hands of rebels…There are fifty thousand bayonets in the
Union armies from the Border Slave States. It would be a
serious matter if, in consequence of a proclamation such as
you desire, they should go over to the rebels.

His apparently negative attitude was really more of an airing of
potential problems and an indication of his sensitivity to the need for
careful timing of a decision so fraught with political dangers. At the
end of his meeting, he more accurately described his state of mind:

Do not misunderstand me, because I have mentioned these
objections. They indicate the difficulties that have thus far
prevented my action in some such way as you desire. I have
not decided against a proclamation of liberty to the slaves,
but hold the matter under advisement. And I can assure you
that the subject is on my mind, by day and night, more than
any other. [264]

The bloodiest day of the Civil War provided the opportunity Lincoln sought to change the nature of the conflict and, at the same time,
revitalize the definition of American liberty. The Battle of Antietam in
Sharpsburg, Maryland, lasted 14 hours on September 17, 1862, saw over
22,000 killed or wounded, and decimated the Confederate forces.
Although disappointed that General McLellan failed to pursue the
retreating General Lee into Virginia, which might have completely
destroyed the main Confederate Army, Lincoln recognized the battle as
a psychological turning point for the Union. With that in mind, he began
work at the Soldiers' Home that evening on the final draft of the Preliminary Proclamation. He returned to the White House on Saturday, the
20th, and, during the day Sunday, he finished the draft he would submit to
the Cabinet the following day. Secretary of State Seward made some
edits in Lincoln's handwritten document and it was issued the same day.
      Unlike many of Lincoln's speeches and public statements, the
Preliminary Emancipation Proclamation does not contain noble or
memorable words. It was not intended as an inspiring declaration of
freedom. Frederick Douglass, the most prominent black American,
met with Lincoln frequently during the war as an unofficial advisor
and, later wrote about Lincoln's approach:

While he hated slavery, and really desired its destruction, he always proceeded against it in a manner the least likely to shock or drive from him any who were truly in sympathy with the preservation of the Union, but who were not friendly to emancipation.[265]

The President justified the order as a military action taken under his war powers, and he wanted the substance to read that way. The Proclamation makes clear that it is rooted in the military powers of the Commander in Chief and refers to previous policies and Congressional acts. The President states his intention to declare on January 1, 1863, that all people in slavery in rebel states would be "thenceforward, and forever free." The President would, on that date, designate states and areas that were in rebellion. For slaves in states that remained loyal to the Union, the final document would recommend compensated, gradual emancipation and would advocate voluntary colonization. Emancipation would not by federal law immediately extend to slaves within government control, primarily because Lincoln was convinced that he could constitutionally do so only where justified by military necessity. The document re-emphasized the Congressional acts that authorized the army to assist all free persons, to treat slaves as captives of war and free them, and to refuse to return any slave unless the owner proved he was not in rebellion. In other words, the army would refrain from enforcing the Fugitive Slave Law.

During the period from the Preliminary Proclamation to January 1, 1863, the date set for the Final Proclamation, the Congressional elections in November showed that the action was greeted with favor in New England, Michigan and Kansas, but opposed in Indiana, Pennsylvania, and Ohio, which voted Democratic. Republicans also lost some ground in New York, New Jersey, Illinois and Delaware. Lincoln used the occasion of his Annual Message to Congress on December 1, 1862 to assuage fears and neutralize arguments against what he had done.

Lincoln again proposed voluntary and compensated emancipation in loyal slave states, together with voluntary colonization—this time by means of Constitutional Amendments. He wanted to have plans in place that would delineate the path to freedom in the event the war ended rapidly, through a compromise settlement, leaving parts of the United States still slave holding areas. Although the measures did not pass, they served to reassure border state citizens. Confronting fears that freed blacks would take jobs from whites, he observed that if the slaves stayed in their original states, no white workers would be displaced and if they moved north, opportunity would be created in the South for white labor. He noted that if his colonization plan were successful, opportunities for white workers would actually increase. Once he had built the foundation of political reassurance, he turned his attention to inspiring political courage:

> The dogmas of the quiet past, are inadequate to the stormy present...The occasion is piled high with difficulty, and we must rise with the occasion. As our case is new, so we must think anew, and act anew. We must disenthrall ourselves, and then we shall save our country. Fellow-citizens, we cannot escape history...The fiery trial through which we pass, will light us down, in honor or dishonor, to the latest generation...We know how to save the Union...In giving freedom to the slave, we assure freedom to the free—honorable alike in what we give, and what we preserve. We shall nobly save, or meanly lose, the last best, hope of earth.[266]

Lincoln was not without doubts about the wisdom of what he was about to do. He felt the weight of responsibility and expressed to his Cabinet his willingness to cede his role to any one of them if they possessed more of the public's confidence than he did. But since such a transfer was neither practical nor constitutional, even if there had been such an individual, Lincoln concluded that "I must do the best I can, and bear the responsibility of taking the course which I feel I ought to take."[267]

The most important change from the Preliminary to the Final Proclamation was Lincoln's directive that freed slaves would be accepted as soldiers. He thereby set the military history of the country on a new and more democratic course. By welcoming blacks into the armed services, while avoiding any emphasis on colonization abroad, Lincoln essentially insured that they would be true Americans, fighting for their country and permanently living in it under freedom.

The President reiterated that the document was issued "as a fit and necessary war measure for suppressing the rebellion." In this way, he assuaged his own doubts about his Constitutional power over slavery and diluted potentially adverse political reaction. To respond to specific public concern, Lincoln also added a provision that urged freed slaves to refrain from violence and accept work at reasonable wages.

As a military measure, its application was limited to those geographic areas that were in rebellion as of January 1, 1863. Thus, none of the loyal slave states—Delaware, Maryland, Kentucky, and Missouri—were covered, nor was the contested state of Tennessee. Some months later, he replied to criticism about the limited scope of his action by saying:

> The original proclamation has no constitutional or legal justification, except as a military measure...If I take the step [expanding the area of emancipation] must I not do so, without the argument of military necessity, and so, without any argument, except the one that I think the measure politically expedient and morally right? Would I not thus give up all footing upon constitution and law? Would I not thus bet in the boundless field of absolutism?...Could it fail to be perceived that without any further stretch, I might do the same in Delaware, Maryland, Kentucky, Tennessee, and Missouri; and even change any law in any state? Would not many of our own friends shrink away appalled? Would it not lose us the elections, and with them, the very cause we seek to advance?[268]

The operative provision granting freedom remained essentially the same: "I do order and declare that all persons held as slaves within said designated States...are, and henceforward shall be free; and that the Executive government of the United States, including the military and naval authorities thereof, will recognize and maintain the freedom of said persons."[269]

There was great anticipation in the country as the fateful day came near for the issuance of Final Proclamation. More than the usual number of people gathered at the White House for the traditional New Year's Day celebration during which the public was usually admitted for two hours and would be greeted by the President. The time stretched to three hours to accommodate the crowd and Lincoln's hand became extremely swollen from greeting his visitors. Finally, he walked upstairs to sign the official document. His hand shook so much that he felt he could barely write, causing him to wonder if this was a negative, superstitious sign, but he quickly attributed it to the three hours of public handshaking. "He declared that he had never been more confident of the righteousness of any act in all his life, and he was unwilling that his signature should appear to indicate any weakness or indecision."[270]

Even though the Final Proclamation only applied in designated rebel territory, where the federal government had little power to enforce the law on a day-to-day basis, and did not affect slavery in loyal states, it had enormous impact as a political and psychological symbol throughout the country. "Northerners and Southerners, white and black, now knew that a Union victory meant the end of slavery."[271] The effect on blacks was immediate. John Eaton, a military chaplain and Superintendent of Freedmen for General Ulysses S. Grant's army in Tennessee and Mississippi described the dramatic results:

> [Negroes] flocked in vast numbers—an army in them-selves—to the camps of the Yankees...springing from antecedent barbarism, rising up and leaving its ancient bondage, forsaking its local traditions and all the associa-tions—and attractions—of the old plantation life, coming garbed in rags, with feet shod or bleeding, individually or in families and larger groups—an army of slaves and fugitives, pushing its way irresistibly toward an army of fighting men...The arrival among us of these hordes was like the oncoming of cities. There was no plan in this exodus, no Moses to lead it. Unlettered reason or the mere inarticulate decision of instinct brought them to us.[272]

Immediately after the issuance of the Proclamation, thousands of slaves who fled to Union armies were held in "contraband camps" where they were the object of a large scale philanthropic effort from the North. They received clothes, economic aid, and medicine, together with educational help from northern teachers and religious assistance from northern missionaries. The Union Army often pro-vided the former slaves with jobs supporting the soldiers, such as farm-ing and providing protection to the camps. Sometimes they were put to work raising cotton on the same plantation from which they had escaped. Some of these plantations were run by the government, some were leased to Northerners who hired the blacks, some remained in the hands of southern plantation owners who took an oath of alle-giance to the Union, and some were subdivided and leased to the freedmen. Eventually, the government established a Freedmen's Bureau to oversee the welfare and re-integration of these new citizens.

One of the major objectives of the Proclamation was the expansion of black recruitment into the army, from both North and South. The new opportunities had some limits, since blacks were required to be led by white officers and black soldiers were paid less than whites. Nevertheless, Lincoln pushed hard to tap this new resource. In a letter to Governor Andrew Johnson of Tennessee he said: "The colored population is the great *available* and yet *unavailed* of, force for restoring the Union. The bare sight of fifty thousand armed, and drilled black soldiers on the banks of the Mississippi, would end the rebellion at once."[273]

There were many examples of heroic fighting by black units, the most well-known being those of the 54th Massachusetts Infantry. Led by Robert Gould Shaw, the son of a prominent abolitionist family, the brigade attacked Fort Wagner, protecting the Confederate port of Charleston, South Carolina. They were able to hold the parapet for a short time; Colonel Shaw was killed and the brigade lost half its men as they were finally beaten back. But the courage and tragic losses of the 54th helped convince the Northern public that black soldiers could greatly aid the war effort.

Lincoln realized the value of the incentive of freedom. In a letter to James Conkling of Illinois, he defended his policy: "Why should they do anything for us, if we will do nothing for them? If they stake their lives for us, they must be prompted by the strongest motive—even the promise of freedom. And the promise being made, must be kept."[274] When Lincoln thought that slaves weren't volunteering fast enough, Frederic Douglass advised him that too few of them knew of the Emancipation Proclamation. The President authorized Douglass to organize secret teams of scouts to venture behind enemy lines to pass the word to the slaves that they would be better off if they came to the Union side before the conclusion of a peace settlement that might trap them as slaves in rebel territory.[275] The plan was never implemented since the tide of the war turned significantly before it could be started. It is estimated, however, that a total of 134,000 blacks from the South and 52,000 from the North responded to Lincoln's call for fighting men.[276]

The eagerness of slaves to seek freedom and to help Union forces in the South neutralized the doubt in the mind of many northerners about the capacity and motivation of blacks. The fact that former slaves were willing to fight and die for their freedom helped make Union loyalists more radical in their political thinking. Equally impressive to Northerners was the eagerness of slaves for education and betterment. Northern missionary teachers following Union armies told stories about the capacity and determination of former slaves to learn:

The children…hurry to school as soon as their work is over…The plowmen hurry from the field at night to get their hour of study. Old men and women strain their dim sight with the book two and a half feet distant from the eye, to catch the shape of the letter. I call this heaven-inspired interest.[277]

The reaction of politicians to the Proclamation was more mixed. Even Lincoln's Party was not unified. Conservatives believed that it was unnecessary to convert a war for the Union into a war over slavery; they were also critical of the interference with civil rights that Lincoln's war policies produced, such as press censorship and denial of habeas corpus.[278] Radicals thought Lincoln was too timid in his slavery policy and favored a wholesale revolution in the Southern social system. Despite these differences, Lincoln took an active legislative role and guided his party to pass precedent-setting legislation that strengthened the national government and economy in lasting ways. These measures included the Homestead Act, the Internal Revenue law, a transcontinental railroad, the creation of land grant colleges, a conscription law, the Department of Agriculture, and the National Banking Act, which established a national currency and network of national banks, finally making permanent Washington and Hamilton's national economic framework.

The reaction of the general public also varied, largely dependent on geography. The Springfield Illinois State Journal was effusive in praise:

President Lincoln has at last hurled against the rebellion the bolt which he has so long held suspended. The act is the most important and the most memorable of his official career—no event in the history of this country since the Declaration of Independence itself has excited so profound attention either at home or abroad.[279]

Border state citizens were less impressed. The Louisville Journal opined:
The measure is wholly unauthorized and wholly pernicious… Kentucky cannot and will not acquiesce in this measure. Never!…The loyalty of Kentucky is not to shaken by any mad act of the President…but she will never lift her own hand against the glorious fabric because he has blindly or criminally smitten it.[280]

As might be expected, the South was outraged. According to the Richmond Examiner:

> The Government of the United States has shot its bolt...It will have no effect on the South; its only serious importance is its indication that the North will stop at nothing in prosecuting the War...[it was] a call for the insurrection of four million slaves, and the inauguration of a reign of hell upon earth![281]

Official foreign reaction was disappointing, at first. British Prime Minister Palmerston criticized the Proclamation as encouraging lawlessness. However, public opinion in Great Britain was much more favorable, eventually forcing the government to abandon any inclination it might have had to modify its neutrality by recognizing the Confederacy. The document "rallied the liberal thought of Britain and the globe to the Union side."[282] Lincoln had succeeded in identifying the Union's cause with the struggle for freedom throughout the world.

Some fourteen years after the Proclamation, Frederick Douglass did as well as anyone in summarizing the response of his countrymen:

> Viewed from the genuine abolition ground, Mr. Lincoln seemed tardy, cold, dull, and indifferent; but measuring him by the sentiment of his country, a sentiment he was bound as a statesman to consult, he was swift, zealous, radical, and determined.[283]

As the weeks and months of 1863 passed, the impact of the Proclamation grew dramatically. Although the words of the document were unemotional and limited in scope, it came to symbolize much more than its words revealed. The general understanding of the purpose of the war changed, from one solely focused on preserving the political Union to one that was also being waged to end slavery. Consistent with the more ambitious goal, Lincoln ceased to emphasize colonization and began to encourage the enfranchisement and improvement of black citizens. "He had evolved from being a racial separatist into someone who viewed African Americans as potentially equal citizens of a color-blind democracy."[284]

Lincoln looked for an additional opportunity to explain to the public the meaning of the bloody and tragic conflict—to relate the purpose of the war to the basic values inherent in American liberty. That occasion arose on November 19, 1863, with an Address at Gettysburg, Pennsylvania during the dedication of a burial ground for those who died in the critical battle near the site. The first line of the Address, dating the founding of the nation in 1776, has become legendary in American history and is critical to Lincoln's purpose: "Four score and seven years ago, our fathers brought forth on this continent a new nation, conceived in liberty and dedicated to the proposition that all men are created equal." The Declaration of Independence was the document most relevant to the revitalization of liberty that Lincoln had achieved with the Emancipation Proclamation. In essence, he enlarged the concept of American liberty, at least as it had been practiced in the 19th century, to include the commitment to equal opportunity for all, which, he maintained, was inherent in the country's founding. He reminded his countrymen that, in 1776, America was "a new nation, conceived in Liberty, and dedicated to the proposition that all men are created equal." In 1863, as a result of the distortion represented by the expansion of slavery in the 19th century, it needed to move to a nation that had "a new birth of freedom." The purpose of the Civil War, then, after the Emancipation Proclamation, was to realize America's revitalized mission and show the world that the principle of equality would make it possible that "a government of the people, by the people, for the people, shall not perish from the earth."

By the end of 1863, after decisive Union military victories at Vicksburg, Gettysburg, and Chattanooga, Lincoln started planning for the reintegration of the Confederacy when victory was achieved. He developed his own Reconstruction policy and announced it in his Annual Message to Congress in December. It was a politically balanced program, sensitive to the need for reconciliation as well as to the promise of the Emancipation Proclamation. It provided that a state could re-enter the Union when at least 10 percent of its population vowed loyalty to the Union, including adherence to emancipation. Although Lincoln suggested that citizens should take loyalty oaths, he remained open to alternatives and to continuing dialogue. He later directed that "any proposition which embraces the restoration of peace, the integrity of the whole Union, and the abandonment of slavery...will be received and considered by the Executive government of the United States."[285]

The Presidential Reconstruction Plan did not go nearly as far as some Republicans in Congress wanted. They preferred to hold out for a drastic social and economic reorganization before any rebel state was readmitted. When Congress passed its own more radical Reconstruc-

tion Plan in June (the Wade-Davis Bill), requiring that a majority of
the citizens of a rebel state take an oath of past as well as future loyalty
to the Union as a condition for readmission, Lincoln refused to sign it
and the bill died on July 4, 1864 as a result of his pocket veto. The radicals in Congress were incensed, but, after General Sherman's victory
in the Battle of Atlanta in September, the country grew more unified
behind the President. He was re-elected by an overwhelming majority in November.

The limited nature of the Emancipation Proclamation created
momentum for a more complete solution. A Constitutional Amendment
abolishing slavery had been debated in Congress in the spring of 1864
but did not receive sufficient votes for passage. After his re-election, Lincoln endorsed the amendment and urged its passage in his Annual Message in December. On January 31, 1865, the Amendment passed
Congress and was sent to the states for approval. Lincoln did not live to
see the Thirteenth Amendment ratified, but it was declared adopted by
President Johnson's administration in December, 1865. Ironically, the
required two-thirds vote of the states was achieved with the support of
two Union slave states, Delaware and Kentucky, and eight states of the
former Confederacy that were recognized as states under Johnson's moderate reconstruction plan but not by the radicals in Congress. After the
Amendment was declared ratified, however, more than enough additional states approved to make the votes of the "Confederate 8" no longer
necessary. Thus, the promise of Lincoln's Emancipation Proclamation
was fulfilled and slavery was prohibited everywhere in the United States.

The passage of the Thirteenth Amendment was only the beginning of the struggle for equality of black Americans. Soon followed
the Fourteenth and Fifteenth Amendments granting the rights of due
process of law, equal protection of the laws, and the right to vote without discrimination based on race or previous status as a slave. And
each Southern state was subject to the requirements of Reconstruction, which was intended to ensure its government was dedicated to
the Union and to freedom. However, the years of Reconstruction
after the Civil War proved disappointing to many blacks as well as abolitionists and Northern reformers, largely due to the unrealistic expectations and hopes that followed emancipation. Some even called the
period "The Tragic Era." Instead of a vibrant economy, satisfied black
and white workers, and fair and efficient political systems, people often
saw stagnation, lethargy, and corruption. Blacks, in particular, had
hoped for significant land distribution and greater economic equality

than actually took place. And the Southern governments that eventually came to power were dominated by the white racism and greed that was all too familiar in the ante-bellum years.

Recent historians have shown, however, that these perceptions did not adequately take into account the great changes that came upon the South to the benefit of blacks, in particular, and American liberty, in general. Slavery was, in reality, overthrown, and replaced by a market economy with significant government regulation to help increase fairness. Black men and women succeeded to an impressive extent in raising themselves up and improving prospects for their families. And their relationship with white society was forever changed. They were put on a course, however gradual, which allowed each person an equal opportunity to develop his own potential.

Even though blacks suffered practical as well as legal discrimination in broad areas of civil rights during the Reconstruction period, they managed to endure these obstacles, create new businesses, educate their children, strengthen their churches and prepare for an ongoing struggle for freedom and equality within American society. None of this could have taken place without the Civil War, the Emancipation Proclamation, and the post war Constitutional Amendments. Although the struggle was to last well into the twentieth century, and is not yet fulfilled, the essential building blocks were put in place as a result of Lincoln's Presidency.

7. Lincoln's Legacy

How one evaluates Lincoln is likely to depend, first, on whether one believes that the Civil War was avoidable, and at what cost. The country paid an enormous price in humanity to settle its sectional and moral differences. More soldiers died in the Civil War than in any other American war and almost as many as in all the others combined. Over 620,000 died—more than 360,000 Union men and over 260,000 Confederates, although very recent scholarship analyzing census data shows that the figure was more likely 750,000[286] That was the equivalent at the time of one out of every fifty Americans! If the same proportion to population had prevailed in the Vietnam War, the battlefield death toll would have been 4 million.

The nation had tried unsuccessfully through six decades of increasingly vituperative political struggles to find a peaceful way to reconcile the political philosophy of North and South. The country's greatest political leaders had failed to abolish the cruel institution of slavery or even to negotiate a consensus for the future. It is highly unlikely that the country could have found a way to emancipate the slaves and preserve its principles of liberty without the cataclysm of war. Lincoln's election made it inevitable that the conflict would come during his term and his leadership ensured that, when it came, it would be fought for the redemption of American liberty and its singular role in the modern world.

To set an enduring example for mankind, Lincoln knew that the United States had to continue its expansion in order to acquire the resources necessary to keep its economy strong and growing. Only in that way could an individual American, through hard work and dedication, realize his full potential as he, himself, was able to do. Lincoln also realized that the country needed to find a way to prevent that expansion from being held hostage to the oppressive institution of slavery.

As a master of practical politics, Lincoln was always able creatively to balance political forces to arrive at the position best calculated to further his goals. He wanted to save the Union, but it had to be a Union that reflected his vision of American liberty. In the 1850's, this meant developing the ideas and the political means to reverse the momentum in favor of slavery that had bedeviled the country. When the war began, it meant nurturing the strongest possible Union coalition, by avoiding alienating the loyal slaveholding states as well as Unionist conservatives and Democrats. As the nature of the war changed and new political opportunities arose, it meant revitalizing American liberty by injecting an element of equality, while doing so in a way that respected both Constitutional constraints and the limits of human altruism. And as victory appeared likely, it meant ensuring the promise of the new birth of freedom while maximizing prospects for a harmonious national reunion.

Lincoln would disapprove of any assessment of him that concluded that he deserved any great credit or recognition of his accomplishments, particularly the issuance of the Emancipation Proclamation. Of that act, he wrote on April 4, 1864, "I claim not to have controlled events, but confess plainly that events have controlled me."[287] Consistent with his character, he appeared too modest and too humble. In truth, Lincoln was as politically skilled as any who has occupied the office of the President. He led the country through the greatest threat it had faced to its liberty and its unity, freeing it from what most believed was an unbreakable political paralysis. In a very real sense, Lincoln's entire political life was dedicated to doing so.

The founders of the nation believed that they were part of a unique experiment in the history of mankind. They wanted to prove that men could govern themselves and ensure human liberty. They hoped that their example would inspire people everywhere to do the same. Lincoln was deeply committed to the success of that experiment. He believed that his generation had to show that liberty need not devolve into factionalism and that self-government could succeed, even in a growing country with many different interest groups.

Lincoln realized that a country organized on that basis would have to take into account both the good and the bad in human nature. To him, the art of politics was to help his fellow men make decisions that would further the ideals on which the United States was founded. His genius lay in developing both the theory and practice to enable the public to support the political steps necessary to free themselves from the horrendous straitjacket of slavery. His heroism lay in providing the skilled leadership to see those steps through to a successful conclusion.

Lincoln believed that men were moved by ideas and that the great patriotic documents of the founding provided the greatest source of inspiration for his countrymen. By combining the idea of equality of all men in the Declaration of Independence, with the elements of liberty established in the Constitution, he was able to revitalize American political theory so it could inspire solutions to the problem of slavery. Anticipating the arguments of proslavery opponents, he developed persuasive historical explanations for the apparent vagueness of those documents as they applied to slavery and to American blacks. And he found a way to make the Constitution into a tool that enabled the national government to establish equality of opportunity for every American.

Like Jefferson, Lincoln had the capacity to articulate, in persuasive and stirring words, the ideals of America as he understood them, and convert them to universal truths. Unlike Jefferson, he was able to guide a politically divided country successfully toward the realization of those ideals. That is not to say that the country has even now fully realized the promise of equal opportunity that the Emancipation Proclamation symbolized. Yet it was firmly set on a course "to afford all, an unfettered start, and a fair chance, in the race of life."[288]

Lincoln redefined the mission of America, making its commitment to liberty more broadly applicable, and enabled the country to retain the admiration of the world well past his term of office, into the 21st century and, likely, beyond. He has also left his country with some principles to guide it as it attempts to live its redefined mission. These principles are as meaningful today, when America is the only superpower in a multicultural world, as they were in Lincoln's time.

First is the notion that the most important responsibility of American leaders is to ensure that both liberty and equal opportunity are real and vital for all Americans. And the most important moral duty of each citizen is to accept his fellow as worthy of the same rights and opportunities as he, regardless of a different origin, race, or religion. If the country is to set an example for the world, that example must be genuine and be there for all to see.

Second is the concept that political ideals are worth little if not coupled with practical political strategies to implement them. This demands leaders who resist temptation to self-interest or to demagoguery. And it requires that its citizens be educated in history and in political issues, and be aware of how to exercise their civic responsibilities.

Finally, we learn from Lincoln that a great President is one who has a vision consistent with American ideals, the life experience that allows him or her to be realistic about human nature and politics, and the character that permits fortitude, forbearance, and flexibility as each become necessary. The continued vitality of America's mission depends on the existence of such leaders.

CHAPTER 5.

Woodrow Wilson and the Application of America's Mission to the World

The First World War, coming early in Woodrow Wilson's first term, presented both a momentous challenge and a leadership opportunity for the United States and for the new President. America had become one of the most powerful nations in the world and was beginning to emerge from its century-long, relative isolation from international affairs. The war hastened that emergence. Wilson needed to determine how America would play its role on the world stage. His great contribution to American history was to develop a unique approach to international leadership, one that was based on commitment to human liberty and to world peace. He designed a path to a new world order, which he hoped would henceforth be identified with the United States.

The Coming of Age of America and Wilson's Unique Place

Woodrow Wilson was a child during the Civil War, when the future of slavery convulsed the country. Domestic survival and, later, critical economic growth, occupied the efforts of the country's political leaders throughout the last half of the 19th century. By the time Wilson was ready to lead the country, in the early 20th century, international issues and rivalries became relevant to the nature of American liberty.

When he was elected President in 1912, Wilson did imagine that he would face a world transformed by military cataclysm and political and technological revolution. Nor did he anticipate the need to confront foreign challenges more serious than any since the onset of the

War of 1812. In the intervening century, the country's foreign policy had essentially reflected George Washington's admonition in his Farewell Address that America should avoid "permanent" alliances.[289] Washington was convinced that the young country, blessed by distance from Europe and by its own natural resources, could avoid the recurrent warfare and hatred engendered by the traditional European balance of power system. James Monroe applied that advice to both North and South America when he declared in the Doctrine bearing his name that European interference with the independence of countries in the hemisphere would no longer be acceptable. For the balance of the nineteenth century, American political leaders viewed Europe as the 'old world,' in whose machinations and power politics the United States need not and should not become involved. Senator Henry Cabot Lodge of Massachusetts, later to become Woodrow Wilson's nemesis, said in 1889: "Our relations with foreign nations today fill but a slight place in American politics, and excite generally only a languid interest."[290]

The United States had grown rapidly in economic and political strength during its first hundred years, particularly after the Civil War abolished the institution of slavery, the great threat to the Union. By 1900, the country was one of the most powerful in the world, producing more than half the world's cotton, corn, copper, and oil; more than one third of its steel, iron, and silver; and almost one third of its coal and gold.[291] Its economic status brought about political influence and thrust it in the middle of the quest for colonies and export markets then motivating the European powers.

William McKinley, elected President in 1896, participated in colonial annexation and big power diplomacy, but only reluctantly. He commenced the Spanish-American War in 1898 after "jingoist" journalism elevated the sinking of the Battleship Maine in Havana harbor to a humiliation of national honor. Victory brought control of both Puerto Rico and the Philippines. When combined with its previous ownership of Hawaii and Samoa, the United States became a leading imperialist power.

Theodore Roosevelt became President in 1901 and continued to exert international power, but without McKinley's reluctance. His "big stick" diplomacy transformed the Monroe Doctrine from one that proscribed European intervention in Latin America to one that justified United States military action whenever it deemed that police power by a "civilized nation" was necessary. He used his "Roosevelt Corollary" to obtain effective control of Panama and the right to build a trans-oceanic canal across its isthmus. William Howard Taft succeeded Roosevelt in 1909 and conducted what has been called "dollar diplomacy," under which American foreign policy, particularly in Latin America and China, seemed governed solely by the objective of furthering American financial gain.

During Woodrow Wilson's first year as President, he declared that the foreign policy of his administration would be different from that of his predecessors and would set a better example for his successors. It would be concerned more with "human rights, national integrity, and opportunity" than with "material interests."[292] Wilson viewed his political role through a religious prism. He believed it was his duty to work to implement God's moral law here on earth—to use ethics and Christian principles to solve worldly problems. Politics provided his opportunity for moral action in the service of mankind, based on his passionate belief that the United States was unique, in its birth and in its mission of nurturing and spreading liberty.

The outbreak of War among European countries in September 1914 provided Wilson with an opportunity to change America's approach to the world. The policy direction he chose has set the pattern for the nation to the present day. He gave its foreign policy a moral basis beyond selfish accumulation of power and wealth, calling upon the nation to make painful human and financial sacrifices. After Wilson asked Congress to declare war on Germany 1n 1917, more than 3 million men were drafted into the military—over 3 per cent of the population, the equivalent of almost 9 million men in 2005. The scope of federal power was dramatically increased, a steeply progressive national income tax was enacted, and many civil liberties were curtailed to stifle dissent and encourage support of the military effort.

Wilson well understood the negative effects of war, yet he led the nation to an intense involvement in European and world politics, one that he believed could be justified only in the service of a new world order of liberty and peace. His leadership inspired not only his own citizens, but people around the globe. He became the dominating force in the international arena at a time of crisis and uncertainty. Winston Churchill has written:

It seems no exaggeration to pronounce that the action of the United States with its repercussions on the history of the world depended, during the awful period of Armageddon, upon the workings of this man's mind and spirit to the exclusion of almost every other factor; and that he played a part in the fate of nations incomparably more direct and personal than any other man.[293]

Wilson's influence was to be felt more deeply well after his Presidency ended, although this could not have been predicted in the immediate aftermath. His own country rejected the Peace Treaty and The League of Nations he labored so hard to establish, and, in the two decades following the First World War, essentially abdicated the leadership role he prescribed for it. It was not until the experience of the Second World War that America and the world clearly understood the lessons Wilson tried to teach. His vision was vindicated with the establishment of the United Nations as the world's best hope for peace, and, most importantly, with the realization of the United States' role as global leader in the service of liberty. His view of America's international mission is even more relevant to the problems of the early 21st century than it was during his lifetime—he would advise strongly against a militaristic, unilateral foreign policy in dealing with the proliferation of nuclear weapons, global economic inequality, and the rise of terrorism.

2. The Coming of Age of Woodrow Wilson

Woodrow Wilson[294] was born on December 26, 1856 in Staunton, Virginia and always considered himself a Southerner. His family moved to Augusta, Georgia when he was two years old, then to Columbia, South Carolina when he was fourteen. One of his earliest recollections was the prediction of a neighbor in November 1860, that, because Lincoln had been elected, he was sure there would be war.[295] He had vivid Civil War memories of wounded Confederate soldiers, Union prisoners in a stockade near Augusta, and widespread fear of an impending vengeful march by Union General Sherman. Those images remained with him, and he brought to the Presidency a profound aversion to the suffering of war. As a child, he shared his father's loyalty to the Confederacy, and, after the war, witnessed the confusion and political disorganization of the Reconstruction period. Yet, he had little patience for those who continued to keep alive hatred of the North and who could not adjust to the Civil War verdict. Although he was proud of his heritage, he believed it fortunate that his region had lost the war because his love for the South told him that its way of life had to change.[296] Wilson continued to show a Southern identity by his allegiance to the Democratic Party and by his tolerance of segregation as an inevitable part of the South's post-war transition.

Woodrow's father, Joseph Ruggles Wilson, was a learned Presbyterian Minister who had a deep and abiding effect on his son's development and personality. Reverend Wilson supervised the education of all his children, but gave particular attention to Woodrow, his eldest son.[297] He had exacting standards, emphasizing literature, religion, and language skills, both oral and written, insisting that his son use correct grammar and an expansive vocabulary to express ideas.[298]

His mother, Jessie Woodrow Wilson, was the daughter of one Presbyterian minister and the sister of another. The comfort and love she provided to her son balanced the drive for intellectual and moral perfection his father promoted. Jessie's devotion was matched by that of Woodrow's two sisters and set a pattern of female emotional support and admiration that he needed throughout his life, later to be provided by his two wives and his daughters, as well as his friends. His prime biographer has written that "his most enduring friends were admiring, uncritical women." [299]

From childhood, Woodrow possessed a determination to succeed and to do great things, partially as a result of the demands and expectations of his father. Although some have characterized the elder Wilson as domineering, Arthur S. Link concluded that the father "evoked these talents with measured encouragement and love. This relationship was ...liberating and creative for both partners."[300] Woodrow said as an adult that his father was "the best instructor, the most inspiring companion...that a youngster ever had."[301]

The future President's educational achievements were complicated by a learning disability, possibly dyslexia, a condition not understood at that time.[302] To compensate for the burden of reading, the youngster developed an ability to focus exclusively on his text and perfected a photographic memory. To overcome the difficulty of writing, he taught himself shorthand at age 16 and used the newly invented typewriter in his young adulthood. He acquired the capacity to write sentences only after they were fully developed in his brain, and learned to be a great orator without often using more than brief notes. In the words of one historian, "In conquering his disabilities in learning and communicating, Wilson liberated a powerful intelligence from what could have been withering bondage."[303]

Domestic life included daily prayer and Bible reading, and regular church attendance. Each Sunday, Woodrow would listen to his father's sermons, and each day to oral prayers. The family believed that they were expected to do God's will on earth by living the ethical values of Christianity and serving their fellow men. They believed in God's design for a moral universe, whose laws governed nations as well as men. Young Woodrow was taught that "God controls history and uses men and nations to achieve His preordained purposes."[304] He never lost faith in that idea. Later in his life, he reportedly said of religion:

> *My* life would not be worth living if it were not for the driving power of religion, for *faith*, pure and simple…There are people who believe only so far as they understand—that seems to me presumptuous and sets their understanding as the standard of the universe…I am sorry for such people.[305]

His ambition as a young man to play a role in the politics of his country was motivated by his faith and his wish to serve God by improving the prospects of others. At the height of his efforts to end the First World War, he said, "We are to be an instrument in the hands of God to see that liberty is made secure for mankind."[306]

At the age of 16, Woodrow entered Davidson, a Presbyterian College in North Carolina, but left the following June, possibly after experiencing poor health. He remained at home the following year, learning Greek, Latin, and shorthand, leaving in 1875 to attend Princeton University. He did quite well academically, studying modern history, politics and literature and graduating in the top third of his class in 1879. He hoped to use his literary and oratorical skill to become a leader of men. According to John Morton Blum:

> The boy dreamed of being the prime minister of a cabinet
> of English gentlemen, of being the articulate leader of a

party subscribing to and ennobled by his purposes, the admired orator, effective alike debating with his peers or instructing his constituency. All Wilson's life this dream lasted, altered only in detail to fit changing circumstances.[307]

Wilson dropped his given first name of "Thomas" and became formally known as "Woodrow" shortly after his graduation. Ignoring his father's wish that he enter the ministry, he followed a path that might more readily lead to a political career by enrolling in law school at the University of Virginia. In 1882, Wilson moved to Atlanta to practice law, and was admitted to the Bar, but quickly found that the legal profession did not satisfy his intellectual interests; he was less intrigued by the problems of individuals than he was the destiny of groups or nations.[308] In the fall of 1883 he left his law practice, intent on becoming a professor of politics or history, and attended graduate school at Johns Hopkins University in Baltimore.

Prior to leaving Atlanta, Wilson met his first wife, Ellen Louise Axson, daughter of a Presbyterian Minister from Rome, Georgia. She was a cultured and sensitive woman who shared his interests in literature and art. They were married in Savannah on June 24, 1885 and later had three children—Margaret, born in 1886, a son Jessie Woodrow, born in 1887, and a second daughter, Eleanor Randolph in 1889. Throughout their marriage, Ellen provided the love and devotion without which her husband would have felt unfulfilled.

Wilson is the only President to earn a Ph. D. Degree, which he did in 1886, after having written two books—*Congressional Government* and *The Modern Democratic State*. In these works, he extolled the democratic form of government, particularly the British model combining legislative and executive power, but cautioned that "democracy required a well-educated and enlightened people, wide public debate, [and] a citizenry with a common purpose." He concluded that countries could achieve democracy only gradually, "through a period of political tutelage."[309]

Wilson began teaching at Bryn Mawr College, then became professor of history at Wesleyan University. He reached the pinnacle of his academic career after joining the faculty at his alma mater, Princeton, in 1890. He taught constitutional law, international law, English common law, administration and public law, all with enthusiasm and grace that earned the respect of his students. The philosophic basis for Wilson's efforts to bring peace and international order after the First World War is reflected in the substance of his Princeton lectures. He taught that Christianity was the precursor for modern notions of international law by setting out moral principles for all people to follow. The purpose of international law was to overcome the chaos of war and the denial of human rights by means of a sense of moral obligation towards order and justice emanating from the "universal conscience of mankind." This conscience developed from an appreciation of God and the use of human reason, which he believed was particularly prevalent in countries with representative government and freedom of thought.

As President of Princeton from 1902 to 1910, Wilson would further develop these ideas in light of his view that the United States was unique among nations; it had overcome the class-based systems common in Europe and had developed a commitment to genuine equality of opportunity. The country had welcomed people of all nationalities, religions, and races and had achieved a level of justice and human welfare that had no peer. America, thereby, had a special mission to serve all mankind by leading a moral crusade for world peace, unity and justice.

Wilson gradually became well known and admired as an important political thinker. He also gained a national reputation as an educational reformer after having modified Princeton's traditional curriculum, reduced the size of classes, and implemented a tutorial system. His attempt to eliminate exclusive, sometimes class-based, eating clubs and to establish a more democratic residential pattern, although popular with many outsiders, encountered significant opposition within alumni and faculty circles and eventually led to his resignation.

Urged by prominent Democrats to run for Governor of New Jersey in 1910, Wilson seized the opportunity as the start of a possible path to the Presidency, a goal that was the logical objective of his moral and political philosophy. After his election as Governor, he rejected the support of corrupt political bosses and implemented many reforms supported by the new progressive movement, including direct primaries, utility rate regulation, campaign finance limits, a workmen's compensation law, and antitrust laws. His accomplishments in such a brief period attracted attention across the country, and he became a featured speaker at Democratic Party events, particularly in the West and South. Capping a meteoric political rise, he was nominated as the Democratic Candidate for President in 1912 at the conclusion of a long and contentious convention, from which he emerged as a progressive reformer, owing little to party bosses or to Wall Street financiers.

The campaign proved to be one of the most spirited in American history, pitting Wilson against incumbent President William Howard Taft, the Republican candidate, former Republican President Theodore Roosevelt, now the candidate of the new Progressive, or "Bull Moose" Party, and Eugene V. Debs, the Socialist. Wilson ran as the advocate for individual opportunity, against corruption in both government and corporations. With Taft and Roosevelt splitting traditional Republican votes, Wilson garnered 42% of the popular vote yet won all but 7 states, achieving a landslide in the Electoral College.

The campaign provided Wilson the opportunity to share his philosophy of liberty and of America's mission with the American public:

> I believe that God planted in us visions of liberty…that we
> are chosen and prominently chosen to show the way to the
> nations of the world how they shall walk in the paths of liberty.[310]

The voters granted Wilson the opportunity to implement his faith-based political ideas.

3. The Coming of the World War and Wilson's Struggle for Neutrality

Woodrow Wilson came into office in 1913 determined to revitalize liberty at home and to encourage peace and democracy abroad. In his Inaugural Address, he lamented that the great material gains of America's growing economy had been accomplished at the cost of "lives snuffed out, of energies overtaxed and broken, the fearful physical and spiritual cost to the men and women and children upon whom the dead weight and burden of it all has fallen pitilessly the years through."[311] He wanted to end the exploitation of workers, improve the inadequate provisions for the health and welfare of the majority of the population, and begin the process of humanizing the American capitalist system. Wilson's domestic agenda was broad, ambitious, and strikingly successful. By establishing strong leadership of his party's majority in both Houses of Congress, thus blending the power of the executive and legislative branches, he was able to pass an impressive amount of precedent-setting progressive legislation. He began a revolution in the scope of the federal government and permanently transformed the role of the President as political leader. In his first term, Wilson led Congress in lowering tariffs, enacting the first graduated income tax, establishing the Federal Reserve System, creating the Federal Trade Commission to prevent unfair competition, strengthening antitrust laws, passing the Federal Farm Loan act to provide easy credit for farmers, enacting an eight hour day for railroad workers and prohibiting child labor. These measures helped to increase competition among businesses and economic opportunity for individuals. They made the capitalist economy fairer and more humane for the average American and established the framework for further social and economic reform under Presidents Franklin Roosevelt, Harry Truman, John Kennedy and Lyndon Johnson.

In the area of international affairs, the President intended to continue to avoid European balance of power politics and to abandon the aggressive foreign policy of Presidents McKinley, Roosevelt and Taft. He believed that, from the time of the Spanish-American War, the United States was primarily motivated by selfish economic goals, too often implemented by military intervention—in Cuba, the Philippines, Latin America and the Far East. Early in his administration, in marking the opening of the Panama Canal, he declared "the United States will never again seek one additional foot of territory by conquest."[312] He intended to lead the world to peace by moral example and persuasion, and to further democracy by diplomacy and personal intervention—a new paradigm for the behavior of a great power.

Wilson at first had difficulty applying these innovative principles. Supreme confidence in his own altruistic motives, and the ready availability of American naval power, led him to use overbearing methods, although short of actual military invasion, to try to help establish democratic governments in Haiti, the Dominican Republic, the Philippines, and China. He had to re-learn as President a lesson that as Professor he had taught to his students—democracy cannot be imposed on a country by a foreign power, no matter how well intentioned the motive. It must be nurtured from within and grow over time. Wilson is not the only President, before or since, that learned that lesson as a result of hard experience. But the greatest challenge to Wilson's ideals, and the greatest opportunity for their success, came with the onset of war in Europe—a war that was to become the widest and most terrifying yet faced by mankind.

For more than two hundred years, European nations tried to maintain a political balance of power wherein no single country was permitted to dominate. Alliances were made and broken, economic relations adjusted, wars fought and settled, and colonies distributed on the basis of that principle. At the beginning of the 20th century, the European balance focused on five countries—England, France, Germany, Austria-Hungary, and Russia. Their relationships primarily determined the peace of the world, with only the United States and Japan having comparable influence.

The German Empire, founded in 1871 by Otto von Bismarck after victory in the Franco-Prussian War, industrialized faster than its rivals. Its economy benefited from strong technological capability, a high quality educational system, efficient government organization, and a disciplined, productive work force. Germany pursued a diplomatic and military policy intended to win a pre-eminent geo-political status that it had already earned in the economic sphere. In response, England, France and Russia formed the Triple Entente whose goal was to checkmate the rise of German power in the world. To avoid isolation and protect its growth, Germany joined with the Empire of Austria-Hungary and with Italy to create the Triple Alliance. Competition between the two alliances—in the build-up of military might, in the quest for colonies around the world, and in economic development—resulted in regular diplomatic crises, threats of war, and actual limited wars after the turn of the century. The urge to national power and imperial aggrandizement appeared to be leading to military conflict, although recent historians have cautioned against assuming that world war was inevitable.[313]

The political balance of power of a world of aristocracy and slow economic growth was ill-suited to the twentieth century reality of rapid social change, distribution of power to mass workers, and swift technological development. The Austro-Hungarian Empire, or the "Dual Monarchy," was particularly vulnerable to the political pressures emanating from new social and economic forces. It was home to a variety of nationalities that were susceptible to the lure of the ideologies of nationalism, democracy, and socialism. Its Hapsburg rulers had done little to bring about political and economic reform, and the flash point for cataclysm proved to be the assassination of Archduke Franz Ferdinand, heir to the Austrian throne, in Sarajevo on June 28, 1914, by a disgruntled Serbian national. Soon thereafter, the Dual Monarchy declared war on Serbia.

The system of alliances took hold, with the Triple Alliance (minus Italy, which had changed sides) supporting the Hapsburgs and the Triple Entente backing the Serbs and their Russian allies. [In the remainder of this Chapter we will use the more common wartime identifiers, with the Triple Alliance becoming the "Central Powers," and the Triple Entente becoming the "Allied Powers."] The momentum of military mobilization plans laid by the participants since the turn of the 20th century made it difficult for the crisis to be ended without war.[314]

None of the belligerents expected the long-lasting horror that the war became.

> All the general staffs had planned on a short, decisive war; no country had made military or economic preparations for a long one…statesmen had been haunted by the fear…that war might stir up more popular revolutions. Only a good quick victory could avert this dreadful possibility [and] serve to distract their people from the political problems at home.[315]

The world would learn very soon after the outbreak of the conflict that the nature of war had changed. Whereas, in the United States' Civil War, armies consisted of up to 100,000 men and battles included at most tens of thousands, the new face of "total" war meant that armies numbered in the millions and battles in the hundreds of thousands. At the first Battle of the Marne in September, 1914, the warring sides suffered more than 500,000 dead or wounded, and by the end of the first calendar year, France recorded almost 1 million casualties and Germany more than 500,000. By the close of the war, a staggering 7,000,000 soldiers had been killed in battle.

At the outset, the United States saw no reason to become directly involved; its traditional approach to foreign affairs maintained studied disinterest in the rivalries of European politics or alliances. President Wilson issued a Proclamation of Neutrality on August 4, 1914 and two weeks later told the Senate and the country that "Every man who really loves America will act and speak in the true spirit of neutrality." He said this knowing that many Americans would feel a natural sympathy with one side or the other. "The people of the United States are drawn from many nations, and chiefly from the nations now at war...Some will wish one nation, others another, to succeed in the momentous struggle. It will be easy to excite passion and difficult to allay it."[316]

[During this period, President Wilson lost his wife, Ellen, who died on August 6, 1914. Her death left him bereft and it was remarkable that he was able to function as well as he did. A man who needed a woman's love as an integral part of his life, he soon met and courted a wealthy widow, Edith Bolling Galt, a more assertive and less traditional woman than Ellen. He married Edith in late 1915 and she was to play an increasingly critical and influential role for the remainder of his years in office.]

Four weeks after Wilson declared American neutrality, he ironically foreshadowed the issues that were to end the neutrality three years later, saying of the war: "It affects us directly and palpably almost as if we were participants...We shall pay the bill, though we did not deliberately incur it."[317] America's traditional way of viewing itself as in a new world, separate and apart from the old one, could no longer be tenable; its trade and economic health were directly affected by the conflict. First, the control of the seas by Great Britain, resulting in a *de facto* blockade of continental Europe, made it difficult for any neutral country, including the United States, to trade to any great extent with the Central Powers.

Second, in order to maintain lucrative trade, the United States extended loans to Great Britain and France that were critical to their ability to carry on their economies while supplying their armies.[318] These actions created common interests between the United States and the Allied Powers, and brought significant benefits to the United States' economy. At the same time, they aroused great resentment in Germany and among the sizeable number of Americans with German background.

Finally, Wilson had to maneuver his neutrality policy carefully between the British and German maritime war strategies as each side ignored aspects of international law that hindered the strategic goals it set for itself. The British systematically interfered with the traditional right of neutral nations attempting to trade with the Central Powers by restricting passage of both military and civilian items, whether shipped directly to those countries, or, indirectly through third nation intermediaries. Given these restrictions, which significantly harmed their ability to wage war and feed their population, the Germans felt they had no choice but to try to overcome the superiority of the British fleet by laying mines and employing the submarine or "U-boat." Use of this new weapon, difficult to detect and defend against, challenged traditional rights of neutral nations by bringing modern warfare to bear on merchant shipping and innocent civilians. Diplomatic historian Thomas A. Bailey summarized the issues this way:

> ...when the Germans argued that because of the 'unusual' conditions of this war they too were justified in departing from then rules, they were met with the Allied Argument that torpedoing vessels without warning was so inhumane as to be unjustifiable. The Germans replied that the slow starvation of a vast civilian population by means of an illegal blockade was far more inhumane.[319]

On May 7, 1915, defying maritime rules protecting passenger ships, a German submarine torpedoed without warning the British liner *Lusitania*, off the coast of Ireland, causing the death of 1198 travelers, including 124 Americans. This act against innocent civilians shocked the world and turned a great deal of public opinion against Germany. Yet, neither the American public nor Congress favored entering the war at that point and abandoning America's traditional isolation from Europe. The President placed the popular sentiment in a moral context in a speech three days after the sinking:

> The example of America must be the example not merely of peace because it will not fight, but of peace because peace is the healing and elevating influence of the world and strife is not. There is such a thing as a man being too proud to fight.[320]

Wilson soon came to realize that recurring German submarine attacks were making it politically and psychologically more difficult to avoid war. He relaxed his opposition to armed preparedness during formal neutrality as well as his opposition to a large, standing army, setting a new direction for America. On December 7, 1915, he submitted to Congress a national defense plan consisting of a five-year naval buildup, an increase in the then small regular army, and a strengthening of the army reserves. These legislative proposals met with success six months later, when Congress passed the National Defense Act, providing for expansion of the army to 175,000 immediately and to 223,000 over five years. It authorized a National Guard of 450,000 men and an Officers Reserve Training Corps (forerunner to the present R.O.T.C.) at the nation's universities.

To avoid being drawn into the war, Wilson took action to help bring it to an end. He sent his most trusted political advisor, Colonel Edward House of Texas, to London, Paris, and Berlin to begin an attempt at mediation. The effort resulted in a Memorandum issued on February 22, 1916 by House and British Foreign Secretary Edward Gray, which provided that the United States would call a peace conference to end the war on the principles of disarmament and a postwar "League of Nations." The conference would be convened at a time the Allies believed was propitious, and the document stated that the United States would 'probably' enter the war if the Germans refused an armistice or proved unreasonable at the table. Wilson added the word 'probably' to the original draft, in order to keep his options open and to increase his bargaining power with the British and French.

The House-Gray Memorandum was a declaration that the era of United States isolation from Europe and the world was over.[321] The future of American liberty would thenceforth be linked with European politics, economics, and war. But if the United States eventually entered the existing conflict, it would do so in the name of the larger principles of peace and democracy, not merely for the shipping rights of neutral nations.

The Europeans were not yet ready for Wilson's mediation at a peace conference, as both sides became progressively more committed to what seemed like unending slaughter. As diplomatic historian and former Secretary of State Henry Kissinger has written:

Once plunged into war, the leaders of Europe became so obsessed with fratricide, so maddened by the progressive destruction of an entire generation of their young men, that victory turned into its own reward, regardless of the ruins on which that triumph would have to be erected.[322]

After the Germans torpedoed the French steamer *Sussex* without prior warning on March 24, 1916, resulting in both injury and loss of life, including some Americans, President Wilson threatened to break diplomatic relations. In its *Sussex* Pledge, the German Government yielded to the threat by promising not to attack passenger and freight vessels without warning and offering protection for passengers and crew, provided Great Britain showed "respect for the laws of humanity." While the Pledge brought a period of maritime calm, during which Germany expressed regret for the prior sinking of the *Lusitania*, the prospects for maintaining neutrality were growing dimmer and the window for ending the war was rapidly closing.

4. Wilson's Visionary Plan for Peace

The President wanted his effort for peace to have a distinctly American theme, one that was consistent with the country's founding principles and with his own dedication to a non-aggressive foreign policy. He found that theme in the idea of a world organization designed to further both peace and liberty. In a speech on May 27, 1916 before the League to Enforce Peace, a group advocating the establishment of just such an organization, he assured the world that the United States "was prepared to abandon its historic isolation and join a postwar League of Nations to prevent aggression and war."

For those Americans who hoped that it was still possible to remain distant from European conflict, he noted that "our own rights as a nation, the liberties, the privileges, and the property of our people have been profoundly affected…We are participants, whether we would or not, in the life of the world." Wilson called for "a new and more wholesome diplomacy" to protect world peace, specifically, "some feasible method of acting in concert." He urged that "the nations of the world must band themselves together to see that [the principle of public right] prevails as against any sort of selfish aggression." The first principle of

public right was "that every people has a right to choose the sovereignty under which they shall live," foreshadowing his later campaign
to make the world 'safe for democracy.' To establish his and the
nation's credibility as an unselfish mediator, Wilson pledged that
"There is nothing that the United States wants for itself that any other
nation has." He concluded by prescribing a "universal association of
the nations...to prevent any war begun either contrary to treaty
covenants or without warning and full submission of the causes to the
opinion of the world—a virtual guarantee of territorial integrity and
political independence."[323]

The immediate response to the speech was a tremendous out-
burst of applause and excitement, and the accolades only increased
with time. The journalist Walter Lippmann wrote at the time that "In
historic significance it is easily the most important diplomatic event
that our generation has known."[324] Historians have since recognized
it as America's "farewell to isolation"[325] and as a historical landmark
equivalent in the twentieth century to the Monroe Doctrine in the
nineteenth.[326] It is as if Wilson's entire life had been leading up to this
propitious moment in the midst of the most tragic war civilization had
known. Here was an opportunity to combine his moral dedication to
peace and justice, his passionate commitment to liberty, and his determination to lead other men toward noble political goals. To do so, his
countrymen had to be persuaded that their own peace and security
required the nation to take an active role in international affairs.

The idea for the international organization of nations about
which Wilson spoke had originated with Theodore Roosevelt.
Awarded the Nobel Peace Prize in 1910 for his successful effort to end
the earlier Russo-Japanese War, he had said in his acceptance address:

> It would be a master stroke if those great powers honestly
> bent on peace would form a League of Peace, not only to
> keep the peace among themselves, but to prevent, by force
> if necessary, its being broken by others.[327]

After the World War began, Roosevelt continued his advocacy,
urging "a great world agreement among the civilized military powers
to back righteousness by force...an efficient world league for the peace
of righteousness."[328] In June, 1915, his Republican colleague, Senator
Henry Cabot Lodge of Massachusetts, joined the call for international

enforcement of peace; yet, Lodge was later to oppose Wilson's League. Prophetically, Lodge gave his recommended organization the name "united nations."[329]

The war stimulated many private groups in the United States and Europe to work for a new international structure, including the American Women's Peace Party and the British League of Nations Association. Peace advocates viewed the unprecedented brutality as proof that war could no longer be seen as an acceptable outcome of national policy, particularly not in a world that was becoming economically interdependent. They put pressure on their governments to reform the international system and establish an organization to keep the peace.[330]

The most influential American organization was the aforementioned League to Enforce Peace (LEP), formed in June, 1915, by many prominent Americans, including former President Taft and A. Lawrence Lowell, President of Harvard University. The LEP supported a "League of Nations" whose members would use both economic and military power against any other member who commits aggression and starts a war. Inherent was a willingness to abandon America's isolation from international affairs beyond its own hemisphere and a readiness to take on responsibility in other parts of the world.

Notable among prominent American politicians who opposed the idea was William Jennings Bryan, a two-time unsuccessful Democratic candidate for President and Wilson's former Secretary of State. Bryan likened the concept to "a policy of fighting the devil with fire." Senator William E. Borah, a leading isolationist and Republican from Idaho, later went further in criticizing the idea of a League: "other nations [could] make war upon the United States if we refuse to submit some vital issue of ours to the decision of some European or Asiatic nations. This approaches...moral treason."[331]

According to his brother-in-law, Stockton Axson, Wilson adopted the idea of a League with enforcement power shortly after the outbreak of the war.[332] He made that commitment public in his speech before the LEP, although he had revealed to diplomats his willingness to join the League in the House-Gray Memorandum three months earlier.

When he ran for re-election in 1916, Wilson wrote and inserted into the Democratic Platform a clear commitment to the idea:

...it is the duty of the United States to join with the other
nations of the world in any feasible association...to prevent
any war begun either contrary to treaty covenants or without warning and frank submission of the provocation and
causes to the opinion of mankind.[333]

Most Americans were still opposed to military intervention and
very grateful to Wilson for having avoided it. During the election
campaign, he was hailed as the man "who kept us out of war." On that
basis, together with support for his progressive domestic programs,
Wilson was re-elected in a close vote, defeating Republican Charles
Evans Hughes, formerly Governor of New York and United States
Supreme Court Justice. Despite his victory, the President knew it
would be much more difficult to avoid military involvement in his second term as the belligerents attempted to break military stalemate by
employing more fearful weapons, a wider range of tactics, and greater
numbers of soldiers.

An emboldened Germany planned to resume and increase submarine warfare, having interpreted Wilson's election as a directive to
him to continue to avoid military involvement. The President "had
begun to despair at the evidently endless, fruitless, man-devouring car-
nage of the Western Front."[334] He feared that the unlimited escalation
of violence would kindle resentment "that can never cool and despairs
engendered from which there can be no recovery." On December 18,
1916, he directed Secretary of State Lansing, to request that each
involved nation specify its war aims so that he could facilitate a peace
conference and reach a compromise end to the war. Wilson offered
the establishment of a "league of nations to ensure peace and justice
throughout the world." He hoped that the prospect of an international
organization providing collective action against aggression would be
reassuring to those nations concerned about their future security.[335]

Wilson publicly described his concept of a just peace in the historic "Peace Without Victory" Address delivered before the Senate on
January 22, 1917. He called for a peace settlement that met the military objectives of *neither* side, because "victory would mean peace
forced upon the loser, a victor's terms imposed on the vanquished. It
would be accepted in humiliation, under duress...and would leave...a
bitter memory upon which peace would rest...as upon quicksand.
Only a peace between equals can last." He pointed to an international

"concert of power which will make it virtually impossible that any such catastrophe should ever overwhelm us again." That organization would require that "a force be created as a guarantor of the permanency of the settlement so much greater than the force of any nation now engaged or any alliance hitherto formed."

To encourage previously isolationist-minded Americans to support such a "League for Peace," Wilson outlined a peace based on the principles of liberty on which the United States was founded: "No peace can last, or ought to last, which does not recognize and accept the principle that governments derive all their just powers from the consent of the governed, and that no right anywhere exists to hand peoples about from sovereignty to sovereignty as if they were property."

He asked the people of the world to accept the principle of the Monroe Doctrine as universal: "that no nation should seek to extend its polity over any other nation or people, but that every people should be left free to determine its own polity, its own way of development, unhindered, unthreatened, unafraid, the little along with the great and powerful." Embodying what he perceived as the hopes of all those who yearned for peace and liberty he said, "I would fain believe I am speaking for the silent mass of mankind everywhere."[336]

The Peace Without Victory Address, for the first time in history, linked the idea of liberty and its future prospects with the concept of an international organization to keep the peace. For Wilson, the welfare of the United States and the vibrancy of the liberty on which it was founded would be greatly strengthened by a dynamic, cooperative world organization that encouraged the development of liberty everywhere. It was not solely an idealist's vision, but the prescription of a realist, as well. As John Milton Cooper, Jr., has written, "He contended that international order must rest upon self-government because satisfaction of that fundamental 'common interest' was indispensable to the assurance of lasting peace."[337] He envisioned a world reformed along the American model—liberal and capitalist, with free trade, freedom of the seas, and equal access to markets and raw materials.[338] Wilson assumed that a world made up of free nations would cooperate effectively in the interests of world harmony. It is an assumption that has yet to be fully tested.

All President Wilson's subsequent efforts, both during and after the war, were intended to ensure the realization of both liberty and

international peace. His great challenge was to persuade his own people and European leaders of the rightness of his path. The former
were being torn by both isolationist tendencies and interventionist
politicians, and the latter were being pressured by the desires for
revenge of their own war-ravaged populations.

5. Momentum for War

On January 31, 1917, the German government responded to the
request for a statement of war aims by describing its own version of
territorial victory and by declaring that it was resuming unrestricted
submarine warfare, including the option of sinking any ship, from
whatever nation, without warning. That its actions might precipitate
a crisis, including American involvement in the fighting, was a risk the
German government was willing to take. It believed Germany could
wreak havoc on the high seas, starve out England, and achieve victory
before the Americans could organize effective military intervention.[339]
Blinded by their desire for a decisive military victory, the Germans
overlooked the likelihood that a less bellicose strategy might also have
weakened Britain economically while, at the same time, kept the
United States out of the war.[340]

Wilson and his Cabinet considered the appropriate reaction.
Secretary of State Lansing felt that peace could be achieved only by
means of a victory for the Allied Powers, and urged United States
entry on their side. But President Wilson 'shocked' the Secretary by
stating that "probably greater justice would be done if the conflict
ended in a draw," although "he could make no clarion calls for a mere
draw when the nation entered the war—the national end had to be victory; but his hope remained peace without victory."[341] Lansing should
not have been so surprised. Wilson had always believed that all the
belligerents had been, to some degree, responsible for the origins of
the war. According to Arthur S. Link, the President was convinced
that:

> All belligerents believed they were fighting for their exis-
> tence, that they all wanted a smashing victory in order to
> increase their power, win new territory, and impose crush-
> ing indemnities upon their enemies. Such a settlement, he

was convinced, would inevitably generate another war within the near future. Hence Wilson believed that the best settlement would be a stalemate ending in a peace settlement based largely upon the status quo ante bellum.[342]

Wilson and the Cabinet decided to break diplomatic relations with Germany with the lingering but flickering hope to avoid war.

Events were soon to force Wilson's hand. First, on February 24, 1917, the British disclosed to the President a diplomatic cable it had decoded from German Foreign Secretary Arthur Zimmerman to Germany's Ambassador to Mexico. It instructed the Ambassador to seek an alliance with Mexico should the United States enter the war against Germany, and to have Mexico put pressure on Japan to switch to Germany's side. The inducement for Mexico was to be recovery of New Mexico, Texas, and Arizona should the Central Powers win the war. The Telegram created a political furor in Congress as well as in public opinion. Two days later, it was learned that a German submarine had torpedoed the British passenger liner *Laconia*, causing the death of two Americans. And, finally, on March 16, three American merchant ships, *City of Memphis*, *Illinois*, and *Vigilancia*, were sunk without warning, resulting in more than 20 American fatalities.

The submarine was a lethal harbinger of the age of total war, from which we have yet to escape, and it made President Wilson's attempt to play the role of a neutral peacemaker politically untenable. Assembling his Cabinet on March 20, he asked each member for advice on whether the United States should enter the war. With the answer unanimously in the affirmative, the President retreated to his office, alone, to contemplate the enormity of his pending decision. He had confided to a journalist a few days before his fateful choice, the reasons for his long-standing antipathy to war:

> It would mean that we should lose our heads along with the rest and stop weighing right and wrong...It required illiberalism at home to reinforce the men at the front. We couldn't fight Germany and maintain the ideals of government that all thinking men shared...Once lead this people into war and they'll forget there ever was such a thing as tolerance. To fight you must be brutal and ruthless and the spirit of ruthless brutality will enter into every fibre of our

> natural life…a declaration of war would mean that Germany would be beaten and so badly beaten that there would be a dictated peace, a victorious peace…It means an attempt to reconstruct a peace-time civilization with war standards…There won't be any peace standards left to work with.[343]

His words would prove prophetic, both during the war and in its aftermath.

Neither side was going to respond positively to Wilson's efforts at mediation—each was committed to its ambitious war aims and constrained by the very horror of their sacrifices to pursue a military victory. The President hoped United States involvement might quickly thwart the German land offensive, counter the humiliating and inhumane submarine attacks, and bring the war to an end much sooner than it would otherwise. Entering the war would give the United States a central role in peace-making and enable Wilson to shape the post-war world in ways that might prevent future war and enhance the growth of liberty. If he wanted a just peace, he would have to fight for it. To be a leader in international affairs, the United States would have to demonstrate to the world that it had not only the power, but the will, to shoulder that responsibility.

In his Second Inaugural Address, just a few weeks earlier, Wilson had prepared Americans for a new level of leadership in international affairs:

> We are provincials no longer. The tragical[sic] events of the thirty months of vital turmoil through which we have just passed have made us citizens of the world. There can be no turning back. Our own fortunes as a nation are involved, whether we would have it so or not.

He was committing the country to exercising its new responsibility in a manner that assumed the universal applicability of the nation's founding principles. If the undemocratic German, Austro-Hungarian, and Ottoman Empires were permitted victory, the future of liberty in Europe, and in many parts of the less developed, colonial world, would become bleak, and the American example less promising. Building on those themes, he was ready to rally the nation to war and the world to peace. Motivated by his religious faith and his study of political history, Wilson had always imagined himself acting in meaningful ways to improve the welfare of mankind; he now grasped the opportunity to do so that was practically forced upon him.

Congress assembled in an extraordinary joint session on the evening of April 2, 1917, to hear their President ask for a declaration of war against the Imperial Government of Germany, characterizing the fight as one for liberty and against autocracy:

> Neutrality is no longer feasible or desirable where the peace of the world is involved and the freedom of its peoples, and the menace to that peace and freedom lies in the existence of autocratic governments backed by organized force which is controlled wholly by their will, not by the will of their people.

Wilson did not limit the purpose of his call to arms to the protection of countries already free and independent, but offered:

> ...to fight...for the ultimate peace of the world and for the liberation of its peoples, the German peoples included: for the rights of nations great and small and the privilege of men everywhere to choose their way of life...**The world must be made safe for democracy.** Its peace must be planted upon the tested foundations of political liberty. [emphasis added]

The President proposed an international organization to prevent war, although this time he called it a concert of "free" peoples, in a formulation more consistent with the theme of his address. Wilson concluded by candidly admitting the gravity of his request:

> It is a fearful thing to lead this great peaceful people into war, into the most terrible and disastrous of all wars, civilization itself seeming in the balance. But the right is more precious than peace, and we shall fight for those things which we have always carried nearest our hearts—for democracy, for the right of those who submit to authority to have a voice in their own Governments, for the rights and

liberties of small nations, for a universal dominion of right by such a concert of free peoples as shall bring peace and safety to all nations and make the world itself at last free.[344]

He received a raucous, standing ovation as he finished, reflecting the broad support his decision had in the country. In recognition of the poignancy of the occasion, Wilson later said, "My message to-day was a message of death for our young men. How strange it seems to applaud that."[345]

Once Congress authorized war on April 6, 1917, Wilson spared no effort to mobilize the nation's resources toward a quick and successful end to the hostilities, notwithstanding the infringement on liberty inherent in the measures taken. The entire government was reorganized to focus on the mission, with profound effects on the lives of all Americans. Steeply progressive income taxes were adopted to finance the war, with maximum tax rates up to 77 per cent, in addition to a graduated profits tax on business of up to 65 per cent.[346] These taxes, the most onerous in the country's history, generated significant political opposition from wealthier Americans, and became a major factor leading to Republican electoral victories after the war. The Selective Service Act was passed on May 18, significantly more far reaching than the ineffective Civil War conscription system. The bill authorized the registration and classification for military service of all men between the ages of 21 and 30, amended a few months later to include men from 18 to 45. Draft boards were established in every local community. Of the 24 million men registered, almost 3 million were called for service. The sacrifices required of Americans to fight the First World War impressed on all Americans the profound nature of the issues Wilson and the Congress believed were at stake and the need to face them squarely as the war was being fought.

Within a year of Wilson's address, over 1 million soldiers would be sent to join the American Expeditionary Force in Europe, commanded by General John J. Pershing, building to 2 million before war's end. American soldiers helped turn back German offensives, particularly in Belleau Wood and the Second Battle of the Marne in July, 1918. The Americans were critical to Allied campaigns in late 1918 at St. Mihiel, the Meuse River, and the Argonne Forest. In all, the United States suffered more than 112,000 fatalities, with another 230,000 wounded, or one casualty in every six soldiers sent to Europe.[347]

In fulfillment of his own prophecy about the domestic effects of a declaration of war, Wilson signed the Espionage Act of 1917 and, later, the Sedition Act of 1918, placing restrictive controls on any speech and actions that were deemed 'disloyal.' The former prohibited espionage, sabotage, refusing service in the armed forces, obstructing the draft or providing aid to the enemy and gave the Postmaster General broad powers to censor the mail and restrict distribution of publications he decided were seditious. The latter punished any conduct or speech tending to undermine the government or the military. The Socialist leader, Eugene V. Debs, who had run for President in 1912, was jailed under this law for ten years for opposing the war. Although Wilson was troubled by the effect of these prosecutions, neither did he approve of Americans who would compromise support for the soldiers. The great burden he felt for sending the men to fight would only be made heavier if he excused those who tried to undercut support for the war effort. His measures were actually less extreme than those urged by others, like Theodore Roosevelt, who recommended the establishment of total martial law and firing squads to punish dissenters.[348]

Concurrent with legal restrictions, Wilson established The Committee on Public Information to stimulate public support for the war. Headed by journalist George Creel, the group undertook one of the most far-reaching propaganda campaigns in American history in order to convert the antiwar minority, utilizing a nationwide public relations campaign that included news releases, movies, advertising, brochures, and speakers. The Committee stimulated and encouraged anti-German hysteria. Troubled by the extreme tactics, Wilson emphasized that he had no quarrel with German people or culture, only the autocratic and aggressive government of Kaiser Wilhelm. Nevertheless, hatred against things Germanic became widespread, with orchestras reluctant to play Beethoven and Wagner, some schools discontinuing teaching the German language, and some German-Americans subjected to maltreatment and discrimination. Similar paranoia resulted in discriminatory actions directed at American citizens of Japanese origin during the Second World War, including the unprecedented governmental decision to remove more than 100,000 from their West Coast residences and detain them in relocation camps, many for the duration of the war.

A massive program was launched to organize both food and railroad resources in the service of the military effort. The Lever Act of

August 1917 gave the administration wide authority over the production of food, fertilizer, fuel and farm equipment, enabling food production to triple over pre-war levels. To cut domestic consumption and increase supplies of food for the military, Herbert Hoover, then head of the Food Administration, instituted meatless Tuesdays, wheat-less Mondays and Wednesdays, and pork-less Thursdays and Saturdays, voluntary programs that were a tremendous success. Victory gardens were widespread and restrictions on the manufacture of alcoholic beverages, together with voluntary restraint, helped accelerate prohibition. Wilson also took control of the railroads under the United States Railroad Administration to ensure the continued ability to transport all the goods necessary to support the military.

The greatest domestic challenge was marshaling American industry to focus on the war. Wilson appointed Bernard M. Baruch, a Wall Street banker, as Chairman of the War Industries Board, with broad power over industrial production. For two years Baruch was, in effect, economic 'tsar' of the United States, regulating war industries, developing new factories and sources of supply, fixing prices, determining priorities for production and delivery, and controlling all defense purchases. Baruch was able to both persuade and, when necessary, compel businessmen to organize and mobilize whatever was needed. In one measure to conserve steel, eight thousand tons were diverted from the manufacture of women's corsets, and to save coal, elevator usage in all buildings was restricted. Civilian factories were transformed to military uses and thousands of products were limited or standardized: tin was eliminated from children's toys and the variety of wheels for horse drawn carriages was reduced from 232 to 4. The economy was subjected to a degree of control never before attempted, yet the public overwhelmingly cooperated in the effort.

What was truly remarkable about all these American sacrifices is that they were made with no desire for conquest or material gain. The President had said in his war address, "We seek no indemnities for ourselves, no material compensation for the sacrifices we shall freely make."[349] The American people were ready to follow him, sincerely believing that they were fighting a war to end war and to make the world safe for democracy.

American war aims were not necessarily compatible with those of the Allied Powers. France, Great Britain and Italy, in particular, wanted to punish Germany for its part in commencing the war, limit

her future power, and acquire German and Austro-Hungarian territory in order to increase their own security. They had made secret
agreements among themselves early in the war to distribute what they
anticipated would be the territorial spoils. In recognition of these differences, the United States did not want to be formally a part of the
"Allied Powers," but chose to be called an "Associated Power," in a
group denoted the "Allied and Associated Powers." Nonetheless, Wilson believed that he could not allow victory for the autocratic Central
Powers because that might indicate that aggressive war could still pay
dividends and might halt the growth of liberty. To modify the more
vindictive aims of the Allied Powers, to encourage the growth of freedom in the German and Austro-Hungarian Empires, and to establish
a fair and just peace, he needed to have a prominent place at the peace
table. Moreover, Wilson believed that future threats to liberty from
similarly undemocratic regimes could best be countered by a properly
structured international League of Nations. To accomplish all these
goals required American entry into the war.[350]

6. Momentum for Peace

As he led the nation into war, the President still hoped for a
'peace without victory.' He was encouraged by the action of the German Reichstag in the summer of 1917 when it supported a compromise peace and when Pope Benedict XV called for a settlement based
on Christian principles. On September 2, Wilson asked Colonel
House to form a group of experts—historians and social scientists—to
formulate specific peace plans. This body, known as The Inquiry, analyzed a variety of geographic, economic, and political issues and prepared recommendations to the President for a comprehensive set of
American objectives to further peace and freedom.

In November 1917, the new democratic government in Russia
that had succeeded the Tsarist Empire after the February Revolution,
was itself overthrown by the Bolsheviks. This small, revolutionary,
Marxist faction was led by Vladimir Lenin, who called for a workers'
revolution, an end to Russia's war effort, and a peace without annexations or indemnities, claiming that the war was the inevitable result of
imperialism among rival capitalist countries. The Bolsheviks promptly
concluded an armistice with Germany and, at the same time, publicly

disclosed the secret treaties among Imperial Russia and the other Allied Powers that divided the anticipated territorial gains. The immediate success of the Bolshevik Revolution sent shock waves throughout European governments who feared that the new ideology of class struggle would attract those in their own countries who yearned for an end to the war. The ultimate totalitarian nature of the communist government the Bolsheviks established in the Soviet Union was not immediately obvious.

President Wilson decided that he needed to articulate a comprehensive plan for peace that would be recognized by the world as a compelling moral vision. He hoped, thereby, to moderate the objectives of his Allies, dissuade Russia from negotiating unilaterally with Germany and leaving the Allied side, undermine support for the autocratic Central Powers among their own people, and counter the growing appeal among the European working class of the revolutionary ideology of the nascent communist government in Russia. On January 8, 1918, to a Joint Session of Congress, he delivered his Fourteen Points Address, the most notable speech of the entire war.[351] In it, he firmly linked the two issues of the future of liberty and the nature of the post-war international settlement. He expressed his purposes this way:

> What we demand in this war…is nothing peculiar to ourselves. It is that the world be made fit and safe to live in; and particularly that it be made save for every peace-loving nation which, like our own, wishes to live its own life, determine its own institutions, be assured of justice and fair dealing by the other peoples of the world as against force and selfish aggression…the principle of justice to all peoples and nationalities, and their right to live on equal terms of liberty and safety with one another…The moral climax of this the culminating and final war for human liberty has come.

The President described five "general" points, including open diplomacy, freedom of the seas, removal of trade barriers, reduction in armaments, and the impartial settlement of colonial claims. In eight "geo-political" points, he relied on the principle of national independence and freedom to recommend evacuation of occupied Russian territory, restoration of Belgian independence, return of Alsace-Lorraine to France, readjustment of Italian frontiers to recognize independent nationalities, freedom for the subject peoples of Austria-Hungary, territorial independence of Rumania, Serbia, and Montenegro, separation and independence for the Turkish and non-Turkish people of the Ottoman Empire, and an independent Poland.

Finally, and most critical to Wilson, Point XIV called for "A general association of nations…under specific covenants for the purpose of affording mutual guarantees of political independence and territorial integrity to great and small states alike."[352] Combining international enforcement with the liberty and independence of all nations, this point was the clarion for all future international organizations.

The Fourteen Points Address spread hope for liberty among oppressed minorities in many places, but chiefly in the undemocratic regimes of Germany, Austria-Hungary and the Ottoman Empire. As its contents became known in the trenches, it significantly eroded the morale of the armies fighting for those Empires, many of whose soldiers felt more loyalty to their own particular nationality than to their government. Wilson's call for freedom was also heard by the German people. When the military fortunes of their country declined later in the war, public pressure for greater freedom hastened German willingness to install a more democratic government and ask for peace based on the Fourteen Points. The speech served also "to rally all groups at home and abroad behind a peace settlement grounded in a league of nations and other new principles of international conduct, and to induce the Allied governments to embrace that cause."[353] Finally, Wilson's speech answered the ideological challenge of Bolshevik communism by enumerating a set of ideals based on liberty and peace, and on righting long-standing political wrongs, that could serve as an alternative to class-based, potentially violent, revolution and one party government. Henceforth, Wilson would be the most influential voice in the articulation of war objectives and in planning for a postwar world.

Hopes for an expeditious negotiated settlement to the war were undermined on March 3, 1918 with the signing of the one-sided Brest-Litovsk Peace Treaty between Germany and Russia, under which Russia lost sovereignty over almost 55 million people, much of its heavy industry and coal production, and its most fertile farmland. Germany gained parts of the Caucasus, Ukraine, Finland, Poland, Lithuania, and Estonia, previously part of the Tsarist Empire, thus freeing its troops from fighting Russians on the eastern front, and permitting it to launch the second Marne offensive in an attempt to defeat France before American reinforcements arrived. This decision represented a rejection by the German government of any compromise settlement, based on its belief that a peace without territorial benefits would weaken the regime domestically and leave it less secure geographically.[354] The offensive was unsuccessful, hastening Germany's defeat and hardening the peace objectives of the Entente Allies, making the Fourteen Points much more difficult to realize.

Attention intensified on both sides of the Atlantic on the nature of an international organization. A British commission headed by Sir Walter Phillimore issued a report calling for an 'alliance' in which member states pledge to refrain from war with each other, promise to use sanctions against violators, consider coming to the aid of victims of aggression and adopt arbitration and mediation procedures. Prime Minister Lloyd George sent the report to Colonel House, who President Wilson subsequently asked, together with the legal expert on the Inquiry, David Hunter Miller, "to come up with an alternative plan for a league." Miller drafted a document entitled "Suggestion for a Covenant of a League of Nations" that included sanctions as suggested by Phillimore as well as Wilson's views on territorial integrity.[355] Even in Germany, support emerged for the concept of a League. Matthias Erzberger, leader of the Catholic Zentrum Party and soon to be head of the German delegation that was to sign the Versailles Treaty, wrote a book published in the fall of 1918 entitled *The League of Nations, the Way to the World's Peace*. The book "praised Wilson's advocacy of the League, and specifically repudiated the popular notion [in Germany] that the American President was a hypocrite [in regard to a just peace]."[356]

Wilson's final revision, called the "Magnolia Draft" because it was written at Colonel House's summer home in Magnolia, Massachusetts, was the version Wilson later took with him to the Paris Peace Conference. It required the member nations to "unite in guaranteeing to each other political independence and territorial integrity," and it authorized territorial adjustments "pursuant to the principle of self-determination" with approval from three-fourths of the members. The organization was, thus, not intended to etch the *status quo* in stone, but, rather, to be a dynamic force for the furtherance of liberty. Above all, "The Contracting Powers accept without reservation the principle that the peace of the world is superior in importance of every question of political jurisdiction and boundary."[357]

President Wilson emphasized to Americans that isolation from foreign affairs was no longer practical in an interdependent world. On September 17, 1918, he pledged to "clear the air of the world for common understandings and the maintenance of common rights," declaring that "the United States is prepared to assume its full share of responsibility for the maintenance of the common covenants and understandings upon which peace must henceforth rest."[358] Wilson's new morality of international relations caught the imagination of much of the world. As former President Herbert Hoover has written:

> The proposition that lasting peace could be had only by organized unity of the world and the rights of nations to self-determination and independence came as a brilliant light and an inspiring hope to peoples who had suffered from domination and war over the centuries.[359]

7. The Paris Peace Conference and the Versailles Treaty

The rapid deterioration of its military fortunes during the summer of 1918 impelled the German government to probe President Wilson in early October for an armistice and peace conference based on the Fourteen Points. Wilson responded that it would be impossible for the conference to deal directly with Germany unless the government was more representative of its people and that steps were taken to prevent any future resumption of hostilities. His terms were accepted on October 23, leading to dramatic political events in rapid succession: a mutiny by the German Navy at Kiel on November 3rd; the surrender of Austria-Hungary on November 4th; a revolution in Bavaria on November 7th; and the abdication and escape from Germany of Kaiser Wilhelm II on November 9th, whereupon a new republic was proclaimed. It can be argued that Wilson's firmness brought the opportunity for liberty to all the citizens of Germany.

Colonel House was dispatched to Europe to urge the Allied Powers to accept the Fourteen Points as the basis for an armistice. On

November 5, they did so, with two major reservations: they insisted that Germany be compelled to make reparation for all civilian damages caused by its aggression; and they reserved the right to decide at the peace conference the meaning of the doctrine of freedom of the seas.

Allied military commander, Marshall Foch, was delegated to work out armistice terms that were presented to the German armistice commission, led by Matthias Erzberger, in a railway car near Compiegne, France. The Germans were outraged by the severity of the provisions, and they futilely tried to change them; the new Socialist, republican government that had succeeded the Kaiser realized that it had little bargaining power and authorized acceptance, hoping for revision later. The Armistice, signed at dawn on November 11, called for a peace treaty based on the Fourteen Points, including the two Entente reservations, but stated that Germany would not be invited as a contributor to the conference drawing up the treaty. In addition, it required evacuation of all occupied territory as well as Alsace-Lorraine and some formerly German parts of both banks of the Rhine River, nullification of the Treaty of Brest-Litovsk, the surrender of all submarines and most navy ships, the destruction of aircraft, tanks, and heavy artillery, and the loss of most railway cars, locomotives and trucks. The German delegation said at the signing, "A nation of seventy millions of people suffers, but does not die."[360]

The Peace Conference was scheduled to meet in Paris in January 1919. President Wilson decided to lead the American delegation and he selected Colonel House, Secretary of State Lansing, Army General Tasker H. Bliss, and Henry White, a Republican career diplomat, as the other members. Some historians, viewing Wilson's later losing battle for Senate approval of the Versailles Treaty and the League of Nations, have criticized him for not selecting any prominent Republican politicians, such as Senator Henry Cabot Lodge, former President William Howard Taft, former Secretary of State Elihu Root, or former Presidential Candidate Charles Evans Hughes, all Republican internationalists with sympathy for the League.[361] Some writers have suggested that deterioration in Wilson's neurological health may have contributed to an inability to be more insightful in his selections.[362] Nonetheless, a variety of factors, including Wilson's determination to be in charge, his desire for maximum maneuverability in the negotiations, and substantive disagreements with Republicans on the appropriate nature of the League, impelled him to choose as he did. [363] He did not want pressure to adjust his belief that the League needed real power to resolve disputes over political independence and territorial integrity, and to effect changes in the status of governments over time.

Wilson faced difficult challenges as a result of the post-war attitudes of the Allied nations. After years of bloody sacrifice, the people and the governments who had been victorious now had strong material goals. The British wanted to profit from the war and their rivalry with Germany for world power by receiving tangible economic and colonial gains. The French wanted to punish Germany for Alsace-Lorraine and its Belgian aggression by weakening it economically and geographically so it would no longer pose a security threat. The Italians wanted pieces of territory from Austria-Hungary, and Japan wanted to maintain its control over parts of China. Public opinion in those countries was dominated by hatred of the enemy and the desire for revenge. Instability was common throughout the European continent, with the Austro-Hungarian Empire falling apart, the Russian and German Empires both overthrown, and the fear of Bolshevik Revolutions widespread. To add to Wilson's difficulties, the Democratic Party suffered a defeat in the November mid-term elections (for a variety of regional and local reasons), leaving uncertain the nature of his political support in the country, thereby making it easier for European advocates of a vindictive peace to oppose his more moderate views at the conference. [364]

Amidst these complex issues, Wilson set sail from New York for Paris with his wife, Edith, and the large American delegation, accompanied by boat horns in the harbor, confetti from the shore, and bi-planes roaring overhead, as if calling out "the American people's confidence and hope that this slender, ascetic-looking man could indeed accomplish a miracle and bring an end to war." [365] His French welcome was even more idolatrous. Two million people lined the streets of Paris as he rode triumphantly through the city; the French public received him as a hero. Wherever he traveled in Europe, crowds showered him with adulation and treated him as the sole object of their hopes. Herbert Hoover explained it this way:

> His eloquent development of his basis of peace, with its "independence of peoples," "self-determination," "no annexations," "justice," "right," a "new order," "freedom of

mankind" and a "lasting peace," had stirred hope among the masses everywhere in the world. To them, no such man of moral and political power and no such evangel of peace had appeared since Christ preached the Sermon on the Mount. Everywhere men believed that a new era had come to all mankind. It was the star of Bethlehem rising again.[366]

For Wilson to have realized all the hopes placed upon him would, indeed, have been miraculous. That he accomplished as much as he did, given the obstacles in his path, was truly admirable and would have a lasting impact on his country, on liberty, and on the world. Because Wilson brought great moral leadership to the gathering, and sought no territorial gain or financial reparation, he could view any potential settlement broadly and on the merits, without selfish distortion. No other statesman of the time could match his tireless work ethic or his general level of knowledge, even of European affairs. Although his only real bargaining chip was the threat to leave the conference, he was reluctant to verbalize it, knowing that it was most effective if not actually used.

The Peace Conference began on January 18th by establishing a Council of Ten consisting of the heads of government and foreign ministers of the Great Britain, France, Italy, Japan, and the United States, eventually superceded by a Council of Four consisting of Wilson, Premier Georges Clemenceau of France, Prime Minister David Lloyd George of Great Britain, and Premier Vittorio Orlando of Italy. These were experienced, hardened leaders, each of whom had his own agenda. Clemenceau, intent on revenge and on forever prohibiting German from invading France, as he had twice witnessed, is reported to have said, "God gave us his Ten Commandments and we broke them. Wilson gave us his Fourteen Points—we shall see."[367] Clemenceau also wanted a League made up solely of the victorious countries—a sort of European security cordon that the French could greatly influence. Lloyd George shared Wilson's hope for a new world order based on the rule of law, but was also committed to maintaining British power around the world and was capable of opportunism and expediency. Orlando could be an idealist, except where Italian objectives conflicted, and was a master politician. Even some of Wilson's advisors had individual agendas—Secretary of State Lansing resented Wilson's domination and Colonel House would readily compromise with Great Britain or France in order to reach a quick settlement.

Wilson insisted at the outset that the League be an integral part of a peace treaty with the authority to supervise the enforcement of its provisions, fearing that if the League were not immediately established, its birth might be delayed or forestalled indefinitely. On January 22, the Council agreed with Wilson and formed a League of Nations Commission, with him as Chairman, responsible for preparing a "covenant" that described the powers of the new organization.

The Commission produced what has become known as the First Paris Draft of the Covenant, bearing the stamp of the President himself. Although he borrowed ideas from the work of Lord Robert Cecil, junior British Cabinet member, and Jan Christian Smuts, South African General then a member of the Imperial War Cabinet, Wilson composed the document of eleven pages on his own typewriter and later amended it in his own handwriting.[368] He, alone, was responsible for its most far-reaching provision—that each member would guarantee the political independence and territorial integrity of the others and, if necessary, use economic sanctions and military force against any violator. This formulation would later become the famous "Article X" of the final League of Nations Covenant that provoked a political firestorm in the United States regarding the alleged dilution of America's ability to make an independent decision for war.

After almost two weeks of intense wrangling over wording among the delegations, a new Final Draft Covenant was jointly produced. Although the President was pleased with its substance, he felt the previous language more felicitous and Colonel House thought the preceding version "more human and a little less legal."[369] Wilson's nemesis, Senator Lodge, assuming incorrectly that the President wrote the Final Draft, issued a pointed criticism of it, saying: "As an English production it does not rank high. It might get by at Princeton but certainly not at Harvard."[370]

The President presented the Final Draft Covenant to the full Conference on February 14, 1919. Mrs. Wilson had to peer at her husband and listen from an alcove behind red brocade curtains because only delegates were permitted at the session. She later wrote of the occasion:

It was a great moment in history…and he stood there— slender, calm, and powerful in his argument—I seemed to see the people of all depressed countries—men, women, and little children—crowding round and waiting on his words.[371]

Wilson told the Conference that the success of the League depended "chiefly upon one great force, and that is the moral force of the public opinion of the world—the cleansing and clarifying and compelling influences of publicity." He acknowledged that there were other elements at work, as well: "If the moral force of the world will not suffice, the physical force of the world shall. But that is the last resort, because this is intended as a constitution of peace, not as a league of war." He emphasized that the League was conceived as a dynamic force for change and for liberty: "We are done with annexations of helpless people, meant in some instances by some powers to be used merely for exploitation."[372]

The most critical part of the Covenant, to Wilson and to world history, was undoubtedly Article X, which required League Members to provide protection to countries that might become victims of aggression. It read in pertinent part as follows:

> The...Parties undertake to respect and preserve as against external aggression the territorial integrity and existing political independence of all States members of the League. In case of any such aggression or in case of any threat or danger of such aggression the Executive Council shall advise upon the means by which this obligation shall be fulfilled.[373]

This provision committed the nations of the world, for the first time in history, to a common approach to keeping the peace and to protecting the independence of any country threatened with aggression. Other important provisions dealt with disarmament, arbitration of disputes, the first world court, a system for de-colonization, and international labor standards.[374]

As he returned temporarily to the United States to garner political support for the League, Wilson reportedly told his personal physician, Dr. Grayson, "The failure of the United States to back it [the League] would break the heart of the world."[375] In Washington, the President encountered an unpleasant political reality—enough Republicans had indicated lack of support for the League that any peace treaty containing it would likely fail in the Senate.[376] At the initiation of Senator Lodge, Chairman of the Foreign Relations Committee, 39 Republican Senators (out of a total Senate of 96) had signed the Round Robin document opposing the League and urging the Paris Conference to first negotiate peace terms with Germany that were acceptable to Britain and France.

Opponents of the League, including both isolationist Senators and Republicans favoring great power domination of international affairs, argued that a worldwide organization was not necessary, preferring regional power blocs and traditional diplomacy to keep the peace. Objections to the reach of Article X included concern that American troops might be required to intervene in disputes that did not directly affect the nation's interests. They further worried about subverting the Monroe Doctrine by involving Europeans in American issues. Public opinion, as reflected by newspaper editorials, generally favored the League, particularly in the South, New England and the Midwest, but also reflected the need to protect the Monroe Doctrine and uncertainty about military involvement overseas.[377]

Acknowledging the Republican opposition, Wilson obtained agreement to changes in the Final Draft Covenant when he returned to Paris. As a result, the final document included the right of each member nation to withdraw from the organization with two years' notice, added language that stated that nothing in the Covenant would be deemed to affect "regional understandings like the Monroe Doctrine," and made it clear that matters solely within a member's domestic jurisdiction would be excluded from consideration by the League. Whether these changes would satisfy critics in the United States was unclear, but there was no doubt that obtaining, for the first time, European agreement with the Monroe Doctrine, constituted a major political accomplishment for Wilson.

With the issue of the League settled, the Conference addressed the more contentious question of the treatment of Germany and the defeated powers.[378] The main issues to be addressed were reparations, or payment for war damages caused, and territorial adjustments. Consistent with his long-held views about the necessity of a balanced settlement, Wilson warned of the dangers of treating Germany too harshly:

We are risking, then, not being paid if we ourselves take measures which will prevent Germany from recovering...Germany must restore what she has taken and rebuild what she has destroyed. But if we make her unable to do that, the penalties we want to impose on her will be purely nominal.[379]

During the deliberations over reparations, Wilson fell ill, probably with influenza, limiting his capacity to participate, leaving Colonel House to represent him at many sessions. In the end, Wilson agreed to French demands that Germany bear the cost of disability pensions to Allied veterans and their families and that Germany and her allies must admit "entire responsibility for the war" and all civilian war losses and damages. The latter provision, Article 231, came to be known as the "War Guilt Clause" and was later used by right wing German politicians, including Adolf Hitler, to stir up emotions against the "unjust" Versailles Treaty.[380]

The territorial provisions dramatically affected the lives of millions of people within Europe and in the former German colonies.[381] "In all, Germany lost about 13 per cent of its area and 10 per cent of its population in Europe (though most of those transferred were not ethnically German), in addition to all its overseas possessions."[382] Her military was limited to a volunteer force of 100,000 and almost all major military and naval equipment was divested.

The German delegation was stunned when these terms were revealed to them and felt betrayed by Wilson. They believed he had abandoned his own principles, particularly the open diplomacy and self-determination declarations in the Fourteen Points, and the fair settlement principle in the Peace Without Victory speech. The delegation recommended rejection of the Treaty to its government, but, faced with the prospect of invasion, famine, and partition of the country, the new Weimar government acquiesced and signed the Treaty at the Palace of Versailles on June 28, 1919. German disappointment and bitterness lasted throughout Wilson's life; at his death in 1924, its embassy in Washington was the only one that declined to lower the flag.[383]

Some members of participating delegations were also alarmed at the terms. On the day of their presentation, Jan Smuts of the British delegation, who had contributed so much to the League Covenant,

Herbert Hoover of the American delegation, and John Maynard Keynes, a British economist, met to discuss the document. According to Hoover, "We seemed to have come together by some sort of telepathy...Each was greatly disturbed. We agreed that the consequences of many parts of the proposed Treaty would ultimately bring destruction."[384] Keynes went on to prophesy misfortune when he wrote *The Economic Consequences of the Peace*, the most famous critique of the Versailles Treaty. As the President left Paris, he was reported to have said to his wife, "Well, little girl, it is finished, and, as no one is satisfied, it makes me hope we have made a just peace; but it is all in the lap of the gods."[385]

There were many criticisms of the Treaty at the time and much historical fault finding since. First and foremost has been the long-standing notion that the treaty was too harsh on Germany, leaving it too weak economically, and providing fodder for propaganda that eased Hitler's rise to power by rallying his country around the need to correct the alleged injustices done to it at Versailles. As the allegation goes, the seeds were sown for an inevitable Second World War. Some have seen that war as inevitable for the opposite reason—the treaty was not harsh enough as Germany was able to re-arm rather quickly and revive its economy fast enough to build the most effective war machine in Europe, enabling it to seek once again the power and glory it sought in 1914.

The Treaty, and Wilson himself, has also been criticized for having only partially implemented the Fourteen Points, particularly regarding the liberation and self-determination of oppressed peoples in the Austro-Hungarian, German and Ottoman Empires. Some compromise with the principle of self-determination was, in fact, made when France was given authority in the Rhineland and the Saar Basin, when Italy was given possession of parts of Austria and the Balkans, when Japan was given possession of the former German colony of Shantung in China, and when Great Britain and France divided areas of the Middle East and Africa. Many liberals believed that these transfers unfairly denied to deserving peoples the benefits of independence. One modern revisionist historian, Niall Ferguson, has even criticized the use of the principle at all in connection with the peacemaking because Germany had to be treated in a hypocritical way. He argues, "the adoption of 'self-determination' as a guiding principle of the peace was fatal because it could not be applied to Germany without aggrandizing her far beyond the territory of the pre-1919 Reich...[thus it] could not be applied in Central and Eastern Europe without renewed violence."[386]

A third area of criticism has focused on the inconsistency between Wilson's admonition that "only a peace between equals can last," and the reality that Germany was never permitted to be a full participant in the Conference. The terms of the pre-armistice agreement and the Treaty itself were essentially presented as a take it or leave it proposition, or, as the Germans called it, a "diktat." Nor was Germany immediately offered membership in the purportedly universal League of Nations.

The Treaty deserves to be seen in a more balanced light, remembering that the world had come through the most terrible war in history. An entire generation of young European men was destroyed and the structure of the European political system had been undermined. The war's main by-products were death and revolution. Europe was devastated and was called "a laboratory resting on a vast cemetery."[387] In that environment, it would have been impossible to produce a perfectly just and reasonable settlement that would gain popular support in Europe.

It is all too easy to view the greater horrors of the Second World War and blame the failure to prevent them on the Versailles Treaty. The war guilt clause and the failure to accept the German delegation as an equal may have caused shame and humiliation, but they did not force Hitler to invade Czechoslovakia, Poland and Russia and send millions of innocents to gas chambers. And nothing in the Treaty impelled Hitler to erect the Third Reich as one of the greatest violators of liberty in human history. Only Hitler deserves the blame for utilizing the anti-German effects of the Treaty in the service of megalomaniacal and genocidal objectives.

It is true that the reparations provisions were open-ended at first, but they later were made more realistic and, in any event, Germany regained its place as one of the strongest industrial nations in the world long before 1939. It is also true that the territorial settlement meant that millions of Germans would live outside the new borders of their homeland. However, that was partly a result of the resentment of millions of non-German residents of the German and Austro-Hungarian Empires who had been denied self-determination, and to quash such yearnings for liberty those Empires started the war.

The short-sighted foreign policy of the democracies between 1919 and 1939 had more to do with the origin of the Second World War than any provision of the Versailles Treaty.[388] Great Britain and France failed to deal effectively with Hitler's designs on his neighbors, the United States essentially retreated to its shores, and all the great powers failed to check Japanese advancements in the Far East.

The Treaty honored the self-determination principle of the Fourteen Points more than it violated it. Belgian independence was restored; an independent Poland was created, although in more land than was historically Polish; self-determination was established in Central Europe with the creation of Czechoslovakia and in the Balkans with Yugoslavia, albeit not without later border disputes; and the seeds were sown in Africa and the Middle East for national independence, although too long delayed by the countries receiving colonial mandates.

The territorial provisions of the Treaty were a compromise between Wilsonian principles of self-determination and the traditional geo-political objectives of the victors in the war. The boundaries it imposed on Europe and, indeed, much of the globe, continue in large measure as the basis for the world's national framework today. It is hard to see how any different type of settlement would have gained support from all the victorious allies.

It is certainly possible that, had Germany been treated less as a villain and more as a partner in building a peaceful world, the democratic Weimar government might have avoided the coming of Hitler. If the peace had been negotiated with them, not dictated; if the overthrow of the Kaiser had been more tangibly recognized, and if the "war guilt" clause had been modified or eliminated, the fledgling democracy might have begun on a stronger footing. But the hard reality was that Imperial Germany had pushed Europe past the breaking point and, in the end, expended all its military or economic strength, leaving little bargaining power to ensure better treatment. European suffering would not permit any magnanimous gestures. President Wilson tried mightily to render the Treaty as fair as he could, and he deserves credit for moderating the most extreme desires of the victors. The result was no doubt more just and more supportive of liberty than it would have been without his participation.

8. The President and the Senate Battle
Over the League

On July 10, 1919, President Wilson formally presented the Versailles Treaty to the Senate, seeking the consent the Constitution required, aware that the League of Nations would be the part of the document stimulating the most controversy. He linked the League to the mission of America: "It was of this that we dreamed at our birth. America shall in truth show the way."[389] On the surface, the ensuing political debate solely concerned the details of the Treaty, particularly the League Covenant; however, on a deeper level, the debate was about whether the United States was, in fact, ready and willing to provide leadership to solve world problems as part of its mission. The outcome of the battle limited that mission for two decades and stands as an example of how petty partisanship can delay addressing issues critical to liberty's future.

While there was some opposition to other Treaty provisions, with German-Americans believing the Treaty too harsh and Irish-Americans disappointed that self-determination for Ireland was not established, the most vigorous opposition was reserved for the League. Opponents wanted it crystal clear that only the United States could determine what the Monroe Doctrine meant in any given circumstance. They also wanted no limitation whatever on the right to withdraw from the organization. Most important, they wanted the decision to employ American armed forces to be solely that of the Congress of the United States.

The President met with the Senate Foreign Relations Committee on August 19 in an attempt to garner their support. He reminded them that he had returned to Paris with the very issues in mind that still animated the opposition and he described the modifications he obtained in response to those concerns. Focusing on criticism of Article X, the President argued that the Executive Council of the League had the power only to "'advise upon' the means by which the obligations of that great article are to be given effect," that "a unanimous vote of the council is required," and that the Conference understood that Congress must "exercise its independent judgment in all matters of peace and war." But he emphasized that "Article X seems to me to constitute the very backbone of the whole covenant. Without it the

League would be hardly more than an influential debating society."
He acknowledged his opponents by indicating that he would accept a
Senatorial "interpretation" highlighting Congress' sole power to make
war, but rejected such a statement if made as part of the formal ratification language.[390] Wilson showed no interest in accepting any binding reservations despite warnings from Republicans that they would
not vote for the treaty without them. Some have speculated that his
intransigence, even at this early stage in the fight, might have been due
to ill health, possibly an undiagnosed stroke.[391] But Wilson frequently
found it difficult to accept the points of view of other politicians, or
even his close advisors, when they were significantly different from his
own.

Moderate and internationalist Republicans feared that Article X
established a new "entangling" alliance that undermined America's
right to decide when and where it should exercise power. They were
willing to abandon isolationism and take on a strong international role,
but only one of America's own choosing. Liberals and left-leaning
individuals saw a problem from a different perspective. They believed
that "The chief danger lay in Article X because it seemed 'in effect to
validate existing empires.'"[392] Wilson disagreed with the liberals,
believing the League would change boundaries and colonial administration whenever warranted.

The most virulent opposition came from those Senators who
have been called "Irreconcilables." They disagreed with the attempt
to link the future of liberty to the fate of an international organization
because they perceived the Europeans who would make up most of the
League's members as "men dominated by bigotry, hatred, intoler-
ance." In the words of Senator Joseph France of Maryland, "America's
peculiar national destiny" was to demonstrate to the world "the tran-
scendent excellency and universal applicability of free republican government and of persuading all other peoples to the adoption of those
institutions and ideals."[393] It would be more difficult to concentrate on
the quality of its own government if America was hindered by League
responsibilities. Senator William Borah of Idaho argued, similarly:
"To try to yoke democracy with the discordant and destructive forces
of the Old World, and democracy would lose its soul...we may become
one of the four dictators of the world, but we shall no longer be master of our own spirit."[394]

At the end of the summer the President embarked on a cross-country tour to rally public support to influence the Senate's decision. His allies viewed it as a courageous and dramatic journey, one that symbolized his commitment to world peace and to liberty. His detractors criticized his decision as quixotic, politically confrontational, and too strenuous for a man who had already expended a tremendous amount of his physical and emotional energy in ending the war and establishing the peace. Nonetheless, the speeches he gave on that trip were among his most eloquent and helped the average citizen understand the passion and moral basis of his motivation. They still have relevance in early 21st century America; they help us understand the negative effects of leaning too far in the direction of a unilateralist foreign policy and doing too little to support and strengthen the United Nations.

Once again, the President emphasized how the League's role in protecting freedom was linked to America's founding principles. In an address in San Diego, California on September 19, he said:

> We in America have stood from the day of our birth for the emancipation of people throughout the world who were living unwillingly under governments which were not of their choice. The thing that we have held more sacred than any other is that just government rests upon the consent of the governed. All over the world that principle had been disregarded by the strong, and only the weak have suffered...If we as a nation indeed mean what we have always said—that we are the champions of human right—now is the time when we shall be brought to the test, the acid test, as to whether we mean what we said or not.[395]

Wilson saw the further development of liberty as a crucial responsibility of the League:

> If the desire for self-determination of any people in the world is likely to affect the peace of the world or the good understanding between nations...it becomes the function of the League to bring the whole pressure of the combined world to bear upon that very matter.[396]

Conscious of the sacrifices in lives, wealth, and civil liberties he had asked the American people to make, the President placed great importance on the League as an insurance policy against any future war. He said that it would be effective because "the whole purifying and rectifying influence of the public opinion of mankind is brought to bear." In reflecting on the war just ended he concluded that "If anything approaching [the League] had been the arrangement of the world in 1914, the war would have been impossible."[397] He urged his countrymen to give their support and he delivered a prophetic warning: "...if by chance, we should not win this great fight for the League of Nations, it would be [our children's] death warrant. They belong to the generation which would then have to fight the final war...the very existence of civilization would be in the balance."[398]

Wilson also had to convince the nation that the League could bring measurable benefits at home. And, as a corollary, failure to join the League would have tangible, negative results. He believed that the country should seize the opportunity for economic and political leadership:

> We will be the senior partner [in the League]. The financial leadership will be ours. The commercial advantage will be ours. And the other countries of the world will look to us, and, shall I say, are looking to us for leadership and direction.[399]

If the United States did not join the League, and rejected international leadership:

> It means that we shall pay, not lighter, but heavier taxes. It means we shall trade in a world in which we are suspected and watched and disliked, instead of in a world which is now ready to trust us, ready to follow our leadership, ready to receive our traders, along with our political representatives, as friends.[400]

In Wilson's view, failure to join would drastically change the nature of American society and the civil rights of its people. In one of his most poignant predictions, one that has great applicability to America today, he warned of a primarily unilateral foreign policy:

If we must stand apart and be the hostile rivals of the rest of the world, then…we must be physically ready for anything to come. We must have a great standing army…that means a mobilized nation…you can't be unfriendly to everybody without being ready that everybody shall be unfriendly to you…You have got to have a concentrated, militaristic organization of government to run a nation of that sort. You have got to think of the President of the United States, not as the chief counselor of the nation…but as the man…ready to order [the military] to any part of the world where the threat of war is a menace to his own people. And you can't do that under free debate. You can't do that under public counsel. Plans must be kept secret. Knowledge must be accumulated by a system which we have condemned, because we have called it a spying system. The more polite call it a system of intelligence…You know how impossible it is to effect social reform if everybody must be under orders from the government. You know how impossible it is, in short, to have a free nation if it is military nation and under military orders.[401]

Wilson's journey was a popular success, but soon resulted in personal tragedy. He was greeted everywhere he went as a hero and great patriot. He spoke to large crowds, some more than 40,000, often in large auditoriums on the strength of his own voice, unassisted by sound amplification systems; the physical and mental stress of his task began to take its toll. His health deteriorated, with intense frequent intense headaches, respiratory problems, and difficulty in walking and standing. After speaking the previous evening in Pueblo, Colorado, he awakened on September 26th feeling light-headed and nauseated, suffering involuntary convulsions in his face. He is reported to have said, "I have never been in a condition like this. I just feel as if I am going to pieces."[402] His physician insisted that he terminate his trip immediately. The President acquiesced, but on October 2, after his return to Washington, he suffered a major stroke, paralyzing his left side. His prognosis was uncertain for many days and his capacity for the remainder of his Presidency was severely limited, likely changing the fortunes of the League and the course of 20th century history.

Wilson was unable to exercise the powers of his office for at least a month, and, thereafter, the effects of the stroke and a subsequent infection negatively affected his stamina, judgment and temperament. During the initial stages of his recuperation, Mrs. Wilson took it upon herself to determine who was granted permission to see him and what issues drew his attention. She forbade his physician, Dr. Grayson, from disclosing the true nature of the President's disability; together with Wilson's Chief Secretary, Joseph Tumulty, she and Dr. Grayson made it appear to the American people that recovery was proceeding apace and that the President would soon be functioning normally. Mrs. Wilson was criticized at the time for taking power into her own hands, but the Constitution did not then give much guidance in the event of the temporary incapacity of the President, providing only that the duties would "devolve on the Vice President" in case of the President's "death, resignation, or inability to discharge the powers and duties of ...office." Then Vice President Thomas Marshall refused suggestions that he take over, for fear of provoking a civil war or, at the least, a terribly awkward situation when the President regained his health. Not until 1967, with the ratification of the Twenty-Fifth Amendment, did the country have a clear procedure to follow in the event of the disability of a President.

The period of the President's diminished capacity coincided with the time the Senate had to decide whether to approve the Treaty and the League. Wilson's inability to interact effectively with key Senators had a dramatic effect on the outcome. One historian of his Presidency described the consequences of his illness in this way:

> Its effects made it almost impossible for him to read, impaired his ability to concentrate, and above all compromised his mental capacity so that he lost all sophistication and was forced back on the back on the bedrock of his character, where all issues were perceived in moral terms as right or wrong. Serious as the physical effects of the stroke were, they were minor compared to the mental damage. For almost four months after 2 October 1919 Woodrow Wilson was physically and mentally incapable of carrying out the duties of president of the United States.[403]

On October 24, 1919, Senator Lodge introduced on the Senate floor his formal Reservation to the provisions of Article X, the focal point for Wilson's adversaries. It provided:

> The United States assumes no obligation to preserve the territorial integrity or political independence of any other country or to interfere in controversies between nations under the provisions of Article X, or to employ the military...unless...the Congress...shall by act or joint resolution so declare.[404]

This reservation passed on November 13 by a vote of 46 to 33. It was obvious at that point, however, that the Treaty would not garner the 67 votes required for passage; Wilson and the Democrats refused to accept any formal reservation placing restrictions on Article X, and there were not enough votes to pass the Treaty without such a provision.[405]

In December, President Wilson was awarded the Nobel Peace Prize in Oslo, Norway for his efforts to end the war and establish the League of Nations. This international recognition had no effect on the political stalemate at home. The Senate scheduled a final vote on the Treaty with reservations on March 19, 1920. Eleven days prior to this vote, Wilson sent a letter to Senator Hitchcock, the Democratic leader in the Senate, that made compromise unlikely, stating his position as follows:

> [A]ny reservation which seeks to deprive the League of Nations of the force of Article X cuts at the very heart and life of the Covenant itself...I have been struck by the fact that practically every so-called reservation was in effect a nullification of the terms of the treaty itself.[406]

This letter, and a similar one the prior November, are generally regarded as significant errors in judgment by Wilson and have variously been ascribed to the effects of his medical problems as well as his personality. Modern medical scholars have concluded that Wilson was increasingly stubborn and inflexible as a result of the effects of worsening cardiovascular disease and psychological disability resulting from his stroke.[407] Other writers have claimed that Wilson's inability to compromise stemmed from unresolved psychological conflict with his father or the inability of his second wife, Edith, to provide the same calming influence as his first wife, Ellen.[408] The most plausible explanation of Wilson's rigidity was offered by John Morton Blum when he wrote of the President that "...he fixed his own security in the doctrines he promulgated. He could not afford to modify these doctrines for fear of losing hold of his personality."[409] Wilson always had confidence in his own ability to find moral guidelines that would point men in the right direction. Once he had divined the proper course of action in a given political situation, he was resolute in pursuing it, relying more on his intuition than on reason or the opinion of others.

In the final Senate vote, the Treaty with Lodge's reservations failed to pass, although 57 Senators, 7 short of the required two-thirds, were identified in favor. Wilson and Democratic Senators who were strong League advocates believed that the United States should take the lead in giving fully committed support to the new international organization and make it the cornerstone of America's approach to the world. For Lodge and most Republicans, American foreign policy should be based primarily on American power and leave a wide berth for unilateral action. Nevertheless, the differences were not so great to have precluded compromise. To have bridged the gap, Wilson would merely have had to accept a formal qualification to Article X that restated an obvious Constitutional truth—that only the United States Congress has the power to commit American troops to war. Nothing in the language of such a provision would have prevented the United States from conducting its foreign policy with the League's success as a primary goal. Lodge and the Republicans would merely have had to call their provision an "interpretation" rather than a reservation. As it was, nothing in Article X guaranteed or even authorized unilateral United States action. Nonetheless, Democrats followed Wilson's lead and made little or no effort to meet the Republicans half-way, and Republicans were so smitten with partisan dislike of the President that they were determined not to let him have the League he wanted.

The Versailles Treaty was accepted by all the delegations to the Paris Peace Conference except the United States. In July 1921, almost three years after the armistice, Congress finally passed a joint resolution declaring the First World War formally over and, subsequently, separate peace treaties were entered into with Germany, Austria, and Hungary.

The Senate's rejection of the Versailles Treaty and the League, together with the succeeding Republican political ascendancy, weakened America's international commitment to both peace and liberty. It also perpetuated for decades the myth that the United States had to choose between a foreign policy that favored unilateral action and one that focused on collective security. Shortly after the final Senate vote, Wilson is reported to have said, "it is evidently too soon for the country to accept the League."[410] Apparently few other nations were ready for the task, either, for even those who did join the League proved unwilling to look beyond their own selfish interests to preserve the liberty and independence of others. During the period between the two world wars, the League was unable to counter aggression by the Japanese in Manchuria, Germany in the Rhineland, Italy in Ethiopia, and Japan in China.

Wilson envisioned that the League of Nations would provide a mechanism to prevent aggression and remedy any legitimate grievances remaining from the Treaty. The difficulty the League had in ultimately achieving those objectives was not inevitable from its origin, but was a product of the lack of commitment of its members—and of the United States, its most famous non-member—to the principles underlying its existence. Whether the League might have been more successful under the influence of active United States leadership will never be known. Nevertheless, the historical significance of Wilson's conception of international cooperation, and its relationship to America's mission, has been critical to American policy since the end of the Second World War, and is likely to remain so for the foreseeable future.

The remaining year of Wilson's Presidency after the final Senate vote was a time of waning influence and weakening physical strength. Though he contemplated seeking a third Democratic nomination in 1920 in order to conduct a national referendum on the League, he was not capable of the task. The country was turning away from great ideas and foreign conflict and towards a period of 'normalcy' under a Republican resurgence. For the remaining three years of his life after he left office, Wilson lived as a recluse in Washington, together with his devoted wife, Edith. He died on February 3, 1924.

9. Wilson's Impact on American Liberty a nd America's Mission

Woodrow Wilson gave the United States a new philosophic basis for its foreign policy. He took the nation to war not for plunder or power, but for a moral cause, the survival of freedom. The unprecedented sacrifices the country made and the dramatic increase in federal power over the lives of citizens that it experienced were all in the service of that ideal. Never before had a country acted with such motivation.

Wilson believed that America's newly found economic, military, and political power could become instruments to develop liberty and peace through international cooperation. Unique among his contemporaries, and rare in all of history, he maintained what Herbert Muller has called "a long and large view of the world's needs."[411] To him, liberty was not merely an American mission, but the aspiration of mankind—a right to which they are entitled "by the Laws of Nature and of Nature's God," as proclaimed in the Declaration of Independence. For that reason, he believed that an international organization of free people would be the best hope for removing the prospect of war from the world's future.

Wilson understood that Americans would more likely support a new direction in foreign policy if it had a moral foundation, grounded in America's founding principles. Thus, he led the nation through a war for the liberty of others and ensured that the Covenant of the League would have as its basis the development of independence and democracy. He recognized that the very technology that ushered in the age of total war had the potential to facilitate the gradual democratization of world opinion. He had faith, grounded in his study of history and his religious principles, that global interdependence, if given the proper framework, would result in the growth of liberty. American values would acquire universal applicability if America was willing to lead the world in that direction. In the 21st century world of a globalized economy, the validity of Wilson's ideas will be tested and the outcome will be crucial to the survival and expansion of liberty.

Wilson's concept of the League of Nations has been criticized for "treating the tragedies of history as aberrations," of placing too much reliance on "the force of public opinion and the worldwide spread of democratic institutions." It is alleged that his concept of collective security "fell prey to the weakness of its central premise—that all nations have the same interest in resisting a particular act of aggression."[412] But this criticism misses the mark for three major reasons. First, it sets up the same false dichotomy between internationalism and unilateralism that pervaded the political battle over American acceptance of Article X of the League Covenant. And Wilson, himself, never underestimated the potential of evil in history. The League he envisioned would summon an aggressor before world opinion and require the members to face each such challenge. If, in the end, a consensus could not be formed, nothing precluded any individual member from acting in its own best interests.

Second, Wilson always viewed the League as a dynamic instrument, not merely a reflection of the political *status quo*. It had the power and duty to encourage self-determination and political independence, with the likelihood that nations choosing liberty would multiply and the political and economic interdependence of the world would increase. Thus, the concept of "collective security" itself would be dynamic and, if in one crisis it failed, in others it would succeed. Wilson's "idealism" inherently fostered the "realism" of growth and change.

Finally, such criticism is devoid of any hopeful vision for the future of mankind. It assumes that the traditional view of national interests will remain static and will always represent the most effective deterrent to aggression. Wilson provided a new way to look at national interests. He alone among the leaders of his time recognized the revolutionary impact of the first total war and he provided the framework for a new world order to manage that impact. If he was ahead of his time, asking his country and the world to see national security through an unselfish lens, his vision still was sharper than any other and has proven prophetic.

It took the horrors of another total war to persuade Americans that the United States should give wholehearted support to an international organization dedicated to peace and the ideals of liberty.[413] The political realities of the 20th century also taught Americans that, as Wilson prescribed, they had to accept moral leadership in world affairs if liberty was to prevail over oppression and if discussion was to substitute for war. Even those who criticize Wilson's vision have had to admit its influence and continued vitality. Former Secretary of

State Henry Kissinger has concluded that "When communism col-lapsed, the Wilsonian idea that the road to peace lay in collective secu-rity, coupled with the worldwide spread of democratic institutions, was adopted by administrations of both major political parties."[414]

Wilson foresaw the cataclysmic potential of 20th and 21st century international issues. He realized that technology-driven total war ren-dered war itself a blunt, not to say particularly inhumane, instrument for achieving diplomatic ends. And he realized, too, that forces opposed to economic and political liberty could poison international affairs and undermine world stability, in the way that terrorism threat-ens to in the early 21st century. In order to prevent any individual area of conflict from becoming a flashpoint for total war, as the Sarajevo assassination had, world opinion needed to be organized to prevent it.

Wilson's vision has served as a model for American foreign pol-icy in modern times, producing initiatives such as the creation of the United Nations, the Marshall Plan to reconstruct Europe after World War II, treaties to limit the spread of nuclear weapons, the World Bank, and even the downfall of communism. Wilson's concept of internationalism can be viewed as the best approach to modern prob-lems of disarmament, environmental degradation, and terrorism. George Kennan, a previous skeptic of Wilsonian ideals and an advo-cate of balance of power politics, wrote that, with respect to control of nuclear weapons, "the vision he put forward might be not just the dream of an idealist but...the price for the survival of civilization." Kennan also wrote that "In his vision of the future needs of world soci-ety, I now see Wilson as ahead of any other statesman of his time."[415]

Critics have pointed to inherent defects in Wilson's vision, and in the United Nations that is its current incarnation, and have argued that the United States must rely more on unilateral action to protect its interests and its liberty. They cite the difficulty in achieving consensus in an organization in which nations "disagree about the nature of the threat or about the type of sacrifice they are prepared to make to meet it."[416] The problem of achieving consensus within the international organiza-tion, particularly when not all members have democratic forms of gov-ernment, can, indeed be a challenge. However, the challenge will be multiplied exponentially if the United States, the world's only super-power, doesn't take leadership in the service of helping the organization succeed. Moreover, reliance by the United States on essentially unilateral action has not shown itself to be a more effective alternative.[417] It should be remembered that, as the growth of democratic movements, global trade, and the Internet draw people closer together, consensus could become more and more likely, particularly if the United States is perceived as sincerely interested in the needs of the rest of the world.

Unprecedented technological developments present the world of the 21st century with a degree of unpredictability and insecurity never before faced. The international vision of Wilson does not guarantee the solution to those problems, but it is hard to formulate a more rational approach than his. There is a growing recognition that critical modern problems, especially those resulting from 1) the proliferation of nuclear, chemical, and biological weapons, 2) startling developments in bioengineering, 3) the alarming impact of environmental damage, and 4) political instability caused by terrorists, can only be solved through international cooperation. Solutions depend on the willingness of the members of the world organization to see their sovereignty less selfishly—in the way Wilson envisioned nine decades ago. Whether they will do so is the issue that will determine the effectiveness of the United Nations.[418] In recent years, the organization has achieved significant success on some of these issues, particularly the enforcement of safeguards under the Nuclear Non-Proliferation Treaty by the International Atomic Energy Agency and the environmental and greenhouse gas limitations under the United Nations Framework Convention on Climate Change and its Kyoto Protocol. The challenge for America is to recognize that the world organization that now embodies Wilson's prescription is of fundamental importance to liberty and peace, both for America and for the world.

If the United States acts unilaterally too often, and is seen as ignoring the shared interests of the global community, it will likely create ill-will, awaken latent resentment, and stimulate countervailing power blocs that threaten its own security.[419] Moreover, such an approach requires the sacrifice of important civil liberties in the service of a society focused primarily on military preparedness. If, on the other hand, America remains true to its founding principles, and to Wilson's concept of internationalism, it will likely continue to serve, in Lincoln's phrase, as the "last, best hope of mankind."

America was not ready to embrace Wilson's ideals when Wilson was ready to articulate them. He called his fellow citizens to a vision of liberty in which short-term self-interest should no longer be the prime motivation for American foreign policy. No one has been more eloquent, or more influential, for the proposition that American liberty is best served when American foreign policy is carried out to promote international cooperation, peace, and freedom. For that, his greatness in history's pantheon is secure.

CHAPTER 6.

Franklin Roosevelt and the Democratization of the American Economy

The Great Depression of the 1930's devastated the economy of the United States, threatened its liberty and stability, and caused great human suffering. Bravely rebounding from disabling polio, Franklin Roosevelt revived his crippled country, reformed its failing capitalist economy, and established a lasting role for the federal government as the guarantor of a measure of economic and social security for its citizens, permanently broadening the meaning of American liberty.

1. The Human Impact

When Franklin Roosevelt served in Woodrow Wilson's Administration as Assistant Secretary of the Navy, he was a physically energetic advocate of a strong military and an aggressive approach to foreign affairs. He admired Wilson's wartime leadership and he looked forward to his own political future. By the time he ran for President in 1932, he had battled disease-caused physical disability and the great threat to the country's liberty came not from abroad but from domestic economic catastrophe.

Early in his Presidency, Roosevelt received the following letter from a woman in Philadelphia:

> There has been unemployment in my house for more than three years—my family have suffered from lack of water supply...for more than two years. Last winter I did not have coal...now winter is here again and we are suffering of cold, no water in the house, and we are facing to be forced out of the house...I am mother of little children, am sick and losing

my health, and we are eight people in the family, and where can I go when I don't have money because no one is working in my house …Waiting and Hoping that you will act quickly.[420]

In the same year, a social worker from Massachusetts wrote the following assessment of the human impact of widespread unemployment:

> This picture is so grim that whatever words I use will seem hysterical and exaggerated. And I find them all in the same shape—fear, fear driving them into a state of semi-collapse; cracking nerves; and an overpowering terror of the future…I haven't been in one home that hasn't offered me the spectacle of a human being being driven beyond his or her powers of endurance and sanity… They…are watching their children grow thinner and thinner; fearing the cold for children who have neither coats nor shoes; wondering about coal.[421]

In the early 1930's, America suffered the greatest economic catastrophe in its history. By 1933, fully 25 percent of the workforce—some thirteen million people had no job, and some observers believe that, given the unreliability of the figures, the number might even have been as high as seventeen million. And for those who were fortunate enough to have a job, their wages were likely to have declined by more than thirty percent between 1929 and 1932. Although the depression was really worldwide in scope, "no other industrial country experienced as much long-term unemployment as the United States."[422]

Statistics don't fully convey the emotional tragedies the depression spawned. They affected everyone, but particularly the most vulnerable of the population—children and the elderly. One historian of the New Deal vividly described the human toll:

> The fog of despair hung over the land. One out of every four American workers lacked a job…Families slept in tarpaper shacks and tin-lined caves and scavenged like dogs for food in the city dump…Thousands of vagabond children were roaming the land, wild boys of the road…Farmers stopped milk trucks along Iowa roads and

poured the milk into the ditch. Mobs halted mortgage sales, ran the men from the banks and insurance companies out of town...[423]

Another observed:

> Unemployment's effect upon the family was often...profound and far-reaching...Fathers discovered that without the usual financial power to buy bikes or bestow nickels, their control and authority over children were seriously weakened and sometimes completely undermined.[424]

The true depth of despair people felt was conveyed in a letter the President received in 1934 from a Pennsylvania man: "Can you be so kind as to advise me as to which would be the most human way to dispose of my self and family, as this is about the only thing that I see left to do."[425]

Many Americans had lost all hope in their future. To understand how circumstances descended to that level, and the demanding challenges Franklin Roosevelt faced as President, it is necessary to look back to the decades preceding the 1930's, during which the United States economy evolved from one of the strongest in the world to one of the most unbalanced.

2. Economic Growth and the Coming of Economic Depression

After America's great Civil War, its economy grew faster than that of any other major country, propelling the United States to world power status by the outset of the First World War. At the same time, however, the unfettered freedom enjoyed by economic capitalists resulted in some negative consequences for workers, farmers and average citizens. The Progressive Movement at the turn of the 20th century was formed to address those consequences, advocating measures to curb the excesses of big business and protect the health and well-being of the majority of citizens.

President Theodore Roosevelt, in an attempt to address the problems caused by rapid industrialization, large-scale immigration, and a political system frequently unresponsive to the needs of the electorate, used government as a tool for greater fairness and social improvement. He championed laws that restricted the business power gained through monopolistic practices, protected the interests of consumers, and encouraged the provision of social services. Woodrow Wilson built on the foundation Roosevelt laid by creating the Federal Trade Commission to ensure fair dealing in the marketplace, establishing the Federal Reserve System to provide controls on investment and banking, and enacting prohibitions against the use of child labor. And American entry into the First World War led President Wilson dramatically to increase the power and economic functions of the federal government.

The promising beginning represented by these developments was slowed or even halted by the policies of the Republican administrations following the War. In an effort to return to "normalcy," governmental activism in the service of the economic and social welfare of the majority of citizens was curtailed. Instead, the policies of Presidents Harding and Coolidge featured measures to protect big business by lowering taxes and increasing tariffs, but largely ignored measures to protect workers and farmers. Although the American economy continued to grow during the 1920's, driven by improvements in technology and resulting increases in productivity, the bulk of economic gains were realized by businessmen and investors. The economic status of the average American increased very little in comparison. During the decade, profits as a whole rose 80 percent, twice that of productivity, and profits in the financial sector increased 150 percent.[426]

Rapid growth in profits created pressure for the use of those profits to expand production as well as to speculate in the price of securities. Goods flooded markets in which consumers had too little buying capacity and the stock market absorbed more and more of the gains resulting from increased productivity.

By 1929, the 2.3 percent of the population with incomes over $10,000 were responsible for two-thirds of the 15 billion dollars of savings. The 60,000 families in the nation with the highest incomes saved almost as much as the bottom 25 million. The mass of the population simply lacked the increase in purchasing power to enable them to absorb the increase in goods.[427]

By the end of the 1920's, the American economy was showing serious signs of crisis. Farmers were the hardest hit. Almost half of Americans were dependent on the farm economy, yet they suffered from an almost decade long depression, with greatly restricted demand for farm products and rapidly growing surpluses. Foreign markets were limited by tariffs and the domestic market declined as a result of the restrictive immigration policies of the Republican administrations. Rural America was poor and getting poorer; the personal income of farmers rose during the decade only 1/3 as much as that of all Americans.[428] In 1930, more than 45 million rural residents still had no indoor plumbing and almost none had electricity.[429]

Industrial workers fared only somewhat better. The manufacturing sector grew rapidly from 1900, with mass production of durable goods such as the automobile leading the way. The cities where factories were located attracted millions of people from farms, including many African-Americans from former slave states, and most of the immigrants coming to the country after the turn of the century. Yet, the income of workers did not rise fast enough to sustain industrial growth over the long term. Although wages for workers increased slightly during the 1920's, their work week was long and they had few, if any, paid vacations. If they were laid off, no government program protected them against the consequences of unemployment. And if they were fortunate enough to keep a job over the long-term, they had no security to look forward to in retirement.

The end of the 1920's was also characterized by weakness in banking, real estate, and manufacturing. More than 5000 banks failed between 1923 and 1930.[430] During 1929, net investment for residential construction decreased significantly, business inventories tripled from those of 1928, and the growth of consumer spending slowed from over 7 percent in 1927-28 to 1.5 percent in 1928-29.[431] The stock market, by contrast, started to rise, attracting capital from many sources. Investors more and more resorted to borrowing to buy stocks "on margin," with these high interest loans secured by the value of the stocks. As the market continued to rise, investors became smitten with the dream of wealth and engaged in irresponsible speculation with borrowed funds. They were soon to suffer dire consequences when stock prices fell, creditors called in their margin loans, and borrowers had little cash to pay them.

Thursday, October 24, 1929, known as "black Thursday," saw stock prices fall dramatically, causing losses amounting to $9 billion; "black Tuesday," October 29, soon followed with even greater losses and, by November, stocks had lost one-third of their September value. As one historian has observed, "The multiplication of values that buying on margin made possible in a rising market worked with impartial and fearful symmetry when values were on the way down."[432] The famous stock market crash heralded the coming of the Great Depression of the 1930's, although it is probably not true that the crash "caused" the depression. The great economist John Maynard Keynes even thought that the crash was a healthy correction to an over-stimulated, speculation-based economy.[433] Only a small percentage of Americans owned stock in 1929 so the crash had little direct effect on the average citizen. However, it had a negative psychological effect, undermining confidence in the strength of the economy, thus slowing any potential recovery. And it clearly signaled that the decades-long economic expansion of the country was built on a questionable foundation.

American businessmen had utilized increases in productivity to keep prices and profits high, and wages relatively low. Not only was the average worker denied the benefits of increased productivity, but the economy as a whole was denied the indispensable advantage of growth in mass purchasing power. The impact of these factors was compounded by weaknesses in the banking sector and failure to curb irresponsible practices in the trading of securities. As a result, America suffered the most serious economic depression in its history.

3. The Early Depression and the Ordeal of President Hoover

Between the stock market crash of 1929 and the end of Herbert Hoover's Presidency in March, 1933, the American economy declined drastically and the suffering of the American people increased alarmingly. For farmers, the downturn of the early 1930's followed an already bleak decade. The worldwide economic collapse meant that whatever foreign markets existed in the 20's completely disappeared and, as the income of American workers plummeted, domestic demand for farm products declined significantly after 1929. Total farm income in 1932 was $2 billion compared with $6 billion in 1929. In the automobile industry, only one-third as many cars were manufactured in 1933 as in 1929, and that created parallel losses in related industries; as an example, steel production was cut 59 percent from 1929 output. In the electrical manufacturing and appliance industries, which had been in the forefront of the technologically-driven growth of the 1920's, revenues were reduced by two-thirds from 1929 to 1932.[434] In the traditional coal mining industry, production fell to levels not seen since 1904.

Thousands of bank failures meant that depositors saw their savings disappear and homeowners faced foreclosures on their mortgages. Between 1930 and 1932, over 600,000 homeowners lost their property and state and local governments thus saw their tax revenue shrink, resulting in further debt default and reductions in both services and wages. From 1929 to 1932, industrial construction decreased more than ninety percent and residential construction by more than eighty percent.

The human impact of the Depression can be seen most directly in statistics regarding unemployment. In 1929, only 3.2 percent of the workforce was unemployed; at the end of 1930, the figure rose to 8.7 percent of non-farm laborers—high, but not yet alarming. However, by the end of 1931, fully 15 percent of workers were out of a job, convincing most everyone that recovery was not near. The impact was not uniform—particularly hard hit were people who lived in large cities where durable goods manufacturing was concentrated. In Chicago and Detroit, for example, unemployment may have reached 50 percent and affected African-Americans newly arrived from the rural South disproportionately.[435]   Nationwide, black unemployment likely reached 50 percent by 1932.[436] Across the South itself, they clearly suffered more than any other race or class. The job picture was so bleak that some Americans, contrary to the image of the United States as the primary land of opportunity, decided to seek opportunities in other countries, including France, Italy, and even the Soviet Union.[437]

The federal government during the administration of President Herbert Hoover, from 1929 to 1933, failed to take sufficient steps either to ameliorate the human impact of the Depression or to convince a majority of the American people that it was committed to doing so. The President remained wedded to what was by then an outmoded economic philosophy that government should do little to interfere with the private, market economy. In fact, the government took some measures that were clearly counter-productive. In 1930, Congress passed and Hoover signed the Hawley-Smoot Tariff, which significantly increased duties on imported goods and made it more difficult for American exports—particularly farm surpluses— to be welcomed abroad. And the Federal Reserve, worried more about foreign withdrawals than domestic purchasing power, did little to help the banking system make credit more available.

President Hoover tried to do a number of things to reassure the public that recovery would come, to prevent further runs on banks, to encourage business voluntarily to maintain wage levels, and to urge local governments to ameliorate the plight of the unemployed. He did not support direct federal aid to the unemployed, for fear that the acts of local governments and volunteers would be discouraged. Although he wanted the Federal Reserve to ease credit and to assist the plight of failing banks, he was deferential to its legal independence and thus proposed no relevant legislation and exerted no real pressure to affect its actions. Hoover maintained his optimism about recovery even as the situation deteriorated steadily and rapidly during his term.

A particularly misguided, although likely well-intentioned, step by President Hoover was his decision to push a large tax increase through Congress. He believed that, through this legislation, the budget deficit would be reduced and more money would be available at low interest rates. But no such result ensued, the crisis of the banks continued, and too little money found its way to the public. Toward the end of his administration, the President supported measures to expand the role of the federal government and abandoned his iron-clad resistance to direct government action. The creation of the Reconstruction Finance Corporation and the Federal Home Loan Bank Board in 1932 made federal funds available to banks for distribution to the public to support home mortgages and a variety of infrastructure construction projects. These agencies set important precedents for later New Deal legislation, but offered too little, too late to affect the Depression in any significant way during the Hoover years.

The image of President Hoover in the mind of the electorate was probably made indelible by his administration's treatment of unemployed

World War I veterans who came to Washington to seek relief from Congress. These thousands were labeled the "Bonus Army" because, without jobs and suffering from poverty, they wanted to accelerate the payment of the war service bonus that otherwise would not come due until 1945. When Congress defeated the bill to do so, many of the veterans decided to camp at Anacostia Flats until 1945 in protest.

> The veterans built shacks out of lumber, packing boxes, scrap tin, and strips of canvas. Some lived in secondhand Army pup tents…they held formation, waited in chow lines, organized baseball games, dug latrines (known as 'Hoover villas') and rose and slept by bugle call. Wives and children began to join husbands, piecing together family life in the swampy land under the steaming sun…The rancid odor of decaying food, sweat, chloride, and urine began to settle over the flats…fifteen thousand or more of them…wanly hoping that Congress might recur to the bonus before adjournment.[438]

The President refused to meet with the veterans, although his wife did participate in passing out blankets and food. In late July, local police attempted to move protestors from a building and violence ensued, with one person dead. The District of Columbia authorities asked President Hoover for help and he sent in the Army under the command of General Douglas MacArthur, who later described the protestors as "a mob…animated by the essence of revolution."[439] MacArthur's troops, including Major George Patton at the head of the 3rd Cavalry and Major Dwight Eisenhower as MacArthur's aide[440] proved efficient and brutal:

> With four troops of cavalry clattering by with drawn sabers, followed by six tanks, with machine guns hooded, and a column of infantry, with fixed bayonets, steel helmets, gas masks and at their belts, blue tear-gas bombs…the soldiers cleared the downtown buildings with bayonets and gas. Then, as evening fell, they moved into Anacostia, turning out the inhabitants with military dispatch…tossing gas bombs into little groups of defiant veterans…women and children, their eyes streaming with tears ran frantically from

their dwellings, without time to gather their pathetic belongings.[441]

President Hoover was seen by most Americans as insensitive to the plight of these veterans, whatever Americans may have thought of the protestors' tactics, and it permanently affected his reputation. One Washington newspaper declared, "If the Army must be called out to make war on unarmed citizens, this is no longer America." [442]

Some believe that history has treated Hoover too harshly, given the unprecedented nature of the depression crisis and the steps he finally began to take that later served as building blocks for the New Deal. However, he was never able to convince most Americans that he cared sufficiently about their plight. The country gave its verdict on the Hoover Presidency when, in the election of 1932, it swept into office the Democratic Governor of New York, Franklin D. Roosevelt, with one of the largest popular and electoral vote mandates in history. The new President faced a country with little hope and an economy in shambles. He had no comparable experience in American history to use as a model. Would he be able to restore that hope and rebuild that economy? Was he the man for the time?

4. Background and Preparation for Leadership

Franklin Delano Roosevelt was born on January 30, 1882 of wealthy Hudson River parents who differed from their privileged peers in their identification with the Democratic Party—the pre-Civil War party affiliation of Franklin's father's family. But in most other ways, they were very much a part of a tradition of New York upper class security, leisure, and civic responsibility. They lived near the Astors and Vanderbilts, in Hyde Park, and were every bit as financially secure as their neighbors.

Franklin's father, James, had been married once and had one son from that marriage. After the death of his first wife, when he was 52 years of age in 1880, he met and fell in love with Sara Delano, a woman then 26, the same age as James' son 'Rosy.' Educated at Union College and Harvard Law School, James had acquired a fortune both by inheriting significant assets and by making investments, some wise and some not so wise. He tried to avoid excessive displays of wealth and had a deep commitment to civic and religious responsibility, serving on the Hyde Park School Board, as a village supervisor, and as a warden of his Episcopal Church.[443]

Sara Delano Roosevelt also came from a wealthy family, but one that provided for her a particularly cosmopolitan upbringing. Her father was involved in the China trade and, when she was seven, Sara sailed from New York to China on a clipper ship to be with him. She lived abroad a good deal, with three years in Hong Kong, and later some time in both France and Germany. Although always a part of upper class New York, she maintained throughout her life a deep compassion for people and a strong belief in the need for civic responsibility. She was to impart to Franklin, her only child, many of these character aspects, and was particularly close to him her entire life.

Franklin was an adored child, given all the advantages inherent in his family and the property they owned. During the summer, the family would vacation at Campobello Island, off the coast of New Brunswick, Canada, where Franklin developed his skill and passion for sailing and his fascination with the sea. Although outdoor activities held great interest for young Franklin, he also spent long hours reading the many books available to him and, at nine years of age, became a collector of stamps—a hobby he pursued avidly for the remainder of his life.

One biographer describes the development of Franklin's personality by saying that James and Sara "…gave him their undivided attention and instilled in him an abiding sense of self-worth. 'As a matter of fact,' Sara later recalled, 'I do not believe I have ever seen a little boy who seemed always to be so consistently enjoying himself.'"[444] Another concludes, "few boys could boast of a happier childhood."[445] Franklin's parents provided many opportunities to broaden his horizons and become aware of his place in the world. "By the time he was 10, he had met writer Mark Twain, members of European royalty, and his first President, Grover Cleveland. By the time he was 15, he had been to Europe eight times."[446] As a corollary to privilege, Franklin was taught that he should live a life of both moral and social responsibility. His parents were religious and sought to pass on their faith in God, their commitment to setting a moral example for others, and their dedication to family and community. These values undoubtedly had a strong impact on Franklin's later choice of a career in politics.

Franklin's early education was, in many ways, typical for an aristocratic young man—private tutors until preparatory school, summers in Europe, and close family ties. He was the center of his mother's life and her devotion was matched by a degree of over-protectiveness that kept him from formal schooling longer than most boys his age. Franklin entered Groton School in Massachusetts as a boarding student when he was fourteen, with the usual entry age being twelve. As a result, he seems to have been treated somewhat as an outsider by his classmates. In addition, his thin physical frame and lack of experience in team sports, contributed to his plight. Franklin tried hard to fit in and gain the acceptance of his peers, with varying degrees of success, and his efforts likely contributed to the development of his adult personality. He perfected the ability to camouflage his insecurity with a cloak of geniality.

Franklin's character and outlook were influenced by his relationship with Groton's stern yet charismatic headmaster, Reverend Endicott Peabody. Imbued with the spirit of Christian humanitarianism and the social gospel, Peabody structured his school to build the character of his students, children of the upper class, so they might serve their church, their country and their fellow man in leadership capacities. The training was rigorous, the discipline was strict, and the moral purpose ever-present. Roosevelt later said that the influence of Mr. and Mrs. Peabody on him was greater than anyone other than his parents.[447]

Franklin was an intelligent student, consistently placing in the upper quarter of his class. He became a very good writer, a talent he exhibited and enjoyed for the rest of his life, and eagerly participated in the required debate curriculum, acquiring skills as an effective public speaker. He joined the school's Missionary Society and volunteered to become a counselor at Groton's summer camp in New Hampshire for poor, inner city boys from nearby Boston and other cities, including New York. He even sought out the opportunity during the school year to shovel coal and perform household chores for an elderly African-American woman who lived nearby, much to the pleasure of his mother, Sara. One can say that his time at Groton helped make him more of a well-rounded and socially conscious man than he otherwise might have become.[448]

Franklin's adolescent years were not only influenced by Reverend Peabody, but by his own increasingly famous fifth cousin, Theodore

Roosevelt. At a time when his own father's health was declining, Franklin reveled in the courageous exploits of the Assistant Secretary of the Navy who left the government to lead the Rough Riders during the Spanish-American War, then was elected as reformist Governor of New York. He, too, would dedicate his life to serve and lead his fellow man. In an outward sign of his idolization, Franklin began to copy some of Theodore's physical mannerisms, including wearing pince-nez eyeglasses.[449]

Upon graduation from Groton, Franklin followed in his father's and his famous cousin's footsteps by entering Harvard University in the fall of 1900. In a social rejection similar to what he faced as a late-comer at Groton, he was turned down in his attempt to join the prestigious Porcellian Club, an organization to which both his father and his cousin, Theodore, had belonged. As with other setbacks he was to suffer later in his life, this one did not impair what was becoming his indomitable spirit and drive to succeed. In fact, it likely made him stronger. In December of his freshman year, his invalid father passed away, posing another challenge to his spirit; Franklin was able to handle the death in a mature way, continuing at school while providing essential emotional support to his mother, Sara. During his sophomore and junior years, she moved into a house in Boston to be near her only son. During that eventful first year, Franklin successfully ran for the Board of the school newspaper, beginning what he considered his most important activity at Harvard. He achieved success and notoriety in that role, writing editorials on a variety of subjects, including civic responsibility, and thus increasing confidence in his own ability to lead others and to achieve his primary life goals.

Franklin was a slightly above-average student, but an extremely hard worker, as was necessary to maintain a heavy academic, social, and extra-curricular schedule. And he was continually looking to a public-oriented future. Although still a member of the patrician class, he was gradually strengthening his commitment to improve the lives of others. In later years, Franklin distanced himself from those of his peers at Groton and Harvard who might have been more occupied with material gain than social conscience. In 1928, just prior to the Stock Market Crash and the onset of the Depression, he lamented their lack of public-spirited leadership and attributed it "not to the lack of possible leaders, but to the enormous wet blanket which is offered to any individual or group which might seek to encourage leadership."[450]

Eleanor Roosevelt came into Franklin's life in the spring of his sophomore year at Harvard. She was Franklin's fifth cousin, once removed, the daughter of Theodore Roosevelt's brother, Elliott, who was also Franklin's godfather. Born of a wealthy New York family in 1884, she was held to almost unreachable standards of grace and beauty by her mother, Anna, giving Eleanor a long-standing belief that she was homely. Her father, Elliott, was often away from home as a result of alcoholism and likely mental illness, but provided tangible affection for Eleanor when she was with him, and served as her only real figure of parental empathy during her childhood. Eleanor's mother died when the child was eight years old, and, she went to live with her grandmother, who proved to be a strict disciplinarian and an unfeeling surrogate parent, although she did allow Eleanor's father to visit occasionally. Those visits were precious to the young girl, who was unaware of her father's illness and unpredictable behavior. She later wrote that after one of his early visits to the grandmother's house she imagined that she and he would be together at some future date.[451] Always close emotionally to her father, Eleanor was distraught when he died less than two years later, deepening the unhappiness of her childhood. When she was fifteen years old, she was sent to a private girl's school in England, where the Headmistress impressed on Eleanor the importance of service to others and the need for a woman to have independence of mind and strong defenses against misfortune and hurt. By age eighteen, she returned to New York to live with cousins, join the Junior League, and teach at a Settlement House for immigrants.

Franklin courted Eleanor during his junior year at Harvard and in the fall of 1903, proposed marriage to her and she accepted. When he told his mother of his plans, Sara reacted negatively, believing that at twenty-two and nineteen, they were too young to marry. Franklin was determined to marry Eleanor, however, and, despite his deep feeling for his mother and her dependence on him, he did not waver from his decision. From the early days of their relationship through the course of his Presidency, Eleanor's social concern was a major influence on Franklin. After accompanying her on a visit to a poor child who was one of her Settlement House students, she recalled that Franklin "was absolutely shaken when he saw the cold-water tenement where the child lived, and kept saying he simply could not believe human beings lived that way."[452]

The marriage took place in New York City in the spring of 1905. Despite Sara's initial opposition, she decided to buy a house for the couple in New York City. The Roosevelts would have six children, five boys and one girl, Anna, who was their first born in May, 1906. All but one, Franklin Delano, Jr., who died in infancy, lived to adulthood. Eventually, Sara built two adjoining houses for them, without first consulting Eleanor about the matter. During the early years of their marriage, Eleanor was subservient to Sara's wishes, although she frequently reacted emotionally when she was not taken into account. Franklin consistently attempted to compromise issues rather than confront the conflict directly, no doubt a useful skill in his later political life.

After graduation from Harvard, Franklin chose to study law at Columbia Law School and entered private practice in New York in 1907. Although a competent and fairly successful lawyer, it was soon clear to Franklin that he would not be satisfied with a legal career. He supposedly told his colleagues that he wanted to run for political office and, eventually, become President. He had a clear model to follow in his cousin Theodore, who had been a member of the New York legislature, Assistant Secretary of the Navy, and Governor of New York. With the exception of allegiance to the Democratic Party, Franklin's path followed Theodore's fairly closely.

Franklin's first office was as state representative after the election of 1910. He focused on conservation of natural resources, arguing for the public interest over that of commercial development. He became identified with progressive reformers and supported legislation establishing workmen's compensation and limiting working hours for women and children. During his service in Albany, he met Louis Howe, a newspaper reporter who was to become a close friend and his main political advisor for the remainder of his life. Howe later said that from the outset he was convinced that "nothing but an accident could keep him from becoming president."[453]

Roosevelt's political ambition quickly turned from the local to the national stage when he endorsed Governor Woodrow Wilson of New Jersey for President in 1912, hoping for a position in the administration if Wilson were elected. Upon Wilson's victory, the newly appointed Secretary of the Navy, Josephus Daniels of North Carolina, sought out Roosevelt and offered him the position of Assistant Secretary. Roosevelt accepted at once, conscious of the example cousin Theodore had set in the same job, and eager to expand the navy as an essential element in the security of the nation. He remained in the position from 1913 until 1920, throughout the First World War, taking a brief time out in 1914 to run as a reformist candidate for the Senate from New York under the new Amendment providing for direct election of Senators, only to lose the primary election.

Roosevelt's political philosophy was further defined and shaped by the example Wilson set. Building on Theodore Roosevelt's concept of the Presidency as "bully pulpit" and "voice of the people," Wilson clearly viewed himself as the primary leader of the country, separate and apart from Congress. In order to prepare for and wage war, he greatly expanded the role and power of the Executive Branch in ways that have been an example for other Presidents to the present time. Franklin Roosevelt himself put it this way in 1920: "Most of our great deeds have been brought about by Executive Leaders, by the Presidents who were not tools of Congress but were true leaders of the Nation, who so truly interpreted the needs and wishes of the people that they were supported in their great tasks."[454]

In his personal life, the differences in personality between Eleanor and Franklin gradually resulted in emotional distance from one another during the war years. Franklin was outgoing, sociable, and eager to experience what the world had to offer. Eleanor was reserved, serious, and rather straight-laced. From early in their marriage, she maintained a separate bedroom and shied away from public life. She shouldered most of the responsibility for the rearing of their five children,[455] while, at the same time, dealing with a strong-willed mother-in-law. At some point during his service in the Wilson Administration, Franklin began a love affair with Lucy Mercer, then Eleanor's social secretary. One biographer of Roosevelt has written:

> Lucy was intelligent, charming, and beautiful, the sort of woman, people said, with whom men naturally fell in love. Franklin apparently found in Lucy the kind of uncritical acceptance that Eleanor was unable to provide.[456]

When Eleanor discovered revealing correspondence between the two, she demanded that Franklin end the affair or give her a divorce—at the time a politically lethal state of affairs. With some pressure from his mother, Franklin agreed to Eleanor's ultimatum. The crisis affected both of them profoundly. From that time forward, they carried on a more businesslike, professional partnership rather than an emotionally intimate marriage. Franklin learned that not everything in his life would go his way and Eleanor suffered another blow to her self-image; yet, at the same time, she became determined to live her own life and make her independent mark.

As the war ended and the Wilson Administration came to a close, Franklin Roosevelt's political star was clearly on the rise. He had made an admirable record as Assistant Secretary of the Navy, he was well known and came from a politically admired family; he was also good-looking, well-spoken, and almost as physically vigorous as his famous cousin. At the 1920 Democratic Convention, he was selected as the Vice Presidential nominee on a ticket headed by James M. Cox, Governor of Ohio. He campaigned extensively, visiting thirty-two states, in planned contrast to Warren G. Harding, the Republican nominee, who campaigned almost exclusively from his front porch. Roosevelt conducted the most active national campaign that had ever been undertaken, speaking many times in a day, traveling by car and, in the first such use, by airplane. He urged his countrymen to support the efforts of President Wilson to join the League of Nations. Decrying isolationism, he urged his fellow Americans to "see that modern civilization has become so complex and the lives of civilized men so interwoven with the lives of other men in other countries as to make it impossible to be in this world and out of it."[457] On the domestic side, Roosevelt called for an activist federal government, one that could efficiently protect its natural resources from exploitation and its human resources from ignorance and workplace abuse. Although Roosevelt was enthusiastically received throughout the country, Republican Harding was elected President in a landslide. The result reflected the yearning of war-weary Americans to follow him in a return to what he called "normalcy." As Roosevelt himself put it, "Every war brings after it a period of materialism and conservatism; people tire quickly of ideals and we are now repeating history."[458]

5. The Challenge of Polio

Roosevelt's career up to the summer of 1921 can be regarded as blessed with good fortune and relatively easily won political fame. His long-held ambition to become President seemed quite realistic and soon to be accomplished. But all that was soon to be threatened by the onset of chronic disease and disability that would test his character as never before. On August 10, 1921, while vacationing with his family at Campobello Island, Franklin felt strangely tired and cold while opening his mail in his bathing suit. He felt unable to get dressed. He put himself to bed that night, confident that the feeling was temporary; however, upon awakening in the morning, he had difficulty moving his left leg, he was feverish and his body ached all over. Soon he lost feeling in both legs. "I tried to persuade myself that this trouble with my leg was muscular, that it would disappear as I used it...but presently, it refused to work, and then the other."[459] Rather than disappear, the paralysis became worse, affecting his basic bodily functions as well as his ability to walk and stand. He was later diagnosed by medical specialists as having acute anterior poliomyelitis, with an uncertain prognosis. The only hopeful thing was that his bodily functions soon returned to normal, although his ability to stand and walk unaided did not.

Franklin turned for encouragement to Eleanor and to Louis Howe. They facilitated his effort to do whatever was necessary to resume a normal life, both physically and politically. Franklin resolved to devote himself to rebuilding his body in the hope of walking again, and to plan for the eventual resumption of his political career. Howe said at the time, "...by gad, legs or no legs, Franklin will be President."[460] Eleanor devoted herself to helping her husband rehabilitate his body and his career, while, at the same time, deepened her commitment to establishing her own identity, separate from her husband and separate from the sheltered, aristocratic upbringing of her youth. Although the marriage never regained the emotional closeness it had prior to the revelation of Franklin's affair with Lucy Mercer, the lives of Eleanor and Franklin would be forever intertwined; he provided her with the means to affect the lives of others and she provided him with perceptive eyes and ears on the world outside his physical orbit. Franklin's need for empathy and love would come from others, including, for an extended period, his confidential secretary, Marguerite (Missy) LeHand.

For the seven years following his initial affliction, Franklin Roosevelt exhibited extraordinary will power and physical stamina to make the most of his disease-ravaged body. Always fond of the water, he dedicated himself to swimming as his basic rehabilitative exercise. He discovered the therapeutic benefits of the warm, natural springs at Warm Springs, Georgia and, eventually, purchased the property and established the Warm Springs Foundation as a resource for other victims of polio. He invested the majority of his assets in Warm Springs which became, for him, a second home. Franklin transformed his upper body from one that was proportional and slim to one that featured muscular bulk and biceps that he claimed were larger than those of heavyweight boxing champion Jack Dempsey. He soon taught himself how to walk a bit on crutches, while his legs were encased in iron braces, and even had his automobile fitted with hand controls allowing him to drive. However, much of Roosevelt's activity was, of necessity, sedentary. He devoted time to his stamp collection, built ship models, read voraciously and constantly reached out for friends and acquaintances to come to his home. Never in this period was he known to pity himself—only to look to his future, one in which he vainly hoped he would regain his physical powers.

Roosevelt took extraordinary steps to hide the extent of his disability. He would not allow himself to be photographed in his wheelchair or being carried up stairs. It seems extraordinary from the vantage point of today's world of instant, real-time news coverage, but the press cooperated in the charade and the fact is that most Americans did not fully know of the effects of his disease.

Always an optimistic sort, Roosevelt's affliction deepened his tendency to see life positively and to obscure difficulties. As one historian stated, "it endowed him with an aura of radiant indomitability."[461] When he was asked during his Presidency whether problems worried him, he replied, "If you had spent two years in bed trying to wiggle your big toe, after that anything else would seem easy!"[462] Many have also seen a change in his character, a transformation from a man who was somewhat distant from the lives of ordinary people to one who had real understanding for those who were disadvantaged. He became even more committed to use politics to lead a more mature, purposeful life; in doing so, he developed a fine-tuned capacity for political calculation. Arthur Schlesinger, Jr. described his new political personality:

> He had always delighted in people. But now...his extroverted Rooseveltian sociability was compounded by his invalid's compulsion to charm anyone who came to his bedside...But

behind the cordiality and exuberance there remained an impassable reserve which...none could penetrate. The relentless buoyancy was less an impulse of the soul than a mask of cheer to the world...a defense against pity without and discouragement within...He enjoyed people, but rarely gave himself to them...Nearly everybody was expendable...Noncommitment also gave him the inner independence which could free him from idealism as well as cynicism...it also meant private sadness. It condemned him to a final loneliness and melancholy."[463]

6. Path to the Presidency

In 1928, Roosevelt's efforts at rehabilitation were interrupted by the call of political opportunity. Al Smith, the Democratic Governor of New York, was nominated for President and he urged Roosevelt to run for the gubernatorial seat. Smith believed that Roosevelt would attract support in upstate New York, thus strengthening the entire Democratic ticket and increasing Smith's chances of carrying the state in the Presidential contest. Although Roosevelt was reluctant to enter the political fray before he was successful in restoring his physical ability, particularly in a year when he thought prospects for Democrats would be slim, he acquiesced to Smith's plea. In later years he said of the race, "I didn't want it...I wanted, much more, to get my right leg to move!...But the moral pressure was too strong."[464]

Anticipating concern about the state of his health, Roosevelt decided to wage a most vigorous campaign, demonstrating his strength and stamina. He carried on a tireless effort, speaking from one end of the state to the other, quieting concern about his frailty. In November, he won his contest by 25,000 votes, although Smith lost the state by more than 100,000.

When Roosevelt took office as Governor of New York on January 1, 1929, the stock market crash had not yet occurred and the full force of the economic depression had yet to be felt. Nevertheless, in his Inaugural Address he indicated that he was willing to use government as a positive force to aid those people who were most vulnerable to economic hardship. He called upon New Yorkers to "help those who have helped us. To secure more of life's pleasures for the farmer;

to guard the toilers in the factories and to insure them a fair wage and protection from the dangers of their trades…to open the doors of knowledge to their children more widely; to aid those who are crippled and ill…"[465] As the economic downturn resulted in widespread unemployment, Roosevelt became the first governor to support direct state work relief aid to those who were unemployed. He established the Temporary Emergency Relief Administration (TERA) under the leadership of Harry Hopkins, a tough-minded, big-hearted social worker who was to become his closest confidant throughout the years of his Presidency and the primary advocate of work relief on the federal level. TERA provided jobs for the unemployed as well as housing, food, and clothing wherever needed. Conscious of the precedent he was setting, Roosevelt defended his work relief program by saying that "the State accepts the task cheerfully because it believes that it will help restore that close relationship with its people which is necessary to preserve our democratic form of government."[466]

Governor Roosevelt's defense of his relief program captured in a nutshell the philosophy of soon to be President Roosevelt in the establishment of the New Deal. In August 1931 he summarized that thinking in a message to the New York legislature:

> What is the state? It is the duly constituted representative of an organized society of human beings—created by them for their mutual protection and well-being. The state or the government is but the machinery through which such mutual aid and protection is achieved…Our government is not the master but the creature of the people. The duty of the state towards the citizens is the duty of the servant to its master."[467]

These words stand in stark contrast to the rhetoric of conservative politicians in late 20th and early 21st century America, portraying the government as the cause of economic troubles rather than an ameliorator of human suffering. To Governor Roosevelt, the economic downturn following the stock market crash was caused more by the stupidity, greed, and short-sightedness of the business leaders from his own economic class than by any policies of government. He believed that those who avoided the hardships of economic depression had an obligation to those who did not. And he argued that the role of government is to provide the vehicle for protecting and rescuing its citizens from unemployment, economic insecurity, and physical hardship. His political philosophy was an outgrowth of many influences from his earlier life—his family's commitment to public service, Headmaster Peabody's social gospel, Eleanor's empathy for the poor, his experience in the wartime administration of Woodrow Wilson, and his battle against disability.

Roosevelt's bold leadership in New York attracted national attention—particularly in contrast to what was considered the insensitivity and inaction of President Hoover in Washington. One might say that, all his life, Roosevelt prepared himself for the Presidency itself. He viewed public life and the opportunity to be President with great relish. Hoover, on the other hand, seemed to many to be uncomfortable in that role and to lack confidence in his own ability to master it. Roosevelt never doubted his own fitness for the office.[468] One can never imagine Hoover saying, as Roosevelt did, "no man ever willingly gives up public life—no man who has ever tasted it."[469]

After a decisive re-election as Governor in 1930, Roosevelt set out to capture the Democratic nomination for President in 1932 by advocating the principles of his New York program to the national economic depression. He would boldly make government work to assist those who suffered the most. In an address on April 7, 1932 known as "The Forgotten Man" Speech, he outlined a national recovery program that was based on helping "the *forgotten man* at the bottom of the economic pyramid." Identifying a major cause of the depression as the loss by farmers of their purchasing power, he concluded that "the result of this loss…is that many other millions of people engaged in industry in the cities cannot sell industrial products to the farming half of the Nation," thus causing urban unemployment. In addition to restoring purchasing power to farmers, he advocated ensuring that mortgage foreclosures do not dispossess both home owners and farm owners. Government, he said, should have as its objective providing "at least as much assistance to the little fellow as it is now giving to the large banks and corporations," a pointed criticism of President Hoover's policies.[470]

While The Forgotten Man Speech attracted a great deal of political support, it also crystallized opposition to Roosevelt among conservative Democrats. Al Smith, once again running for the nomination, accused him of fomenting class conflict, and pitting the

poor against the rich.   But Roosevelt was not deterred. In a Commencement Speech at Georgia's Oglethorpe University in May, he
argued that the Depression stemmed from "an insufficient distribution
of buying power coupled with an oversufficient speculation in production." He prescribed "a wiser, more equitable distribution of the
national income...to insure that all who are willing and able to work
receive from it at least the necessities of life." In words that cannot
have soothed the concerns of investors and conservatives, he warned
that "In such a system, the reward for a day's work will have to be
greater, on the average, than it has been, and the reward to capital,
especially capital which is speculative, will have to be less." After a
contentious primary season and a nearly deadlocked, four-ballot convention, Roosevelt finally prevailed and was given the opportunity to
begin the "bold, persistent experimentation" he advocated in his
Oglethorpe Address. [471]

Breaking with tradition to become the first Presidential nominee
to deliver his acceptance speech in person, Roosevelt issued a most
famous call to action, one which also broke tradition by re-defining the
role of the federal government. He castigated the Republican Administration for assuming that the depression was caused by "economic
laws [that]...cause panics which no one could prevent" and for believing that the duty of government was "to see to it that a favored few are
helped and hope that some of their prosperity will leak through, sift
through, to labor, to the farmer, to the small business man." Roosevelt
observed that what he called "the failure of Republican leaders to solve
our troubles" had not yet led to "unreasoning radicalism." He praised
his countrymen for suffering so much yet maintaining "an orderly and
hopeful spirit" despite "crushing want." As President, he would have
to deal with the very real potential of such radicalism. He blamed the
Depression on excessive corporate profits and surpluses during the
decade of the twenties, leading to "unnecessary plants" and financial
speculation, then to unemployment, loss of purchasing power, and
credit contraction. His solution was to use the federal government to
lead economic reconstruction by ensuring both "work and security."
He pledged to all Americans a "more equitable opportunity to share in
the distribution of national wealth," which he famously called "a _**new
deal**_ for the American people."[472]

To project the energy and optimism he promised in his New
Deal, Roosevelt embarked on a personal speaking campaign that took

him to almost all of the states. Traveling by airplane, train, bus and auto, he carried his infectious smile and warm personality to as many people as he could reach. The contrast with President Hoover's detached melancholy was dramatic. Roosevelt offered action, hope, and help for the "forgotten man." He would lift the nation by using the federal government to address the harshness caused by economic forces—to provide relief, old age assistance, protection against unemployment, to restore the purchasing power of farmers and to ensure that markets were not governed by speculation and manipulation. In November, the nation elected him with enormous margins: 7 million popular votes (out of a total of 39.7 million) and 413 electoral votes (out of a total of 531).

As the country waited an agonizing four months for the new President to be inaugurated, the economic crisis and accompanying human suffering became rapidly much worse. More and more banks failed, depriving thousands of their life savings; the winter brought more hunger, disease, and homelessness, particularly in large cities and rural farms; yet many financiers and corporate executives continued to draw enormous salaries and bonuses, seemingly indifferent to the plight of their fellow citizens. The mood of the country was pessimistic and depressed. The President-elect was to overcome that pessimism and give people hope; he prepared for action to reassure America, relieve its suffering, and rescue its economic system.

7. Preparing the New Deal

Franklin Roosevelt came to the Presidency determined to restore public confidence by using the federal government to establish the public interest as the paramount political concern of the nation. He and his advisors were more certain of their diagnoses of problems than they were of their solution. Nevertheless, they were committed to action, to experimentation, to challenging tradition, and to rescuing the capitalist economy before it would be too late.

Roosevelt sought advice and ideas from a broad variety of Americans, especially from the brightest minds in academia. In the run-up to the election, he had organized a Brains Trust [later changed to "Brain" Trust] of leading economists and political scientists, chiefly Columbia University professors Adolf A. Berle, Jr., Raymond Moley, and Rexford G. Tugwell, who concluded that a primary cause of the depression was an imbalance of income that resulted loss of consumer purchasing power. In a speech in September, 1932, Roosevelt adopted that conclusion and called for "meeting the problem of underconsumption [by] distributing wealth and products more equitably."[473] He thus foreshadowed New Deal policies that used the federal government to get money into the hands of ordinary people rather than to offer incentives to business for increased production. There were other recommendations coming from experts that Roosevelt was less attracted to, although, from time to time, formed the basis of some of his policies. Conservatives, including Joseph Kennedy and Bernard Baruch, urged cutting government spending and raising taxes. Some liberals, including John Maynard Keynes and Marriner Eccles, urged massive government spending and encouraged inflation as a path to economic growth. Roosevelt avoided this path until the political situation pushed him in that direction after his re-election in 1936. Others, including Brain Trust members Berle and Tugwell, recommended major structural reform of the economy with government planning at the center. Roosevelt tried that approach early in his first term, under the National Industrial Recovery Act, with rather chaotic results, and later abandoned it after the Supreme Court found constitutional flaws in the legislation.

As his inauguration neared, Roosevelt kept foremost in his mind a pledge he made in his speech at Oglethorpe University early in his campaign, for "a wiser, more equitable distribution of the national income" as well as his sense that "the country needs [and] demands bold, persistent experimentation."[474] He later recalled the condition of the country at that time:

> By Inauguration Day...the banks of the United States were all closed, financial transactions had ceased, business and industry had sunk to their lowest levels. The widespread unemployment which accompanied the collapse had created a general feeling of utter helplessness.[475]

On March 4, 1933, after taking the oath of office, Roosevelt was assisted by his son as he took a few halting steps to the podium outside the White House to speak to an anxious nation. His clear opening message was intended to help erase the demoralization about the present and the future that pervaded the minds of his countrymen. "First of all," he declared, "let me assert my firm belief that the only thing we have to fear is fear itself—nameless, unreasoning, unjustified terror which paralyzes needed efforts to convert retreat into advance." He assured his listeners that "this great nation will endure as it has endured, will revive and will prosper," promising that he would "act and act quickly." Under his program of action, "our greatest primary task is to put people to work...in part by direct recruiting by the Government itself." An equally important effort would be "to raise the value of agricultural products and with this the power to purchase the output of our cities." He would, at the same time, "prevent...the tragedy of the growing loss through foreclosure of our small homes and farms." In response to what many believed was a major cause of the depression, he pledged "a strict supervision of all banking and credits and investments, so that there will be an end to speculation with other people's money."[476] Although specifics were left to the legislative proposals that were to follow, the Inaugural Address had the effect of reviving the hope of the American people. The new President was seen as a man who knew how to lead the nation and one who had confidence in its future.

Roosevelt wasted no time in taking action to ameliorate hardship and to bring needed reform to the American economic system. The period from the Inauguration to June 16, 1933 has been dubbed "The Hundred Days," the most famous period of Presidential/Congressional legislative creativity in the history of the country. The new President sent fifteen messages to Congress to address the economic crisis and was able to sign fifteen bills passed in response to his initiatives. Together with what was called "The Second Hundred Days" in 1935, it established much of Roosevelt's political legacy and further broadened the meaning of liberty for the average American.

8. Rescuing Life Savings

Franklin Roosevelt took office in the midst of a bank panic. From the onset of the Depression in 1929, more than 5000 banks had failed. As the Inauguration approached, the rate of failure dramatically increased and banks in every state were in financial distress. Citizens who had been in the habit of putting their life savings in these institutions began saw their futures in serious jeopardy. As William Leuchtenburg has described it, "people stood in long queues with satchels and paper bags to take gold and currency away from the banks to store in mattresses and old shoe boxes. It seemed safer to put your life's savings in the attic than to trust the greatest financial institutions in the country."[477] In an effort to prevent wholesale panic well beyond the capacity of the banks to pacify, state governors declared bank holidays so that by Saturday, March 4th, Inauguration Day, thirty eight states had closed their banks and many of the rest severely limited bank operations and the amount of withdrawals.

As Roosevelt was driven to the Inauguration he was told the New York Stock Exchange and the Chicago Board of Trade had suspended trading for fear of the spread of the bank panic to investors. He summoned representatives of the nation's bankers to an emergency meeting at the White House the next day. He announced to them and to the nation that he was issuing executive orders to declare a four day banking holiday throughout the country and to suspend all gold transactions. He also reviewed with them the specifics of emergency legislation his advisors had worked out during the post-election period with former President Hoover's staff that he planned to submit to the Congress as soon as it met on the following Thursday. The proposed Emergency Banking Act conferred on the President the power to regulate gold and foreign exchange transactions, authorized the Reconstruction Finance Corporation to shore up banks by buying their preferred stock, increased the power of the Federal Reserve Board to issue money, and permitted the re-opening of the banks under strict, new federal requirements to safeguard depositors. Congress took only eight hours to pass the bill the same day it reconvened. At the same time, the bank holiday was extended through the week-end to permit the Treasury Department more time to determine which banks were solvent enough to reopen.

The banking crisis gave Roosevelt the opportunity to begin his practice of broadcasting Fireside Chats over the radio during which he would speak directly to the American people to explain actions his administration was taking and to provide avuncular reassurance at a time of great suffering. This technique ensured that his message would be unmodified by editors at newspapers that may have been politically opposed to his program. He said during the first such "chat" on Sunday, March 12, that, as a result of the government's actions, "it is safer to keep your money in a reopened bank than under the mattress."[478] And the country listened. On Monday, the day after the banking holiday ended, deposits in banks were larger than withdrawals and, within a few weeks, seventy percent of banks had reopened.[479] The new President was able to influence both the minds and hearts of the American people as much as any President had ever done. In the midst of a crisis of economic hardship, he had, in just his first week, convinced most of his countrymen that he would take care of them.

Roosevelt knew that he needed to provide more permanent changes in the banking system in order to ensure that depositors would be protected over the long-term from the dangers of speculative loans and undercapitalized banks. In what became the Glass-Steagall Banking Act of 1933, the Administration convinced Congress to enact a variety of measures intended to reassure a bank's customers and investors, including: increased requirements for bank capital and reserves, strict regulation of bank officials, separation of commercial and investment banking, and, perhaps most important, a system of federal guarantees for bank deposits under the Federal Deposit Insurance Corporation (FDIC). The FDIC remains the single most important protector of the savings of average Americans. Bankers themselves had bitterly resisted the legislation, instead supporting industry self-regulation and fearing that deposit insurance would mean that the larger, urban banks would have to pay for the weaknesses of small, rural institutions.

As the Depression continued, and domestic political pressure for greater action increased, Roosevelt proposed legislation in 1935 that would strengthen federal control over monetary policy. The Banking Act of 1935 established the current Board of Governors of the Federal Reserve System with seven of its members appointed by the President for terms of fourteen years to ensure public rather than private control over economic policy. The Board was given authority over interest rates and reserve requirements of regional Federal Reserve Banks, greater control over state banks, and decisive influence over the money supply and the availability credit through its authority to buy and sell government bonds under its Federal Open Market Committee. Thus, before the end of his first term, Roosevelt completed the development of comprehensive federal power over the economy that was first made necessary by the need to protect the life savings of average Americans at the outset of his Presidency.

9. Rescuing the Farmer

An agricultural depression commenced long before the stock market crash of 1929. Throughout the decade of the 1920's, agricultural
income suffered in comparison with other sectors of the economy. After
the crash, conditions became much worse, with a greater than sixty percent reduction in such income—by 1933, the rate of farm foreclosures
was twenty thousand per month.[480] The problem was not scarcity of
farm products; rather, it was overproduction and the other side of the
same coin, lack of purchasing power of both farmers and workers to buy
the amounts produced. Roosevelt focused on the farmer, himself, first on
his over-production and second on his finances.

To lead in the formulation of agricultural policy, the President
chose Henry A. Wallace as Secretary of Agriculture, an agricultural
scientist, editor of a magazine for farmers entitled *Wallace's Farmer*,
and the son of a former Secretary of Agriculture under former President Harding. Although he was motivated by a deeply held moral
belief in the betterment of the lives of all people and was fully committed to liberal, Keynesian, government activism in the economy, he
was also practical and very tough-minded. Wallace proved to be one
of the most important political figures of the 30's and 40's, eventually
becoming Vice President from 1940 to 1944, only to be dropped by
Roosevelt in favor of Harry Truman in an attempt to appease conservative Democrats. Wallace followed his commitment to liberal international policies and opposition to what he believed was President
Truman's pro-business policies to become the presidential nominee of
the Progressive Party in 1948.

Well acquainted with the effects of rural poverty, Wallace advocated technological improvements in agricultural production and economic reform to increase the market for the farmer's products—by
preventing agri-business monopolies and by increasing the capacity of
urban workers to consume. He believed that an increase in demand
was the only effective means of long-term agricultural well-being. He
attracted many of the best and brightest minds of the decade to the
Agriculture Department and was able to coalesce various interest
groups and political opinions around practical programs of reform.

Wallace and Roosevelt resisted the more radical voices urging government price fixing, forcing farmers to reduce output, and government
transfer of land ownership to sharecroppers. Instead, they produced a

program that formed the basis for what became the Agricultural Adjustment Act of 1933 ("AAA"). The AAA gave Secretary Wallace a variety of tools to assist the farmer. First, he could offer benefit payments for farmers who, in 1933, plowed under surplus crops, and, in later years, voluntarily reduced acreage under cultivation ("domestic allotment plan"). These payments resulted, for example, in the destruction of over 10 million acres of cotton, causing a significant rise in the price of the crop. The only other major destruction dealt with a surplus caused by the low price of corn—an oversupply of pigs. The Agriculture Department bought and slaughtered more than eight million piglets, resulting in a ten percent increase in producer income. More of the Department's effort, however, went into the domestic allotment program, with twenty percent reduction in production of wheat, forty percent in cotton, and twenty percent in hogs.

Second, the Secretary was given the authority to establish agreements under which farmers would be paid a minimum price for their products—"price supports." In addition, he could subsidize the export of a variety of crops. Third, by virtue of the Farm Credit Act passed in June, 1933, the Farm Credit Administration was authorized to refinance farm mortgages to prevent foreclosures. By the end of 1934, that agency had refinanced twenty percent of mortgages on farms, saving many farm families from economic ruin. Prior to this legislation, farmers sometimes took the law into their own hands to protect a neighbor threatened with loss of his acreage. In a "penny auction," neighbors would use force and the threat of force to forestall any legitimate foreclosure bidder, then buy the property for a nominal sum and return it to its "rightful" owner.

Under the Commodity Credit Corporation established in October, farmers were loaned money in amounts higher than the price their crops would have brought in the market, in return for removing land from cultivation. To finance the program, the Department of Agriculture was authorized to administer a tax on the initial processing of commodities, with the processor able to pass the cost on in the market to the benefit of the price to the farmer.

Roosevelt's agricultural policy during his first term increased farm income, raised the price of farm products and reduced the farmer's indebtedness. Although long-term recovery awaited more massive economic growth after World War II, the crisis of suffering brought on by the Depression was significantly ameliorated.

10. Rescuing the Unemployed

President Roosevelt knew that he needed to address the needs of the millions of unemployed as rapidly as possible. From the outset, he had two complementary goals in mind—to relieve suffering and to make it possible for people to find jobs. The first goal was accomplished by using federal resources to provide emergency relief payments that had been so inadequate under the variety of local and state programs. Under the Federal Emergency Relief Administration (FERA) federal unemployment assistance to the states was coordinated and increased. The effect of distribution of these funds was both moral and political. By giving the families of the unemployed money to be used to prevent starvation, lack of clothing and poor housing, lives and futures were saved. By erecting a clearly federal framework under a Democratic administration for these measures, the political loyalty of the common man to the Democratic Party was guaranteed for decades.

Finding jobs for people proved a greater challenge, both economically and politically. The first program to do so was the Civilian Conservation Corps, recommended as part of the President's message to Congress soon after he took office in March, 1933. Of modest size, it was intended to provide direct federal employment for approximately one quarter of a million men, "in simple work, not interfering with normal employment, and confining itself to forestry, the prevention of soil erosion, flood control and similar projects."[481] Conscious of the precedent-setting nature of this program, Roosevelt emphasized the public benefits to be gained, the fact that there would be no conflict with private enterprise, and the moral value of the work. Foreshadowing even larger programs of this nature, he told the Congress that "The overwhelming majority of unemployed Americans, who are now walking the streets and receiving private or public relief, would infinitely prefer to work."[482]

To head the New Deal's relief program, Roosevelt chose Harry Hopkins, the hard-nosed social worker who had run the relief program in New York, and one of the most colorful and important political personalities of his entire Presidency. A chain-smoker, fond of horseracing, card games, and profanity, Hopkins, like other New Deal leaders, was committed to the welfare and economic security of each and every American. He had great empathy for those who depended on his programs, determined to change traditional prejudice toward them. He decried those who thought "the applicant was in some way morally deficient...we tried to see that relief officials were people who understood that the predicament of the worker without a job is an economic predicament not of his own making."[483]   No one was more influential with the President, or more trusted. Hopkins was able to convince Roosevelt to try bold, experimental programs in federal job creation and provided effective leadership of all of them. He later was asked to shoulder broader responsibilities with the administration, including as Roosevelt's closest foreign policy representative during the Second World War.

By 1935, FERA was spending more than $3 billion in public relief, to be compared with a federal expenditure of approximately 200 million in 1932. As Anthony Badger has stated, "its existence rescued many Americans from the threat of starvation."[484] There can be little question that the agency acted as a social safety net when one was needed most. In addition, it contributed to recovery by giving the poor some purchasing power whose absence had helped cause the Depression itself.

Hopkins persuaded the President in late 1933 to establish by Executive Order, the Civil Works Administration (CWA) to provide jobs directly on the federal payroll. It was a "work-relief" program, taking half of its beneficiaries from existing financial relief recipients and half from the rolls of the unemployed. The program featured no means test or mandatory social services, both mainstays of traditional relief programs. It focused on public works maintenance and construction projects that were relatively small scale, in order that they could be commenced quickly. During its short life, which ended on March 31, 1934, CWA modernized 500,000 miles of roads, refurbished 40,000 schools, created or improved 3,500 playgrounds and athletic fields and 1,000 airports, hired 50,000 teachers, including all Boston teachers who were unemployed, and provided work for 3,000 artists and writers.[485]

The program created political problems which the administration had not had enough time to anticipate or solve. In some areas, wages paid by CWA were higher than those prevailing in local areas, creating political opposition, particularly in the South where blacks were attracted to the city for such jobs at wages higher than those they could earn as agricultural workers, and higher than those earned by urban whites. Conservatives complained that the program inhibited the creation of jobs in the private sector. And the President became concerned that the cost of CWA was higher than the government could then afford. Although the President rescinded the program after less than one year's duration, the administration learned political lessons it would later apply to an even larger program of work relief, whose need the CWA highlighted. Harry Hopkins has written of CWA:

> American communities had had a taste of what could be accomplished under a government program for the unem-ployed...Once the cover was drawn away from the need, and we no longer talked about merely keeping the idle busy, that need revealed itself to be stupendous. The workers were there, imploring for both work and wages. Private money was standing still because it could not hope for profit, and by its apathy it was paralyzing consumption.[486]

11. Rescuing the Investment System

When Roosevelt took office, he inherited widespread lack of con-fidence in America's investment system. It had become obvious that rampant speculation in stocks and other investment vehicles, together with the easy credit mechanisms that fueled such speculation, had helped cause the stock market crash of 1929, and, to some degree, the ensuing worldwide economic depression. Moreover, there was general recognition that, during the decade of the 1920's, economic benefits went primarily to investors, financiers, and businessmen in the form of higher profits and increased stock values, and decidedly not to work-ers and farmers in terms of wages and income. Underlying these con-cerns was the perception, sometimes vague or based on class prejudice and, at other times, persuasively and sensationally disclosed by gov-ernment investigations, that the system was generally dishonest, sub-ject to manipulation by a wealthy few, and completely inaccessible to the honest, individual investor.

The new President began to address these issues soon after his Inauguration. His first topic was the sale of investment securities. In his message to Congress, the President identified the problem this way: "the public in the past has sustained severe losses through practices neither ethical nor honest on the part of many persons and corporations selling securities...[the legislation] puts the burden of telling the whole truth on the seller. It should give impetus to honest dealing in securities and thereby bring back public confidence."[487] The bill attempted to remedy the paucity of objective, reliable information available to the investor. Most corporations did not publish financial reports, and those that did provided incomplete data. As a result, only a few investment bankers had the resources and connections necessary to acquire adequate information for sound investment decisions. The proposal thus challenged the favored position of bankers like J.P. Morgan and Charles Mitchell. Conveniently, Roosevelt's bill received a great deal of political momentum as a result of the contemporaneous investigation of investment practices being conducted by the Committee on Banking and Currency, vocally led by Ferdinand Pecora, its legal counsel. Joseph P. Kennedy, soon to be the first chairman of the Securities and Exchange Commission and father of President John Kennedy, vividly described the hearings:

> For month after month, the country was treated to a series of amazing revelations which involved practically all the important names in the financial community in practices which, to say the least, were highly unethical...The belief that those in control of the corporate life in America were motivated by honesty and ideals of honorable conduct was completely shattered."[488]

The Pecora hearings not only helped Roosevelt pass his bill, named the Securities Act of 1933, but also resulted in the passage of the Glass-Steagall Act that mandated the separation of investment from commercial banking and established the Federal Deposit Insurance Corporation.

The Securities Act of 1933 required, with the issue of any new stock, the disclosure of complete financial information, including balance sheets and income statements and the identity and financial interests of major owners, option holders, directors and officers. Information was required to be verified by independent auditors and the act contained civil and criminal penalties for misrepresentation.

Thus was born "the first system of national control over corporate finance."[489] The act did not attempt to bring any structural changes to the capitalist system, only to make the free market work the way its advocates claimed that it was supposed to. Its requirements are still at the heart of today's system of regulation of public stock offerings.

By the time Congress adjourned on June 16, 1933, Roosevelt, while signing several bills and looking back on the achievements of his first one hundred days in office—including measures to rescue the banks, the farmer, the unemployed, and the investment system—commented that "more history is being made today than in [any] one day of our national life."[490] Roosevelt capitalized on the great political support for him throughout the nation and attempted to develop his programs with input from a broad spectrum of interests, representing a wide array of political viewpoints. Those groups that had been denied a voice in the recent past, such as small farmers, labor unions, and small businessmen were extremely pleased. Those that had been used to privileged access to power, such as wealthy financiers, investment bankers, and corporation heads, were less comfortable.

In the second year of his Presidency, Roosevelt created conflict with those business interests as a result of his commitment to build on the 1933 regulation of the investment system. His primary purpose was to reform the stock exchanges, particularly those practices that contributed to the rampant speculation that led to the stock market crash, such as lax requirements for loans to buy securities "on margin". In addition, Roosevelt wanted to respond to Congressional and public concern that the privileged position of corporate "insiders" and members of brokerage firms resulted in a decidedly uneven investment field, to the detriment of the public and the average investor. His goal was to restore confidence in the capitalist system so that it operated as it should. Nonetheless, many financiers, eager to preserve their power and favored position, opposed these measures with the help of their many Congressional allies. Roosevelt said of them that "the fundamental trouble with this whole Stock Exchange crowd is their...inability to understand the country or the public or their obligation to their fellow men."[491] Finally a bill emerged in June that, notwithstanding the compromises necessitated by turf battles both inside and outside Congress, established historic regulatory requirements that eventually brought order and fairness to the financial markets.

The Securities Act of 1934 created the Securities and Exchange Commission (SEC), an independent, bi-partisan agency with five Commissioners appointed by the President, to administer the law as well as the Act of 1933 that preceded it. The 1934 Act strengthened the information disclosure requirements for securities by requiring registration statements for all traded stock, outlawed deceptive practices by exchange members and corporate insiders, prohibited stockbrokers from trading to benefit themselves, limited membership in the exchanges to those brokers who worked on commission and processed orders only for the public, and gave the Federal Reserve Board new powers to prescribe requirements for margin loans. The passage of the Act was the occasion for many businessmen finally to abandon political support for the President, convinced as they were that the SEC would bring upon them unnecessary regulation contrary to their best interests. Much would turn on the nature of the SEC Commissioners and their approach to their responsibilities.

Roosevelt appointed as the first Chairman of the SEC Joseph P. Kennedy, a businessman who some believed had benefited from some of the practices the SEC was established to prevent. In response to his own advisors questioning of the appointment, Roosevelt is reported to have said, "Set a thief to catch a thief."[492] Kennedy proved to be a very effective first Chairman. He attracted an exceptionally objective and professional staff, a characteristic the SEC enjoys to the present day, and he established effective communication with all shades of political opinion, including the apprehensive financiers his agency regulated. Although much of the details of the regulatory framework were established under his two successors, James M. Landis and William O. Douglas, later Supreme Court Justice, Kennedy set the SEC on the constructive course it has followed ever since. Soon after his appointment, he vividly set forth his politically sensitive mission: "We of the SEC do not regard ourselves as coroners sitting on the corpse of free enterprise. On the contrary, we think of ourselves as the means of bringing new life into the body of the securities business."[493] Roosevelt's action and Kennedy's leadership set the nation on a course that restored faith in the honesty and integrity of America's dynamic system of capital investment, permanently strengthening this element of American liberty.

12. Opposition from the Left

The 1934 Congressional election was a great vote of confidence in the President and in his Democratic party—Republican House members were reduced from 117 to 103 and Republican Senate seats diminished from 53 to 25. Roosevelt's programs to provide relief to the unemployed, aid to the besieged small farmer, and solvency to the banks benefited masses of the poor, immigrants, and minority groups in northern cities and farm workers in the west who voted in droves for the Democrats. So began the Roosevelt political revolution that greatly expanded the traditional Democratic southern base and changed the balance of national politics for decades.

The New Dealers realized that, despite the rescue programs they had already enacted, and the psychological uplift Roosevelt had brought to the county, economic circumstances were still very grave. Almost ten million people—more than twenty percent of the labor force, were still unemployed; a devastating drought continued to afflict the agricultural heartland, and industrial workers were demanding long-denied rights. Although many were saved from starvation and homelessness, long term economic recovery had not yet begun. The election results presented a new opportunity for further social reform and change in the American political landscape.

The prolonged economic crisis and suffering of millions offered encouragement to political radicals of all stripes, many of whom offered programs that were as impractical as they were threatening to political stability. Progressives like Senator Hiram Johnson of California, Burton Wheeler of Montana, and Robert LaFollette of Wisconsin favored much more government spending and were impatient with what they believed was Roosevelt's conservatism. Socialists such as Norman Thomas, John Dewey and Professor Paul H. Douglas of Illinois favored greater state ownership and re-distribution of income. A former Socialist, novelist Upton Sinclair, came close to winning the Governorship of California on a platform that would turn over all idle land and factories to the unemployed. The Communist Party drew prominent supporters such as authors John Dos Passos, Sherwood Anderson, and Langston Hughes, although it likely had fewer than 30,000 committed adherents in 1934.[494]

Gaining much more popularity, sometimes amounting to real political challenge to the administration, and likely responsible for pushing Roosevelt to his most lasting reforms, were the activities of three charismatic individuals with real mass appeal—Dr. Francis Everett Townsend, Reverend Charles Edward Coughlin, and Senator Huey P. Long of Louisiana. The movements these individuals led prompted Harold L. Ickes, Roosevelt's Secretary of the Interior, to write in his diary of his fear for the country's stability if Roosevelt's policies didn't counter their appeal: "[A] breakdown on the part of the Administration would result in an extreme radical movement, the extent of which no one could foresee."[495]

Dr. Townsend was a physician from California who had an epiphany after he looked out his window and saw three elderly women foraging for food in a garbage can.[496] He became committed to solving the social and economic problem whose symptom he witnessed and came up with the Townsend Old Age Revolving Pension Plan to stimulate lasting recovery. Under his plan, the federal government would pay each American over sixty years of age a monthly "pension" of $200. In return, the recipients would promise to retire from any job they maintained and spend their pension in the month they received it. Townsend believed that his plan would not only benefit the elderly recipients, but free up jobs for younger people, increase wages by reducing the pool of available workers, and facilitate a true recovery by putting all those dollars directly into the economy. The plan would be financed by a national sales tax of 2% on all goods and services. Experts maintained that the scheme was economically untenable, since such a tax would have provided less than $75 per month as a pension and would have been such a great burden on those under sixty that incomes might have been cut in half.[497] At the time, however, Townsend attracted millions of followers. Townsend Clubs were established across the country, conducting emotional meetings of members, stimulated by Townsend's messianic zeal. Twenty-five million signatures were collected on petitions urging Congress to pass a law enacting the Townsend program. In response, such a bill was filed in January 1935 and considered several times by Congress, although it never came close to passage. The movement lost energy only after the passage of the Social Security Act later in 1935.

Charles Edward Coughlin, a Catholic priest who led the Shrine of the Little Flower in the immigrant community of Royal Oak, Michigan, rose from obscurity to become a national political figure. He did so by means of weekly radio addresses that spread his unique blend of social justice, religious righteousness, isolationism, and thinly veiled anti-Semitism. His audience at the time of Roosevelt's election was estimated to be from 30 to 45 million.[498] Although initially supportive of the New Deal, he began to be critical of it, particularly after the government exposed one of Coughlin's advisors as participating in illegal speculation in silver futures.

In November, 1934, Father Coughlin formed the National Union for Social Justice which called for the nationalization of some industries, protection of the rights of labor unions, greater government spending to inflate the economy, and removing power from Wall Street. He also denounced an internationalist foreign policy, vigorously opposing President's Roosevelt's effort to obtain Senate approval for United States membership in the World Court, an effort that ultimately failed to attract the two-thirds majority required. As one historian has written, "He appealed to an audience bewildered by the conflicting theories about the nature of the depression and hungry for some comprehensible explanation."[499] At its height, the National Union for Social Justice had a membership estimated to be more than 8 million and had the potential, particularly in tandem with other similar groups, to present a significant political challenge to the New Deal.

The man who propelled himself the farthest politically by manipulating the fears, helplessness, and frustration of the common man was the flamboyant Huey P. Long of Louisiana. He was an incongruous mixture of courage, irreverence, foolishness, extravagance, theatricality, intelligence, and oratorical prowess. He upset political power brokers to become a demagogic Governor of Louisiana, building for himself an unprecedented political machine that brought both progressive reform and ruthless bossism to the state. He dominated the legislature and showed little respect for the principle of separation of powers. Long spoke to the anger and resentment of the masses, decrying the greedy manipulations of the privileged elites, but he also played to their hopes, promising that under his administration "every man a king, but no one wears a crown." He did improve education, health and public works in the state and became so popular in Louisiana that he was also elected Senator in 1930, holding both offices until 1932. He delighted in his nickname "Kingfish", taken from the Amos 'n' Andy radio show, and constantly poked cynical fun at those with status in society. His national appearances on NBC were among the most popular of the network's programs.

Long was a key supporter of Roosevelt during the convention in Chicago in 1932 through the election. But they soon parted ways in a mutual pattern of distrust. Long resented what he saw as Roosevelt's cautious approach to challenging the power of the financial elite. In addition, he carried the resentment of a self-proclaimed southern populist against the Ivy League-educated New Deal bureaucrats. But most important, Long began to have national political ambitions that would put him on a path of opposition to the Roosevelt, leaving him free to claim that the President's program merely was a sham intended to preserve the power of the moneyed classes. For his part, the President believed that Long was a demagogue with too little respect for democratic processes and too much appetite for graft and corruption. He was reported to have called Long one of the two most dangerous men in the country (the other being General Douglas MacArthur, who had brutally suppressed the 'Bonus Army').[500]

In January, 1934, Long created a national political organization to carry him to further prominence and power. His Share the Wealth Society advocated a program of massive redistribution of wealth under which each American family would be guaranteed a 'household estate' of $5,000 in order to buy a home, an automobile and a radio. Each family would also be promised an annual income of $2,500. In order to finance the program, no American would be permitted to retain assets greater than $5 million and no one's income could exceed $1.8 million, thus confiscating the estates of many wealthy families. In addition, income taxes would be drastically graduated so that the marginal tax rate for a level of income exceeding $1 million would be 100%. The program also featured broad federal aid for education and for old-age pensions. Long traveled the country and spoke frequently on the radio to publicize his Share the Wealth platform and received a great deal of support, claiming five million members for the Society by 1935. It did not matter much to Long or his followers that his plan was totally unrealistic from an economic point of view. They believed with the Kingfish that a few privileged individuals owned so much of the nation's wealth that too little was left for most of the public. What did matter, however, was the political impact the Kingfish and his followers were making. Roosevelt's closest political advisors were concerned that Long might hold the balance of power in 1936. There is evidence from the U.S. Ambassador to Germany of the time that Roosevelt, himself, was convinced Long intended to make it difficult for the President to be re-elected, throw the election to a conservative Republican, then lead a movement to make him a Hitler-type candidate for President in 1940.[501] Such fears were not realized, however, since the Kingfish was killed by an assassin in Baton Rouge on September 7, 1935.

The leaders of these mass political movements captured a widely held belief that the economic and social difficulties facing the country were not caused by the capitalist system, per se, but, rather by the uncontrolled excesses of that system that resulted in wealth and power being concentrated in too few hands. President Roosevelt certainly felt pressure for more far-reaching social and economic reforms before the 1936 election. If he could bring about a redress of inequalities and injustices without a radical revolution of either the right, as in Germany, or the left, as in Russia, then America could regain its economic health within a fairer, more democratic capitalist system that channeled and controlled economic growth to benefit everyone. Roosevelt was to defend his more robust program—called by some the "Second New Deal," by saying: "I am fighting Communism, Huey Longism, Coughlinism, Townsendism…to save our system, the capitalist system, from crackpot ideas."[502] In a fireside chat in September, 1934, the President spelled out the philosophical basis for the precedent-setting programs he intended to enact in the following year:

> I believe with Abraham Lincoln, that 'the legitimate object of Government is to do for a community of people whatever they need to have done but cannot do at all or cannot do so well for themselves in their separate and individual capacities.' I am not for a return to that definition of liberty under which for many years a free people were being gradually regimented into the service of the privileged few. I prefer and I am sure you prefer that **broader definition of liberty** under which we are moving forward to greater freedom, to **greater security for the average man** than he has ever known before in the history of America."[503] (emphasis supplied)

In early 21st century America, the growing disparity between the rich, on the one hand, and the middle classes and the poor, on the other, presents a similar opportunity to implement the broad definition of liberty about which Roosevelt spoke so eloquently in 1934.

13. Establishing a Federal Commitment to Work Relief

By early 1935, President Roosevelt was ready to acknowledge that, without greatly enhanced federal government effort, the goal of putting the nation back to work would not be realized. The first element to that effort was the Emergency Relief Appropriation Bill, under which the federal government would provide jobs directly to those in need. Behind that unassuming title, the legislation, soon to be called 'Big Bill' constituted the largest non-war related expenditure in the history of the country—a total of nearly $5 billion. The goal was to provide work for all of the 3.5 million able-bodied unemployed who were then receiving direct relief payments. Roosevelt was careful to design the program with both social and political goals in mind. Wages were to be more generous than 'the dole', "to preserve not only the bodies of the unemployed from destitution but also their self-respect." However, the new 'security wage' was to be "not so large as to encourage the rejection of opportunities for private employment or the leaving of private employment to engage in Government work." Preference was to be given to projects that would be "self-liquidating in the sense that there is a reasonable expectation that the Government will get its money back at some future time." The work was designed to have a public purpose and be of benefit to local and state governments.[504]

Big Bill supported or established a variety of administrative programs. It strengthened the Civilian Conservation Corps, which ultimately attracted more than 2.5 million young men to outdoor projects throughout the country, including building more than 30,000 wildlife shelters, restoring historic battlefields, building forest fire prevention roads, trail, and towers, and digging flood prevention canals. Primarily, however, the Corps was responsible for planting trees to prevent erosion, restore forests, and remedy the effects of reckless harvesting of lumber. It has been estimated that more than half of forest planting in the history of the country was accomplished by the CCC.[505] Eligibility for the Corps was limited to unmarried men between the ages of 18 to 25 who came from families receiving relief. Many young men from urban areas enlisted, most with little or no previous familiarity with the country's natural resources. They learned good work habits along with specific skills that would aid them in future employment, not the least of which was how to get along with people from a variety of different backgrounds. CCC was one of the most successful New Deal creations.

The President was given broad administrative authority to create agencies by executive order that would further the purpose of the legislation. One of those agencies was the Rural Electrification Administration (REA), which brought electric power to American farms. Nine out of ten farms had no electricity in 1935, primarily because power companies found it unprofitable to build power lines in rural areas, with relatively few potential customers. REA provided low-cost loans to non-profit, farmer controlled cooperatives in order to do what was required. After a cooperative would string power lines, "finally the great moment would come: farmers, their wives and children, would gather at night on a hillside in the Great Smokies, in a field in the Upper Michigan peninsula, on a slope of the Continental Divide, and, when the switch was pulled on a giant generator, see their homes, their barns, their schools, their churches, burst forth in dazzling light. Many of them would be seeing electric light for the first time in their lives." The REA was ultimately responsible for bringing power to nine out of ten of the nation's farms.[506]

Another agency created by the President was the National Youth Administration that provided part-time jobs to high school and college students. The goal was to encourage these poor youngsters to complete their education and not drop out to contest others for rare or non-existent full-time jobs. The NYA provided work opportunity to more than 2 million students.

By far the major impact of Big Bill was in the area of public works under two separate agencies. The Public Works Administration (PWA), created in 1933 and under the leadership of Harold Ickes, received much increased funding under Big Bill, although the lion's share went to Harry Hopkins' new agency, the Works Progress Administration (renamed the Works Projects Administration in 1939). Ickes ran a tight ship and concentrated primarily on large public works projects, having long-term benefit for the areas in which they were located, and significant potential to stimulate private economic activity. Some of the well-known projects for which PWA was responsible include the Triborough Bridge linking Long Island to New York City, the Lincoln Tunnel linking New York City and New Jersey,

LaGuardia Airport outside of New York City, the Skyline Drive in Virginia, the San Francisco-Oakland Bay Bridge, and the Florida Keys Highway. From 1933 to 1939, PWA was involved in the building of 70 per cent of the nation's new schools, 65 per cent of courthouses, 35 per cent of hospitals and public health buildings, and a variety of ships, airplanes and airports for the United States armed forces.

The driving force behind Harry Hopkins' government service was to get people back to work. As head of the new Works Progress Administration (WPA), he had the greatest impact on employment of any New Dealer. In the first year of WPA Hopkins was able to give jobs to 3 million people and over the eight years life of his agency he provided 8.5 million jobs. In order to accomplish this, Hopkins chose projects which did not require long lead times, procurement of costly materials, or approvals from a variety of public or private entities. He also had to maneuver around legislative restrictions that forbade the agency from competing with private industry or interfering with work undertaken by city or state governments. Given the obstacles, Hopkins' achievements were truly remarkable. The WPA built or remodeled almost 6,000 schools, 13,000 playgrounds, 2,500 hospitals and 1,000 airports.[507] In 1937 alone it was responsible for sixty percent of the construction in New York City, including many model recreational facilities under the direction of Parks Commissioner Robert Moses.[508]

The WPA also established some of the most innovative government programs ever adopted to further support for the fine arts. These provided work to unemployed artists, writers, actors, and musicians. When critics complained about this program, Hopkins replied, "Hell, they've got to eat just like other people," and went on to defend the basis of the effort: "Few things could add such a permanent volume of employment as would a program of educating the public to use the services and participate in the pleasure of the culture we possess."[509] The Federal Arts Project commissioned works that depicted ordinary American life, for post offices and public buildings, including more than 2,500 murals, 17,544 sculptures and 108,899 easel paintings, including $7,800 to Jackson Pollack to produce paintings whose value was orders of magnitude higher.[510] Under the Federal Music Project, 15,000 musicians gave 225,000 performances, scores of symphony orchestras and jazz bands were established, and regularly scheduled free dances took place in many cities across the country. The Federal Writers Project disseminated information on America, its history and folklore, including a popular series of guidebooks about each state, many major cities, and travel routes, and a project that recorded the memories of former slaves through oral interviews numbering more than 150,000 pages. More than 5,000 writers produced 276 volumes and 701 pamphlets—Saul Bellow obtained his first job from the Project and it enabled Richard Wright to produce his great novel, *Native Son*. Finally, the Federal Theater Project put playwrights and others to work producing and performing plays in 22 production centers. An estimated 30,000,000 people watched the performances between 1935 and 1939, with weekly audiences estimated to be 150,000 across the country. Actor John Houseman and directors Orson Welles, Joseph Losey, and John Huston all received their start from the Project.

WPA was not without its critics, particularly when workers staged demonstrations or strikes, often encouraged by Communist organizers, or when local politicians benefited from agency patronage. Others complained of "make-work" projects or of scandalous subject matter, such as the integration of the races. It did not succeed in providing jobs to all who needed them. But it did do so for more than 3 million of the average 10 million jobless. Under the influence of Eleanor Roosevelt, the government, through WPA, focused on improving opportunities for women, creating thousands of jobs in adult education, illiteracy, pre-school and after-school programs. Its benefits to individuals and to the country were indisputable. Labor Secretary Perkins, in her memoir of her New Deal experience, summarized the impact of work relief in the story of one recipient:

> Thousands of the most respectable groups had to accept it and were deeply grateful for the opportunity to maintain their self-respect. An almost deaf, elderly lawyer, a Harvard graduate, unable to find clients, got a WPA job as assistant caretaker at a small seaside park...I had occasion to see him from time to time, and he would always ask me to take a message to the President—a message of gratitude for a job which paid him fifteen dollars a week and kept him from starving to death. It was an honorable occupation that made him feel useful and not like a bum and derelict, he would say with tears in his eyes.[511]

14. Establishing a Federal Commitment to Social and Economic Security

Franklin Roosevelt knew that his work relief programs, far-reaching as they were, would only be temporary until real economic growth in the private sector took over the job. Government employment could serve a variety of beneficial ends, not the least of which was the health and welfare of able-bodied citizens. Nevertheless, it was a palliative that would be difficult to support economically over a long period of time and would not bring the kind of sustained recovery the nation needed. But the President also knew that, when robust private economic growth returned, it would bring with it cyclical downturns of varying severity. Roosevelt feared that American liberty might not survive another Depression. Radical solutions, of the right or left, might be turned to that would endanger American political stability and make difficult the maintenance of American freedom. He wanted to establish permanent programs that would protect the livelihood of American workers, even in the event of a future economic failure. And he wanted to give Americans the security of knowing that when they reached old age, or when they became disabled, they would have a measure of economic security and would not have to worry about their ability to support themselves. Therefore he proposed the two most lasting contributions of his administration—Social Security and Unemployment Insurance.

To design his far-reaching effort, Roosevelt turned to a cabinet committee headed by Frances Perkins, Secretary of Labor. Perkins was the first woman cabinet member and, like Henry Wallace and Harry Hopkins, was a compelling individual. A graduate of Mount Holyoke College, who, in her early years wrote 'pot-boiler' romance, she became inspired by social work at Jane Addams' Hull House and went on to become a politically savvy labor lobbyist in New York state, serving on several governmental commissions advocating protective labor laws protecting workers. Like Hopkins, she was a committed and confident crusader for lifting the status of the poor and afflicted. With her ever-present felt tricorne hat, she led a Cabinet Committee made up of Relief Administrator Harry Hopkins, Agriculture Secretary Henry Wallace, Attorney General Homer Cummings, and Treasury Secretary Henry Morgenthau, together with an expert advisory

Committee on Economic Security, in a long and difficult process of crafting what was to become the Social Security Act of 1935.

In his initial charge to the Perkins committee in June, 1934, the President laid out the idea of a social insurance program in which "there is no reason why everybody in the United States should not be covered. I see no reason why every child, from the day he is born, shouldn't be a member of the social security system. When he begins to grow up, he should know he will have old-age benefits direct from the insurance system to which he will belong all his life. If he is out of work, he gets a benefit. If he is sick or crippled, he gets a benefit...Everybody ought to be in on it—the farmer and his wife and family...from the cradle to the grave they ought to be in a social insurance system." At the time, Roosevelt envisioned that his plan would also include a national health insurance program, saying, "I am confident we can devise a system which will enhance and not hinder the remarkable progress which has been made in the practice of the profession of medicine and surgery in the United States."[512]

Perkins wrestled with the President's ambitious goals, knowing that he would want her to come up with something big enough to make a difference yet practical enough to be politically saleable. The cabinet committee deemed a national health insurance program a worthy goal, but one that could not be implemented at any acceptable economic cost and could not overcome strong political opposition from the medical profession and the insurance industry. It decided that the most they would recommend would be grants to states to improve medical care to the physically handicapped and to provide preventative public health programs in rural areas. A broader national health program would await the Medicare and Medicaid legislation benefiting the elderly and the poor under President Lyndon Johnson in the late 1960's and Barack Obama's Patient Protection and Affordable Care Act of 2010.

The Cabinet Committee next took up the problem of unemployment insurance, having received a recommendation from the experts to establish a centralized, federal system of social insurance to avoid the inefficiencies in a variety of state-run systems. Perkins and the Cabinet knew, however, that the states would strenuously object to such an approach; moreover, Attorney General Cummings was concerned that doubts would be raised about whether the federal government had power under the Constitution to establish such a program.

Yet, the problem they faced in establishing a state-based system was how to ensure that an individual state would adopt such a program when to do so might put it at an economic disadvantage compared to a neighboring state without such a plan. The solution came from then Supreme Court Justice Louis D. Brandeis, who had been an advocate of unemployment insurance since his days as a labor lawyer decades before. Although the separation of powers doctrine prevented his personal participation in the Cabinet Committee's deliberations, he suggested his idea to his daughter, Elizabeth, the wife of Paul Raushenbush of Wisconsin, the originator and director of the only existing state unemployment compensation program. Elizabeth then briefed Secretary Perkins on this idea of a "tax-offset" mechanism and a joint federal-state program. The legislation would essentially guarantee state adoption of unemployment insurance plans because federal tax deductions would be given to people living in states that adopted such programs for the full amount of state unemployment taxes. Thus, each state would likely adopt such a program rather than permit tax dollars otherwise available to it to flow to Washington for a federal plan. Perkins' Committee adopted this idea both because it avoided the political problems inherent in an exclusively federal program and had great potential to solve any constitutionality problem.

The issue of old age insurance was simultaneously more politically urgent and more politically charged. The United States had been the only modern, industrialized country to face the Depression without either a program to compensate the unemployed for at least a portion of lost wages or to provide insurance to protect the elderly against insufferable poverty. Moreover, as the President told Secretary Perkins, "the Congress can't stand the pressure of the Townsend Plan unless we have a real old-age insurance system, nor can I face the country without having devised...a solid plan which will give some assurance to old people of systematic assistance upon retirement."[513] Yet, in other countries, programs included government provided pensions financed by direct tax revenues. The President believed that, in the United States, such a system would be politically difficult to pass, would be economically challenging to sustain over time, and might give rise to unnecessary political pressure from workers to continually raise the pension benefit. Therefore, in his message, he stated that "the funds necessary to provide this insurance should be raised by contribution rather than by an increase in general taxation."[514] Roosevelt knew that by calling them "contributions" rather than "taxes", the program would look more like insurance and satisfy the sensibilities of skeptical politicians. The basis for the plan was not to be that the individual is entitled to an old age pension as a civil right; rather, it was that the working man who contributes to his own retirement is entitled to receive the fruit of his contributions to his country and to his own account as an economic or property right. That was deemed more consistent with the American tradition.

Roosevelt recognized that the payroll "taxes" required to finance the Social Security System would be, to some extent, regressive and not have any of the income redistribution effect of the progressive income tax. And he knew, also, that taking money from workers would reduce their capacity to increase the consumer spending so necessary to the country's recovery. He defended his plan by saying, "those taxes were never a problem of economics. They are politics all the way through. We put those payroll contributions there so as to give the contributors a legal, moral, and political right to collect their pensions and their unemployment benefits. With those taxes in there, no damn politician can ever scrap my social security program."[515]

The President and his advisors certainly believed that workers deserved a measure of economic security in their old age. But Social Security also had a very practical and very beneficial effect on the remainder of the work force—in an economy that was not growing, where jobs were scarce, removing seniors from the labor market made opportunity for an increased wage or for a job itself much more tangible for the others. Roosevelt believed in a comprehensive approach to economic and social security, including work relief, unemployment insurance and old-age pensions. He assumed that work relief would meet a relatively short-term need, anticipating strong economic growth in the future. But he envisioned unemployment insurance and the Social Security System as enduring parts of the American economic system and of American liberty. He was right on both counts.

Perkins's Committee had to work through a number of elements that required sacrificing the President's original goals for the plan. First, although the experts recommended that benefits be equal, thus creative some income redistributive effects, the Committee decided that paying benefits in proportion to a worker's earnings would be more consistent with American tradition and with the President's concern that a plan closely following insurance principles would be more politically acceptable. Second, the Committee had to face the fact that early recipients of benefits would not have had enough time to build contributions to the level required for the system to be self-sustaining. Thus, it appeared that either their benefits needed to be cut, a large unfunded liability needed to be passed on to a future Congress, or payroll tax rates had to be set at a high level. Reluctantly, the Committee, with the President's acquiescence, accepted the solution offered by Treasury Secretary Morgenthau to exclude from coverage groups of workers for whom collecting taxes would have been difficult and thus would have had to have been subsidized by the contributions of others. Thus, the accrued liability for the program would be reduced, including amounts required for early beneficiaries. The President's original vision of a universal system was significantly modified by the exclusion of farm workers, domestic servants, and employees of organizations with fewer than ten workers. Only twenty years later was coverage extended to those originally excluded, thus more closely resembling the universal scope Roosevelt had envisioned.

On January 17, 1935, the President delivered his historic recommendations to Congress. Acknowledging the economic "hazards involved in our national life," he promised that, although "no one can guarantee this country against the dangers of future depressions...we can reduce those dangers...We pay now for the dreadful consequence of economic insecurity—and dearly."[516] Legislation embodying the President's proposals was filed by Senator Robert Wagner of New York and Congressman David Lewis of Maryland. There was some opposition in Congress, much of it on the ground that the system was inconsistent with the American principle of self-reliance and individual responsibility, some of it based on unwillingness to pay into a system that supported people who did not work. Nevertheless, the bill passed both houses with overwhelming margins and was signed by the President on August 15. Its major provisions included: 1) old age pensions financed by employee contributions of one percent of wages in 1937, rising in three year steps to three percent in 1949, with similar taxes on employers; 2) federal unemployment insurance with state programs stimulated by the tax-offset feature; 3) a program of federal grants to states for Aid to Dependent Children (ADC), including payments to families and services for the care and protection of homeless, neglected, dependent, and physically handicapped children; 4) a program of federal grants to states and local agencies for public health programs, and 5) federal grants to states for relief of the indigent elderly. The ADC program was the first attempt by the federal government to provide aid for families without fathers, many of whom had left to find work away from home. Its name was later changed to Aid to Families with Dependent Children (AFDC), and served as the primary part of a welfare system that is still in place, although significantly redesigned by President Clinton's welfare reform in 1996.

The programs authorized under the Social Security Act were implemented quickly and much more efficiently than even its supporters had reason to hope. By 1937, all states had adopted unemployment compensation laws proving the effectiveness of Brandeis' tax-offset mechanism. By 1939, all states had established old age assistance programs to utilize the federal grants the legislation provided. More than 26 million Social Security applications were processed in the first two years, unique individual Social Security numbers issued and cards distributed, and a national bureaucracy set up to administer the program on a continuing basis. The first beneficiary check was issued on January 17, 1940, when $41.30 was sent to 70 year old Ida M. Fuller of Vermont. The Act set the country on a course from which it could not retreat. As part of the framework of American liberty, its citizens could thenceforth expect that they would be protected from the most acute effects of losing their job and that their senior years would be relatively free from the insecurity resulting from fear that they would lack the resources to survive. As the President said upon signing the bill:

> We can never insure one hundred percent of the population against one hundred percent of the hazards and vicissitudes of life, but we have tried to frame a law which will give some measure of protection to the average citizen and to his family against the loss of a job and against poverty-ridden old age.[517]

15. Establishing a Federal Commitment to Economic Fairness

President Roosevelt went on to enact a variety of measures in 1935 and 1936 that firmly, although cautiously, placed the federal government on the side of bringing greater fairness and equality into the economy. Under the Wagner National Labor Relations Act of 1935,

the right of labor unions to organize and bargain collectively was recognized. The National Labor Relations Board (NLRB) was authorized to conduct elections to permit workers to choose to be
represented by a union, to ensure that employers did not engage in
"unfair labor practices" such as refusing to "bargain in good faith" with
the worker's representative, attempting to set up company-sponsored
unions, or discriminating against workers who were union members.
As a result of this act, workers throughout the nation organized on a
massive scale, permanently redressing the balance of power between
capital and labor, and establishing a level of wages and job security that
previously did not exist.

The political effects of the labor legislation were far-reaching. In
the first place, the existence of labor unions with tangible rights
reduced the appetite of workers for any more radical solutions, such as
socialism or communism. It made the workers feel more loyal to the
American system of liberty. Second, it established economic and social
mobility as a realistic hope for the worker and for his children. And
third, it brought to Roosevelt and the Democratic Party millions of
supporters who changed the face of American politics. It had all these
effects while preserving the essential elements of the American capitalist system; it merely made those elements fairer to all.

The New Deal labor legislation was not without its weaknesses.
It did little to guarantee that all sectors of the labor force would be
organized; there were many areas of commerce in which unions found
organization difficult, whether for economic, political, or psychological reasons. As a result, millions of women, farm workers, southerners
and minorities did not receive the benefits of the legislation for quite
some time. And industry did what it could to narrow the impact of the
law by vigorous legal challenges all along the way. In 1938 the President obtained enactment of the Fair Labor Standards Act that prohibited child labor and required that employers in basic industries adopt
a national minimum wage and a maximum forty-hour work week.
Although that law did not extent to agriculture, domestic service and
other occupations, it helped to bolster the benefits for workers established earlier by the National Labor Relations Act. And both acts created a foundation of worker protection and security on which later
Congresses could build. The American economy was permanently
restructured and American liberty redefined. There would be no
going back.

In the areas of banking and the investment system, the President and his advisors were pleased with the legislation passed in the first year of the New Deal, but they believed that there still existed a major area of the economy in which the public interest was being ignored in favor of private bankers and financiers. The Federal Reserve System, established in 1913, had not been modified since and was not really under the control of either the President or Congress. During World War I the nation's largest private banks established an Open Market Committee as an adjunct to the Federal Reserve System in order to aid in the war effort by buying and selling government bonds. The actions of this Committee soon had a decisive effect on the money supply and on interest rates; some believed that their failure to make credit more available helped worsen the Depression. Therefore, the Committee was written in to the Banking Act of 1933, as an arm of the Federal Reserve's regional banks, but the membership was still determined by private bankers.

Roosevelt proposed a major overhaul of the Federal Reserve in the Banking Act of 1935 in order to bring the entire operation, including the Open Market Committee, under greater Presidential control and thus, presumably, make their actions more responsive to the public interest. After a lengthy legislative battle, a compromise bill emerged that gave the President much of what he wanted. Under the new law, the President appointed a seven-member Board of Governors of the Federal Reserve System, but, to insulate them from complete Presidential, they served for terms of 14 years. The Board was given greater control over the regional banking system, including minimum reserve requirements and approval over the appointment of major officers. A Federal Open Market Committee consisting of seven Board members and five regional Reserve bank representatives effectively placed control of interest rates and credit availability in the hands of the federal government. Thus, Roosevelt's goal of ensuring public control over monetary policy was achieved.

On June 19, 1935 the President submitted to Congress another element of his campaign to bring greater equity and fairness to the economy, the so-called "Wealth Tax". This measure raised more emotional opposition and engendered more ill feeling from the members of Roosevelt's own economic class than almost anything else the New Deal proposed. One can imagine how directly they felt attacked when they read the following part of the President's message: "Our revenue laws have operated in many ways to the unfair advantage of the few, and they have done little to prevent an unjust concentration of wealth and economic power."[518] In an attempt at a redistribution of both wealth and power, Roosevelt proposed a new inheritance tax on monies received by beneficiaries, significantly increased taxes on the decedent's estate, the imposition of a gift tax, steeply graduated taxes "levied upon very great individual net incomes", and a revised corporate tax graduated for the amount of corporate income to replace the then current flat tax.

The effort was stimulated by a combination of motives, ranging from deeply held political philosophy, the desirability of raising more revenue, and the need to neutralize Huey Long, Upton Sinclair and allied "Share the Wealth" advocates. Despite anguished cries of opposition from the wealthy and from many newspapers and conservative politicians, the President seemed buoyed by the reaction. He really felt like he was an advocate for the common man. As he said in his message to Congress, "...inherited economic power is as inconsistent with the ideals of this generation as inherited political power was inconsistent with the ideals of the generation which established our Government."[519] The opposition was strong enough, however, to water down the legislation and the bill that passed eliminated the precedent-setting inheritance tax and reduced the impact of the graduated corporate income tax. But it did increase estate taxes and raise the income tax at the highest level from 63 to 79 per cent. The impact, however, was more symbolic and political than redistributive. During the decade of the thirties, "the top 1 per cent retained one eighth of all personal income...the top 5 percent retained over one quarter...[and] the share of the top 1 per cent rose from 28.3 per cent in 1933 to 30.6 per cent in 1939."[520]

The combination of measures enacted in the so-called "Second New Deal", but particularly the reforms of labor-management relations, currency and credit control, and tax policy, went to the heart of the President's push to make the capitalist economy fairer for everyone. He made his motive clear in his tax message when he said that "social unrest and a deepening sense of unfairness are dangers to our national life which we must minimize by rigorous methods."[521]

16. Roosevelt's Legacy

This chapter has focused on actions taken by Franklin Roosevelt during his first term and the beginning of his second. Those are the ones in which the New Deal exhibited its greatest energy and creativity and those are the ones that had the greatest impact on future domestic policy and on the definition of American liberty. Roosevelt also left a great legacy as the leader of the free world during the Second World War, but that story is beyond the scope of this chapter. Nevertheless, his leadership in the creation of the United Nations continues the story previously told in this book of Woodrow Wilson's internationalism, while avoiding shortcomings inherent in the structure of the League of Nations.

The story told here is of programs that were successful, both because of their impact on Americans of the time and their influence on future Presidents and Congresses. The New Deal was not, however, without misguided policies and counter-productive programs. The attempt to micro-manage the economy from Washington under the National Recovery Administration and the attempt to obtain a more sympathetic Supreme Court by enlarging and packing its membership stand out as two examples of such political mistakes.

Nor can it be said that Roosevelt brought the country to full economic recovery. Only in the aftermath of world war, with the country freed from the constraints of balanced budgets and limited raw materials, did the American economy fully rebound. Nonetheless, when it did, the many reforms instituted by New Deal made the recovery, when it came, both fairer and more sustainable.

Finally, the chapter did not focus on the impact Eleanor Roosevelt had on policy, but she certainly was the most policy-oriented first lady in history and she undoubtedly had a great influence on her husband's decision-making.

The intent of this chapter is to describe how Franklin Roosevelt redefined American liberty to include a crucial role for the federal government in guaranteeing to all Americans a measure of economic fairness and social security in the face of the potential harmful impacts of unrestrained capitalism. As he took office, he faced economic crisis by seizing the opportunity permanently to reform America's social, economic, and political system. Brought up with economic and social security himself, he wanted to give some of what he enjoyed to the masses of his countrymen who had not—to make life less threatening and more predictable for all. Conscious of both the privileges and, at times, unfairly gained advantages of his financial class, he wanted to use the power of government to save the capitalist system by reforming it, to ensure that it operated fairly and to establish programs to shelter those for whom its benefits might be meager. The Depression had made clear that the dynamic growth in the American economy since the Civil War came before the country had created the means to provide either economic fairness or stability. Roosevelt would build on the tradition of the Progressive reformers and establish institutions that would make economic security and justice part of the fabric of American liberty.

In his Inaugural Address beginning his second term, Roosevelt summarized the motivation behind his Presidency:

> I see one-third of a nation ill-housed, ill-clad, ill-nourished…The test of our progress is not whether we add more to the abundance of those who have much; it is whether we provide enough for those who have too little.[522]

He was determined to do whatever it would take to ensure that the future would be brighter for the vast majority of Americans; that their economic system would never again subject them to Depression-era deprivation and that the favored few would have to earn their favors honestly and play by new rules requiring fairness and openness in financial markets. Like Lincoln, who revitalized American liberty by including in it greater political equality, Roosevelt was to revitalize American capitalism by including in it greater economic equality. In accepting the Democratic nomination for his second term, Roosevelt made the problem clear:

> For too many of us the political equality we once had won was meaningless in the face of economic inequality. A small group had concentrated into their own hands an almost complete control over other people's property, other people's money, other people's labor—other people's lives. For too many of us life was no longer free; liberty no longer real; men could no longer follow the pursuit of happiness.

Against economic tyranny such as this, the American citizen
could appeal only to the organized power of Government.

He concluded by articulating an opportunity for leadership that he
willingly accepted: "To some generations much is given. Of other
generations much is expected. This generation of Americans has a
rendezvous with destiny." [523]

The first six years of the Presidency of Franklin Roosevelt
brought more political and institutional change to the nation than any
other similar period in its history. Even the Civil War took many
decades for its civil rights revolution to take hold. Roosevelt brought
energy and hope to a people with little of either. To many, the Depression was a sign that America's capitalist economy was a thing of the
past. To Roosevelt, it was an invitation not to revolution, but to
reform and leadership.

In the field of banking and savings, he halted bank failures and
the evaporation of life savings—fewer banks failed in his first two
terms than in any previous administration.

In the field of investments and financial markets, his securities
legislation and the regulations of the Securities and Exchange Commission brought efficiency and predictability to the engines of capitalism, restoring the confidence of the investing public and making
possible sustained economic growth in the future. Contrary to the
fears of Roosevelt's opponents, there was a growing recognition even
on Wall Street that the law, effectively enforced, facilitated financial
operations by policing unethical investors and setting minimum standards for smooth running markets.

In agriculture, the New Deal rescued farmers from the most
extreme impacts of the Depression—the lack of income, the foreclosure
of their farms, and the backwardness of rural area—and structured the
framework of American agricultural policy to the present day.

In labor relations, Roosevelt's actions established worker protec-
tions on hours, wages, and child labor and established the right to
unionize as a recognized part of American liberty and a desirable part
of the American economy.

One of the New Deal's greatest impacts was on unemployment.
Countless millions were saved from starvation and emotional breakdown by the existence of the various forms of work relief and unemployment compensation. If the programs did not result in long-term

economic recovery, they provided a sure fire way to rescue the multitudes from the immediate effects of economic depression, and their model will continue to be used in the future in the event of a recurrence of extreme economic downturn.

To the elderly and infirm of the country, Roosevelt's Social Security program held out a measure of income security that would become an indivisible part of American liberty into the next century. Roosevelt enshrined the federal government's role in guaranteeing for the most vulnerable Americans at least a minimum standard of subsistence. From then on, American liberty was to include the goal of a basic welfare standard for the country.[524]

Integral to the substantive reforms of the New Deal was the personality and character of Franklin Roosevelt. His outward confidence and buoyant good cheer set an example for the nation at a time of pessimism and sadness. He carried an inner serenity, in one part stemming from his privileged upbringing, but, in another, from his mastery of a crippling disability. Although he had to be assisted almost everywhere, dragging heavy braces on his legs and enduring the pain of his limitations, he always appeared nonchalant about his difficulties. He gave the impression of a vigorous, strong man. Partly this was because the press of the time maintained a voluntary restraint from revealing the effects of the President's affliction, but, partly it was because Roosevelt always acted vigorously, in both his public and private life.

No doubt, Roosevelt was a father figure to the country. People trusted him as they would an empathetic parent, one who cares very much for the welfare of each of his children and one who is able to provide for them a good measure of protection. Roosevelt gave Americans the feeling, too, that they were part of his Presidency; they wrote to him in unprecedented numbers, bearing their soul, disclosing their pain, and offering ideas to help him make decisions; and they did not fail to listen to him explain problems directly to them on the radio. In a very real sense, Roosevelt's personal skills made his political success possible. Roosevelt's bond with the people was illustrated in a report from a social worker in the field to Harry Hopkins:

> Every house I visited—mill worker or unemployed—had a picture of the President. These ranged from newspaper clippings (in destitute homes) to large coloured prints, framed in gilt cardboard. The portrait holds the place of

honour over the mantel; I can only compare this to the Italian peasant's Madonna. And the feeling of these people for the President is one of the most remarkable emotional phenomena I have ever met. He is at once God and their intimate friend; he knows them all by name, knows their little town and mill, their little lives and problems. And, though everything fails, he is there, and will not let them down.[525]

The relationship of the American people to their President and to the federal government was forever changed by Franklin Roosevelt. He made government a real and a positive force in the life of each citizen. He made people feel the Constitutional principle that the government was formed "to promote the general welfare," and left as a legacy a belief that government was capable of compassion and caring. As David M. Kennedy has written, "...ever after, Americans assumed that the federal government had not merely a role, but a major responsibility, in ensuring the health of the economy and the welfare of its citizens. That simple but momentous shift in perception was the newest thing in all the New Deal, and the most consequential too."[526]

Roosevelt set a prodigious example for all future Presidents. In effect, he revolutionized the Presidency, making it the focus of national attention, the wellspring for political ideas, the initiator of legislation, the key administrator, and the most powerful communicator. Future Presidents, without Roosevelt's character, personality, and charm would not be as successful in the office as he. Yet his is the example most have tried to emulate.

In assessing the achievement of Franklin Roosevelt, one must consider his actions in the context of his own time. In 1933, John Maynard Keynes called him "the trustee of those in every country who believed in social peace and in democracy." Unlike many other national leaders of the thirties, he lead his country through perilous economic times with its economic system reformed, not overturned, its social fabric strengthened, not torn apart, and its democracy more effective and more equal, not abandoned. By making the Great Depression tolerable, he preserved and redefined the nation's liberty at a time when the survival of democratic government was far from assured.

It is no surprise that the best description of what Franklin Roosevelt has meant to American liberty comes from the man himself. In a fireside chat in 1938, he told the nation:

Democracy has disappeared in several other great nations, not because the people of those nations disliked democracy, but because they had grown tired of unemployment and insecurity, of seeing their children hungry while they sat helpless in the face of government confusion and government weakness through lack of leadership...Finally, in desperation, they chose to sacrifice liberty in the hope of getting something to eat. We in America know that our democratic institutions can be preserved and made to work. But in order to preserve them we need...to prove that the practical operation of democratic government is equal to the task of protecting the security of the people...The people of America are in agreement in defending their liberties at any cost, and the first line of that defense lies in the protection of economic security.[527]

CHAPTER 7.

Conclusion. Building upon the Framework Decisions and 21st Century Issues

E ach of the decisions narrated in this book is a permanent guide-post on the path of development for American liberty. This is true not only because of the contemporary impact of the decision itself, but as a result of the example it set for successor Presidents faced with their own policy choices.

Although Washington's establishment of national economic policy was vigorously debated in his own time, and the national bank he created was later rejected by President Jackson and his political allies, the country firmly adopted his example from the Civil War to the present day. The Federal Reserve Bank and monetary system established by President Wilson and strengthened by Franklin Roosevelt owe everything to Washington's example. Moreover, the precedent of ensuring that national economic policy actually works to benefit the economic growth of the entire nation that was at the heart of Washington and Hamilton's actions has inspired many policies not directly related to the monetary system or the bank. These include the regulation of interstate commerce begun under Grover Cleveland, Theodore Roosevelt's anti-monopoly trust-busting, Woodrow Wilson's Federal Trade Commission to ensure competition and fair trade, Franklin Roosevelt's regulation of investment markets, and Barack Obama's strengthening of that regulation as a result of the recession of the early 21st century.

Jefferson's facilitation of the expansion of the nation established a powerful incentive for James Monroe's acquisition of Florida and setting of the country's boundary at the Pacific Ocean in the northwest. Although the War with Mexico has been a controversial episode in American history, the resulting acquisition of Texas and California undoubtedly increased the resources of the country and permitted the more vigorous development of its liberty. And Andrew Johnson's acquisition of Alaska was motivated to some degree by Jefferson's example. Even though the aggressive methods of some of acquisitions has been the subject of criticism, such as that of the Philippines and Puerto Rico after the Spanish-American War, and the annexation of the Hawaiian Islands, there can be no doubt that the expansion of freedom that resulted from even these actions was consistent with Jefferson's original motivation.

Monroe's great Doctrine achieved its object—protecting the liberty and independence of Latin American republics from threat by European colonial powers. The fact that some of those countries have not always been able to maintain their own democracy effectively does not reflect negatively on the Doctrine. Although some ill-advised American policies have been justified in the Doctrine's name, there is no doubt that two of the greatest contributions to the survival of liberty in the twentieth century owe their inspiration to it—the Marshall Plan protecting the economic and political liberty of western Europe after World War II and the Truman Doctrine preserving the independence of Greece and Turkey from Communist threat.

Lincoln's Emancipation Proclamation was a turning point in American history, permanently setting a direction of non-discrimination and individual liberty for all. Unfortunately, the Reconstruction efforts following the death of Lincoln did not benefit from his wisdom, and led to many decades of disappointment in the achievement of true equal opportunity. Nevertheless, the full promise of Lincoln's action was brought much closer in the twentieth century as a result of actions by the Supreme Court, Congress and Presidents Eisenhower, Kennedy and Johnson fully to realize the civil rights of all Americans.

Woodrow Wilson created a revolution in the early twentieth century fully as important as those of the eighteenth. To place liberty and internationalism side by side was a precedent-setting action that has profoundly influenced America and the world ever since. Although it wasn't until the aftermath of the tragic Second World War that the establishment of the United Nations finally overcame the inherent weaknesses of Wilson's League of Nations, there is today widespread agreement that the future of liberty, in America and in the world, can be best served by international cooperation for peace and economic development. Taking inspiration from that example, Presidents

Kennedy, Nixon, and Reagan established the basis for the international limitation of weapons of mass destruction, and President George H.W. Bush set an important post-Cold War example of international cooperation to stop aggression and threats to a country's freedom with the effort he led to protect Kuwait.

It must be acknowledged, however, that Wilson's example is sometimes misinterpreted or even intentionally distorted to support action Wilson would never have condoned. One controversial recent example was George W. Bush's invasion of Iraq, to some extent justified as bringing democracy to a country that never before enjoyed it. Yet Wilson would never have taken such basically unilateral action without true international sanction and without effective indigenous support.

It took a cataclysmic depression to help Americans realize that their economic good fortune was not guaranteed but required an active national government to protect it by cushioning the negative effects of market forces. Franklin Roosevelt permanently added to the definition of American liberty the idea that each individual was entitled to a measure of economic and social security established by the federal government. Without it, the liberty and freedom established by the Declaration of Independence and the Constitution would not be secure.

The Presidential decisions defining American liberty offer guidance to today's political leaders for solving the problems of the 21st century.

To address the failure of the health care system to provide universal, affordable care to all, these decisions point to federal government leadership in assigning greater resources and more effective regulation. Public acceptance of government programs as well as market-based ones will be essential. We don't yet know whether President Obama's Patient Protection and Affordable Health Care Act will meet those needs or achieve political acceptance.

Similar approaches will be required to address the need for improved K-12 education for all the country's children as well as wider access to a college education. The continued vitality of American liberty has always required an educated and vigilant citizenry and the continued strength of the country depends on its ability to meet the demands of a competitive global economy.

The benefits of globalization have been tangible and significant in most of the world. However, they have not come without costs, particularly <u>the inability of "third world" countries to keep pace</u>. The Presidential actions described in this book would point to solutions that feature international agreements to ensure that the poorer areas of the world benefit from globalization. This will require that the United States and the major powers have the political willingness to make the economic sacrifices necessary to assist developing nations grow more rapidly and more equally distribute the benefits of global economic expansion.

As technology and the internet have made the world a smaller and more accessible place, <u>terrorism has become a more prevalent strategy of the angry and the dispossessed</u>. To meet the challenge of international terrorism, our Presidential decisions would lead to a multi-lateral rather than a unilateral foreign policy, one that relies less on military solutions and more on encouraging liberty, education, and economic development in the third world.

The future of mankind depends on our response to the by-products of industrialization and global economic growth—<u>environmental degradation and climate change</u>. Our Presidential guidance points to international agreements to lessen those effects and reverse that degradation, again requiring the political willingness of the United States and, particularly, the rapidly developing powers such as China and India, to restrain some of their growth in favor of a survivable planet.

Prospects for liberty in the world, and even for life itself, are related directly to our ability <u>to restrain and reverse the proliferation of nuclear, chemical, and biological weapons</u>. For this most critical challenge, the policies described in this book would lead to international safeguards with effective enforcement mechanisms, together with the political willingness in the United States and all major countries to give up the degree of sovereignty necessary for effective enforcement.

It is the author's hope that this book will stimulate debate in the direction of these solutions and, in light of the six foundational decisions, cast that debate in a patriotic light.

BIBLIOGRAPHY

General

Amar, Akhil Reed. *America's Constitution, A Biography*. New York: Random House, 2005

Becker, Carl L. *The Declaration of Independence, A Study in the History of Political Ideas*. New York: Random House, Vintage Books edition, 1958

_____. *The United States, An Experiment in Democracy*. New Brunswick: Transaction Publishers, 2001, paperback edition; New York: Harper & Brothers, 1920

Berlin, Isaiah. *Four Essays on Liberty*. Oxford: Oxford University Press, 1969

Boyer, Paul S., ed. *The Oxford Companion to United States History*. Oxford, New York: Oxford University Press, 2001

Brinkley, Alan and Davis Dyer, eds. *The Reader's Companion to the American Presidency*. Boston: Houghton Mifflin Company, 2000

Commager, Henry Steele. *The American Mind, An Interpretation of American Thought and Character Since the 1880's*. New Haven: Yale University Press, 1950

Hofstadter, Richard. *The American Political Tradition and the Men Who Made It*. New York: Alfred A. Knopf, 1948; Vintage paperback edition, 1989

_____, ed. *Great Issues in American History, Vol., II, From the Revolution to the Civil War, 1765-1865*, and *Vol. III, From Reconstruction to the Present Day, 1864-1981*. New York: Vintage Books, 1958, 1969

Johnson, Paul. *A History of the American People*, London: Phoenix Press, Orion Publishing Group, Ltd. 2000, originally published London: Weidenfeld & Nicolson, 1997

Kammen, Michael. *People of Paradox, An Inquiry Concerning the Origins of American Civilization*. New York: Alfred A. Knopf, 1972

_____. *Spheres of Liberty, Changing Perceptions of Liberty in American Culture.* Madison: University of Wisconsin Press, 1986; Jackson, University Press of Mississippi, 2001, paperback edition

Morison, Samuel Eliot, and Henry Steele Commager. *The Growth of the American Republic, Volume I, 1000-1865, Volume II, 1865-1950,* Fourth Ed., 7th Pr. New York: Oxford University Press 1956

Parrington, Vernon Louis. *Main Currents in American Thought, Volume I, The Colonial Mind, 1620-1800; Volume II, The Romantic Revolution in America, 1800-1860.* Norman: University of Oklahoma Press 1987

Chapter 1

Bailyn, Bernard, ed. *The Debate on the Constitution, Federalist and Antifederalist Speeches, Articles, and Letters During the Struggle Over Ratification, Part One, September 1787 to February 1788 and Part Two, January to August, 1788.* New York: The Library of America, 1993

Banning, Lance. *The Sacred Fire of Liberty, James Madison and the Founding of the Federal Republic.* Ithaca and London: Cornell University Press, 1995, paperback edition, 1998

Beer, Samuel H. *To Make a Nation, The Rediscovery of American Federalism.* Cambridge: The Belknap Press of Harvard University Press, 1993

Carroll, John Alexander and Mary Wells Ashworth. *George Washington, Volume Seven, First in Peace,* Completing the Biography by Douglas Southall Freeman. New York: Charles Scribner's Sons, 1957

Cook, Don. *The Long Fuse, How England Lost the American Colonies, 1760-1785.* New York: Atlantic Monthly Press, 1995

Cooke, Jacob E. *Alexander Hamilton, A Profile.* New York: Hill and Wang, 1967

Cunliffe, Marcus. *George Washington, Man and Monument.* Mount Vernon: The Mount Vernon Ladies' Association, 1998

Elkins, Stanley and Eric McKitrick. *The Age of Federalism.* New York: Oxford University Press, 1993

Ellis, Joseph. *Founding Brothers, The Revolutionary Generation.* New York: Alfred A. Knopf, 2000

_____. *His Excellency, George Washington*. New York: Alfred A. Knopf, 2004

_____. *Passionate Sage, The Character and Legacy of John Adams*. New York: W.W. Norton & Company, 1993

Ferling, John E. *A Life of George Washington*. Knoxville: University of Tennessee Press, 1988

_____. *Almost a Miracle, The American Victory in the War of Independence*. New York: Oxford University Press, 2007

_____. *John Adams, A Life*. Knoxville: The University of Tennessee Press, 1992; New York: Oxford University Press paperback, 2010

Fischer, David Hackett. *Washington's Crossing*. New York: Oxford University Press, 2004

Flexner, James Thomas. *George Washington and the New Nation, 1783-1793*. Boston, Toronto: Little, Brown and Company, 1969, 1970

_____. *George Washington, Anguish and Farewell 1793-1799*. Boston, Toronto: Little, Brown and Company, 1972

Freeman, Douglas Southall. *George Washington, A Biography, Volume One, Young Washington*. New York: Charles Scribner's Sons, 1948

_____. *George Washington, A Biography, Volume Six, Patriot and President*. Clifton, N.J.: Augustus M. Kelley, 1975; First published, New York: Charles Scribner's Sons, 1954

Gilbert, Felix. *To the Farewell Address, Ideas of Early American Foreign Policy*. Princeton: Princeton University Press, 1961

Hamilton, Alexander. *Alexander Hamilton Writings*. New York: The Library of America, Literary Classics of the United States, Inc., 2001

Hamilton, Alexander, James Madison and John Jay. *The Federalist Papers*. Toronto: Bantam Books, 1982, paperback edition

Higginbotham, Don, ed. *George Washington Reconsidered*. Charlottesville: University Press of Virginia, 2001

Jensen, Merrill. *The New Nation, A History of the United States During the Confederation, 1781-1789*. New York: Alfred A. Knopf, 1950; Boston: Northeastern University Press, 1981, paperback edition

Ketcham, Ralph. *James Madison, A Biography*. Charlottesville, University Press of Virginia, 1971, paperback edition, 1990

Knott, Stephen F. *Alexander Hamilton & The Persistence of Myth*. Lawrence: University Press of Kansas, 2002

Leibiger, Stuart. *Founding Friendship, George Washington, James Madison, and the Creation of the American Republic*. Charlottesville: University Press of Virginia, 1999

Madison, James. *Notes of Debates in the Federal Convention of 1787 Reported by James Madison*. New York: W.W. Norton & Company, 1987, bicentennial edition

Marshall, John. *The Life of George Washington*. Indianapolis: Liberty Fund, Inc., , 2000

McDonald, Forrest. *Alexander Hamilton, A Biography*. New York: W.W. Norton & Co., Inc., 1979; Norton paperback, 1982

_____. *Novus Ordo Seclorum, The Intellectual Origins of the Constitution*. Lawrence: University of Kansas Press, 1985

_____. *The Presidency of George Washington*. Lawrence: University Press of Kansas, 1974

McDonald, Forrest and Ellen Shapiro McDonald. *Confederation and Constitution, 1781-1789*. Columbia: University of South Carolina Press, 1968

Middlekauff, Robert. *The Glorious Cause, The American Revolution, 1763-1789*. New York: Oxford University Press, 1982

Miller, John C. *Alexander Hamilton and the Growth of the New Nation*. New York: Harper & Row, 1964, Torchbook Edition, 1964,; originally published in 1959 by Harper & Row as *Alexander Hamilton: Portrait in Paradox*

_____. *Origins of the American Revolution*. Boston: Little, Brown and Company, 1943; Stanford University Press, 1959, paperback edition

_____. *The Federalist Era, 1789-1801*. New York: Harper & Row, 1960

Mitchell, Broadus. *Alexander Hamilton, A Concise Biography*. New York: Oxford University Press, 1976

Morgan, Edmund S. *The Birth of the Republic, 1763-1789*. Chicago: The University of Chicago Press, 1956

_____. *The Genius of George Washington*. New York: W.W. Norton & Company, 1980

_____. *The Meaning of Independence, John Adams, George Washington and Thomas Jefferson*. New York and London: W.W. Norton and Company, 1976

Morris, Richard B. *The Forging of the Union, 1781-1789*. New York: Harper and Row, 1987

Phelps, Glenn A. *George Washington & American Constitutionalism*. Lawrence: University Press of Kansas, 1993

Rakove, Jack N. *Original Meanings, Politics and Ideas in the Making of the Constitution*. New York: Alfred A. Knopf, 1996

_____. *Revolutionaries, A New History of the Invention of America*. New York, Boston: Houghton Mifflin Harcourt, 2010

Rhodehamel, John H. *The Great Experiment, George Washington and the American Republic*. New Haven & London: Yale University Press, 1998

Sharp, James Roger. *American Politics in the Early Republic, The New Nation in Crisis*. New Haven, Yale University Press, 1993

Washington, George. *George Washington Writings*. John H. Rhodehamel, ed., The Library of America, Library Classics of the United States, New York, 1997

Weisberger, Bernard A. *America Afire, Jefferson, Adams, and the First Contested Election*. New York: William Morrow, 2000

Wood, Gordon S. *The Creation of the American Republic, 1776 to 1787*. Chapel Hill and London, The University of North Carolina Press, 1969, 1998

_____. *The Radicalism of the American Revolution*. New York: Alfred A. Knopf, 1992

_____. *Empire of Liberty, A History of the Early Republic, 1789-1815*, Oxford and New York: Oxford University Press, 2009

Chapter 2

Adams, William Howard. *The Paris Years of Thomas Jefferson*. New Haven: Yale University Press, 1997

Banning, Lance. *Jefferson and Madison, Three Conversations from the Founding*. Madison: Madison House, 1995

Barbe-Marbois, Francois. *The History of Louisiana*. E. Wilson Lyon, Ed., Baton Rouge: Louisiana State University Press, 1977, reprint of 1830 edition, Philadelphia: Carey & Lea, Philadelphia

Bernstein, R.B. *Thomas Jefferson*. New York: Oxford University Press, 2003

Bowers, Claude G. *Jefferson and Hamilton, The Struggle for Democracy in America*. Boston: Houghton Mifflin Company, 1925, paperback edition, 1953

Brant, Irving. *James Madison, Secretary of State, 1800-1809*. Indianapolis: The Bobbs-Merrill Company, Inc., 1953

Brodie, Fawn M. *Thomas Jefferson, An Intimate History*. New York: W.W. Norton & Company, 1974, paperback edition, 1998

Burstein, Andrew. *The Inner Jefferson, Portrait of a Grieving Optimist*. Charlottesville, University Press of Virginia, 1995

Carpon, Lester J. ed. *The Adams-Jefferson Letters, The Complete Correspondence between Thomas Jefferson and Abigail and John Adams*. Chapel Hill: The University of North Carolina Press, 1959, paperback edition, 1987

Commager, Henry Steele. *Jefferson, Nationalism, and the Enlightenment*. New York: George Braziller, Inc.,1975

Cunningham, Jr., Noble E. *Jefferson and Monroe, Constant Friendship and Respect*. Chapel Hill: Thomas Jefferson Foundation, The University of North Carolina Press, 2003

_____. *The Jeffersonian Republicans, The Formation of Party Organization, 1789-1801*. Chapel Hill: The Institute of Early American History and Culture, The University of North Carolina Press, 1957

Ellis, Joseph J. *American Sphinx, The Character of Thomas Jefferson*. New York: Alfred A. Knopf, 1997

Fehrenbacher, Don E. *The Era of Expansion, 1800-1848*. New York: John Wiley & Sons, Inc., 1969

Gordon-Reed, Annette. *Thomas Jefferson and Sally Hemings: An American Controversy*. Charlottesville: University of Virginia Press, 1997

Jefferson, Thomas. *Jefferson Writings*. Merrill D. Peterson, ed., New York: The Library of America, Literary Classics of the United States, Inc., 1984

Kaplan, Lawrence S. *Thomas Jefferson, Westward the Course of Empire*. Wilmington: Scholarly Resources, Inc., 1999

Koch, Adrienne. *Jefferson & Madison, The Great Collaboration*. Oxford: Oxford University Press, 1950, paperback edition, 1964

Lewis, Jan Ellen and Peter S. Onuf. *Sally Hemings & Thomas Jefferson, History, Memory, and Civic Culture*. Charlottesville: University Press of Virginia, 1999

Malone, Dumas. *Jefferson and His Time*, six volumes (*Volume One, Jefferson the Virginian, Volume Two, Jefferson and the Rights of Man, Volume Three, Jefferson and the Ordeal of Liberty, Volume Four, Jefferson the President, First Term, 1801-1805, Volume Five, Jefferson the President, Second Term, 1805-1809, Volume Six, The Sage of Monticello*). Boston: Little, Brown and Company, 1948, 1951, 1962, 1970, 1974, 1981

Mayer, David N. *The Constitutional Thought of Thomas Jefferson*. Charlottesville, University Press of Virginia, 1994

Mayo, Bernard, ed. *Jefferson Himself, The Personal Narrative of a Many-sided American*. Boston: Houghton Mifflin Company, Boston, 1942; Charlottesville: University Press of Virginia, 1970, paperback edition

McDonald, Forrest. *The Presidency of Thomas Jefferson*. Lawrence: University Press of Kansas, 1976

Miller, John Chester. *The Wolf by the Ears, Thomas Jefferson and Slavery*. Charlottesville: University Press of Virginia, 1991

Peterson, Merrill D. *Thomas Jefferson & the New Nation, A Biography*. Oxford and New York: Oxford University Press, 1970, paperback edition, 1975

Tucker, Robert W. & David C. Hendrickson. *Empire of Liberty, The Statecraft of Thomas Jefferson*. New York: Oxford University Press, 1990, paperback edition, 1992

Onuf, Peter S. *Jefferson's Empire, The Language of American Nationhood*. Charlottesville: University Press of Virginia, 2000, paperback edition, 2001

_____, ed. *Jeffersonian Legacies*. Charlottesville: University Press of Virginia, 1993

Parry, J.H. *Trade and Dominion, The European Overseas Empires in the Eighteenth Century*. New York: Praeger, 1971

Peterson, Merrill D. *Adams and Jefferson, A Revolutionary Dialogue*. New York: Oxford University Press, 1978, paperback edition

_____. ed. *Thomas Jefferson, A Profile*, Hill and Wang, New York, 19

Smelser, Marshall. *The Democratic Republic, 1801-1815*. New York: Harper & Row, Harper Torchbooks, 1968

Wallace, Anthony F.C. *Jefferson and the Indians, The Tragic Fate of the First Americans*. Cambridge: The Belknap Press of Harvard University Press, 1999

Van Alstyne, Richard W. *The Rising American Empire*. New York: W.W. Norton & Company, 1974, paperback edition

Chapter 3

Adams, Henry. *History of the United States of America During the Administrations of James Madison*. New York: The Library of America, Literary Classics of the United States, Inc., 1986

Adams, John Quincy. *Memoirs of John Quincy Adams Comprising Portions of His Diary from 1795 to 1848*, Charles Francis Adams, ed., 12 volumes, Philadelphia: J.B. Lippincott & Co., 1874-1877

_____. *Writings of John Quincy Adams, Vol.VII, 1820-1823*, Worthington Chauncy Ford, ed., New York: MacMillan, 1917

Ammon, Harry. *James Monroe: The Quest for National Identity*. Charlottesville: University Press of Virginia, 1990

Bailey, Thomas A. *A Diplomatic History of the American People*. New York: Appleton-Century-Crofts, Inc., 1955

Bemis, Samuel Flagg. *John Quincy Adams and the Foundations of American Foreign Policy*. New York: Alfred A. Knopf, Inc., 1949, W.W. Norton & Company, Inc., paperback edition, 1973

Cresson, W.P. *James Monroe*. Chapel Hill: University of North Carolina Press, 1946

Dangerfield, George. *Defiance to The Old World, The Story Behind the Monroe Doctrine*. New York: G.P. Putnam's Sons, 1970

_____. *The Awakening of American Nationalism, 1815-1828*. New York: Harper & Row, 1965

Dozer, Donald Marquand. *The Monroe Doctrine, Its Modern Significance*. New York: Alfred A. Knopf, 1965

Fischer, David Hackett. *Washington's Crossing*. New York: Oxford University Press, 2004

Herring, George C. *From Colony to Superpower, U.S. Foreign Relations since 1776*. New York: Oxford University Press, 2008

Lucier, James P. *The Political Writings of James Monroe*. Washington, D.C.: Regnery Publishing, Inc., 2001

May, Ernest R. *The Making of the Monroe Doctrine*. Cambridge: Harvard University Press, 1975

Merk, Frederick. *Manifest Destiny and Mission in American History, A Reinterpretation*. New York: Alfred A. Knopf, 1963

Morgan, George. *The Life of James Monroe*. Boston: Small, Maynard and Co., 1921

Nagel, Paul C. *John Quincy Adams, A Public Life, A Private Life*. New York: Alfred A. Knopf, 1997; Cambridge: Harvard University Press, 1999, paperback edition

Parsons, Lynn Hudson. *John Quincy Adams*. Madison: Madison House Publishers, Inc., 1998

Perkins, Dexter. *Hands Off, A History of the Monroe Doctrine*. Boston: Little, Brown and Company, 1941

Remini, Robert V. *John Quincy Adams*. New York: Henry Holt and
    Company, 2002
Sellers, Charles. *The Market Revolution, Jacksonian America 1815-1846*.
    New York: Oxford University Press, 1991
Smith, Gaddis. *The Last Years of the Monroe Doctrine, 1945-1993*. New
    York: Hill and Wang, 1994
Wilson, Charles Morrow. *The Monroe Doctrine, An American Frame of
    Mind*. Princeton: Auerbach Publishers, 1971

Chapter 4

Boritt, Gabor S. *Lincoln and the Economics of the American Dream*. Mem-
    phis: Memphis State University Press, 1978; Urbana and Chicago:
    University of Illinois Press, 1994, paperback edition
Carwardine, Richard J. *Lincoln, Profiles in Power*. London: Pearson
    Education Limited, 2003
Charnwood, Lord. *Abraham Lincoln, A Biography*. Lanham: Madison
    Books, 1996
Craven, Avery. *The Coming of the Civil War*. New York: Charles Scrib-
    ner's Sons, 1942, second edition, 1947; Chicago: Phoenix Books
    paperback edition, University of Chicago Press, 1966
Davis, David Brion. *The Problem of Slavery in Western Culture*. Ithaca:
    Cornell University Press, 1966
_____. *The Problem of Slavery in the Age of Revolution, 1770-1823*.
    Ithaca: Cornell University Press, 1975
Donald, David Herbert. *Lincoln*. New York: Simon & Schuster, 1995
_____. *"We Are Lincoln Men," Abraham Lincoln and his Friends*, Simon
    & Schuster, New York, 2003
Douglass, Frederick. *Autobiographies*. New York: The Library of
    America, Literary Classics of the United States, Inc., 1994
Farber, Daniel. *Lincoln's Constitution*. Chicago: The University of
    Chicago Press, 2003
Fehrenbacher, Don E. *Lincoln in Text and Context, Collected Essays*.
    Stanford: Stanford University Press, 1987
_____. *Prelude to Greatness: Lincoln in the 1850's*. Stanford: Stanford
    University Press, 1962, paperback edition, 1999
_____. *The Dred Scott Case, Its Significance in American Law and Politics*.
    New York: Oxford University Press, 1978; paperback edition, 2001

_____. *The Slaveholding Republic, An Account of the United States Government's Relations to Slavery*. Completed and edited by Ward M. McAfee. New York: Oxford University Press, 2001

Fredrickson, George. *Big Enough to be Inconsistent: Abraham Lincoln Confronts Slavery and Race*. Cambridge: Harvard University Press, 2008

Foner, Eric. *Free Soil, Free Labor, Free Men: The Ideology of the Republican Party Before the Civil War*. London: Oxford University Press; paperback edition 1971

_____, ed. *Our Lincoln: New Perspectives on Lincoln and His World*. New York: W.W. Norton Company, Inc., 2008

Franklin, John Hope. *The Emancipation Proclamation*. Garden City, N.Y.: Doubleday & Company, Inc., 1963

Goodwin, Doris Kearns. *Team of Rivals: The Political Genius of Abraham Lincoln*. New York: Simon & Schuster, 2005

Harold Holzer. *Lincoln President-Elect: Abraham Lincoln and the Great Secession Winter, 1860-1861*. New York: Simon & Schuster, 2008; paperback edition, 2009

Jaffa, Harry V. *Crisis of The House Divided, An Interpretation of the Issues in the Lincoln-Douglas Debates*. Chicago: The University of Chicago Press, 1982

_____. *A New Birth of Freedom, Abraham Lincoln and the Coming of the Civil War*. Lanham: Rowman & Littlefield, 2000

Jordan, Winthrop D. *White over Black, American Attitudes Toward the Negro, 1550-1812*. Chapel Hill: University of North Carolina Press, 1968; paperback edition, 2000

Kaplan, Fred. *Lincoln: The Biography of a Writer*. New York: HarperCollins, 2008

Klingaman, William K. *Abraham Lincoln and the Road to Emancipation, 1861-1865*. New York: New York, 2001

Kolchin, Peter. *American Slavery, 1619-1877*. New York: Hill and Wang, 1993; revised edition 2003

Lincoln, Abraham. *The Collected Works of Abraham Lincoln*. Roy P. Basler, ed. New Brunswick: Rutgers University Press, 1953

_____. *Speeches and Writings, 1832-1858*. Don E. Fehrenbacher, ed., New York: The Library of America, Literary Classics of the United States, Inc., 1989

McPherson, James M. *Abraham Lincoln and the Second American Revolution*. New York: Oxford University Press, 1990

_____. *Battle Cry of Freedom, The Civil War Era*. New York: Oxford University Press, 1988

_____. *Drawn with the Sword, Reflections on the American Civil War*. New York: Oxford University Press, 1996

_____. *Ordeal By Fire, The Civil War and Reconstruction*, New York: Alfred A. Knopf, 1982

_____. *Tried by War: Abraham Lincoln as Commander in Chief*. New York: The Penguin Press, 2008

_____,ed. *"We Cannot Escape History:" Lincoln and the Last Best Hope of Earth*. Urbana: University of Illinois Press, 1995

Miller, William Lee, *Arguing About Slavery, John Quincy Adams and the Great Battle in the United States Congress*, Alfred A. Knopf, New York, 1996, Random House, Inc., New York, Vintage Books edition, 1998

_____. *Lincoln's Virtues*. New York: Alfred A. Knopf, 2002

Mitgang, Herbert. *Abraham Lincoln, A Press Portrait*. New York: Fordham University Press, 2000

Morrison, Michael A. *Slavery and the American West, The Eclipse of Manifest Destiny and the Coming of the Civil War*. Chapel Hill: The University of North Carolina Press, 1997, 1999

Neely, Mark E. Jr. *The Last Best Hope of Earth, Abraham Lincoln and the Promise of America*. Cambridge: Harvard University Press, 1993

Paludan, Phillip Shaw. *The Presidency of Abraham Lincoln*. Lawrence: University Press of Kansas, 1994

_____, ed. *Lincoln's Legacy: Ethics & Politics*. Urbana and Chicago: University of Illinois Press, 2008

Peterson, Merrill D. *Lincoln in American Memory*. New York: Oxford University Press, 1994

Potter, David M. *Lincoln and His Party in the Succession Crisis*. New Haven: Yale University Press, 1942

_____. *The Impending Crisis, 1848-1861*. New York: Harper & Row, 1976

Randall, J.G. *Lincoln The President, Springfield to Gettysburg, Volume One*. New York: Dodd, Mead & Company, 1945

_____. *Lincoln The President, Springfield to Gettysburg, Volume Two*. New York: Dodd, Mead & Company, 1945

_____. *Lincoln The President, Midstream*. New York: Dodd, Mead & Company, 1952

Randall, J.G., and Richard N. Current. *Lincoln The President, Last Full Measure*. New York: Dodd, Mead & Company, 1955

Randall, J.G. and David Herbert Donald. *The Civil War and Recon-struction*. Lexington: D.C. Heath and Company, Second Edition, 1969

Stampp, Kenneth M. *America in 1857, A Nation on the Brink*. New York: Oxford University Press, 1990

_____. *The Imperiled Union, Essays on the Background of the Civil War*. New York: Oxford University Press, 1980; paperback edition 1981

_____. *The Peculiar Institution, Slavery in the Ante-Bellum South*. New York: Alfred A. Knopf, 1956

Wilson, Douglas L. *Honor's Voice, The Transformation of Abraham Lincoln*. New York: Alfred A. Knopf, 1998

Woodward, C. Vann. *The Strange Career of Jim Crow*. London: Oxford University Press, second revised edition, 1966

Vorenberg, Michael. *Final Freedom, The Civil War, the Abolition of Slavery, and the Thirteenth Amendment*. Cambridge: Cambridge University Press, 2001

Chapter 5

Bailey, Thomas A. *Woodrow Wilson and The Great Betrayal*. New York: The MacMillan Company, 1945; Chicago: Quadrangle Books, Inc., 1963, paperback edition

_____. *Woodrow Wilson and The Lost Peace*. New York: The MacMillan Company, 1944: Chicago: Quadrangle Books, Inc., 1963, paperback edition

Blum, John Morton. *Woodrow Wilson and the Politics of Morality*. Boston: Little, Brown and Company, 1956

Brands, H.W. *Woodrow Wilson*. New York: Times Books, Henry Holt & Co., 2003

Clements, Kendrick A. *The Presidency of Woodrow Wilson*. Lawrence: University of Kansas Press, 1992

Cooper, John Milton, Jr. *Breaking the Heart of the World, Woodrow Wilson and the Fight for the League of Nations*. Cambridge: Cambridge University Press, 2001

_____. *Pivotal Decades, The United States, 1900-1920*. New York: W.W. Norton Company, 1990

_____. *The Warrior and The Priest, Woodrow Wilson and Theodore Roosevelt*. Cambridge: The Belknap Press of Harvard University Press, 1983

_____. *Woodrow Wilson, A Biography*. New York: Alfred A. Knopf, 2009

Cooper, John Milton, Jr., and Charles E. Neu, eds. *The Wilson Era: Essays in Honor of Arthur S. Link*. Arlington Heights, Illinois: Harlan Davidson, Inc., 1991

Ferguson, Niall. *The Pity of War: Explaining World War I*. London: Allen Lane, The Penguin Press, 1998; New York: Basic Books, 1999

Freud, Sigmund and William C. Bullitt. *Thomas Woodrow Wilson, A Psychological Study*. Boston: Houghton Mifflin Company, 1967

Herring, George C. *From Colony to Superpower, U.S. Foreign Relations since 1776*. New York: Oxford University Press, 2008

Hoover, Herbert. *The Ordeal of Woodrow Wilson*. New York: McGraw-Hill, 1958; Washington, D.C.: The Woodrow Wilson Center Press, paperback edition, 1992

Kissinger, Henry. *Diplomacy*. New York: Simon & Schuster, 1994

Knock, Thomas J. *To End All Wars, Woodrow Wilson and the Quest for a New World Order*. New York: Oxford University Press, 1992; Princeton: Princeton University Press, 1992, paperback edition

Latham, Earl, ed. *The Philosophy and Policies of Woodrow Wilson*. Chicago: The University of Chicago Press, 1958

Levin, N. Gordon, Jr. *Woodrow Wilson and World Politics*. New York: Oxford University Press, 1968; New York: Oxford University Press, 1970, paperback edition

Link, Arthur S. *Wilson*. Princeton: Princeton University Press, five volumes, 1947-1965

_____. *Woodrow Wilson, A Brief Biography*. Cleveland: The World Publishing Company, 1963; Chicago: Quadrangle Books, Inc., 1992, paperback edition

_____. *Woodrow Wilson, A Profile*. New York: Hill and Wang, 1968

_____. *Woodrow Wilson and The Progressive Era, 1910-1917*. New York: Harper & Brothers, 1954; Harper & Row, 1963, paperback edition

_____. *Woodrow Wilson, Revolution, War, and Peace*. Arlington Heights, Illinois: Harlan Davidson, Inc., 1979

_____, ed. *The Deliberations of the Council of Four (March 24-June 28, 1919), Notes of the Official Interpreter, Paul Mantoux, Volume One, To the Delivery to the German Delegation of the Preliminaries of Peace*. Princeton: Princeton University Press, 1992

_____, et. al., eds. *The Papers of Woodrow Wilson*. Princeton: Princeton University Press, 69 volumes, 1966 to 1994

MacMillan, Margaret. *Paris, 1919: Six Months That Changed The World*. New York: Random House, 2001

Mason, Alpheus Thomas. *Brandeis, A Free Man's Life*. New York: The Viking Press, 1946

Muller, Herbert J. *Freedom in the Modern World*. New York: Harper & Row, 1966

Ninkovich, Frank. *The Wilsonian Century: U.S. Foreign Policy Since 1900*. Chicago: University of Chicago Press, 1999

Schmitt, Bernadotte E., and Harold C. Vedeler. *The World in the Crucible, 1914-1919*. New York: Harper & Row, 1984

Smith, Daniel M. *The Great Departure, The United States and World War I, 1914-1920*. New York: Alfred A. Knopf, 1965

Smith, Gene. *When The Cheering Stopped: The Last Years of Woodrow Wilson*. New York: William Morrow & Company, 1964, paperback edition

Stevenson, David. *Cataclysm: The First World War as Political Tragedy*. New York: Basic Books, 2004

Thompson, John A. *Woodrow Wilson*. London: Pearson Education Limited, 2002

Chapter 6

Badger, Anthony J. *The New Deal: The Depression Years, 1933-40*. New York: Hill and Wang, 1989

Bernstein, Irving. *A Caring Society, The New Deal, the Worker, and the Great Depression*. Boston: Houghton Mifflin Company, 1985

Beschloss, Michael R. *Kennedy and Roosevelt: The Uneasy Alliance*. New York: W.W. Norton & Company, 1980

Blum, John Morton. *From The Morgenthau Diaries: Years of Crisis, 1928-1938*. Boston: Houghton Mifflin Company, 1959

Brinkley, Alan. *The End of Reform, New Deal Liberalism in Recession and War*. New York: Alfred A. Knopf, 1995

_____. *Voices of Protest, Huey Long, Father Coughlin, and the Great Depression*. New York: Alfred A. Knopf, 1982; Vintage Books, Random House, 1983, paperback edition

Burns, James MacGregor. *Roosevelt, The Lion and the Fox, 1882-1940*. New York: Harcourt Brace Jovanovich, 1956

Davis, Kenneth S. *FDR: The New Deal Years, 1933-1937.* New York: Random House, 1986

_____. *FDR: The New York Years, 1928-2933.* New York: Random House, 1985

Edsforth, Ronald. *The New Deal, America's Response to the Great Depression.* Malden: Blackwell Publishers, Inc., 2000

Einaudi, Mario. *The Roosevelt Revolution.* London: Constable and Company, Ltd., 1960; Westport, Greenwood Press, 1997, reprint

Friedel, Frank. *Franklin D. Roosevelt.* Four volumes (*The Apprenticeship, The Ordeal, The Triumph, Launching the New Deal*). Boston: Little, Brown and Company, 1952-1973

Galbraith, John Kenneth. *The Great Crash, 1929.* Boston: Houghton Mifflin, 1954, 1988

Graham, Otis L., Jr. *An Encore for Reform, The Old Progressives and the New Deal.* New York: Oxford University Press, 1967

_____. *Toward A Planned Society, From Roosevelt to Nixon.* New York: Oxford University Press, 1976

Gordon, Colin. *New Deals: Business, Labor and Politics in America, 1920-1935.* Cambridge: Cambridge University Press, 1994

Hawley, Ellis W. *The New Deal and the Problem of Monopoly: A Study in Economic Ambivalence.* Princeton: Princeton University Press, 1966

Hofstadter, Richard. *The Age of Reform, From Bryan to F.D.R.* New York: Alfred A. Knopf, 197.

_____. *The American Political Tradition and the Men Who Made It.* New York: Alfred A. Knopf, 1948, 1973; Vintage Books, 1989, paperback edition

Hopkins, Harry L. *Spending to Save, The Complete Story of Relief.* New York: W. W. Norton and Company, Inc., 1936; University of Washington Press, Seattle, 1972

Jackson, Robert H. *That Man, An Insider's Portrait of Franklin D. Roosevelt.* New York: Oxford University Press, 2003

Jenkins, Roy. *Franklin Delano Roosevelt.* New York: Times Books, Henry Holt & Company, 2003

Kennedy, David M. *Freedom From Fear, The American People in Depression and War, 1929-1945.* New York: Oxford University Press, 1999

Leuchtenburg, William E. *Franklin D. Roosevelt and The New Deal, 1932-1940.* New York: Harper & Row, 1963

_____. *The FDR Years: On Roosevelt and His Legacy*. New York: Columbia University Press, 1995

_____. *The Perils of Prosperity, 1914-1932*. Chicago: University of Chicago Press, 1958; second edition, 1993

_____, ed. *The New Deal, A Documentary History*. New York: Harper & Row, 1968; Columbia: University of South Carolina Press, 1968

Maney, Patrick J. *The Roosevelt Presence, A Biography of Franklin Delano Roosevelt*. New York: Twayne Publishers, 1992; Berkeley: University of California Press, 1992, paperback edition

McElvaine, Robert S. *The Great Depression, America, 1929-1941*. New York: Times Books, 1993, paperback edition

_____, ed. *Down & Out in the Great Depression: Letters from the "Forgotten Man."* Chapel Hill: The University of North Carolina Press, 1983

McJimsey, George. *The Presidency of Franklin Delano Roosevelt*. Lawrence: University Press of Kansas, Larwence, 2000

Miller, Nathan. *FDR: An Intimate History*. Garden City, New York: Doubleday & Company, 1983

Moley, Raymond. *After Seven Years*. New York: Harper & Brothers, 1939

Parrish, Michael E. *Anxious Decades, America in Prosperity and Depression, 1920-1941*. New York: W.W. Norton & Company, 1992

_____. *Securities Regulation and The New Deal*. New Haven: Yale University Press, 1970

Patterson, James T. *America's Struggle Against Poverty, 1900-1914*. Cambridge: Harvard University Press, 1994

Perkins, Frances. *The Roosevelt I Knew*. New York: Harper & Row, 1946; paperback edition, 1964

Roosevelt, Franklin D. *The Public Papers and Addresses of Franklin D. Roosevelt*, Samuel I. Rosenman, ed. New York: Random House and Harper and Brothers, 13 volumes, 1938-1950

Rosen, Elliot A. *Hoover, Roosevelt, and the Brains Trust, From Depression to New Deal*. New York: Columbia University Press, 1977

Schlesinger, Arthur M. Jr. *The Age of Roosevelt*. Three volumes (*The Crisis of the Old Order, 1919-1933, The Coming of the New Deal, The Politics of Upheaval*). Boston: Houghton Mifflin Company, 1957, 1958, 1960

Sherwood, Robert E. *Roosevelt and Hopkins: An Intimate History*. New York: Harper Brothers, 1948; Enigma Books, 2001 reprint of 1950 revised edition

Smith, Jean Edward. *Eisenhower in War and Peace*. New York: Random House, 2012

_____. *FDR*. New York: Random House, 2007

Tugwell, Rexford G. *The Democratic Roosevelt, A Biography of Franklin D. Roosevelt*. Garden City, New York: Doubleday & Company, Inc., 1957

Ward, Geoffrey C. *A First-Class Temperament: The Emergence of Franklin Roosevelt*. New York: Harper & Row, 1989

_____. *Before the Trumpet, Young Franklin Roosevelt, 1882-1905*. New York: Harper & Row, 1985

NOTES

Chapter 1. George Washington and the Foundation of a National Economy

1. *George Washington, Writings*, (Library of America, New York, 1997) pp. 3-10

2. Letter to John Augustine Washington, May 31, 1754, in *George Washington, Writings*, p.48

3. Letter to the President of Congress, August 20, 1780, in *The Writings of George Washington from the Original Manuscript Sources, 1745-1799*, John C. Fitzpatrick, ed., Volume 19, June 12, 1780-September 5,1780, (U.S. GPO, Washington, D.C., June, 1937), p. 408-9

4. Richard B. Morris, *The Forging of the Union, 1781-1789*, (Harper & Row, New York, 1987), Chapter 2

5. Ibid., pp. 90-1

6. Forrest McDonald, *Novus Ordo Seclorum*, (University Press of Kansas, Lawrence, 1985), p. 157

7. Gordon Wood, *The Creation of the American Republic, 1776-1787* (University of North Carolina Press, Chapel Hill, 1998 edition), Chapter XII

8. Gordon Wood, *The Creation of the American Republic*, Chapter X, part 3

9. Letter to John Jay, May 18, 1786, in *George Washington, Writings* (Library of America, New York, 1997), p. 600

10. Letter to James Duane, April 10, 1785, in *The Writings of George Washington from the Original Manuscript Sources,1745-1799*, Volume 28, December 5, 1784-August 30, 1786, (U.S. GPO, Washington, D.C., October, 1938), p. 124

11. Stuart Leibeger, *Founding Friendship, George Washington, James Madison, and the Creation of the American Republic* (University of Virginia

Press, Charlottesville, 1999), pp. 75-6; Stanley Elkins and Eric McKitrick, *The Age of Federalism*, (Oxford University Press, New York and Oxford, 1993), pp. 44-5

12. Elkins and McKitrick, *The Age of Federalism*, (Oxford University Press, New York and Oxford, 1993), p. 45

13. James Roger Sharp, *American Politics in the Early Republic, The New Nation in Crisis*, (Yale University Press, New Haven 1993), p. 27; James Thomas Flexner, *George Washington and the New Nation ,1783-1793*, (Little, Brown and Company, Boston, 1969,1970), pp. 3,141

14. <u>Letter from Pierce Butler to Weedon Butler, May 5, 1788</u>, in Max Farrand, ed., *The Records of the Federal Convention of 1787* (New Haven 1911), Vol. III, p. 302

15. They did so in an effort to overturn the Alien and Sedition Acts, which placed restrictions on free speech and on non-citizens in response to a perceived foreign threat to the country's security.

16. The powers are generally separate, but there are some areas where they are, to some extent, shared. For example, the President has some share in legislative power with the ability to veto legislation; Congress has some share in executive power with the right to advise and consent on the appointment of certain executive officials; the judiciary has a share of executive power when it executes (or, more accurately, enforces) the laws; and Congress has a share of judicial power with the capacity to impeach federal officials and to establish federal courts.

17. Forrest McDonald, *The American Presidency, An Intellectual History*, (University Press of Kansas, 1994, Chapters 7 and 10.

18. <u>*Diary Entries*, April 16 and 23, 1789</u>, in *George Washington, Writings*, p. 730

19. <u>First Inaugural Address, April 30, 1789</u>, in *George Washington, Writings*, (Library of America, New York 1997), p. 733

20. Forrest McDonald, *The Presidency of George Washington* (University of Kansas Press, Lawrence, 1974), p. 41

21. John C. Miller, *Alexander Hamilton and the Growth of the New Nation*,(Harper & Row, New York, 1959, Torchbook Edition, 1964), p. 41

22. He found that there were four categories of debt: 1) the <u>foreign</u> debt, consisting of about $10-11 million, $6.5 million owed to France, $3.6 to Dutch financiers and a small amount to Spain; 2) the <u>Continental</u> Congress debt consisted of $11 million in bonds or loan office certificates used to purchase war supplies, $16 million in promissory notes the Congress authorized military commanders to issue for supplies and soldier pay while

in the field, and about $200 million in face value of paper money, which had by 1789 lost most of its value; 3) the <u>state</u> debt, consisting of about $25 million owed by the states for money they raised to prosecute the war, which some states (chiefly Virginia, Rhode Island and North Carolina) had already issued paper money of dubious value to redeem, others (chiefly Massachusetts and South Carolina) had yet to begin to redeem, and still others (most of the rest) had begun to pay responsibly and gradually; and 4) intergovernmental obligations, about $100 million spent by the states and for which the Articles of Confederation had specified would be credited to the states by the national government after a through audit in accordance with a fair apportionment of the costs of the war. See Forrest McDonald, *Alexander Hamilton, A Biography* (W.W. Norton, New York, 1979, paperback, 1981) pp. 144-149

23. <u>Letter to Marquis de Lafayette, January 29, 1789</u>, in *George Washington, Writings*, p. 717

24. Miller, *Alexander Hamilton and the Growth of the New Nation*, pp. 15, 230-1; Elkins and McKitrick, pp. 107-9, 115-6, McDonald, *Washington*, pp. 63-4

25. Alexander Hamilton, Report on Public Credit, in *Alexander Hamilton, Writings*, p. 569

26. Specifically, the funding mechanism was a clever balance among three factors: 1) a realistic amount of taxation, 2) a reasonable interest rate, and 3) a time frame for payment. For the foreign debt, much of which had specific dates of maturity, the Report proposed taking out new loans, at an annual cost of about $.5 million and a projected interest rate of 5%. For the Continental Congress, state and intergovernmental debts, the Report proposed that the federal government issue new certificates at an interest rate of about 4.5%, below the original 6% par value of the debt. The Report sweetened this approach for investors by offering six different methods of payment over time, including a full 6% if the creditor wished. Hamilton argued that, by establishing a sound economy and stable credit, the prevailing interest rate would likely fall to 4.5 or 4% over time, anyway. As a kind of insurance policy for creditors, the Report proposed a <u>sinking fund</u> to stabilize the value of the debt by annual purchases of government certificates to firm the market in the event their value was "sinking". The fund would also directly retire a portion of the debt principal each year.

27. *Hamilton, Writings*, p. 544

28. Elkins and McKitrick, *The Age of Federalism*, (Oxford University Press, New York and Oxford, 1993), pp. 19-20

29. Letters to David Stuart, March 28 and June 15, 1790, in *George Washington, Writings*, pp. 757-8, 761-2

30. Lance Banning, *The Sacred Fire of Liberty, James Madison & the Founding of the Federal Republic* (Cornell University Press, Ithaca, 1995, Cornell Paperbacks, 1998), p. 316

31. Thomas Jefferson, The Anas, 1791-1806, Selections, in *Thomas Jefferson, Writings* (Library of America, New York, 1984), p. 668

32. The Conflict with Hamilton, Letter to the President of the United States, September 9, 1792, in *Thomas Jefferson, Writings*, p. 993

33. Forrest McDonald, *Alexander Hamilton*, pp. 184-5, p. 404, n. 41

34. Letter to Marquis De La Luzerne, August 10, 1790, in *The Writings of George Washington from the Original Manuscript Sources, 1745-1790*, Volume 31, Jan. 22, 1790-March 9, 1792, (U.S. GPO, Washington, D.C., Aug. 1939) p.84

35. George Washington, Second Annual Message to Congress, December 8, 1790, in *George Washington, Writings*, p. 768

36. Sharp, *American Politics*, p. 37

37. The government would be required to purchase $2 million of bank stock, with the remaining $8 million to be purchased by private investors, provided at least 25% was paid for in gold or silver.

38. Madison's point of view on the Necessary and Proper Clause was contrary to the position he took when he wrote Federalist 44 during the campaign to adopt the Constitution. In that document, Madison observed that the Constitutional Convention specifically rejected carrying over the second article of the Articles of Confederation, which prohibited the exercise of any power not *expressly* delegated.

39. Thomas Jefferson, Opinion on the Constitutionality of a National Bank, February 15, 1791, in *Thomas Jefferson, Writings*, p. 416

40. Ibid., p. 419

41. *Hamilton, Writings*, p. 621

42. Letter to David Humphreys, July 20, 1791, in *George Washington, Writings*, p. 778

43. Third Annual Message to Congress, October 25, 1791, in *George Washington, Writings*, pp. 787, 791

44. Alexander Hamilton, Political and Personal Defense, To George Washington, August 18, 1792, in *Alexander Hamilton, Writings*, p. 781

45. Alexander Hamilton, Political and Personal Defense, To George Washington, August 18, 1792, in *Alexander Hamilton, Writings*, p. 782

46. Edmund S. Morgan, The Genius of George Washington (W.W. Norton & Company, New York, 1980), pp. 20-1

47. E.g., Gordon S. Wood, *Empire of Liberty: A History of the Early Republic, 1789-1815*, (Oxford University Press, Inc., New York, 2009), p. 95 et seq.

48. E.g., Joseph J. Ellis, *His Excellency, George Washington*, (Alfred A. Knopf, New York, 2004), p. 206

49. Glenn A. Phelps, *George Washington and American Constitutionalism*, (University Press of Kansas, 1993), pp. 190-94

Chapter 2. Thomas Jefferson and the Expansion of the Nation

50. Dumas Malone, *Jefferson the Virginian, Volume I, Jefferson and His Time*, (Little, Brown & Company, Boston, 1948), p. 37

51. Willard Sterne Randall, *Thomas Jefferson, A Life* (Henry Holt & Co., New York, 1993) p. 348

52. Letter to Chastellux, November 26, 1782, *Jefferson, Writings*, p. 780

53. See, for example, Letter to Maria Cosway (Dialoge between My Head & My Heart) Oct. 12, 1786 and Letter To Maria Cosway, Apr. 24, 1788, in *Jefferson, Writings*, pp. 866 and 921

54. See *The Jefferson-Hemings Matter, Report of the Scholar's Commission*, Robert F. Turner, ed., Carolina Academic Press, Durham, 2001, 2011, concluding no likely sexual relationship, with minority views; but see Annette Gordon-Reed, *Thomas Jefferson and Sally Hemings: An American Controversy* (University Press of Virginia, Charlottesville, 1997) and Fawn M. Brodie, *Thomas Jefferson* (W.W. Norton & Company, New York, 1974) concluding there was.

55. See, especially, Abigail Adams to Jefferson, with Enclosure, June 6, 1785, Jefferson to Abigail Adams, July 7, 1785, Abigail Adams to Jefferson, June 26, 1787, Abigail Adams to Jefferson, June 27, 1787, Abigail Adams to Jefferson, May 20, 1804, Jefferson to Abigail Adams, June 13, 1804, Abigail Adams to Jefferson, July 1, 1804, Jefferson to Abigail Adams, July 22, 1804, Abigail Adams to Jefferson, Aug. 18, 1804, Jefferson to Abigail Adams, Sept. 11, 1804, Abigail Adams to Jefferson, Oct. 25, 1804, Abigail Adams to Jefferson, Sept. 20, 1813, in *The Adams-Jefferson Letters, The Complete Correspondence between Thomas Jefferson and Abigail and John Adams*, Lester J. Cappon, ed. (The University of North Carolina Press, 1959, Reprint paperback edition, 1998), pp. 28, 36, 178,179, 268, 269, 271, 274, 276, 278, 280, and 377

56. The other committee members were John Adams of Massachusetts, Benjamin Franklin of Pennsylvania, Roger Sherman of Connecticut
and Robert R. Livingston of New York.

57. Letter to Henry L. Pierce and Others, April 6, 1859, in *Abraham
Lincoln, Speeches and Writings, 1859-1865* (The Library of America, New
York, 1989), p. 18

58. Autobiography, 1743-1790, in *Jefferson, Writings* p. 18

59. See A Bill for Establishing Religious Freedom in *Jefferson,
Writings*, pp. 346-48 and A Bill for the More General Diffusion of Knowledge in *Jefferson, Writings*, pp. 365-373

60. Jefferson's notes at the time indicated that his belief in religious
freedom went beyond the limited "tolerance" of only those groups adhering
to the "moral rules required by the preservation of society" advocated by
John Locke by including Jews, Moslems, pagans and atheists. Jefferson,
Notes on Locke, in *The Papers of Thomas Jefferson*, Julian P. Boyd, et. al, eds.
(Princeton University Press, Princeton, N.J., Vol. 1, 1950), pp. 545-48; See
also David N. Mayer, *The Constitutional Thought of Thomas Jefferson* (University Press of Virginia, Charlottesville, Va., 1994, 2nd paperback printing,
1997) p. 159. Jefferson himself believed in the superiority of the moral
teachings of Jesus Christ but did not believe in his divinity, See Letter to
Dr. Benjamin Rush, with a Syllabus, April 21, 1803, in *Jefferson, Writings*, p.
1122

61. The others were his authorship of the Declaration of Independence and his founding of the University of Virginia, as the epitaph he
chose for himself reads on his tombstone in the family cemetery at Monticello. *Jefferson, Writings*, p. 706

62. Notes on the State of Virginia, in *Jefferson, Writings*, p. 286

63. Notes on the State of Virginia, in *Jefferson, Writings*, p. 290

64. Andrew Burstein, *The Inner Jefferson, Portrait of a Grieving
Optimist*, (University of Virginia Press, Charlottesville, 1995), p. 279

65. Letter to William S. Smith, Nov. 13, 1787, in *Jefferson, Writings*, p.
911

66. Letter to Thomas Jefferson, Aug. 23, 1792, in *George Washington,
Writings* (Library of America, New York, 1997) p. 815, 817-818 and Letter
to Alexander Hamilton, Aug. 26, 1792, in *Washington, Writings*, p. 818-820

67. Letter to Mrs. Church, Nov. 27, 1793, in *Jefferson, Writings*, p.
1013

68. Some local party organizations referred to themselves as part of
the "Democratic-Republican" Party, but soon most references were to the

"Republican" Party. Jefferson's Republican Party was renamed the "Democratic" Party by President Andrew Jackson and is the antecedent of the modern Democratic Party. It is not to be confused with the party of Abraham Lincoln and the present Republican Party.

69. His somewhat naïve conviction that American commercial pressure against Great Britain could further American interests by getting British troops to leave our Northern Territory and admit our commercial exports to her other colonies, was later, in his second presidential term, to lead to economic disaster.

70. Letter to James Madison, with Enclosure, Jan. 1, 1797, Enclosure to John Adams, Dec. 28, 1796, in *Jefferson, Writings*, p. 1040

71. Letter to James Madison, with Enclosure, Jan. 1, 1797, in *Jefferson, Writings*, pp. 1038,1039

72. The name of the incident derives from a code used in the dispatches of the American envoys John Marshall, Charles Cotesworth Pinckney and Elbridge Gerry to refer to the three French agents of Foreign Minister Talleyrand who laid out the French "requirements".

73. In opposing these laws, Jefferson utilized principles of constitutional interpretation that were to have consequences in our history he failed to foresee. He embraced the concept of ***nullification*** of federal authority by individual states when the federal government exceeded powers delegated to it under a strict construction of the Constitution. This nullification idea later gave a Constitutional rationale to southern opposition to federal tariffs during the administration of President Andrew Jackson as well as to the secession of southern states from the Union leading up to the Civil War. See South Carolina Ordinance of Nullification, Nov. 24, 1832, in *Documents of American History, 6th edition*, Henry Steele Commager, ed., (Appleton-Century-Crofts, New York, 1958), p. 261and David M. Potter, *The Impending Crisis, 1848-1861*(Harper & Row, New York, 1976), p. 483

74. Letter to John Trumbull, Feb. 15, 1789, in *Jefferson, Writings*, p. 939

75. Such a result is possible even today when neither candidate receives the majority of electoral votes and the Congress must decide the President.

76. All excerpts from First Inaugural Address, March 4, 1801, in *Jefferson, Writings*, pp. 493-5

77. The Treaty of San Lorenzo, more popularly referred to as Pinckney's Treaty was named after Thomas Pinckney of South Carolina, U.S. Ambassador to Great Britain, who was our negotiator with the Madrid gov-

ernment, and later became the Federalist candidate for Vice President in the election of 1800 .

78. The precise boundary between East and West Florida was the Perdido River near Pensacola.

79. By this time, Napoleon Bonaparte had consolidated the Revolution, by preserving its many reforms and eliminating many of its excesses, and was in total control of the country. He was to become First Consul for Life in 1803 and then, in December, 1804, Napoleon I, Emperor of the French.

80. Dumas Malone, *Jefferson the President, First Term 1801-1805* (Little, Brown & Co., Boston, 1970) p. 251

81. George C. Herring, *From Colony to Superpower, U.S. Foreign Relations Since 1776*, (Oxford University Press, Inc., New York, 2008), p. 102

82. Letter to the New York Evening Post from Pericles, a.k.a., Alexander Hamilton, as quoted in Dumas Malone, *Jefferson the President, First Term 1801-1805* (Little, Brown & Co., Boston, 1970) p. 277

83. Letter to James Madison, Sept. 1, 1802, in *American State Papers, Foreign Relations*, Lowrie and Clark, eds., Vol. II., 1832, p. 525

84. DuPont was a financial advisor to King Louis XVI and later president of the Constituent Assembly during the French Revolution, where he and Jefferson began a long-term friendship and correspondence about economic policy. His economic and political views resulted in his imprisonment in France, after which he emigrated to the United States. He is the scion of the DuPont family prominent to this day in U.S. industry.

85. Letter to the U.S. Minister to France (Robert R. Livingston), Apr. 18, 1802, in *Jefferson, Writings*, p. 1105

86. Merrill D. Peterson, *Thomas Jefferson and the New Nation*, (Oxford University Press, 1970, 3rd paperback printing, 1975), p. 754

87. Letter to the Special Envoy to France, Jan. 13, 1803, in *Jefferson, Writings*, p. 1112

88. Mainly Choctaws, Chickasaws and Creeks.

89. Instructions to Captain Lewis, June 20, 1803, in *Jefferson, Writings*, pp. 1126-1132; Anthony F.C. Wallace, *Jefferson and the Indians, The Tragic Fate of the First Americans* (Belknap Press of Harvard University, Cambridge, 1999) p.241-242

90. As quoted in Elijah Wilson Lyon, *Louisiana in French Diplomacy*, 1759-1804, (University of Oklahoma Press, 1934) p. 194

91. Barbe Marbois, *The History of Louisiana*, E. Wilson Lyon, ed., (Louisiana State University Press, Baton Rouge, 1977 Reprint of 1830 edition, Carey & Lea, Philadelphia), p. 264

92. Barbe Marbois, *The History of Louisiana*, p. 274

93. Arkansas, Colorado, Iowa, Kansas, Louisiana, Minnesota, Missouri , Montana, Nebraska, North Dakota, Oklahoma, South Dakota, Texas, and Wyoming

94. Henry Adams, *History*, p. 468

95. The United States gained West Florida in 1810, essentially by force, under the administration of President James Madison and, obtained the remainder of Florida by negotiation with Spain in 1819 under then President Monroe.

96. Letter to John Dickinson, Aug. 9, 1803, in *The Writings of Thomas Jefferson*, Volume VIII, 1810-1806, Paul Leicester Ford, ed., (G.P. Putnam's Sons, New York, 1897), p. 262

97. Letter to John Breckinridge, Aug. 12, 1803, in *The Writings of Thomas Jefferson*, Volume X, Library Edition, Andrew A. Lipscomb and Albert Ellery Bergh, eds., (The Thomas Jefferson Memorial Association, Washington, D.C., 1903), p. 411

98. Letter to John B. Colvin, Sept. 20, 1810, in *Jefferson, Writings*, p. 1231

99. Letter to Benjamin Hawkins, Feb. 18, 1803, in *Jefferson, Writings*, p. 1115

100. Anthony F.C. Wallace, *Jefferson and the Indians, The Tragic Fate of the First Americans, The Tragic Fate of the First Americans*, (Cambridge, 1999), p. 251-260

101. Letter to Dr. Joseph Priestley, Jan. 29, 1804, in *Jefferson, Writings*, p.1142

102. Herring, *From Colony to Superpower*, p. 107

103. Frederick Jackson Turner, The Significance of the Mississippi Valley in American History, in Turner, *The Frontier in American History* (New York, 1920)

104. Robert W. Tucker & David C. Hendrickson, *Empire of Liberty* (Oxford University Press, New York, 1990, paperback edition 1992) p. 247

105. The War of 1812 with Great Britain carried on by President James Madison was a result of maritime conflict engendered by Jefferson's embargo.

106. John Chester Miller, *The Wolf by the Ears, Thomas Jefferson and Slavery* (University Press of Virginia, Charlottesville, 1991, third paperback printing, 1995) pp. 142-143

107. Arthur M. Schlesinger, Jr., *A Thousand Days, John F. Kennedy in the White House*, (Houghton Mifflin, Boston, 1965) p. 733

Chapter 3. James Monroe and the Establishment of America's Place in the World

108. Henry Adams, *History of the United States in the Administrations of James Madison (The Library of America*, New York, 1986), pp. 1218-19; Samuel Eliot Morison & Henry Steele Commager, *The Growth of the American Republic, Volume One* (Oxford University Press, New York, Fourth Edition, 1950) p. 431.

109. Harry Ammon, *James Monroe, The Quest for National Identity* (University Press of Virginia, Charlottesville 1971, paperback 1990), p. 2

110. Monroe's close friendship with Marshall did not survive the political disagreements between the two men in the 1790's, Marshall being a strong Federalist and supporter of Hamilton, Monroe being an avid Republican and ally of Jefferson.

111. Letter to James Madison, Jan. 30, 1787, in *Thomas Jefferson, Writings* (Library of America, New York, 1984) p. 886

112. Thomas Paine, The American Crisis, Number 1, December 19, 1776, in *Thomas Paine, Collected Writings*, (The Library of America, New York, 1995), p. 91

113. Harry Ammon, James Monroe, *The Quest for National Identity*, p. 19

114. Ibid., p. 113

115. Hamilton and Jay were both New Yorkers as were the leading "Republican" candidates for the French post, Governor Clinton and Aaron Burr.

116. Message To The Speakers of the House of Delegates, and of the Senate, December 7, 1801, in *The Writings of James Monroe*, Stanislaus Murray Hamilton, ed., Vol. III, 1796-1802 (New York, 1900), p. 306-7

117. Message To The Speakers..., December 7, 1801, in *The Writings of James Monroe*, Vol. III, p.318

118. James Monroe, *Journal of the Negotiations in Spain*, Feb. 10, 1805

119. Henry Adams, *History of the United States in the Administrations of Thomas Jefferson*, (The Library of America, New York, 1986), p. 630

120. Letter to James Madison, June 3, 1804, in *The Writings of James Monroe*, Vol. IV, p. 191

121. Letter to James Monroe, Feb. 18, 1808, in *Writings of Thomas Jefferson*, Paul Leicester Ford, ed., New York, 1892-99, Vol. IX, p. 176-8

122. The patent office was spared because the British were persuaded by its Director, William Thornton, that destruction of patent records would

significantly harm non-U.S. citizens who might benefit from or be subject to American patents.

123. Marshall Smelser, *The Democratic Republic 1801-1815* (Harper & Row, New York, 1968), p. 269

124. Wharton, *Social Life in the Early Republic*, (???), p. 171, as quoted in W.P. Cresson, *James Monroe*, (Chapel Hill, 1946), p. 270

125. The phrase was coined by a Boston newspaper, the *Columbian Centinel* in 1817, on the eve of President Monroe's triumphant tour of New England, to indicate the public's willingness to unite under him without the divisiveness of party conflict.

126. Henry Adams, *History of the United States in the Administrations of James Madison*, pp. 1299, 1300

127. John Quincy Adams, *Memoirs of John Quincy Adams Comprising Portions of His Diary from 1795 to 1848*, Charles Francis Adams, ed., 12 volumes (Philadelphia, 1874-77), Vol. IV, p. 470 (entry of December 6, 1819)

128. Daniel Goodwin, Jr., *The Dearborns*, (Chicago, 1884), as quoted in George Morgan, *The Life of James Monroe*, (Boston, 1921), p. 368

129. Samuel Flagg Bemis, *John Quincy Adams and the Foundations of American Foreign Policy*, (Alfred A. Knopf, Inc., New York, 1949), p.302

130. Samuel Flagg Bemis, *John Quincy Adams and the Foundations of American Foreign Policy*, p. 310

131. The issue of whether Monroe sanctioned Jackson's later actions in Florida has been debated ever since. In 1830, Jackson claimed that Monroe had sent a letter via Congressman Rhea empowering him to seize Florida, but the letter was never produced. The only letter from Rhea in existence is one dated January 12, 1817 and is not only vaguely worded but, given only 6 days from Jackson's letter, there could not possibly have existed an intervening more specific letter with Monroe's authorization. Even Jackson's biographer, Robert Remini, in the first volume of his major work, only claims that Jackson believed in his own mind that he had the President's approval. Monroe later claimed that he handed Jackson's letter to Calhoun without reading it. And we know that no clear response was sent. Was it reasonable to believe, with such momentous issues, that silence is tacit authorization?

132. <u>Letter from Andrew Jackson to John Calhoun, May 5, 1818</u>, in *American State Papers, Military Affairs*, Vol. I, p. 702

133. <u>Letter from Andrew Jackson to John Calhoun, May 5, 1818</u>, in *American State Papers, Foreign Affairs*, Vol. IV, pp. 601-2

134. Samuel Flagg Bemis, *John Quincy Adams and the Foundations of American Foreign Policy*, pp. 326,328-9.

135. The United States claim to Texas was based on an expansive reading of the Louisiana Purchase and was not particularly persuasive, despite the domestic political outcry in its favor.

136. John Quincy Adams, *Memoirs*, Volume IV, p. 274 (entry of February 22, 1819)

137. John Quincy Adams, *Memoirs*, Volume V, p. 128

138. Letter to Thomas Jefferson, May 20, 1820 in *The Political Writings of James Monroe*, James P. Lucier, ed., (Washington, D.C., 2001), p. 521

139. John Quincy Adams, *Memoirs*, Volume IV., p. 275

140. John Quincy Adams, *An Eulogy: On the Life and Character of James Monroe Delivered at the Request of the Corporation of the City of Boston on the 25th of August, 1831* (Boston, 1831), pp. 85,6

141. Monroe was formally unopposed, but one elector, William Plumer, the Federalist Governor of New Hampshire, chose to cast his ballot for John Quincy Adams, much to Adams' embarrassment

142. Virginius, *Richmond Enquirer*, Nov. 7, 1820

143. Letter to Edward Everett, January 31, 1822, in *Writings of John Quincy Adams*, Worthington Chauncey Ford, ed., (New York, 1913-1917), Vol. VII, 1820-1823, pp. 197-207

144. One could argue that President Reagan's defense build-up helped accelerate the demise of Communism by straining Russia's economy and that, therefore, this would be an example of the success of an "aggressive" policy for liberty.

145. Canning's proposed five principles:

We conceive the recovery of the Colonies by Spain to be hopeless.

We conceive the question of the Recognition of them, as Independent States, to be one of time and circumstances.

We are, however, by no means disposed to throw any impediment in the way of an arrangement between them and the mother country by amicable negotiation.

We aim not at the possession of any portion of them ourselves.

We could not see any portion of them transferred to any other Power with indifference.

See Letter from Mr. Canning to Mr. Rush, August 20, 1823, in *The Writings of James Monroe*, Stanislaus Murray Hamilton, ed., (New York, 1902), Volume VI, 1817-1823, p. 365

146. <u>Letter from Thomas Jefferson to James Monroe, October 24, 1823</u>, in *The Writings of James Monroe*, Ibid., Volume VI., p. 391; also in *Thomas Jefferson, Writings*, (Library of America, New York, 1984), pp. 1481,2

147. John Quincy Adams, *Memoirs*, Volume VI, p. 185

148. Ammon, *James Monroe*, pp. 479-80

149. John Quincy Adams, *Memoirs*, Volume VI, p. 178-9

150. In September, 1821, Czar Alexander had issued a ukase extending Alaska to the 51st parallel, within the Oregon Territory, and claimed rights in the waters from there to the Bering Strait. See Morrison and Commager, *The Growth of the American Republic*, Volume I, 1000-1865, (New York, 1950, 4th edition), p. 460

151. John Quincy Adams, *Memoirs*, Volume VI, p. 194

152. <u>Letter to Thomas Jefferson, June 2, 1823</u>, in *The Writings of James Monroe*, Volume VI, p. 310

153. Monroe Doctrine Excerpts from <u>Seventh Annual Message, Dec. 2, 1823</u>, in *Messages and Papers of the Presidents, 1789-1897*, James D. Richardson, ed., (Washington, 1896), Vol. II, pp. 209, 218, and 218

154. As quoted in Dexter Perkins, *Hands Off, A History of the Monroe Doctrine*, (Boston, 1941), pp. 55-6

155. <u>Metternich to Nesselrode, January 19, 1824</u>, as quoted in Dexter Perkins, *Hands Off*, p. 27

156. One modern historian, however, sees the Doctrine with a different lens—as primarily the product of the political objectives of the various actors around Monroe who battled for the Presidency in 1824. See Ernest R. May, *The Making of the Monroe Doctrine*, (Cambridge, 1975)

157. <u>Letter to Samuel L. Gouverneur [Monroe's son-in-law], 8 August 1831</u>, after Monroe's death, in *The Papers of John C. Calhoun*, Volume XI, 1829-1832, Clyde W. Wilson, ed., (University of South Carolina Press, Columbia, 1978), p. 453

158. <u>First Inaugural Address, March 4, 1817</u>, in *A Compilation of the Messages and Papers of the Presidents*, James D. Richardson, ed., (Washington, 1896), Vol. II, p. 10

159. Ibid.

160. Ibid.

161. John Quincy Adams, *An Eulogy: On the Life and Character of James Monroe Delivered…on the 25th of August*, 1831, p. 94

Chapter 4 Abraham Lincoln and the Revitalization of American Liberty

162. In this Chapter, the states that eventually formed the Confederacy in the Civil War are identified, in the aggregate, as the "South" or "Southern." When border slaveholding states that remained in the Union are intended to be included in the subject matter being discussed, the wider group shall be referred to as the "slaveholding states." The states that eventually constituted the Union in the Civil War are identified as the "North" or "Northern."

163. Edmund S. Morgan, "Slavery and Freedom: The American Paradox,", in *The Journal of American History*, Vol. LIX (June, 1972), p. 6

164. Letter to John Holmes, April 22, 1820, in *Thomas Jefferson, Writings* (Library of America, New York, 1984), p. 1434

165. With the possible exception of Russia, see Peter Kolchin, *Unfree Labor* (Harvard University Press, Cambridge, 1987) for a comparative analysis

166. David Brion Davis, *The Problem of Slavery in Western Culture* (Cornell University Press, Ithaca, 1966), p. 8

167. Peter Kolchin, *American Slavery, 1619-1877* (Hill and Wang, New York, First Revised Ed., 2003), p. xi.

168. Peter Kolchin has estimated that between 5 and 20% of the captives died in transit, in Peter Kolchin, *American Slavery, 1619-1877*, p. 18

169. Peter Kolchin, *American Slavery, 1619-1877*, p. 22

170. Peter Kolchin, *American Slavery, 1619-1877*, p. 49

171. Don E. Fehrenbacher, *The Slaveholding Republic* (Oxford University Press, New York, 2001), p. 15

172. Don E. Fehrenbacher, *The Slaveholding Republic* p. 20

173. Peter Kolchin, *American Slavery, 1619-1877*, p. 81

174. Thomas Jefferson, The Autobiography, in *Thomas Jefferson, Writings*, p. 22

175. James Madison, *Notes of Debates in the Federal Convention of 1787* (Ohio University Press, 1966; W.W. Norton & Company, New York, paperback edition, 1987), p. 411

176. James Madison, *Notes of Debates in the Federal Convention of 1787*, p. 355

177. U.S. Constitution, Article I, Section 2, Clause 3

178. Northern legislators also recognized that, had a slave been counted as a full person for purposes of representation in the House, Southern political power would have been strengthened even more than it was under the federal ratio.

179. Don E. Fehrenbacher, *The Dred Scott Case, Its Significance in American Law and Politics* (Oxford University Press, New York, 1978, first paperback ed., 2001), p. 22

180. U.S. Constitution, Article I, Section 9, Clause 1

181. *Boston Liberator*, Feb. 3, 1843; *The Letters of William Lloyd Garrison, Volume II, No Union with Slaveholders, 1841-1849*, Walter M. Merrill, ed., (Belknap Press of Harvard University Press, Cambridge, 1971), p. 118. Ten years previously, Garrison had called the Constitution "the most bloody and heaven-daring arrangement ever made by men for the continuance and protection of a system of the most atrocious villainy ever exhibited on earth." [Letter to the Editor of the London Patriot, August 6, 1833, in *The Letters of William Lloyd Garrison, Volume I, I Will Be Heard, 1822-1835*, Walter M. Merrill, ed.]

182. This act of the Continental Congress in 1787 prohibited slavery in territory which later became the states of Indiana, Illinois, Michigan, Ohio, and Wisconsin, and was modeled after a previous one authored by Thomas Jefferson in 1784 for the same purpose but not then enacted.

183. Don E. Fehrenbacher, *The Dred Scott Case, Its Significance in American Law and Politics*, p. 27.

184. Kenneth M. Stampp, *The Peculiar Institution, Slavery in the Ante-Bellum South* (Random House, New York, 1956, Vintage Books ed., 1984), p. 197

185. Helen Tunnicliff Catterall, *Judicial Cases Concerning American Slavery and the Negro, Vol. I, Cases from the Courts of England, Virginia, West Virginia and Kentucky* (Carnegie Institution, Washington, D.C., 1926), p. 311

186. Northern states sought to undercut the Fugitive Slave Law with "personal liberty" laws increasing the rights of escaped slaves and making their return more difficult, but the Supreme Court upheld the Fugitive Slave Law in 1842, although the Court also decided that states did not need to cooperate in its enforcement.

187. W. E. Burghardt Du Bois, *The Suppression of the African Slave-Trade to the United States of America, 1638-1870* (New York: Longmans, Green & Co., New York, 1896), pp. 109-193 D92.D85 Cutter

188. Don E. Fehrenbacher, *The Slaveholding Republic*, p. 137

189. Peter Kolchin, *American Slavery*, pp. 93, 254

190. Kenneth M. Stampp, *The Peculiar Institution*, p. 30

191. *The Frederick Douglass Papers, Series Two: Autobiographical Writings, Vol. I: Narrative*, John W. Blassingame, John R. McKivigan, Peter P. Hinks, eds. (Yale University Press, New Haven, 1999), pp. 61-2

192. Peter Kolchin, *American Slavery*, p. 198

193. Later political debates centered on the constitutionality of the Thomas Amendment prohibiting slavery north of 36/30, but references to that issue usually mistakenly refer to the "constitutionality of the Missouri compromise," while meaning only the constitutionality of the 36/30 prohibition.

194. <u>Senate Speech 10 January 1838</u> in *The Papers of John C. Calhoun, Volume XIV, 1837-39*, Clyde N. Wilson, ed.(University of South Carolina Press, Columbia, 1981), p. 84

195. Kenneth M. Stampp, *The Peculiar Institution*, p. 28

196. J.G. Randall & David Herbert Donald, *The Civil War and Reconstruction* (D.C. Heath and Company, Lexington, 2nd ed., revised, 1969), p. 23

197. See William E. Miller, *Arguing About Slavery, John Quincy Adams and the Great Battle in the United States Congress* (Random House, New York, 1958, Vintage Books ed., 1995)

198. Don E. Fehrenbacher, *The Dred Scott Case and Its Significance in American Law and Politics*, p. 123.

199. As quoted in Frederick E. Merk, *Manifest Destiny and Mission in American History*, (Alfred A. Knopf, New York, 1963), p. 32

200. David M. Potter, *Impending Crisis, 1848-1861* (Harper & Row, New York, 1976), p. 12

201. *Congressional Globe*, 28 Cong., 2nd Sess., 1845, Jan. 27, 1845, p. 200

202. David M. Potter, *Impending Crisis, 1848-1861*, p. 43

203. <u>Senate Speech, Feb. 19, 1847</u> in *The Papers of John C. Calhoun, Volume XXIV, 1846-47*, Clyde N. Wilson and Shirley Bright Cook, eds., p. 172

204. *Congressional Globe, 31st Cong., 1st Sess., 1850*, Appendix, March 4, 1850, p. 453

205. *Congressional Globe, 31st Cong., 1st Sess., 1850*, March 7, 1850, p. 476

206. Stanley W. Campbell, *The Slave Catchers: Enforcement of the Fugitive Slave Law, 1850-60* (Univ. of North Carolina Press, Chapel Hill, 1968), p. 207

207. Joan D. Hedrick, *Harriet Beecher Stowe: A Life* (Oxford University Press, New York, 1994), p. vii

208. <u>Letter to Joshua Speed, August 24, 1855</u>, in *Abraham Lincoln, Writings, 1832-1859* (The Library of America, New York, 1989), p. 363

209. Although the party Jefferson founded was originally called the "Republican" or "Democratic-Republican" Party, that name had been abandoned by Andrew Jackson and permanently changed to the "Democratic" Party.

210. Eric Foner, *Free Soil, Free Labor, Free Men, The Ideology of the Republican Party Before the Civil War* (Oxford University Press, London, 1970), p. 65

211. *The Works of William Seward*, Charles E. Baker, ed. (Redfield, New York, 1861), Vol. IV, p. 292

212. Eric Foner, *Free Soil, Free Labor, Free Men*, p. 72

213. *The Works of William Seward*, Charles E. Baker, ed., Vol. III, p. 293; Vol. V, pp. 221,228

214. David Herbert Donald, *Lincoln* (Simon & Schuster, New York, 1995), p. 28

215. *Herndon's Informants: Letters, Interviews and Statements About Abraham Lincoln*, Douglas L. Wilson and Rodney O. Davis, eds., (University of Illinois Press, Urbana, 1997), David Turnham (WHH Interview, Sept. 15, 1865), p. 121

216. David Herbert Donald, *Lincoln*, p. 33

217. Douglas L. Wilson, *Honor's Voice: The Transformation of Abraham Lincoln* (Alfred A. Knopf, New York, 1998), pp. 4-7

218. Benjamin Quarles, *Lincoln and the Negro* (Oxford University Press, New York, 1962), p. 18

219. Letter to Jesse W. Fell Enclosing Autobiography, Dec. 30, 1859, in *The Collected Works of Abraham Lincoln*, Roy P. Basler, ed. (Rutgers University Press, New Brunswick, 1953),Vol. III, p. 512

220. Speech to Young Men's Lyceum, January 27, 1838, in *Lincoln, Writings, 1832-1858*, p. 32

221. Speech to Young Men's Lyceum, January 27, 1838, in *Lincoln, Writings, 1832-1858*, p. 36

222. Helen Nicolay, *Lincoln's Secretary, A Biography of John G. Nicolay* (Longmans, Green & Co., New York, 1949), p. 133

223. Eulogy on Henry Clay, July 6, 1852, in *Lincoln, Writings, 1832-1858*, p. 264

224. Speech on The Kansas-Nebraska Act, October 16, 1854, in *Lincoln's Writings, 1832-1858*, p. 315

225. Speech on The Kansas-Nebraska Act, October 16, 1854, in *Lincoln's Writings, 1832-1858*, p. 328

226. The Wilmot Proviso had not passed; the Kansas-Nebraska Act had repealed the 36/30 restriction of the Missouri Compromise; and popular sovereignty was then Congress' policy, under which the slave status of an area was decided only upon admission as a state.

227. *Dred Scott v. Sandford, Reports of Cases Argued and Adjudged in The Supreme Court of the United States*, 19 Howard's Reports 393, 404-5, 407 (1857)

228. David M. Potter, *Impending Crisis, 1848-1861*, p. 293

229. Kenneth M. Stampp, *America in 1857, A Nation on the Brink* (Oxford University Press, New York, 1990), p. 300

230. Speech on the Dred Scott Case, June 26, 1857, in *Lincoln, Writings, 1832-1858*, p. 398

231. Kenneth M. Stampp, *America in 1857*, pp. 330-1

232. Don E. Fehrenbacher, *Dred Scott and Its Significance in American Law and Politics*, p. 464

233. Don E. Fehrenbacher, *Dred Scott and Its Significance in American Law and Politics*, p. 453

234. House Divided Speech, June 16, 1858, in *Lincoln, Writings*, p. 432

235. The concerted action consisted of Douglas' Kansas-Nebraska Act, Pierce's support of the bill's enactment, Taney's opinion in Dred Scott, and Buchanan's advice in his Inaugural Address for the country to accept the yet announced Dred Scott opinion, about which he had advance word from one member of the Court.

236. Don E. Fehrenbacher, *Prelude to Greatness: Lincoln in the 1850's* (Stanford University Press, Stanford, 1962) p. 86

237. What Lincoln did not say was that the quote was taken out of context, since Douglas did not make it in discussing the operation of popular sovereignty but used it to refer to the distorted December vote on the Lecompton Constitution that asked only about the extent of the slavery restriction; Douglas, of course, was against the entire Constitution and, therefore, the vote was, to him, irrelevant.

238. Cincinnati Enquirer, Sept. 30, 1858, as related in Don E. Fehrenbacher, *Prelude to Greatness: Lincoln in the 1850's*, p. 101

239. Seventh Lincoln-Douglas Debate, Alton, Illinois, Oct. 15, 1858, in *Lincoln, Writings, 1832-1858*, pp. 810-811

240. Address at Cooper Institute, Feb. 27, 1860, in *Lincoln's Writings, 1859-1865*, p. 122

241. Sixth Lincoln-Douglas Debate, Quincy, Illinois, Oct. 13, 1858, in *Lincoln, Writings, 1832-1858*, p. 734

242. Don E. Fehrenbacher, *Prelude to Greatness: Lincoln in the 1850's* (Stanford University Press, Stanford, 1962), pp. 119

243. Eric Foner, *Free Soil, Free Labor, Free Men*, pp. 311-312

244. Address at Cooper Institute, February 27, 1860, in *Lincoln, Writings, 1859-1865*, pp. 128-129

245. J.G. Randall and David Donald, *Civil War and Reconstruction*, p. 134.

246. Speech to Germans at Cincinnati, February 12, 1861 in *Lincoln, Writings, 1859-1865*, p. 203; Speech at Independence Hall, Philadelphia, February 22, 1861, in *Lincoln, Writings, 1859-1865*, p. 213

247. Letter to Senator Lyman Trumbull, Dec. 10, 1860, in *Collected Works of Abraham Lincoln*, Roy P. Basler, ed. (Rutgers University Press, Trenton, 1953),Vol. IV, p. 149

248. The remaining four states of the Confederacy—Virginia, Arkansas, Tennessee, and North Carolina—did not secede until after the outbreak of hostilities in April, 1861.

249. First Inaugural Address, March 4, 1861, in *Lincoln's Writings, 1859-1865*, p. 224

250. J.G. Randall and David Donald, *Civil War and Reconstruction*, p. 382, n. 9

251. Letter to John C. Fremont, Sept. 2, 1861, *Collected Works of Abraham Lincoln*, Vol. IV, p. 506

252. Letter to Orville W. Browning, Sept. 22, 1861, *Collected Works of Abraham Lincoln*, Vol. IV., pp. 531-2

253. John Hope Franklin, *The Emancipation Proclamation* (Doubleday & Co., Garden City, 1963), p. 18

254. John Hope Franklin, *The Emancipation Proclamation*, p. 21

255. George M. Fredrickson, *Big Enough to be Inconsistent: Abraham Lincoln Confronts Slavery and Race* (Harvard University Press, Cambridge, 2008), pp. 102-3

256. Peter Kolchin, *American Slavery*, p. 204

257. Letter to Senator James A. McDougall, March 14, 1862, in *Lincoln, Writings, 1859-1865*, p. 310

258. This version of the story apparently comes from the recollections Major Thomas T. Eckert who supervised the telegraph office, but one modern historian has cast doubt on its veracity, see Mark E. Neely, Jr., *The Last Best Hope of Earth*, pp. 108-109

259. *Diary of Gideon Welles, Secretary of the Navy under Lincoln and Johnson*, (Houghton-Mifflin, Boston, 1911) Vol. I, p. 71

340 Elton B. Klibanoff

260. F.B. Carpenter, *The Inner Life of Abraham Lincoln: Six Months at the White* House (Houghton, Mifflin and Company, Boston, 1894), p. 22

261. Don E. Fehrenbacher, *The Slaveholding Republic*, p. 315

262. Address to a Committee of Colored Men, August 14, 1862, in *Lincoln, Writings, 1859-1865*, p. 353

263. Letter to Horace Greeley, August 22, 1862, in *Lincoln, Writings*, 1859-1865, p. 358

264. Reply to Chicago Emancipation Memorial, in *Lincoln, Writings, 1859-1865*, pp. 361-2, 365, 367

265. Frederick Douglass, *Life and Times of Frederick Douglass, in Frederick Douglass* (Library of America, New York, 1994), p. 793

266. Annual Message to Congress, December 1, 1862, in *Lincoln, Writings, 1859-1865*, p. 415

267. *Inside Lincoln's Cabinet: The Civil War Diaries of Salmon P. Chase*, David Herbert Donald, ed. (Longmans, Green & Co., New York, 1954) p. 151

268. Letter to Salmon P. Chase, Sept. 2, 1863, in *Lincoln, Writings, 1858-1865*, p. 501

269. Final Emancipation Proclamation, January 1, 1863, in *Lincoln, Writings, 1858-1865*, p. 425.

270. William Barton, *President Lincoln* (Bobbs-Merrill, Indianapolis, 1933), Vol. II, p. 510

271. Peter Kolchin, *American Slavery*, p. 207

272. John Eaton, *Grant, Lincoln, and the Freedmen*, Reminiscences of the Civil War (Longmans, Green and Co., New York, 1907), p. 2

273. Letter to Andrew Johnson, March 26, 1863, in *Lincoln's Writings, 1858-1865*, p. 440

274. Letter to James Conkling, Aug. 26, 1863, in *Lincoln's Writings, 1858-1865*, p. 498

275. Mark E. Neely, Jr., *The Last Best Hope of Earth, Abraham Lincoln and the Promise of America* (Harvard University Press, Cambridge, 1993), p. 121

276. John Hope Franklin, *The Emancipation Proclamation*, p. 130

277. Joe M. Richardson, *Christian Reconstruction: The American Missionary Association and Southern Blacks, 1861-1890*, Athens, Ga., 1986, p. 13, as quoted in Peter Kolchin, *American Slavery*, p. 208

278. See Daniel Farber, *Lincoln's Constitution* (University of Chicago Press, Chicago, 2003), Ch. 7

279. Herbert Mitgang, *Abraham Lincoln, A Press Portrait*, Fordham University Press, 2000, p. 306

280. Herbert Mitgang, *Abraham Lincoln, A Press Portrait*, Fordham University Press, 2000, p. 313, quoting the National Intelligencer, Oct. 8, 1862.

281. Sept. 29, 1862, as quoted in John Hope Franklin, *The Emancipation Proclamation*, p. 67

282. Allen Nevins, *The Statesmanship of the Civil War*, The Page-Barbour Lectures, University of Virginia 1951 (The MacMillan Co., New York, 1953)

283. Speech at Freedmen's Memorial Monument, April 14, 1876, as quoted in Mark E. Neely, *The Last Best Hope of Earth*, p. 97

284. Frederickson, *Big Enough to be Inconsistent*, p. 28

285. Offer of Safe Conduct for Peace Negotiators, July 18, 1864, in *Lincoln, Writings, 1858-1865*, p. 612

286. Hacker, J. David. A Census-Based Count of the Civil War Dead in *Civil War History*, Volume 57, No. 4, December, 2011, Kent State University Press

287. Letter to Albert B. Hodges, April 4, 1864, in *Lincoln, Writings, 1858-1865*, p. 586

288. Special Message to Congress, July 4, 1861, in *Lincoln, Writings, 1858-1865*, p. 259

Chapter 5 Woodrow Wilson and the Application of America's Mission to the World

289. Many writers—including Woodrow Wilson himself—have mistakenly attributed to Washington a warning against "entangling" alliances, rather than "permanent" alliances, but the former phrase was penned by Thomas Jefferson in his First Inaugural Address. The two phrases have quite different implications for foreign policy, with Washington's giving the country greater flexibility as circumstances warrant, but they were used often in the nineteenth century to argue for an essentially isolationist and non-confrontational approach to world affairs, independent of the shifting alliances of European powers.

290. Quoted in Samuel Eliot Morison and Henry Steele Commager, *The Growth of the American Republic*, 4th ed. (Oxford University Press, New York, 1950, 1956), Vol. II, p. 314

291. Mark Sullivan, Our Times, The United States, 1900-1925, The Turn of the Century, in Berky and Shenton, eds., *The Historians' History of the United States, Volume II* (G.P. Putnam's Sons, New York, 1966), p. 1033

292. <u>An Address on Latin American Policy, in Mobile, Alabama,</u> <u>October 27, 1913</u>, in *The Papers of Woodrow Wilson*, Arthur S. Link, ed., Vol. 28 (Princeton University Press, Princeton, N.J., 1978), p. 451

293. Winston S. Churchill, *The World Crisis* (Thornton, Butterfield Ltd., London, 1927), Vol. III, p. 229.

294. Wilson's given name was actually Thomas Woodrow Wilson, which it remained until after he graduated from Princeton, when he decided to drop "Thomas" as an affirmation of his adulthood.

295. John Morton Blum, *Woodrow Wilson and the Politics of Morality* (Little, Brown and Co., Boston, 1956), p.5

296. John Morton Blum, *Woodrow Wilson and the Politics of Morality*, p. 6

297. Woodrow's sister Marion was born in 1850, Annie in 1854 and his younger brother Joseph in 1866.

298. Arthur S. Link, *Woodrow Wilson, A Brief Biography* (World Publishing Co., Cleveland, 1963, Quadrangle paperback edition, 1972), p. 17

299. Arthur S. Link, <u>Portrait of the President</u>, in Latham, ed., *The Philosophy and Polices of Woodrow Wilson*, p. 9

300. Arthur S. Link, <u>Introduction</u>, in Arthur S. Link, ed., *Woodrow Wilson, A Profile* (Hill and Wang, New York, 1968), p. iii

301. Arthur S. Link, *Woodrow Wilson, A Brief Biography*, p. 17

302. A recent biographer does not believe Wilson's disability was dyslexia because he could read and did not make mistakes in spelling and grammar, See John Milton Cooper, Jr., *Woodrow Wilson, A Biography*, (Alfred A. Knopf, New York, 2009), p. 20

303. John Milton Cooper, Jr., *The Warrior and the Priest, Woodrow Wilson and Theodore Roosevelt*, (Belknap Press of Harvard University, Cambridge, 1983), p. 21

304. Arthur S. Link, *Revolution, War and Peace* (Harlan Davidson, Inc., Arlington Heights, IL, 1979), p. 5

305. Arthur S. Link, <u>Portrait of the President</u>, in Earl Latham, ed., *The Philosophy and Policies of Woodrow Wilson* (University of Chicago Press, Chicago, 1958), p. 7, quoting Mrs. Crawford H. Toy, "Second Visit to the White House," diary entry dated January 3, 1915, Manuscript in the Baker Collection.

306. Remarks to Confederate Veterans in Washington, 5 June 1917, in *The Papers of Woodrow Wilson*, Arthur S. Link, ed., Vol. 42 (1983), p. 452

307. John Morton Blum, *Woodrow Wilson and the Politics of Morality*, p. 10

308. At the time, Wilson told his future wife that "Whoever thinks, as I thought, that he can practice law successfully and study history and politics at the same time is woefully mistaken." As quoted in Cooper, Jr., *Woodrow Wilson, A Biography*, p. 40. [My own experience is consistent with Wilson's observation.]

309. Thomas J. Knock, *To End All Wars, Woodrow Wilson and the Quest for a New World Order*, p. 6 and n. 20

310. <u>A Campaign Address in Jersey City, New Jersey, May 25, 1912</u>, in *The Papers of Woodrow Wilson*, Arthur S. Link, ed., Vol. 24 (1977), p. 443

311. <u>Inaugural Address, March 4, 1912</u>, in *The Papers of Woodrow Wilson*, Arthur S. Link, ed., Vol. 27 (1978), p. 149

312. <u>An Address on Latin American Policy in Mobile, Alabama, October 27, 1913</u>, in *The Papers of Woodrow Wilson*, Arthur S. Link, ed., Vol. 28 (1978), p. 451

313. See Niall Ferguson, *Pity of War* (Allen Lane, London, 1998) and Barbara Tuchman, *The Guns of August* (The Macmillan Company, New York, 1962)

314. See Barbara Tuchman, *The Guns of August*, Chapters. 2-5

315. Herbert J. Muller, *Freedom in the Modern World* (Harper & Row, New York, 1966), p. 334,335

316. <u>An Appeal to the American People, August 18, 1914</u>, in *The Papers of Woodrow Wilson*, Arthur S. Link, ed., Vol. 30 (1979), pp. 393-394

317. <u>An Address to a Joint Session of Congress, September 4, 1914</u>, in *The Papers of Woodrow Wilson*, Arthur S. Link, ed., Vol. 30 (1979), p. 475

318. Trade with Britain and its allies grew from under $1 billion in1914 to over $3 billion in 1916, most of that being military items; financial assistance increased to over $2 billion in the same period. See Bernadotte E. Schmitt and Harold C. Vedeler, *The World in the Crucible, 1914-1919* (Harper & Row, New York, 1984), p. 247

319. Thomas A. Bailey, *A Diplomatic History of the United States* (Appleton-Century-Crofts, Inc., New York, 5th ed., 1955), p. 625

320. <u>An Address in Philadelphia to Newly Naturalized Citizens, , May 10, 1915</u>, in *The Papers of Woodrow Wilson*, Vol. 33 (1980), p. 149

321. Kendrick A. Clements, *The Presidency of Woodrow Wilson*, p. 131.

322. Henry Kissinger, *Diplomacy* (Simon & Schuster, New York, 1994) Touchstone edition, p. 219

323. <u>An Address in Washington to the League to Enforce Peace, May 27, 1916</u>, in *The Papers of Woodrow Wilson*, Vol. 37, pp. 113-116.

324. As quoted in Thomas J. Knock, *To End All Wars, Woodrow Wilson and the Quest for a New World Order*, p. 77

325. William L. Langer, From Isolation to Mediation, in *Woodrow Wilson and the World of Today*, Arthur P. Dudden, ed., (Philadelphia, 1957), p. 38

326. Edward H. Buehrig, Woodrow Wilson and Collective Security: The Origins, in *The Impact of World War I*, Arthur S. Link, ed., (New York, 1969), p. 33.

327. Address Before the Nobel Prize Committee, Nov. 5, 1910, in *The Works of Theodore Roosevelt, Vol. XVI, American Problems*, Hermann Hagedorn, ed. (Charles Scribner's Sons, New York, 1926), pp. 308-9

328. The Belgian Tragedy in *Outlook*, Sept. 23, 1914, in *The Works of Theodore Roosevelt, Vol. XVIII*, pp. 27, 29-30

329. Force and Peace, Address at Commencement, Union College, Schenectady, N.Y., June 9, 1915, in *The Annals of the American Academy of Political Science*, Philadelphia, July 1915, Publ. No. 915: "…the peace can only be maintained…by the force which united nations are willing to put behind the peace and order of the world…The great nations must be so united as to be able to say to any single country, you must not go to war, and they can only say that effectively when the country desiring war knows that the force which the united nations place behind peace is irresistible." p. 14

330. See Thomas J. Knock, *To End All Wars*, Ch. 4; Daniel M. Smith, *The Great Departure*, pp. 87-9; Arthur S. Link, *Revolution, War and Peace*, Ch. 4

331. Bryan speech as quoted in John Milton Cooper, Jr. *Breaking the Heart of the World, Woodrow Wilson and the Fight for the League of Nations* (Cambridge University Press, Cambridge, 2001), p. 13 [The Commoner, XV, July, 1915, p. 9]; Borah Speech Jan. 5, 1917, *Cong. Record, 64th Cong., 2nd Sess.*, 893-895 as quoted in ibid., p. 19

332. Thomas J. Knock, *To End All Wars*, p. 35; John Milton Cooper, Jr., *Breaking the Heart of the World*, p. 16

333. Draft of Platform, June 10, 1916, in *The Papers of Woodrow Wilson*, Arthur S. Link, ed., Vol. 37 (1981), p. 196

334. John Milton Cooper, Jr. *Breaking the Heart of the World*, p. 18

335. An Appeal for a Statement of War Aims, December 18, 1916, in *The Papers of Woodrow Wilson*, Arthur S. Link, ed., Vol. 40, pp. 275, 274

336. Address to Senate, January 22, 1917, in *The Papers of Woodrow Wilson*, Arthur S. Link, ed., Vol. 40, pp. 534-539.

337. John Milton Cooper, Jr., *The Warrior and the Priest, Woodrow Wilson and Theodore Roosevelt*, p. 314.

338. George C. Herring, *From Colony to Superpower, U.S. Foreign Relations since 1776* (Oxford University Press, New York, 2008), p. 412.

339. Daniel M. Smith, *The Great Departure, The United States and World War I, 1914-1920* (Alfred A. Knopf, New York, 1965, p. 76

340. Cooper, Jr., *Woodrow Wilson, A Biography*, p. 373

341. Herbert J. Muller, *Freedom in the Modern World*, p. 343

342. Arthur S. Link, *Revolution, War, and Peace*, p. 23

343. Frank I. Cobb, On the Eve of War, in Arthur S. Link, ed., *Woodrow Wilson, A Profile*, pp. 128,129

344. An Address to a Joint Session of Congress, April 2, 1917, in *The Papers of Woodrow Wilson*, Arthur S. Link, ed., Vol. 41 (1983), pp. 523, 525, 526, and 527

345. J.P. Tumulty, *Woodrow Wilson as I Know Him* (Garden City, N.Y., 1921), p. 256

346. The Sixteenth Amendment, ratified in 1913, had authorized a national tax based on incomes.

347. *Encyclopedia of American History*, Richard B. Morris, ed., (Harper & Row, New York, 1965), p. 315

348. Roosevelt's attitude is described in John Morton Blum, *The Republican Roosevelt* (Harvard University Press, 2nd ed. 1977), pp. 157-8

349. An Address to a Joint Session of Congress, April 2, 1917, in *The Papers of Woodrow Wilson*, Arthur S. Link, ed., Vol. 41 (1983), pp. 525

350. See Frank Ninkovich, *The Wilsonian Century, U.S. Foreign Policy since 1900* (University of Chicago Press, 1999), pp. 53-72

351. Wilson's address was preceded by one given by the British Prime Minister, David Lloyd George at Caxton Hall on January 5, which anticipated many of Wilson's ideas, including an international collective security organization, but Wilson was intent on his own speech and it is his that has maintained the greater historical significance.

352. Fourteen Points Address, January 8, 1918, in *The Papers of Woodrow Wilson*, Arthur S. Link, ed., Vol. 45 (1984), pp. 536, 539, 536-538

353. Thomas J. Knock, *To End All Wars*, p. 145.

354. David Stevenson, Cataclysm, *The First World War as Political Tragedy*, p. 325

355. Information on the Phillimore Report and Miller's draft is taken from John Milton Cooper, Jr., *Breaking the Heart of the World*, p. 28

356. Klaus Epstein, *Matthias Erzberger and the Dilemma of German Democracy* (Howard Fertig, New York, 1971), p. 250

357. "COVENANT" enclosure with Wilson to letter to Edward Mandell House, September 7, 1918, in *The Papers of Woodrow Wilson*, Arthur S. Link, ed., Vol. 49, p. 468

358. An Address in the Metropolitan Opera House, Sept. 27, 1918, in *The Papers of Woodrow Wilson*, Arthur S. Link, ed., Vol. 51, p. 131

359. Herbert Hoover, *The Ordeal of Woodrow Wilson* (The Woodrow Wilson Center Press, The Johns Hopkins University Press, 1992), p. 131

360. Harry R. Rudin, *Armistice, 1918* (Yale University Press, New Haven, 1944), p. 383, quoting Declaration of the German Plenipotentiaries on the Occasion of Signing the Armistice, in *Foch, Memoirs II*, pp. 318-319

361. Daniel M. Smith, *The Great Departure, The United States and World War I, 1914-1920*, pp. 116-117

362. John Milton Cooper, Jr., *Breaking the Heart of the World*, p. 38, and Edwin A. Weinstein, *Woodrow Wilson, A Medical and Psychological Biography* (Princeton, N.J., 1981), pp. 320-323

363. See the generally balanced presentation of factors in John Milton Cooper, Jr. *Breaking the Heart of the World*, pp. 33-38. On differences with his opponents, Theodore Roosevelt, for example, felt that membership in a League should only be offered to allies; that international enforcement of peace was not clearly wise; that the establishment of a League should not be part of the peace treaty; that any League should not be able to affect domestic issues such as the Monroe Doctrine, the tariff, and immigration; and that Germany should be subjected to harsh terms.

364. There is little consensus among historians as to why the Democrats suffered defeat. Some point to a backlash from Wilson's call for a Democratic Congress prior to the election, some to an electorate weary of taxes and wartime sacrifices, some to support for a vindictive peace against Germany, some to Wilson's failure to educate the public to his post-war objectives, some to the Wilson administration's controls on wheat prices, and some to better Republican organization. See Thomas J. Knock, *To End All Wars*, pp. 184-5.

365. Kendrick A. Clements, *The Presidency of Woodrow Wilson*, p. 163

366. Herbert Hoover, *The Ordeal of Woodrow Wilson*, pp. 68-69

367. Thomas A. Bailey, *A Diplomatic History of the United States*, p. 662, quoting W.A.White, *Woodrow Wilson* (Boston, 1929), p. 384.

368. John Milton Cooper, Jr., *Breaking the Heart of the World*, p. 48

369. Col. House Diary, Feb. 13, 1919 in *The Papers of Woodrow Wilson*, Arthur S. Link, ed., Vol. 55 (1986), p. 156

370. Colonel Stephen Bonsal, *Unfinished Business* (Doubleday, New York, 1944), p. 275

371. Edith Bolling Wilson, *My Memoir* (The Bobbs-Merrill Co., Indianapolis, 1939), p. 239

372. Address to Peace Conference, February 14, 1919, in *The Papers of Woodrow Wilson*, Arthur S. Link, ed., Vol. 55 (1986), pp. 175, 176

373. Address to Peace Conference, February 14, 1919, in *The Papers of Woodrow Wilson*, Arthur S. Link, ed., Vol. 55 (1986), p. 167

374. Articles VII and IX required the reduction in military and naval programs; Article XI permitted any member to bring to the League any matter it believed threatened peace; Articles XII through XV established mechanisms for international arbitration of disputes between nations and established an International Court of Justice; Article XVI authorized economic boycotts and military force against offending nations; Article XIX set out a mandate system to encourage the eventual independence of areas colonized by the major powers; and Article XX established an International Bureau of Labor to set standards on working conditions for men, women, and children throughout the world. Margaret MacMillan, in *Paris 1919*, has explained this last article as an attempt to appeal to the working class in the victorious democracies in the wake of the Bolshevik Revolution. (p. 95)

375. Grayson Diary, Feb. 22, 1919, in *The Papers of Woodrow Wilson*, Arthur S. Link, ed., Vol. 55 (1986), p. 244

376. A treaty requires the votes of two-thirds of the Senate, which, at the time totaled ninety-six.

377. John Milton Cooper, Jr., *Breaking the Heart of the World*, pp. 84-85

378. The Versailles Treaty's treatment of Germany served as a "standardized model that to a large extent [the Allied Powers] simply reproduced in dealing with the other Central Powers." David Stevenson, *Cataclysm*, p. 426

379. *The Deliberations of the Council of Four (March 24-June 28, 1918), Notes of the Official Interpreter, Paul Mantoux*, Arthur S. Link, Ed. (Princeton University Press, 1992), Vol. I., p. 373

380. The clause was not primarily intended to force Germany to admit war guilt, but to lay the legal foundation for broad reparations. The provision was drafted by John Foster Dulles of the American delegation, later to be Secretary of State under President Eisenhower. The succeeding provision, Article 232, qualified it by stipulating that Germany and its allies could not pay the costs of the entire war, limiting its liability to damage to property and reimbursement of war pensions. Computation of the total reparations bill, and overseeing its payment, was left to a post-war

Reparations Commission, but the Commission was not required to set a fixed sum or limited time period.

381. France was given some former German territory in the Rhineland, which would become permanent only if Germany defaulted on reparations obligations, as well as fifteen year authority over the Saar mining region, after which a vote of the inhabitants would decide the territory's fate. It also re-acquired Alsace-Lorraine, seized by Germany in the Franco-Prussian War of 1871. Belgium's borders were adjusted to undo German aggression; Austria was prohibited from uniting with Germany; German-speaking Sudetenland, previously part of Austria, was incorporated in Czechoslovakia; German terri-tory was ceded to Poland to give it access to the Baltic, but resulted in dividing East Prussia from the remainder of Germany; the former German port of Danzig was made a free city under League supervision, with Polish control over its infrastructure; and plebiscites were arranged that later resulted in Ger-many's loss of Schleswig to Denmark and Germany's gain of the coalfields of Upper Silesia.

382. David Stevenson, Cataclysm, *The First World War as Political Tragedy*, p. 422

383. Margaret MacMillan, *Paris 1919, Six Months that Changed the World*, p. 465

384. Herbert Hoover, *The Ordeal of Woodrow Wilson*, p. 234

385. Tom Schachtman, *Edith and Woodrow, A Presidential Romance* (B.P. Putnam's Sons, New York, 1981), p. 189

386. Niall Ferguson, *The Pity of War* (Basic Books, New York, 1999), pp. 440, 441.

387. Statement by Thomas Masaryk, Czech leader, as quoted in Wal-worth, *America's Moment*, p. 45 and cited in Herring, *From Colony to Super-power*, p. 420

388. See. E.g., A.J.P. Taylor, *The Origins of the Second World War* (Hamilton, London, 1961)

389. Address to the Senate, July 10, 1919 in *The Papers of Woodrow Wilson*, Arthur S. Link, ed., Vol. 61 (1989), p. 436

390. A Conversation with Members of the Senate Foreign Relations Committee, Conference at the White House, 19 August 1919, in *The Papers of Woodrow Wilson*, Arthur S. Link, ed., Vol. 62 (1990), pp. 343-344

391. John Milton Cooper, Jr., *Breaking the Heart of the World*, p. 150 and note 68, citing Park, Wilson's Neurological Illness, in *The Papers of Woodrow Wilson*, Arthur S. Link, ed., Vol. 62, pp. 633-638

392. Thomas J. Knock, *To End All Wars*, p. 253

393. John Milton Cooper, Jr., *Breaking the Heart of the World*, p. 217, quoting from Cong., Rec., 66th Cong., 1st Sess. (Oct. 9, 1919), 6600-6614

394. John Milton Cooper, Jr., *Breaking the Heart of the World*, p. 265, quoting from Cong., Rec., 66th Cong., 1st Sess. (Nov. 19, 1919), 8781-8784

395. An Address in the San Diego Stadium, Sept. 19, 1919, in *The Papers of Woodrow Wilson*, Arthur S. Link, ed., Vol. 63 (1990), pp. 372, 374

396. An Address in the San Francisco Civic Auditorium, Sept. 17, 1919, in *The Papers of Woodrow Wilson*, Arthur S. Link, ed., Vol. 63 (1990), p. 332

397. A Luncheon Address in San Francisco, Sept. 18, 1919, in *The Papers of Woodrow Wilson*, Arthur S. Link, ed., Vol. 63 (1990), p. 345

398. An Address in the San Diego Stadium, Sept. 19, 1919, in *The Papers of Woodrow Wilson*, Arthur S. Link, ed., Vol. 63 (1990), pp. 382

399. An Address in the St. Louis Coliseum, Sept 5, 1919 in *The Papers of Woodrow Wilson*, Arthur S. Link, ed., Vol. 63 (1990), p. 47

400. An Address in the San Francisco Civic Auditorium, Sept. 17, 1919, in *The Papers of Woodrow Wilson*, Arthur S. Link, ed., Vol. 63 (1990), p. 325

401. An Address in the St. Louis Coliseum, Sept 5, 1919 in *The Papers of Woodrow Wilson*, Arthur S. Link, ed., Vol. 63 (1990), pp. 46, 47

402. From the Diary of Dr. Grayson, Sept. 26, 1919, in *The Papers of Woodrow Wilson*, Arthur S. Link, ed., Vol. 63 (1990), p. 519

403. Kendrick A. Clements, *The Presidency of Woodrow Wilson*, p. 202

404. *Cong. Rec., 66th Cong., 1st Sess.* (Oct. 24, 1919), 7417

405. There were many factions in the Senate, including strong reservationists, mild reservationists, irreconcilables, and a variety of Democratic groups, but without an agreement between the strong reservationists and the President, a 2/3 majority for the League was impossible. See John Milton Cooper, *Breaking the Heart of the World*, pp. 221-282

406. Wilson Letter to Senator Hitchcock, March 8, 1920, in *The Papers of Woodrow Wilson*, Arthur S. Link, ed., Vol. 64 (1990), p. 58

407. Bert E. Park, Wilson's Neurologic Illness during the Summer of 1919, in *The Papers of Woodrow Wilson*, Arthur S. Link, ed. Vol. 61 (1990), Appendix, pp. 628-638; Edwin A Weinstein, *Woodrow Wilson: A Medical and Psychological Biography* (Princeton University Press, Princeton, N.J., 1981); Bert E. Park, *The Impact of Illness on World Leaders* (Philadelphia, 1986), pp. 3-76, 331-342; and Bert E. Park, Woodrow Wilson's Stroke of October 2, 1919, in *The Papers of Woodrow Wilson*, Arthur S. Link, ed., Vol. 63 (1990), Appendix II, pp. 639-646

408. See Sigmund Freud and William Bullitt, *Thomas Woodrow Wilson, A Psychological Study* (Houghton Mifflin, Boston, 1967) and John Milton Cooper, Jr., *Breaking the Heart of the World*, p. 64

409. John Morton Blum, *Woodrow Wilson and the Politics of Morality*, pp. 11, 110

410. Lt. Grayson Memorandum, March 25, 1920, in *The Papers of Woodrow Wilson*, Arthur S. Link, ed., Vol. 65 (1991), p. 125

411. Herbert J. Muller, *Freedom in the Modern World*, p. 351

412. Henry A. Kissinger, *Diplomacy*, pp. 50, 249

413. Historians have differed over whether America's commitment to the United Nations resulted from the fear of an immoral enemy (first Nazi Germany and Imperial Japan, then Russian Communism) or a Wilsonian commitment to a new international order. See, e.g., John Milton Cooper, *Breaking the Heart of the World* vs. Frank Ninkovich, *The Wilsonian Century*

414. Henry A. Kissinger, *Diplomacy*, pp. 54-55

415. George F. Kennan, The Legacy of Woodrow Wilson, *Princeton Alumni Weekly*, October 1, 1974, pp. 11-13 as quoted in Thomas J. Knock, Kennan Versus Wilson, in John Milton Cooper, Jr. and Charles E. Neu, eds., *The Wilson Era, Essays in Honor of Arthur S. Link* (Harlan Davidson, Inc., Arlington Heights, IL, 1991), p. 317; George F. Kennan, Comments on the paper entitled "Kennan versus Wilson" by Professor Thomas J. Knock, in John Milton Cooper, Jr. and Charles E. Neu, eds., *The Wilson Era*, p. 330

416. Henry A. Kissinger, *Diplomacy*, p. 53; see also, Herbert G. Nicholas, Building on the Wilsonian Heritage, in Arthur S. Link, ed., *Woodrow Wilson, A Profile*, pp. 184-192

417. Reference is made to the Vietnam and Second Iraq Wars.

418. Paul Kennedy and Bruce Russett, Reforming the United Nations, in *Foreign Affairs*, September/October 1995, Volume 74, No. 5, pp. 59-60

419. See Zbigniew Brzezinski, *The Choice, Global Domination or Global Leadership* (Basic Books, Cambridge, 2004), Chs. 4-6

Chapter 6 Franklin Roosevelt and the Democratization of the American Economy

420. Robert S. McElvaine, ed., *Down & Out in the Great Depression, Letters from the "Forgotten Man"* (The University of North Carolina Press, Chapel Hill, 1983), pp. 60-1

421. Patterson, James T., *America's Struggle Against Poverty, 1900-1994* (Harvard University Press, Cambridge, 1994), p. 37

422. Anthony J. Badger, *The New Deal, The Depression Years, 1933-1940* (Hill and Wang, New York, 1989), p. 18

423. Arthur M. Schlesinger, Jr., *The Crisis of the Old Order*, (Houghton Mifflin, Boston, 1957), p. 3. [All excerpts from *The Crisis of the Old Order* are reprinted by permission of Houghton Mifflin Harcourt Publishing Company. All rights reserved.]

424. Carl N. Degler, *Out of Our Past, The Forces that Shaped Modern America* (Harper & Row, New York, 1959, rev. ed., 1970), pp. 382-3

425. McElvaine, *The Great Depression, America, 1929-1941*, p. 174, n. 11

426. Schlesinger, *The Crisis of the Old Order*, p. 65

427. Schlesinger, *The Crisis of the Old Order*, p. 67

428. Badger, *The New Deal, The Depression Years, 1933-1940*, p. 30

429. Kennedy, *Freedom From Fear, The American People in Depression and War, 1929-1945*, pp. 16, 22

430. Badger, *The New Deal, The Depression Years, 1933-1940*, p. 31

431. Schlesinger, *The Crisis of the Old Order*, p. 157

432. Kennedy, *Freedom From Fear, The American People in Depression and War, 1929-1945*, p. 38

433. Kennedy, *Freedom From Fear, The American People in Depression and War, 1929-1945*, p. 39

434. Badger, *The New Deal, The Depression Years, 1933-1940*, p. 20

435. Kennedy, *Freedom From Fear, The American People in Depression and War, 1929-1945*, p. 87 relying on black unemployment statistics from Lester Chandler, *America's Greatest Depression* (New York, Harper & Row, 1970), p. 40.

436. McElvaine, *The Great Depression, America, 1929-1941*, p. 187

437. William E. Leuchtenburg, *Franklin D. Roosevelt and the New Deal, 1932-1940* (Harper & Row, New York, 1963), p. 28

438. Schlesinger, *The Crisis of the Old Order*, p. 259

439. Leuchtenburg, *Franklin D. Roosevelt and the New Deal, 1932-1940*, p. 15

440. See Smith, Jean Edward, *Eisenhower in War and Peace*, (Random House, New York, 2012), pp. 106-116, for a full description of the events.

441. Schlesinger, *The Crisis of the Old Order*, pp. 262-3

442. The Washington Daily News, July 29, 1932, as quoted in Smith, Jean Edward, *Eisenhower in War and Peace*, p. 115

443. Patrick J. Maney, *The Roosevelt Presence, A Biography of Franklin Delano Roosevelt* (Macmillan Publishing Company, New York, 1992), p. 2

444. Maney, *The Roosevelt Presence, A Biography of Franklin Delano Roosevelt*, p. 4

445. Freidel, *Franklin D. Roosevelt, The Apprenticeship, Vol. I*, p. 27

446. Maney, *The Roosevelt Presence, A Biography of Franklin Delano Roosevelt*, p. 4

447. Schlesinger, *The Crisis of the Old Order*, p. 322

448. Maney, *The Roosevelt Presence, A Biography of Franklin Delano Roosevelt*, pp. 5,6

449. Maney, *The Roosevelt Presence, A Biography of Franklin Delano Roosevelt*, p. 8

450. Freidel, *Franklin D. Roosevelt, The Apprenticeship, Vol. I*, p. 6, quoting FDR letter to Robert Washburn, 1928

451. Nathan Miller, *FDR, An Intimate History* (Doubleday & Co., New York, 1983), p. 44

452. Miller, *FDR, An Intimate History*, p. 47

453. Schlesinger, *The Crisis of the Old Order*, p. 341

454. Schlesinger, *The Crisis of the Old Order*, pp. 358-9

455. A sixth child, Franklin Delano Jr., born in 1909, died that same year.

456. Maney, *The Roosevelt Presence, A Biography of Franklin Delano Roosevelt* Ibid., p. 22

457. Miller, *FDR, An Intimate History*, p. 173

458. Schlesinger, *The Crisis of the Old Order*, p. 366

459. Miller, *FDR, An Intimate History*, p. 183

460. Schlesinger, *The Crisis of the Old Order*, p. 369

461. Kennedy, *Freedom From Fear, The American People in Depression and War, 1929-1945*, p. 96

462. Schlesinger, *The Crisis of the Old Order*, p. 406

463. Schlesinger, *The Crisis of the Old Order*, pp. 407, 409-410

464. Schlesinger, *The Crisis of the Old Order*, pp. 382-3

465. *The Public Papers and Addresses of Franklin D. Roosevelt, Volume One, The Genesis of the New Deal, 1928-1932*, S.I. Rosenman, Ed., (Random House, New York, 1938), p. 76

466. *The Public Papers and Addresses of Franklin D. Roosevelt, Volume One*, p. 459

467. *The Public Papers and Addresses of Franklin D. Roosevelt, Volume One*, p. 457-8

468. Kennedy, *Freedom From Fear, The American People in Depression and War, 1929-1945*, p. 95

469. Kenneth S. Davis, *FDR, The New York Years, 1928-1933* (Volume 2) (Random House, New York, 1979, 1980,1983,1985), p. 64

470. *The Public Papers and Addresses of Franklin D. Roosevelt, Volume One*, pp. 625,626

471. *The Public Papers and Addresses of Franklin D. Roosevelt, Volume One*, p. 645

472. *The Public Papers and Addresses of Franklin D. Roosevelt, Volume One*, pp. 647-659

473. *The Public Papers and Addresses of Franklin D. Roosevelt, Volume One*, pp. 752

474. *The Public Papers and Addresses of Franklin D. Roosevelt, Volume One*, pp. 645, 646

475. Explanatory Note by Franklin Roosevelt in *The Public Papers and Addresses of Franklin D. Roosevelt, Volume Two, The Year of Crisis, 1933*, S.I. Rosenman, Ed., (Random House, New York, 1938), p. 16

476. *The Public Papers and Addresses of Franklin D. Roosevelt, Volume Two*, pp. 11-13

477. Leuchtenburg, *Franklin D. Roosevelt and the New Deal, 1932-1940*, p. 39.

478. *The Public Papers and Addresses of Franklin D. Roosevelt, Volume Two*, p. 64

479. Badger, *The New Deal, The Depression Years, 1933-1940*, p. 71

480. Kennedy, *Freedom From Fear, The American People in Depression and War, 1929-1945*, p. 141

481. Three Essentials for Unemployment Relief. (C.C.C., F.E.R.A., P.W.A.) March 21, 1933, in *The Public Papers and Addresses of Franklin D. Roosevelt, Volume Two*, p. 80

482. Three Essentials for Unemployment Relief. (C.C.C., F.E.R.A., P.W.A.) March 21, 1933, in *The Public Papers and Addresses of Franklin D. Roosevelt, Volume Two*, p. 81

483. Harry Hopkins, *Spending to Save*, pp. 100-1

484. Badger, *The New Deal, The Depression Years, 1933-1940*, p. 196

485. Leuchtenburg, *Franklin D. Roosevelt and the New Deal, 1932-1940*, pp. 122,3

486. Harry Hopkins, *Spending to Save*, p. 124

487. Recommendation for Federal Supervision of Investment Securities in Interstate Commerce. March 29, 1933, in *The Public Papers and Addresses of Franklin D. Roosevelt, Volume Two*, p. 93

488. As quoted in Michael Beschloss, *Kennedy and Roosevelt, The Uneasy Alliance*, (W.W. Norton & Company, New York, 1980, p. 84

489. Parrish, *Securities Regulation*, P. 3

490. As quoted in Leuchtenburg, *Franklin D. Roosevelt and the New Deal, 1932-1940*, p. 61

491. Roosevelt letter to Adolph A. Berle as quoted in Parrish, *Securities Regulation*, p. 109

492. Beschloss, *Kennedy and Roosevelt, The Uneasy Alliance*, p. 88

493. Beschloss, *Kennedy and Roosevelt, The Uneasy Alliance*, p. 92

494. Kennedy, *Freedom From Fear, The American People in Depression and War, 1929-1945*, p. 223

495. As quoted in Kennedy, *Freedom from Fear*, p. 223

496. Alan Brinkley, *Voices of Protest, Huey Long, Father Coughlin, and the Great Depression*, (Alfred A. Knopf, New York, 1982), p. 222

497. Badger, *The New Deal, The Depression Years, 1933-1940*, p. 295

498. Leuchtenburg, *Franklin D. Roosevelt and the New Deal, 1932-1940*, p. 100

499. Leuchtenburg, *Franklin D. Roosevelt and the New Deal, 1932-1940*, p. 101

500. Rexford G. Tugwell, *The Democratic Roosevelt, A Biography of Franklin D. Roosevelt*, (Doubleday & Company, Garden City, N.Y., 1957), p. 349

501. Kennedy, *Freedom From Fear, The American People in Depression and War, 1929-1945*, p. 241, citing James A. Farley, *Behind the Ballots: The Personal History of a Politician* (Harcourt, Brace, New York, 1938) and William E. Dodd Jr. and Martha Dodd, eds., *Ambassador Dodd's Diary, 1933-1938* (Harcourt, Brace, New York, 1941)

502. E.D. Coblenz, *William Randolph Hearst* (Simon and Shuster, New York, 1952), p. 178, as quoted in Kennedy, *Freedom From Fear, The American People in Depression and War, 1929-1945*, p. 242

503. Second "Fireside Chat" of 1934, *The Public Papers and Addresses of Franklin D. Roosevelt, Volume Three* (Random House, New York, 1938), September 30, 1934

504. Annual Message to the Congress, January 4, 1935, in *The Public Papers and Addresses of Franklin D. Roosevelt, Volume Four* (Random House, New York, 1938), pp. 20-22

505. Leuchtenburg, *Franklin D. Roosevelt and the New Deal, 1932-1940*, p. 174

506. Leuchtenburg, *Franklin D. Roosevelt and the New Deal, 1932-1940*, p. 158

507. Leuchtenburg, *Franklin D. Roosevelt and the New Deal, 1932-1940*, p. 126

508. Badger, *The New Deal, The Depression Years, 1933-1940,* p. 204

509. Hopkins, *Spending to Save*, p. 175

510. Badger, *The New Deal, The Depression Years, 1933-1940,* p. 218

511. Frances Perkins, *The Roosevelt I Knew* (The Viking Press, New York, 1946, reprinted by Harper & Row, 1964), p. 187

512. Perkins, *The Roosevelt I Knew*, pp. 282, 283, 289

513. Perkins, *The Roosevelt I Knew*, p. 294

514. Message to the Congress Reviewing the Broad Objectives and Accomplishments of the Administration, June 8, 1934, in *The Public Papers and Addresses of Franklin D. Roosevelt, Volume Three* (Random House, New York, 1938), p. 291

515. As quoted in Schlesinger, *The Coming of the New Deal*, pp. 308-9

516. A Greater Future Economic Security in the American People—A Message to the Congress on Social Security, January 17, 1935, in *The Public Papers and Addresses of Franklin D. Roosevelt, Volume Four* (Random House, New York, 1938), p. 43

517. Presidential Statement upon Signing the Social Security Act, August 14, 1935, in *The Public Papers and Addresses of Franklin D. Roosevelt, Volume Four* (Random House, New York, 1938), p. 324

518. A Message to the Congress on Tax Revision, June 19, 1935, in *The Public Papers and Addresses of Franklin D. Roosevelt, Volume Four* (Random House, New York, 1938), p. 271

519. A Message to the Congress on Tax Revision, June 19, 1935, in *The Public Papers and Addresses of Franklin D. Roosevelt, Volume Four* (Random House, New York, 1938), p. 272

520. Badger, The New Deal, *The Depression Years, 1933-40* (Hill and Wang, New York, 1989), p. 104

521. A Message to the Congress on Tax Revision, June 19, 1935, in *The Public Papers and Addresses of Franklin D. Roosevelt, Volume Four* (Random House, New York, 1938), p. 274

522. Inaugural Address, January 20, 1937, in *The Public Papers and Addresses of Franklin D. Roosevelt, 1937 Volume* (Random House, New York, 1941), p. 5

523. Acceptance of the Renomination for the Presidency, June 27, 1936, in *The Public Papers and Addresses of Franklin D. Roosevelt, Volume Five* (Random House, New York, 1938), pp. 233, 235

524. Carl M. Degler, *Out of Our Past, The Forces that Shaped Modern America*, (Harper & Row, New York, 1959, rev. ed.), p. 410

525. McElvaine, *The Great Depression, America, 1929-1941*, p. 115 quoting Martha Gellhorn, Report to Mr. Hopkins, Hopkins Papers, Box 60

526. Kennedy, *Freedom From Fear, The American People in Depression and War, 1929-1945*, p. 377

527. As quoted in Samuel Eliot Morrison and Henry Steele Commager, *The Growth of the American Republic, Vol. II* (Oxford University Press, New York, 4th ed., 1950, 6th printing, 1956), pp. 630-1

INDEX

Spain, 51,57-8,63,79,83-4,90-1,93-4,96,
	98,100
Spanish Empire, 91-2
Spanish Intendant, 62
Spanish-American War, 182,252,301
special acts,15
"spoils system," 57
Springfield, Illinois, 146
St. Augustine, Florida, 93
St. Louis, Missouri, 146
St. Marks, Florida, 92
St. Mihiel, Battle of, 208
Stampp, Kenneth M., 133
Stanton, Elizabeth Cady, 132
Stanton, Secretary of War Edwin M.,
	168
Star-Spangled Banner, 86
states' rights, state power, 23,28,50,89
Staunton, Virginia, 187
staying laws, 15
Stock Market Crash of 1929, 252
Stowe, Harriet Beecher, 140
Strategic Arms Limitation Treaty, 4
"strict construction" (U.S.
	Constitution), 32,36
Submarine, U-Boat, 197,202,204-6
Summary View of the Rights of British
	America, A (Thomas Jefferson), 44
Sumner, Senator Charles, 141,162
Supremacy Clause, U.S. Constitution,
	18
Supreme Court of the United States,
	20,151,157-9,264,294,301
Sussex (ship), Sussex Pledge, 199

Taft, William Howard, 186,192-3,216
Talleyrand, Foreign Minister, 52,61,63
Tallmadge, Representative James, 131
Taney, Chief Justice Roger B., 151-3,
	155
Taylor, President Zachary, 138-9
tender laws, 15
Tennessee, 89,128,130,162,173-4
Tenth Amendment, U.S. Constitution,
	20,33,152
terrorism, 303
Texas, 2,69,94-5,104,128,135-7,161,300
Third Reich, 224
Thirteenth Amendment, U.S.
	Constitution, 179

Thomas Amendment, 131
Thomas, Norman, 276
Three-Fifths Clause, U.S. Constitution,
	125,161
Tippecanoe, Battle of, 71
Touissant L'Ouverture, 58
Townsend, Dr. Francis Everett, 277
Trail of Tears, 71
Transcontinental Railroad, 176
Transcontinental Treaty, 76,82,95,
	97,104
Trenton, Battle of, 12,22,75,77-8
Triborough Bridge, 282
Triple Alliance, 194
Triple Entente, 194,214
Truman, President Harry S.,
	193,268,301
Trumbull, Lyman, 150
Tsar Alexander, 99
Tsarist Empire, 211,213
Tugwell, Rexford G., 263-4
Tumulty, Joseph, 231
Turner, Nat, 133
Tuyl, Baron, 99,100
Twenty-Fifth Amendment, U.S.
	Constitution, 231
two-party system, 36,41
Tyler, President John, 135

Ukraine, 213
Uncle Tom's Cabin (Harriet Beecher
	Stowe), 140
Unemployment Insurance, 285
Union, 30,121,135,138-9,140-1,150,
	152,157-8,160,162-81,181
Union Army, 162,164-5,180
Union College, 249
United Nations, 3,4,237-8,294,301
United Nations Framework Convention
	on Climate Change, 238
University of Virginia, 42,103,190
Utah, 137-8

Valley Forge, Battle of, 12-3,77
Venezuela, 104
Versailles, Treaty of, 214,216,222-5,
	233-4
Vesey, Denmark, 133
Vicksburg, Battle of, 178
Vietnam, 98

CPSIA information can be obtained at www.ICGtesting.com
Printed in the USA
LVOW082151190313

325100LV00001B/95/P